coolcamping
britain
SECOND EDITION

Andrew Day, David Jones, Jonathan Knight, James Warner Smith

Additional contributions by

Alf Alderson, Jules Brown, Dan Davies, Sophie Dawson, Keith Didcock, Martin Dunford, Richard Happer, Norm Longley, Scott Manson, Paul Marsden, Robin McKelvie, Mirio Mella, Andrea Oates, Sam Pow, Hayley Spurway, Andy Stothert, Paul Sullivan, Alexandra Tilley-Loughrey,

KEY
AONB – Area of Outstanding Natural Beauty
C&CC – Camping and Caravanning Club
EH – English Heritage location (see www.english-heritage.org.uk)
NT – National Trust location (see www.nationaltrust.org.uk)
SSSI – Site of Special Scientific Interest
Public transport options are only included where viable

introduction

I am often asked 'What is your favourite campsite?' Of course, it's an impossible question to answer. Different campsites are good for different reasons and my favourite campsite for sitting around the campfire until the early hours is not the same site that I stay at when I want to go out walking and exploring. My favourite woodland site is great for hiding away for a few days but, when the sun is shining, I like to take my family to our regular beach campsite. So instead of having one favourite campsite, I have a whole book full of them – and I'd like to share it with you!

In this second edition of *Cool Camping Britain*, we have pulled together a diverse collection of favourites from every corner of the UK, including many interesting new finds. Badgell's Wood campsite is a good example – a wild but well-managed woodland site in Kent that probably doesn't deserve the term 'campsite' as it feels more like you've stumbled into the woods and found a particularly tranquil coppice in which to pitch. The fact that this area was used to train World War II soldiers only adds to the attraction.

Then there's Ruberslaw, set in the rolling landscape of the Cheviot Hills in the Scotttish Borders; a site that boasts not only a stunning location, but also an Edwardian walled garden and glasshouse. It's an enchanting place, made even more appealing by its large communal barn and the choice of croquet, boules or garden jenga on the recreational lawn.

Another new inclusion worth mentioning here is the wonderful Welsh campsite Bach Wen Farm, a small, peaceful place with just half-a-dozen pitches, but huge views out to sea. The site provides direct access to a little-used beach that is perfect for taking long coastal walks and will blow away the cobwebs and clear the head of the stresses of daily life.

Hopefully you'll find a few campsites in these pages that become your own firm favourites, and, if you do, we'd love to know about it. Just head over to the website at www.coolcamping.co.uk to write a review and tell us what you think.

Whether it's this book or the Cool Camping website that inspires you, I hope you have a great time finding exciting new places to pitch your tent.

See you out there!

Jonathan Knight
Chief Camper

england

campsite locator

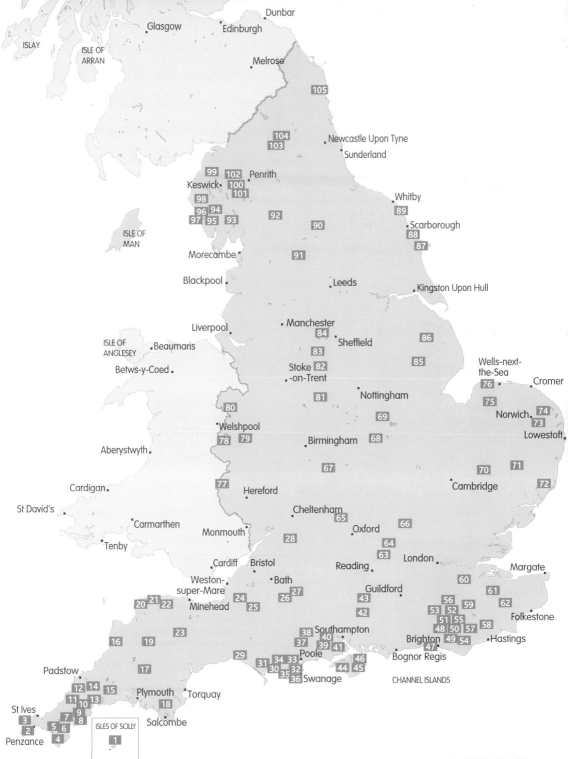

ISLAY

ISLE OF
ARRAN

Glasgow
Edinburgh
Dunbar

Melrose

105

104
103
Newcastle Upon Tyne
Sunderland

99 **102** Penrith
Keswick
100
101
98
Whitby
89
96 **94**
97 **95** **93**
92
90
Scarborough
88
87

ISLE OF
MAN

Morecambe
91

Blackpool
Leeds
Kingston Upon Hull

Liverpool
Manchester
84
Sheffield
86

ISLE OF
ANGLESEY
Beaumaris
83
85

Betws-y-Coed
Stoke **82**
-on-Trent
Wells-next-
the-Sea
76
Cromer

81
Nottingham
75

80
69
Norwich **74**
73

Welshpool
78 **79**
Birmingham **68**
Lowestoft

Aberystwyth
67
70 **71**

Cardigan
77
Hereford
Cambridge
72

St David's
Cheltenham
65
Oxford **66**

Carmarthen
Monmouth
28
64
London

Tenby
63

Cardiff Bristol
Reading
Margate

Weston-
super-Mare
Bath
60

20 **21** **22**
24
27
Guildford
61

Minehead
26
43
53 **52** **59**
62
Folkestone

23
25
42
56
51 **55**
48 **50** **57** **58**

16 **19**
38 Southampton
40
Brighton **49** **54** Hastings
47

17
29
37
39 **41**
Poole
Bognor Regis

Padstow
31 **34** **33**
30 **35** **32**
36
46
44 **45**
Swanage
CHANNEL ISLANDS

12 **14**
15
Plymouth
18
Torquay

St Ives
11 **10** **13**
9
7 **8**
Salcombe

3
5 **6**
ISLES OF SCILLY
1

2
4
Penzance

ENGLAND **11**

campsites at a glance

troytown campsite

Troytown Farm, St Agnes, Isles of Scilly TR22 0PL 01720 422360 www.troytown.co.uk

If camping on the tiny island of St Agnes isn't exciting enough, it's certainly an adventure getting there. Take your pick from a boat or plane for the journey to one of the the Isles of Scilly's two main islands, St Mary's. The plane has the edge for maximum thrill: a tiny eight-seater bouncing about on the winds. Bag one of the front seats for a bird's-eye view of the 100-odd islands that make up this archipelago.

Then it's on to a catamaran for the trip to St Agnes. If it's a bright day, you'll be greeted by the almost Mediterranean sight of boats moored on the turquoise waters of Porth Conger as you arrive. Next is a tractor ride – for your luggage at least. Most people choose to let their bags go ahead and walk the 20 minutes to the campsite, a scenic stroll that provides a stunning introduction to the island.

At just a mile in diameter, St Agnes is one of the smallest inhabited islands of the Scilly archipelago. It's a beautiful, rugged place that has seen little change since Celtic times; a forgotten outpost of England's west. The majority of the island's 70 inhabitants work in flower farming during the winter months, although tourism is now as important to the economy. Even so, there are only a handful of B&Bs on the island and most people come to stay at Troytown Farm, England's westernmost campsite. Its position couldn't be any more remote or spectacular. The campsite clings to the western shore of the island, just feet away from the rock-calmed Atlantic waters and the beautiful sandy curve of Periglis Beach. It's a magical

wilderness that feels like the ends of the earth. In fact, the nearest neighbours to the southwest are New Yorkers.

Small, separate fieldlets with low hedges and walls offer a certain amount of protection from the elements, but this can be a windy island, so come prepared. When the sun shines, though, it's perfect. You can play in the rock pools, spot rare, migrating birds or just sling up a hammock and listen to the waves gently lapping on the shore. At night, there are incredible views of the Milky Way and dazzling displays of shooting stars. Isolation is this island's greatest asset, so bring a love of nature and plenty of books. The island may be remote, but it's fairly self-sufficient. Troytown Farm has a small dairy herd producing milk, yogurt and ice cream that is famous across the island. They also rear pigs and grow vegetables to provide campers with food, so most survival essentials are available at the farmhouse and onsite shop. The other of life's necessities is available by the pint at The Turks Head in Porth Conger, the island's only pub. Perched on the hillside overlooking the bay and the adjacent islet of The Gugh, it might just win the prize for best beer garden in England. St Agnes is also blessed with fantastic beaches. As well as Periglis there's a small, sheltered beach at Cove Vean on the eastern shore and a sandbar at Porth Conger, where you can splash about in the waves or walk across to The Gugh at low tide. But for great sunset views, head back to Periglis – and see if you can spot the Statue of Liberty in the distance.

COOL FACTOR Extreme Atlantic isolation; one of England's most naturally beautiful campsites.

WHO'S IN Tents, dogs (arrange in advance), groups – yes. Campervans, caravans – no.

ON SITE A traditional-style granite building houses good facilities, including toilets, showers, coin-operated washing machines and dryers, shaver points and baby–changing facilities. There's an onsite shop. Pre-erected bell tents include pre-inflated airbeds, picnic bench and chairs, lanterns and solar lighting, cool box with ice-pack service, cooking pots, frying pan, kettle, water carrier, crockery, cutlery, utensils, camping stove with two burners and grill. When you arrive on St Agnes, you will be met at the quay to transport luggage to the site (and back when you leave). Bedding and towels are not included. Bring sleeping bags, pillows and a torch (there is no street lighting on the island). Buckets, spades and crabbing lines are provided to keep the kids busy. If it rains it's worth knowing that the site also has self-catering accommodation in a chalet and cottage.

OFF SITE Check out some great tours of the islands with Island Wildlife Tours (01720 422212; islandwildlifetours.co.uk). Or try snorkelling with the seals with Scilly Diving (01720 422848; scillydiving.com).

FOOD & DRINK For great seafood try High Tide Seafood Restaurant (01720 423869; hightide-seafood.com). The Turks Head, Porth Conger, has good food and beer.

GETTING THERE Cars and other vehicles must be left on the mainland. Contact Isles of Scilly Travel (0845 710 5555; ios-travel.co.uk) for plane and boat travel. Contact Troytown Farm for details of transportation to the campsite.

OPEN March–October; winter by arrangement. Advance bookings essential during July and August.

THE DAMAGE From £9 per person per night. Bell tents £320–£490 per week (depending on season). Luggage transportation £2.50 per person.

treen farm campsite

Treen Farm Campsite, Treen, St Levan, Penzance, Cornwall TR19 6LF 07598 469322 www.treenfarmcampsite.co.uk

Treen Farm has been in the Halls family for as long as anyone can remember. During the last war, one of the fields on the cliff top was commandeered by the RAF as a communications post. A few military buildings were constructed on the land, rendering it useless for farming – but perfect for camping.

Since then, campers and cows have co-existed at Treen Farm and the camping field has been updated. A fancy tap with running water was installed in 1974, and there are now even toilets and hot showers. The spacious site is a comfortable field's length back from the cliff top, so it's only exposed in the worst of weather, but benefits from a 180 degree sea view, stretching from the Isles of Scilly to rocky Lizard Point.

What you can't see are the beaches, but you don't have to go far. The nearest is Pedn Vounder, a tiny cove of golden sand accessed by a ten-minute cliff-top walk and a five-minute rocky scramble from the campsite; it's never busy, but it does get cut off at high tide, so keep an eye out. At low tide, you can walk along the sand to Green Bay and the larger Porthcurno beach, which is a family favourite and much more accessible. If that's not enough beach for your buck, it's just 10 minutes by car to Sennen on the north coast, and the huge, sweeping arch of sand and one of Cornwall's best surfing spots at Whitesands Bay. Bucket-and-spade summer days don't come any better than this.

Treen used to be a popular tourist destination thanks to Logan Rock, a 70-tonne lump of granite naturally balanced so that it could be rocked back and forth. People came from far and wide to try their strength at rocking the stone, until in 1824 bravado got the better of a bunch of drunken sailors who pushed it clean into the sea. Local residents were so outraged at this that the ringleader of the gang was ordered to return the stone to its position at his own expense – a project that took considerably more time than the original prank and nearly bankrupted the young sailor. Needless to say, the rocking action has not been the same since.

Thankfully, toppled rocks aside, there are plenty of modern-day attractions to entertain. Best is the Minack Theatre, an open-air auditorium cut into the cliffs west of Porthcurno, whose dramatic setting and backdrop of the crashing waves make it a unique theatre experience – and, like the fine beaches here, it shouldn't be missed.

COOL FACTOR Walking distance to some outstanding Cornish beaches.

WHO'S IN Tents, campervans, dogs – yes. Groups – by arrangement. Mobile homes, caravans – no.

ON SITE Showers (token operated, 25p for 5 minutes), toilets (including disabled facilities), laundry and washing-up area. The shop sells most things you might need.

OFF SITE Try and catch a performance at the spectacular Minack Theatre (01736 810181; minack.com). Indoor attractions abound at Penzance (8 miles) and Land's End (3 miles), including the latter's Arthur's Quest (0871 720 004; landsend-landmark.co.uk/arthurs_quest), an interactive family-friendly reimagining of the legendary king (as narrated by Brian Blessed). And be sure to visit Porthcurno beach, one of the best stretches of sand in a county that's not exactly short of good beaches.

FOOD & DRINK Sample some of the delicious pasteurised Treen Farm milk, straight from the cows. They sell yogurt and organic eggs, too. Treat yourself to a meal (or a night if you're feeling flash) at 17th-century The Abbey (01736 351163; theabbeyonline.co.uk) in Penzance, which has a Michelin-starred restaurant as well as rooms and suites. The Logan Rock Inn (01736 810495; theloganrock.co.uk) in Treen is a friendly pub selling St Austell Ales and a wide range of meals, with plenty of local fish and seafood options.

GETTING THERE Take the A30 southwest from Penzance, then turn on to the B3315 through St Buryan to Treen. The campsite reception is at the shop in the village.

PUBLIC TRANSPORT From Penzance train station catch the bus to Land's End. Get off at the foot of the hill in Treen and it's a 5-minute walk.

OPEN April–October. No pre-booking.

THE DAMAGE From £13 per night for 2 adults with a small tent and car. Adults are £5–£6; under-4s free; children (4–10) £2; and 11–15s £3.

secret garden

Secret Garden, Bosavern House, St Just, Penzance, Cornwall TR19 7RD 01736 788301 www.secretbosavern.com

The greatest difficulty this small campsite could ever encounter is living up to its name. After all, those two simple words, 'secret' and 'garden', when put together, promise so much: your very own slice of Eden-like paradise full of natural pleasure.

The fact that this tiny campsite is situated on the mystical far-western edge of Cornwall, where travellers only find what they earnestly seek and don't just drop in by chance, only adds to the anticipation and allure of the Utopian vision. And the way to the Secret Garden is indeed enchanting, along the rugged coast westwards, fleeing the crowds of St Ives, or across the empty granite-strewn hills, escaping any Pirates of Penzance.

The sign outside Bosavern House, where the Secret Garden hides away, stating that there are cream teas available, is yet another promising prospect for keen gastro-campers. But this doesn't look like a place where there is – or can be – a campsite. Instead, it's a rather grand-looking granite mansion. 'Where's the campsite?', you ask the distinguished-looking chap who comes to the door. 'It's in the garden round the back', says he, and your heart dares to wonder if all those wild imaginings of a secret garden can really be true.

You push past the hens, brush off the embrace of the palm trees and other exotic plants, and there it is – the Secret Garden. But what's this – other campers taking up residence here too? So you aren't the first person to make it here after all. It seems unbelievable after such an epic journey but it's true. In fact, there are 12 pitches within this lovely little oasis, and quite often in high season they are all occupied.

However, even though the site may not be solely yours, after a day or three has passed and the outside world is just a distant memory, the realisation dawns that this garden campsite, with all its hidden-away intimacy, really feels like a secret – and a perfect one at that. The onsite facilities are spotlessly maintained, and there are pleasingly homely touches, with the lounge in the main house open for campers' use, alongside the library and bar.

The feeling that you've happened upon a secret location endures once you step outside, where little-trod footpaths lead off towards the coast. One such magical trail leads to Porth Nanven, through a mile of scenery that you never want to end, to yet another seemingly undisclosed place. Another footpath strikes out across farmland, before burrowing its way through dark, damp, overgrown tree-tunnels to the cliffs, and to Cape Cornwall: one more well-kept secret. It's fortunate that the Cape doesn't poke out into the Atlantic just a little further or it would have been Land's End, and this beautiful, empty place might have ended up being smothered by visitor footfall. As it is, you can stroll here from your Secret Garden, enjoy a swim in the cove or tidal pool, climb to a lookout to see if you can spot a basking shark, watch the fishermen winch their boats out of the sea, then wander back to the campsite for a cream tea in the garden... And all without encountering more than a handful of other retiring and secretive folk.

So, does the Secret Garden live up to its name? We think it does.

COOL FACTOR A secret hideaway in Cornwall.

WHO'S IN Tents, campervans, caravans – yes. Dogs, groups – no.

ON SITE 12 pitches, all with hook-ups. The homely ablutions block is small but colourful and spotlessly maintained, providing toilets, showers, laundry and washing-up. The lounge in the main house is available for campers' use, as is the library and bar. The proprietors will even cook your breakfast if you order it the night before. No campfires.

OFF SITE Remnants of Cornwall's mining heritage are scattered about. The Levant Engine House (01736 786156; NT) – a very beautiful 4-mile walk along the coast path from the Secret Garden – contains a functioning Cornish Beam engine, which is in steam several times a week in summer. About 4 miles in the opposite direction is Sennen Cove, with its stunning beach and serious surf action, while a bit closer to the site (a mile away) is Porth Nanven, where a bracing dip awaits the adventurous. Just beyond Sennen Cove lies Land's End, with its dramatic cliffs, breathtaking views, and collection of attractions. Between St Just and Penzance are the exotic (and slightly secretive) gardens at Trengwainton (01736 363148; NT), where plants that grow nowhere else in Britain thrive.

FOOD & DRINK For classic Cornish cream teas look no further than the House's front garden from 2.30–5pm during July and August. Local pubs in St Just (½ mile) include the Commercial Hotel (01736 788455; commercial-hotel.co.uk) with good food, and the Star (01736 788767; thestarinn-stjust.co.uk), an ancient, atmospheric inn with none. For a special treat, the Victoria Inn (01736 710309; victoriainn-penzance.co.uk) at Perranuthnoe seves contemporary food that is as remarkable as the ancient surroundings.

GETTING THERE Follow the A30 towards Land's End and turn right on to the B3306 after Crows An Wra. Bosavern House, and its Secret Garden, is on the right after 2 miles.

OPEN March–October; arrivals are accepted between 2pm and dusk.

THE DAMAGE Tent + 2 people £18 per night; additional persons (over 2 years) £3.80; hook-up £4.80.

teneriffe farm

Teneriffe Farm, Predannack, Mullion, Helston, Cornwall TR12 7EZ 01326 240293 www.nationaltrust.org.uk/teneriffecampsite

Don't expect the wow-factor to hit you as soon as you arrive at Teneriffe Farm. On first impression it's just a very pleasant place to pitch up, hemmed by farmland, and with a blaze of Atlantic blue peeking above the hedges. Beyond this there are no obvious frills, save for the swings and slide of the children's play area. But that's just the point: camping should be a simple pursuit, and it's always best if your focus is on nature, starry nights and the Great Outdoors. And Teneriffe Farm is a place for all three.

Located close to the Lizard National Nature Reserve, 10 minutes on foot from the South West Coast Path and a 40-minute stroll from the pretty harbour of Mullion Cove, the location is a real gem. The recent acquisition of this cliff-fringed site by the National Trust is part of a project to breathe life into the landscape by re-joining the land with its neighbour and making a viable farm where there hasn't been one for years. So, starry skies and the simple life aside, the campsite is also helping to enhance the landscape and to boost the local economy.

There are pitches for tents, campervans and caravans, and nice dry pods for those who prefer not to rely on the weather, which are available all year round except February. The pitches are well spaced and well sized, and there are decent toilets, and shower facilities, a washing-up area and a laundry. There's also lots to do in the area, from exploring the delights of the Lizard Peninsula to seeking out some of the best local beaches. In the end, though, the best thing to do is just enjoy the wonderful location – boosting the local economy has never felt so good.

COOL FACTOR Sometimes the simplest sites are the best.

WHO'S IN Tents, campervans, caravans, dogs – yes. Groups – no.

ON SITE No campfires. 24 generous pitches (14 hook-ups) and an overflow field. Shower/toilet block being renovated, but will include a laundry, ice pack and phone-charging facilities.

OFF SITE Mullion Cove is a short drive or a 40-minute walk; from here you can go on a kayaking trip with Lizard Adventure (07845 204040; lizardadventure.co.uk) or walk over the cliffs to Poldhu via the Marconi Centre, where the first transatlantic message was sent in 1901. Turn the walk into a 4-mile loop via Mullion village. There's also Kynance Cove, another National Trust-owned property with beautiful heather-covered cliffs and a beach that was recently voted one of the world's best; plus it has a great local café. Consider also walking along the coast path to Lowland Point, where you can see seals and basking sharks.

FOOD & DRINK For the best fish and chips in the area it's worth the 10-minute drive to The Smugglers in Lizard village (01326 290763). Further south, the Top House Inn (01326 290974; thetophouselizard.co.uk) does great food, while the popular Polpeor Café on the beach of the same name, does fabulous fry-ups, pasties, cakes and more – all with views to die for.

GETTING THERE Following the main Helston-Lizard road, the A3083, make a right turn on the B2296 to Mullion, go through the village and turn left to Predannack just before Mullion Cove.

PUBLIC TRANSPORT The bus between Helston and Lizard stops at Mullion, just over a mile away.

OPEN Easter–November.

THE DAMAGE £9–£17 per pitch including 2 people. £20–£40 per pod.

granary barn camping

Granary Barn Camping, Nantrisack Farm, Sithney, Helston, Cornwall TR13 0AE 07740 514 188
www.cornwall-backpackers.co.uk/camping

Helston is Cornwall in microcosm. Home of the fabled May-time 'furry dance', the county's second oldest town is a picture-postcard patchwork of pasty shops, ancient pubs (like the 15th-century Blue Anchor Inn), and charming old miners' cottages that once housed some 1,000 workers from the local Wheal Vor tin mine. You could spend hours ambling along its steep serpentine streets en route to the harbour at Porthleven. But you could also hop in the car and head westwards through fields of green to the small outlier hamlet of Sithney, home of the beautifully secluded farmhouse campsite, Granary Barn Camping.

Many campsites around these parts have plenty to shout about, be it captivating sea views, artisan farm shops or über luxurious glamping abodes. But Granary Barn's greatest asset is its affable owner Tom. Warmly greeting guests with his faithful Border Collie in tow, this easy-going host is hospitality personified. As Tom puts it, 'This is a personality-driven site, I want the campers to engage with me, share their day. I want to provide students and anyone else with the chance to have a holiday at my prices, which are pitched at affordability. Money may be tight; however it is still possible to have a break in Cornwall, with a friendly site owner who, while they are here, is their new best friend!'.

As befits its breezy host, there's a refreshingly informal attitude to pitches. Tom lets campers pitch up where they like, for there's really no need for regimented spots when you've got a trio of spacious fields like this.

Thankfully this refreshingly cavalier philosophy doesn't extend to the facilities which, although basic, are immaculately maintained. Bins are emptied daily and toilets and electric showers are scrubbed diligently – attentive Tom prides himself on it.

Should the weather fail to read the script, Tom will even let you bunk down in the backpackers' hostel (availability permitting and for a small fee). This cushy dormitory sleeps eight (on single beds) with a communal kitchen and lounge area.

As for things to do nearby, the historic harbour village of Porthleven, with its traditional net lofts and fishermen's cottage, is just a few minutes' walk away and has a 3-mile-long sand and shingle beach, and the Lizard Peninsula beyond is the Cornish coast at its most dramatic. Also, no visit to this stretch of Cornwall would be complete without crossing the tidal causeway to St Michael's Mount, a fairy-tale island immersed in myth and legend that sits offshore a few miles to the southwest. You can tour the medieval castle, visit the Civil War gun batteries, or simply marvel at the views from the sub-tropical gardens.

Even with all this on your doorstep, it's always good to return to the campsite and, of course, to your genial host. Tom calls the farmhouse home and is on call 24 hours a day ('give me a bell if you need anything... even if it's three in the morning!'). And, unlike some campsites we could mention, Granary Barn's relaxed vibe and no-curfew rule means you can kick back and relax into the wee small hours.

COOL FACTOR The essence of Cornwall, including its famous hospitality.

WHO'S IN Tents, campervans, caravans, groups – yes. Dogs – no.

ON SITE A scattering of informal pitches spread across 3 flat, well-trimmed fields. There is also a backpackers' hostel, plus an adjacent farmhouse B&B. Toilets with shower room, laundry and fridge in the barn. Water points and rubbish bins dotted conveniently around the camping fields.

OFF SITE St Ives' breathtaking Blue Flag–approved beaches are also within easy reach. Porthminster is among the UK's finest, while the surfers spot of choice is Porthmeor. If you're in the area and fancy a bit of culture, Tate St Ives (01736 796226; tate.org.uk/St-Ives) features some fine contemporary and modern art within a former gas works.

FOOD & DRINK The nearest pub is the Crown Inn (01326 565538) at Crowntown, a 10-minute walk. The Ship Inn (01326 564204; theshipinncornwall.co.uk) on Porthleven Harbour is straight out of Cornish folklore. The food's not bad either, with a selection of pub grub faves and locally caught seafood dishes. Quirky Kota-Kai Bar Kitchen (01326 574411; kotakai.co.uk) boasts an eclectic menu, hosts movie nights, and kids eat free 5.30–6.30pm. For a special night out, Amélies at The Smokehouse (01326 554000; ameliesporthleven.co.uk) takes some beating.

GETTING THERE Granary Barn is on the B3302 Helston–Hayle Road, 450 metres south of Sithney School. From Helston, pass Lidl on the left and carry on up the hill. At the top, turn right on to the B3302. After 1 mile, opposite a plant nursery, turn right into an avenue of trees.

PUBLIC TRANSPORT Bus service to Sithney village, which is a quarter of a mile away.

OPEN All year.

THE DAMAGE £5 per person per night. school holidays £7. Bank hols £10.

tehidy holiday park

Tehidy Holiday Park, Harris Mill, Illogan, Redruth, Cornwall TR16 4JQ 01209 216489 www.tehidy.co.uk

There's something delightfully nostalgic about Tehidy Holiday Park. It is nestled in the wooded seclusion of the Tolskithy Valley, and arrival at this family-run campsite – with its iconic red phone box and swing-sign advertising Roskilly's ice cream – feels like the beginning of a *Famous Five* tale. And with the storied sands and hidden coves of St Ives and other west Cornwall beaches a healthy walk away through the sprawling woodlands of Tehidy Country Park, adventure is never far away.

But while Tehidy is quaint, it's far from twee and is very well equipped. There is an array of pitches for campers and caravanners, with conveniently located utilities aplenty. Everything about this place is well-maintained, from the neatly trimmed grass and the immaculately clean washing facilities to the well-stocked site shop, formerly the local blacksmith's forge. Even the vibrant wildflowers that adorn the perimeter seem perfectly proportioned – a cluster of foxglove here, a bunch of orchid there. And for those less enamoured with the joys of canvas and tent peg, Tehidy's brand new wigwams make for the perfect fuss-free break. These fully insulated wooden cabins are heated and wired, with all the mod cons you could possibly need – an affordable alternative to costly Cornish B&Bs and ideal for those who are travelling light.

Affable owner Richard takes tremendous pride in every aspect of the park, and it's easy to see why Tehidy is one of Cornwall's most garlanded campsites. If David Bellamy drops by with any more conservation awards, they'll have to build him his own wigwam!

COOL FACTOR Old-fashioned camping at its best.

WHO'S IN Tents, caravans – yes. Dogs, groups – no.

ON SITE 11 hardstandings for tourers; another 19 for tents, plus the wigwams. Facilities block includes high-pressure thermostatic showers, flush toilets, laundry, dish-washing room with freezer for ice packs. There's a play area with trampoline, table tennis, swings and climbing frame, plus a games room with pool table and table football. Wigwams are fully insulated, heated, powered and equipped with microwave and kettle. The small onsite shop stocks groceries and local produce. Wi-Fi is also available at a small cost.

OFF SITE The Blue Flag beach at Porthtowan is an Area of Outstanding Natural Beauty that's popular with the surf junkies. You can dig deeper into the area's industrial heritage at the East Pool Mine (01209 315027; NT), and two of Cornwall's most popular visitor attractions are close by – the Lost Gardens of Heligan (01726 845100; heligan.com) and the Eden Project (01726 811911; edenproject.com).

FOOD & DRINK BBQ slabs and raised BBQs are provided. There's a covered cookout shelter and the onsite shop stocks plenty of lovely local produce. For fresh locally caught seafood, the fisherman's cottage at Chapel Porth is a real gem. Treat yourself to a post-surf snack at Blue Bar Porthtowan (01209 890329; blue-bar.co.uk) or head to Truro's Old Grammar School (01872 278559; theoldgrammarschool.com) for tapas and cocktails.

GETTING THERE Take the A30 towards Redruth; take the exit for Portreath and Porthtowan then turn right at the roundabout to Portreath. At the crossroads turn left, drop down through North Country to the B3300 crossroads, straight over, up the hill past the Cornish Arms and Tehidy is on the left.

OPEN Late March–early November.

THE DAMAGE Camping/touring from £14 for 2 people. Wigwams from £45. Electric hook-ups £3.

tregedna farm

Tregedna Farm, Maenporth, Falmouth, Cornwall TR11 5HL 01326 250529 www.tregednafarmholidays.co.uk

From its dip within the valley, Tregedna Farm is surrounded by countryside as far as the eye can see. Yet daily life here revolves around the nearby beach. And what a beach! Wedged between the yachty buzz of Falmouth and the peaceful Helford river, Maenporth is one of the best-located beaches on Cornwall's south coast, yet the fact that it's a 40-minute walk from Falmouth town is enough to deter the crowds, so it always has a deserted nook of sand.

The pitches here are on a large and spacious south-facing field surrounded by woodland; you can pitch up wherever you like and there are family rooms and dormitories in nearby Tregedna Lodge for non-campers.

It's a simple life at Tregedna Farm. While the smell of bacon and coffee still lingers, families set off along the footpath on a pilgrimage to the beach. Children skip ahead with buckets and spades; parents straggle behind pushing buggies laden with picnics and wetsuits. When teatime approaches, the pilgrims return, trails of sand in their wake, the children lagging behind sporting salt-water mops and ice cream smudged smiles. During the evening, barbecue smoke fills the air and the chatter of children swirls around the tents until long after school-day bedtime. But as the sun drops so do the kids, leaving just the chink of wine glasses and the patter of footsteps to and from the dish-washing area. This easy routine greets you day after day, broken only by rainy interludes and sightseeing excursions that witness the beach gear abandoned as parents scrabble around for the car keys and spin into Falmouth for a dose of maritime culture and retail therapy.

COOL FACTOR Coastal camping with room for the kids to play.

WHO'S IN Tents, campervans, caravans, dogs, groups – yes.

ON SITE There's a play area with swings and a see-saw, and masses of space for ball games and running around. The refurbished toilet block has male/female loos and there's a separate stone hut with showers (2 male, 2 female), a large indoor washing-up area, washing machine and dryer.

OFF SITE Maenporth Beach is the reason for camping here – a sheltered sliver of pebble and sand perfect for bathing and rockpooling, snorkelling and kayaking. Arvor Sea Kayaking (07990 515263; arvorseakayakingcornwall.com) runs sea-kayaking sessions from the beach and along the Helford Estuary. Around the headland, Elemental Adventures (01326 318771; elementaluk.com) runs dinghy sailing, windsurfing and coasteering sessions. It's a 45-minute stroll to Falmouth, whose attractions include the National Maritime Museum, Pendennis Castle and boat trips to St Mawes.

FOOD & DRINK For snacks, burgers and ice cream, head to Life's a Beach at Maenporth or, just behind the beach, the Cove (01326 251136; thecovemaenporth.co.uk), which serves gourmet, locally sourced food. A 20-minute walk around the headland, the Swanpool Beach Café sells legendary ice creams. For a trendy beach hangout, try the Gylly Beach Café on Gyllyngvase Beach (01326 312884; gyllybeach.com).

GETTING THERE From Truro, take the A39 to Falmouth, staying on it until you pass Asda, after which turn right at the next roundabout; straight across the next 2 mini-roundabouts and continue for about 2 miles, following signs to Maenporth. Tregedna Farm is on the right.

PUBLIC TRANSPORT Penmere station on the Truro–Falmouth branch line is about 1½ miles from the campsite. The Falmouth–Helford Passage bus (no. #500) goes past the site.

OPEN Easter–October.

THE DAMAGE Adult £8 per night; child (aged 3–13) £4. Electric hook-up (best to book in advance) £3.50.

arthur's field

Arthur's Field, Treloan Lane, Gerrans, Nr Portscatho, Roseland Peninsula, Truro, Cornwall TR2 5EF 01872 580989
www.coastalfarmholidays.co.uk

You could call site-owners Debbie and Peter Walker's relationship with Arthur's Field something of a love affair. And a pretty passionate one at that. When they first visited the site with their two young sons, to surf and explore the south coast at the point where Cornwall dips her heel into the dazzling waters of Falmouth Bay, the field was little more than a grassy farmer's paddock. One visit, though, and the Walkers were in love. The next time they arrived they were moving in.

Sitting on the cliff-top just above Treloan Cove, and within strolling distance of postcard-pretty Portscatho, Arthur's Field is a site that stressed-out urbanite campers can only dream of. Certain things have changed since the rustic meadow of old, but the place is far from overcome by the Cornwall summer hordes, retaining a simple-but-effective campsite charm. Having pitched your tent, there's really no need to get into your car again until going-home time comes

around. Problem is, you'll probably never want to go home at all. Just like Debbie and Peter, you'll end up wanting to live the dream.

Every dream comes with a certain amount of variation, it must be said, and the couple have left ample room for each to live out their own. Crafting a site for all, the tents and caravans that were always welcome are now joined by a cosy eco-pod and yurt, offering some seaside glamping comforts. There are resident sheep, chickens and pigs to make this an authentic camping-on-the-farm experience, and in the morning it's up to the little ones to collect freshly laid eggs and feed the rabbits, drawn by the sound of Debs' ringing bell. This is also a time for them to socialise with other kids, so that when you reconvene around the fireside in the evening, firm friends have already been made. In fact, the only downside at Arthur's Field is plain for all to see. Since the Walkers aren't going anywhere, you can't move in.

COOL FACTOR A hop and a skip across a field and you can jump straight into the sea.

WHO'S IN Tents, campervans, carvans, families, couples, dogs – yes

ON SITE 57 pitches, all with hook-ups, are spread over 1 field. There is also a 'snug' eco-pod and a glamping yurt, featuring futon-style beds and a wood-burning stove. There are 11 showers, including 3 family, and 6 sinks, including 1 at child-height. In summer the cow's field is mowed to create a football pitch, and there are cricket stumps, too. The site is within walking distance of the cliffs, so little ones should be accompanied.

OFF SITE There's private access to several beaches, all great for swimming, fishing and diving, especially Treloan Cove and Peter's Splosh. Slightly further away are sandy Carne and Towan beaches. Porthcurnick beach is walkable from the other side of Portscatho, and seals are regular visitors. Portscatho is a lovely place to spend the afternoon fishing or rockpooling; if you're lucky you might spot the distant flipping tails of dolphins. If it's raining, don waterproofs and take a ferry from Portscatho to St Mawes and another to Falmouth, which is not bad for shopping, museums and the like.

FOOD & DRINK The Walkers organise a family evening twice a week. Simon, from the famous Hidden Hut (hiddenhut.co.uk) on Porthcurnick beach, comes to cook paella and other more local dishes. The Plume of Feathers (01872 580321) and the Royal Standard (01872 580271) are within walking distance. Locally caught fish lifts their menus above standard pub grub. The Boathouse (01872 580326), in the village, is nice for cream teas, and you can buy fantastic seafood from Ralph's Shop (01872 580702).

GETTING THERE Follow the A3078 until you reach Trewithian. Turn left at Treloan Coastal Farm towards Gerrans and Portscatho. Stay on this road until you reach Gerrans and stop beside the church. Treloan Lane is marked on the wall and runs directly to Arthur's Field, 300 metres down on the left-hand side.

PUBLIC TRANSPORT Train or bus to Truro (about 19 miles from the campsite) then take a bus (50/51) towards St Mawes. Hop off at Portscatho and walk from there.

OPEN All year.

THE DAMAGE Camping pitches from £15 (October–March, excluding Christmas week), up to £25 (late July–3 September). Snug £33–£38 per night. Yurt from £40 per night.

treveague farm

Treveague Farm, Gorran, St Austell, Cornwall PL26 6NY 01726 842295 www.treveaguefarm.co.uk

A family farm perched in divine cliff top countryside, within easy reach of three sandy coves, Treveague Farm has everything a really good seaside campsite needs. So when you consider its extras – a café serving organic food, farm animals, a badger hide and an aviary with bantams, lovebirds and more – it really does notch up a few credits as a superb place to stay.

Spread across three meadows, with glorious sea views in two directions, even with 80 pitches it's impossible to feel hemmed in here. However, it can be an exposed location, so you might want to opt for a space by the hedgerows rather than a front-row view. While kids gravitate to the farm animals, playground and storytelling sessions in the Secret Garden (great distractions for chilling out), make sure you tear them away from all this for a trip to the beach, because that's what this location is really all about. It's an easy stroll down to Hemmick beach (though it's advisable to avoid the short-cut through a field of bulls if you have a dog in tow), and the calf-grinding walk back up is always a great excuse for a generous scoop of the Cornish ice cream they serve back at camp.

COOL FACTOR There are 3 beaches within reach, farm animals, and an organic farm cafe.

WHO'S IN Tents, campervans, caravans, dogs – yes. Groups – no.

ON SITE 80 grass pitches (40 hook-ups). Extra-large tents welcome. No campfires. Facilities include indoor/outdoor sinks, fridges/freezers, laundry and baby-changing. Showers are 50p and you have to pay for Wi-Fi. There are pigs, cows and sheep, a wildlife hide for badger-watching, a resident barn owl and other creatures.

OFF SITE Of the beaches, Hemmick is the closest (10–15 minutes' walk), but Gorran Haven has more facilities. There's also the stunning Vault Beach, although this is a longer walk.

FOOD & DRINK There's little need to stray beyond the onsite café and restaurant, open from breakfast to 9pm. You can also buy meat for the BBQ, or catch your own dinner on a 2-hour mackerel fishing trip (£13 per person, 07973 957550).

GETTING THERE From St Austell take the B3273 to Mevagissey; past Pentewan, turn right at the crossroads at the top of the hill. Follow the signs to Heligan, then to Seaview campsite, and you'll see the signs to Treveague.

PUBLIC TRANSPORT Bus 526 from St Austell station stops a 500m walk from the site.

OPEN Easter–end September.

THE DAMAGE £7–£28 per pitch (including 2 people).

the meadows

The Meadows, Pentewan, St Austell, Cornwall PL26 6DL 01726 844383 www.themeadowspentewanvalley.co.uk

Nestled in the heart of the Pentewan Valley, where the St Austell River yields to the boundless blue of the Atlantic, The Meadows campsite is the traditional Cornish campsite of dreams – traditional, albeit with a little touch of luxury thrown in. With its stunning seascapes and unparalleled access to the Pentewan Trail, the site's enviable location means this Area of Outstanding Natural Beauty is yours to savour. It's also just for adults (sorry kids). Friendly owners John and Lynn are the very embodiment of courtesy, welcoming tenters, glampers and caravanners with smiles and open arms.

Although it is just down the road from the holiday park-opolis that is Pentewan Sands, The Meadows is a million miles away in terms of atmosphere. Natural and fun are the keywords here. For the canvas contingent, John and Lynn have set aside their spacious, sheltered, sunny meadow for a dozen or so lucky tents. A handful of caravanners are seen to with hook-ups, while campervans can park up right beside the stream that leads to the Little Winnick River. Extra-special secluded meadow pitches are also being cultivated for next season, so watch this space.

For those in need of a little pampering, your cordial keepers are only too happy to introduce you to Lottie and Mabel – two vintage caravans, decked out with chic interiors, bunting and ships sail sunscreen. Recline on the stripy deckchairs as you enjoy a bit of al fresco dining courtesy of the smoky Joe barbie (cleaned and prepped daily) on the spacious, screened deck area (Lottie) or private seating area (Mabel).

It's the little touches that really make your stay at The Meadows. The book-swap boasts books on walking, campervan cooking and explorer maps. The small onsite shop sells home-laid eggs, Roskillys ice cream, local milk, plus seasonal treats such as wild garlic pesto (made by John). John's breakfast baguettes are the stuff of local legend while, during high season, Kernowforno visit the site every Tuesday with their woodfired oven to cook pizzas fresh to order.

John and Lynn do their utmost to ensure that your stay is as fuss-free as possible, and your eco-conscious hosts are also eager to emphasise the wild beauty of the site, leaving the far end of the meadow to Mother Nature, so it is positively abuzz with wildlife. The large bird-feeding station is a magnet for all manner of feathered friends, while the adjacent stream is teeming with tiny brown trout, watched over by ravenous kingfishers. As the sun descends over Mevagissey Bay, hooting owls can be heard in the surrounding trees as the resident hedgehog does the rounds, scavenging stale buns and anything else that takes his fancy. If you're really lucky, you may even see the odd deer at dawn. This is also very much a dog-friendly site. There's a 'canine drinking station' for your parched pooches and some tremendous walks to be had with easy access to some great beaches – Hemmick is a particular favourite of camp dog, Harvey.

So with campers of all persuasions catered to and easy access to Cornwall's best beaches and attractions, The Meadows really is all things to all men... and women... and dogs.

COOL FACTOR The Cornish campsite of your dreams.

WHO'S IN Small caravans, campervans and tents; motorhomes and large caravans (very limited pitches); small groups and dogs – yes. Kids – no. Large groups by prior arrangement.

ON SITE 40 pitches: 20 electric grass pitches and a further 20 informal camping pitches, and 2 vintage caravans. Excellent shower block with separate wet-room style cubicles. Laundry facilities; ice-pack freezing. There's a small onsite shop; mobile phone charging service; book swap. Firepit BBQ hire – wood supplied. Communal sun-deck area with wood-burning stove. Vintage caravans include electric hook-up, gas stove, BBQ, screened deck area or private garden and seating area.

OFF SITE The Meadows is right on the Pentewan Valley Trail – ideal for exploring on foot or by bike with Pentewan Valley Cycle Hire (01726 844242; pentewanvalleycyclehire.co.uk), who deliver and collect bikes from the site. The Pentewan Valley trail links up to the South West Coast Path, making walking to Charlestown and Gorran Haven a nice day out. Fowey boasts countless attractions, and the ferry crossing from Mevagissey is a lovely way to get there.

FOOD & DRINK The Lobbs Farm Shop (01726 844411; lobbsfarmshop.com) at Heligan stocks a wide range of local produce. Fresh fish can be bought on the harbour at both Mevagissey and Fowey. Also in Fowey, Sam's on the Beach (01726 812255; samscornwall.co.uk) serves great seafood from an old lifeboat station. The Polgooth Inn (01726 74089; polgoothinn.co.uk), a gentle stroll away near St Austell, is a traditional Cornish inn with good food.

GETTING THERE The Meadows is approx. 3 miles south of St Austell on the B3273. From the main A30, shortly after bypassing Bodmin, take the A391 turning to St Austell. In St Austell itself, follow signs for Mevagissey and take the B3273.

PUBLIC TRANSPORT Train to St Austell and then a local bus which will drop you opposite the campsite gates.

OPEN Beginning of May–end September.

THE DAMAGE £10–£17 for 2 people per night. EHU pitches £13–£21/includes 2 adults and one vehicle. 25% discount for those arriving under their own steam. Dogs stay free.

pleasant streams farm

Pleasant Streams Farm, Lower Sticker, St Austell, Cornwall PL26 7JL 01726 74837 www.cornwallfarmcamping.co.uk

'There's very little to do here, no bells and whistles', says Tony Hedges, proprietor of Pleasant Streams Farm with his wife Lesley. But this is indeed a pleasant field in which to pitch a tent. Campfires are encouraged, and often the crackle-pop of the fire is the only noise of the evenings here. There is, though, quite a lot to do on and around the site. There's a lake in the centre, which not only attracts wildlife but also beckons you to hop in the rowing boat for an afternoon afloat; a summerhouse has books and games for rainy days; and, of course, there are the animals: Matilda, Snowflake, Billy and Gruff the goats, Rodney and Del Boy the pigs, and the chickens and ducks that lay fresh eggs for your breakfast. And that's not even counting the field mice, owls, herons and badgers. You can always break the tranquillity with a ten-minute stroll to the local pub in Sticker, just don't expect wild nights and karaoke. Most people who stray from the site do so by day, biking along the nearby Pentewan Valley Trail or hiring the campsite's kayak and exploring the beautiful coast around Gorran Haven and Charlestown.

COOL FACTOR It's all about simple pleasures when you pitch up by a lake in rural Cornwall.

WHO'S IN Tents, campervans, caravans, groups – yes. Dogs – no.

ON SITE Space for 50 tent pitches in the main camping field. 3 electric hook-up pitches available (book in advance); 3 vintage caravans also available for rent. Campfires allowed. Basic showers, toilets and a water tap for washing-up.

OFF SITE Explore the coast by kayak (on hire from the campsite for £25 per day), or freewheel along the Pentewan Valley Trail with Pentewan Valley Cycle Hire (01726 844242; pentewanvalleycyclehire.co.uk). The site is also close to the Lost Gardens of Heligan (01726 845100; heligan.com) and the Eden Project (01726 811911; edenproject.com). The fishing village of Mevagissey and historic port of Charlestown are a short drive away.

FOOD & DRINK It's a 15-minute stroll to the Hewas Inn (01726 73497; hewasinn.co.uk), which serves a traditional pub fayre and a selection of good ales from St Austell Ales. For something extra special, Austell's (01726 813888; austells. co.uk) boasts a refined à la carte menu.

GETTING THERE From the A390 between St Austell and Truro, take the Hewas Water exit and turn right towards Lower Sticker. Straight over a crossroads and it's on the right.

PUBLIC TRANSPORT A bus service runs from St Austell and stops at Sticker, 10–15 minutes' walk from the site.

OPEN Easter–September.

THE DAMAGE All pitches include 2 adults and 1 car: 2–4 person tent £10; 4–6 person tent £14; 6–8 person tent £16. Additional adult £3; Children (4–14 years) £2; children under 4 free. Caravans £15; motorhomes £20; electric hook-ups £3; additional car £5. Vintage caravans are available to rent from £150 for a short break.

PLANTS
FOR
SALE

trewan hall

Trewan Hall, St Columb Major, Cornwall TR9 6DB 01637 880261 www.trewan-hall.co.uk

The 36 acres of undulating fields, immaculate gardens and enchanting woodland that surrounds the 17th-century manor house of Trewan Hall, makes for a near-perfect camping spot. Positioned just outside the pretty parish town of St Columb Major, this family-orientated campsite has been run by the Hills for 50 years, so it's fair to say that they know a thing or two about camping. And with Cornwall's finest walks, pristine white sand beaches and picture-postcard villages right on the site's doorstep, you don't have to be eagle-eyed to realise why they never left. Trewan's camping area itself is lovely and small enough to feel quite private. There are two slightly sloping fields (one smaller and more family-friendly) plus a larger field with plenty of space and a real 'away from it all' atmosphere. The management here are flexible, meaning campers can pitch where they like. So if you spot a secluded corner that takes your fancy, it's yours. Not being slap bang on the Cornish coast means the site is relatively sheltered from the elements; however it's worth mentioning that a country lane runs alongside the smaller camping field, but unless you're an extremely light sleeper you won't be disturbed by the infrequent traffic.

Caravans and motorhomes are also welcome at Trewan Hall. But fret not canvas campers; given the site's pursuit of natural beauty over profit, there are only a select number of caravans allowed at one time, so the comprehensive views of rolling fields, parish churches and grass-munching cattle remain unbroken. The facilities here are pretty comprehensive too: the brand new ablution block comes equipped with showers, baths, washing-up sinks and electric razor points. Best of all, guests have access to the fully supervised, 25-metre heated swimming pool (open during high season at a pleasing cost of just 60p): just the ticket for cooling off when the Cornish sun comes out to play.

You won't have a shortage of things to do here. Not only do you have the nearby historic town of St Columb Major; with its time-honoured country pubs, you're also only a flip-flop away from the tranquil coastline of Mawgan Porth. And 14 miles down the road you'll discover the world's largest (and most impressive) greenhouse, the Eden Project. These sights, combined with the cosy, grassy comfort that comes with field camping make Trewan Hall an ideal place to pitch up.

COOL FACTOR The grounds of a 17th-century manor where a relaxed atmosphere and sense of pleasant privacy rules.

WHO'S IN Tents, caravans, motorhomes, families, couples and well-behaved dogs – yes. Young groups – no.

ON SITE Freestyle pitching on 2 well-drained, relatively flat fields with space for around 200 tents. 1 recently rebuilt toilet/washing block with showers, baths, washing-up sinks, electric razor points, hairdryers, ironing area, wet-suit washing areas and chemical disposal point. A fully stocked shop is open selling groceries, camping equipment, toys and games. Library, writing room and fully supervised 25-metre heated swimming pool. Various onsite barns for table tennis, table football, pool and darts. Small basketball area in the barnyard, comprehensive woodland playground for children including sandpit. Entertainment in various forms, including magicians, bands and storytelling, and a Nature Workshop once or twice a week.

OFF SITE The site's closest attraction is the world-famous Eden Project (01726 811911; edenproject.co.uk). The flat, easygoing Camel Trail starts in Padstow and runs east through Wadebridge (along the Camel Estuary) before finishing at Poley's Bridge. Both the Padstow–Wadebridge and Wadebridge–Bodmin sections make a splendid half-day excursion. Bikes can be hired from both ends.

FOOD & DRINK Hot food is available all day in the camp shop, and fresh bread and cakes from an excellent local bakery. A fish and chip van and a pizza 'horse box' visit the site once a week. Port & Starboard (01726 860270; theportandstarboard. co.uk), in Indian Queens (a 10 minute drive) serves great fish and chips. The Smugglers Den Inn (01637 830209; thesmugglersden.co.uk) at Cubert is a thatched inn with real atmosphere, traditional food and local ales.

GETTING THERE From the A39, turn off when you see signs for St Eval Talskiddy, and follow for ¾ of a mile. The site is on the left.

OPEN Start of May–mid September.

THE DAMAGE Adults £7–£11; children (between 5 and 15) £3.50–£6. Electric hook-ups £5; dogs £1.50.

broad meadow house

Broad Meadow House, Quay Road, Charlestown, St Austell, Cornwall PL25 3NX www.broadmeadowhouse.com

Walk past Charlestown's museum and along the short cul-de-sac behind it and you'd be forgiven for being sceptical about there being a campsite here at all, let alone one of the nicest small sites in the country. However, just beyond the final house, a gate opens up to a couple of tiny fields that command fabulous views out to sea and along the shoreline towards Black Head, the tip of a headland sporting the golden flash of a wheat field on its back.

Broad Meadow (was it ever broad? Ancient sepia photos suggest not) has two geese, a 'Posh Shed' (self-catering coastal retreat), one permanent tent and plenty of space for people who'd rather bring their own. Since the owners limit the number of campers on site to a mere dozen, you get the distinct feeling of being one of an incredibly privileged few. This is especially true if you order a delicious breakfast basket (including freshly made smoothie) to be brought to your tent in the morning.

Basking sharks and grey seals are sometimes spotted in the bay (just ask to borrow the telescope) while peregrine falcons, sparrowhawks and buzzards contest the air space above. Swallows, sensibly, prefer to skim the surface of the field and are so used to company that they come quite close to feed.

In tiny Charlestown there's some easy coasteering to be had; a gig club that allows beginners to have a go at rowing on novice nights (Wednesdays); and, for those who want to go it alone, sea kayaks and other water vessels for hire from neighbouring Porthpean Beach.

COOL FACTOR With fabulous seaside views, this is one of the best small campsites in the country.

WHO'S IN Only tents and VW campervans accepted or small vans of similar size. Well-behaved dogs are welcome but must be kept on a lead.

ON SITE 1 pre-pitched 'Posh Tent' ('Karsten' Multi-Dome) and 4 DIY pitches, all with electric hook-ups. DIY pitches have use of 2 unisex loos and 1 shower. The pre-pitched 'Posh Tent' has a private shower and loo. There is a washing-up sink, mini fridge and freezer, recycling, free Wi-Fi and recharging points. Children will find plenty of room for games in the safely enclosed meadow. Campfires are not permitted but BBQs are allowed off the grass.

OFF SITE Charlestown Shipwreck Heritage Centre (01726 69897; shipwreckcharlestown.com) is 'the largest collection of shipwreck artefacts in Britain'. You're also within walking distance of one of Cornwall's best-known sights, the Eden Project (see p.26).

FOOD & DRINK The Pier House Hotel, Charlestown, has a harbourside snug bar with recommended food and live entertainment on Saturday evenings (01726 67955; pierhousehotel.com).

GETTING THERE Take the Charlestown exit off the roundabout on the main A390. Follow the road into Charlestown and the site is on the left.

PUBLIC TRANSPORT St Austell station is 1.7 miles away; bus 525 runs hourly to Charlestown.

OPEN Easter–October (weather dependent).

THE DAMAGE DIY pitch: adults £14 per night; under-12s: £7 per night; under-2s: free. Pre-pitched posh tent including breakfast: couple, £95 per night; family, £135 per night. Complimentary: wooden picnic bench, parasol, and 'Welcome Bevvie Basket'.

ruthern valley holidays

Ruthern Valley Holidays, Ruthern Bridge, Bodmin, Cornwall PL30 5LU 01208 831395 www.ruthernvalley.com

After a nice day on the beach at Polzeath or Rock, surrounded by surfers and Sloanes, Ruthern Valley is somewhere you can escape to, hidden among the green canopy of Cornwall's interior. Close to Bodmin Moor, this secluded, beguiling little site is humming with wildlife, so children can have plenty of fun spotting rabbits and squirrels, and budding ornithologists can look out for woodpeckers a-pecking and hear owls a-hooting. Having said that, they'll probably enjoy feeding the chickens just as much. It's a top location, with the wild delights of Land's End an hour or so away, and Bodmin Moor, a perfect place for stomping around with children, as you regale them with heady stories about smugglers and highwaymen, isn't far. Or you could cycle to Padstow for a crabbing session on the quay and perhaps a slap-up portion of Mr Stein's famous fish and chips, which is pretty-much a perfect way to while away an afternoon. Grogley Woods are close to the site and lovely for shady walks. So, at the end of a busy day, when you've had your fill, and more, of sun, sea and sand, what could be better than the peaceful, leafy shade of Ruthern Valley?

COOL FACTOR In the middle of Cornwall, this is a magical place where you can escape the beach crowds.

WHO'S IN Tents, campervans, caravans, glampers, groups – yes. Dogs – no.

ON SITE 16 standard grass pitches on the main field and 6 more secluded pitches on the first field. 4 smaller grass pitches below in the woods. Some electric hook-ups. The family keeps pigs and chickens, which children can help to feed. There are 4 solar-powered showers and 2 washing-up sinks. Laundry facilities include 2 washers, 2 dryers and an ironing board. There are also 'camping pods' – insulated timber huts for 2 adults and 2 kids – and sturdy wooden wigwams, which sleep up to 5 people with memory foam mattresses, kettle, fridge, microwave, heating and lighting.

OFF SITE Part of the appeal of Ruthern Valley is its proximity to the Camel Trail, a disused railway track running 16 miles from Wadebridge to Padstow. Hire bikes at Bridge Bike Hire, Wadebridge (01208 813050; bridgebikehire.co.uk) or hire wet-suits and surf boards onsite and head straight to the beaches.

FOOD & DRINK There's a small shop onsite which sells basic groceries, curries from the Little Cornish Curry Company, Roskilly's ice cream, fresh baguettes and local Rattler cider. Cycle 3 miles along the Camel Trail to the Borough Arms (01208 73118; theborougharms.com), a child-friendly pub.

GETTING THERE Take the A30 and come off at the St Austell exit. Turn right at the first roundabout, taking you back over the A30, and take the left turn for Lanivet. Keep going through Lanivet, 1 mile, at top of the hill turn left signed Nanstallon. Left again, signed 'Ruthern Bridge', and continue for 2 miles, turning left before the small bridge.

OPEN All year.

THE DAMAGE From £12.50 per tent for 2 adults + £4 for children. Wigwams £45–£60; camping pods £30–£35 per night (2 people).

penbugle farm wigwams

Penbugle Organic Farm, St Keyne, Liskeard, Cornwall PL14 4RS 01579 326055 www.penbuglefarm.co.uk

Camping can be a surprisingly romantic experience. Picture the scene: two people sheltering from the elements in a snug Wigwam, cooking fresh local produce on a simple fire, enjoying panoramic views of the Cornish countryside. Thanks to Penbugle Organic Farm, this bucolic blend is available to campers all year round. And, in a cosy wooden room that's only a few feet wide, you won't need any excuse to get cosy with each other...

The brainchild of John and Lizzie Ridout, Penbugle (meaning 'shepherd's hill' in Cornish) is a 260-acre, fully organic farm located between the ancient market town of Liskeard and the fishing village of Looe. Penbugle is very much a functioning farm and visitors are invited to sample its produce, including scrumptious pork sausages and fresh free-range eggs. On a site that's buzzing with livestock, expect to mingle with the locals, including Red Ruby cattle, pigs, ponies, and the cuddly South American alpacas who keep a keen watch for uninvited foxes.

There are three different camping experiences at Penbugle. Most luxurious are its wigwams (sleeping up to five), which come with electric lighting, heating and mattresses. There are also two bell tents in a lovely grass paddock, pitched on wooden decking. And, last but not least, there are ten pitches for regular tents. The atmosphere is intimate and you'll soon get to know your neighbours, whether dining al fresco or meeting on the way to the showers.

COOL FACTOR Cosy wigwams in a gorgeous Cornish location.

WHO'S IN Tents, glampers, couples, kids, groups, dogs – yes. Caravans and motorhomes – no.

ON SITE 10 pitches for tents (all grass, no electric hook-ups), plus wigwams and 2 bell tents. Facilities include 2 gents' showers, 2 ladies'; toilets and a washing-up sink. Fully equipped kitchen with a microwave, kettle, cooker, fridge, pots and pans. Wigwams sleep 4–5 and have electric lighting heater, bed, fridge, toaster, kettle, standpipe by the door, firepits and picnic table; bell tents include coir matting, cotton rugs and LED lights. Guests must provide their own bedding.

OFF SITE Nearby Looe is adorable, with good beaches and watersports opportunities. Take a stroll around the historic headland on the River Fowey, past the remains of St Catherine's Castle. Polmartin Riding School (01503 220428; polmartinfarm.com) hosts riding along its own scenic tracks. The zipwires at Adrenalin Quarry (01579 308204; adrenalinquarry.co.uk) are a 15-minute drive.

FOOD & DRINK Cornish Orchards Cider Farm (01503 269007; cornishorchards.co.uk) sells mouth-watering local produce. The Plough (01503 262556; ploughduloe.co.uk) in Duloe is a traditional village pub serving good-quality food. In summer, enjoy the views from the beer garden at The Smugglers Inn (01503 250646) in Seaton.

GETTING THERE From Plymouth take the A38 to Liskeard and take the Moorswater Industrial Estate slip road and turn right at the T-junction into the village of Dobwalls. At the mini roundabout take the first exit left and then take the 2nd exit on the next roundabout. Follow the road for 2 miles until you reach a crossroads with a stone cross; drive on and Penbugle Farm is on the left at the top of the hill.

OPEN All year (except bell tents; May–September).

THE DAMAGE Tents £10 per adult (16yrs +) and £5 per child per night. Wigwams and bell tents from £40 per night (2 people sharing). Dogs £5 per dog per night.

cerenety eco camping

Cerenety Eco Camping, Lower Lynstone Lane, Bude, Cornwall EX23 0LR 01288 356778 www.cerenetycampsite.co.uk

In the eyes of the wild-camping tribes, campsites are for softies. But wild camping with kids – well, it can just be a bit of a hassle. At the very least it's nice to know there's running water to deal with potty mishaps and stacks of dirty dishes. So with its no frills, close-to-nature approach, Cerenety proves you can still enjoy the wilder side of camping in a uniform campsite, which has tent pitches, welcomes small campervans and has a limited number of beds in its barn accommodation.

With just a smattering of tents permitted across Cerenety's seven sprawling acres, first and foremost there's plenty of space to run around like wild things. Every feature is as squeaky green as the surrounding countryside, from compost loos and solar panels, to recycled materials ingeniously put to use in rustic, efficient amenities. There's even a veggie patch where you can head to pick your own.

Animal-lovers roll-up. Children flock to bottle-feed orphan lambs, and alpacas roam a few feet shy of the tents. Where nature rules and campfire smoke spirals lazily into dusky skies, it comes as a surprise that the surfer dudes, amusement arcades and retro cafés of Bude are just a mile's easy stroll along the canal, so you can get a seaside fix without even having to hunt down the car keys. And, when you get back, the serenity of the site is even more welcome.

COOL FACTOR Serene, green and no overcrowding.

WHO'S IN Family groups, single-sex groups, small campervans, tents, dogs (by arrangement) – yes. Caravans, large campervans – no.

ON SITE 3 sprawling fields with no set pitches. A field shelter houses 2 showers, 3 compost loos and a washing-up sink (hot water is powered by solar panels). Owner Jake will freeze iceblocks for you in the house. A small shop sells basics such as toothpaste and loo roll. Pick your own fresh veggies from the market garden. Spot butterflies, moths and the visiting heron on the wildlife pond. Feed the orphan lambs and pet the animals – Flipper the dog, Torry the pony and Red the rescue horse, as well as rabbits, ducks and chickens. Campfires and BBQs very much encouraged.

OFF SITE It's a 20-minute stroll to the seaside – Bude's stunning Summerleaze, Crooklets and Widemouth beaches serve up a heady cocktail of surf, sand, cool waterfront cafes and amusement arcades. Hit the waves with Raven Surf School (01288 353693; ravensurf.co.uk), take a dip in the tidal pool or row a boat along the canal (boat hire at Lower Wharf: 07968 688782). Cyclists can opt for a gentle route along the canal towpath, or freewheel all the way from Bude to Land's End along the Cornish Way.

FOOD & DRINK Life's A Beach (01288 355222; lifesabeach. info) on Summerleaze beach is a handy beachside cafe by day and a cosy restaurant by night.

GETTING THERE Follow signs for Bude. At the mini roundabout go straight across towards Widemouth Bay. Follow the main road over the bridge and up the hill. At the top of the hill you will see Upper Lynstone Caravan Park on the right hand side-turn left here and follow the narrow lane to the end where you'll come to a T-junction. Turn right and the campsite is the first gate on the right.

PUBLIC TRANSPORT Train or bus to Exeter then the bus (X9) from Exeter to Bude. If you you ask in advance, the owners can pick you up from Bude.

OPEN March–October.

THE DAMAGE From £4 –£10 per person per night.

langstone manor

Langstone Manor Holiday Park, Moortown, Tavistock, Devon PL19 9JZ 01822 613371 www.langstonemanor.co.uk/index.htm

Feeling a bit hemmed in? Then take a trip to the ancient, fascinating landscape of Dartmoor, one of England's great breathing spaces. With some of Europe's finest archaeological remains (including circles and stone rows), burial chambers and moss-covered boulders in woods of twisted trees, a visit here feels like falling into a chapter of Tolkien's *Lord of the Rings*. Set amongst a sheltered valley in Dartmoor's favoured southwest edge, Langstone Manor is an idyllic camping escape, perfect for those wanting to discover the brooding, windswept wilds of the adjacent moorland. There's a relaxed, peaceful atmosphere here, with no long list of rules and regulations. Set in the grounds of a traditional country manor, the entrance to the site (through a field of mobile homes) can be slightly off-putting. However the camping fields are truly superb. Pitches in the daffodil field are flat, predominantly terraced (to ensure a sense of seclusion) and offer panoramic views across the neighbouring moors. The facilities are of a high standard too. The toilet block is kept immaculately clean, with spacious, roomy showers, vanity basins and flushing toilets, while in cooler months the block is heated. There's also a separate bathroom (for a small charge): ideal if you're camping with the kids.

On a summer's day, Dartmoor is a postcard-maker's dream. Ponies wander fancy-free, sheep graze beside walking paths and the welcoming communities of Princetown, Widecombe-in-the-Moor, and petite Postbridge bustle along nicely with craft markets, small festivals and cosy pubs. It's this cinematic scenery that persuaded Steven Spielberg to film *War Horse* here, and Dartmoor was of course the setting for Sir Arthur Conan Doyle's legendary crime novel, *The Hound of the Baskervilles*. When winter arrives and sleeting rain, howling winds and churning mists take over, you can see why Doyle choose this wonderfully eerie wilderness as a location.

Many families bring bicycles to Langstone Manor so their offspring can tear along the purpose-built cycle ways, with The Granite Way and Drake's Trail providing spectacular, traffic-free routes. If they're not doing that, guests can usually be found skinny-dipping in the nearby river, or swinging merrily in the outdoor play area. As for everyone else? Well, they're just kicking back and enjoying that peaceful, relaxed atmosphere.

COOL FACTOR Views of Dartmoor and easy access to the treasures it holds.

WHO'S IN Tents, glampers, caravans, campervans, families, small groups and well-behaved dogs – yes. Noisy groups – no.

ON SITE 40 pitches for traditional campers, 1 camping pod suitable for a couple or a family with 2 small children, larger pods with room for up to 4 adults also available. 2 of the larger pods are pet friendly. Free hot showers, toilets, hairdryers, nappy changers, an accessible family bathroom, laundry and dish washing area. The manor house has a wonderful lounge bar, dining room, Wi-Fi access and games room, with table football, air hockey and pool. The lounge area has a wood-burning stove with overhead drying racks for wet gear, a library where guests can swap and borrow books, board games and toys.

OFF SITE Plymouth is packed with possibilities. You can tour its fabulous local gin distillery (01752 665292), swim in the art deco Tinside lido (01752 261945) or discover the underwater delights of the National Marine Aquarium (0844 893 7938; national-aquarium.co.uk).

FOOD & DRINK The site can provide baguettes, rolls and croissants. The manor house has an excellent lounge bar and dining room (seasonal opening times). The Peter Tavy Inn (01822 810348; petertavyinn.com) is a traditional 15th-century pub with ancient timber beams and a garden looking out over the Dartmoor countryside. The Whitchurch Inn (01822 612181; whitchurchinn.co.uk) is a great place to enjoy a hearty, freshly cooked meal from the seasonal menu.

GETTING THERE Take the A30 towards Okehampton then the A386 to Tavistock. From here, take the B3357 and after approx. 2 miles turn right at the crossroads. Pass over the cattle grid, continue up the hill and turn left following the sign. Langstone Manor is on the right.

OPEN March–November.

THE DAMAGE Pitch from £14–£19 for 2 people, pods start from £35. Green rate available for walkers and cyclists.

karrageen

Karrageen, Bolberry, Malborough, Kingsbridge, Devon TQ7 3EN 01548 561230 www.karrageen.co.uk

Karrageen is all about giving its lucky occupants plenty of room to breathe, think, play and relax. There will be no tangle of guy ropes here and there's even room for those multi-bedroom structures that can take up a good few pitches on their own. You'll find nothing fancy, nothing flash and nothing gimmicky: just a simple, very well maintained and nicely landscaped campsite in an ever-so-lovely location – with space to spare.

The camping field is a terraced hillside split into a series of quite small, intimate and attractive cul-de-sacs where no one overlooks anyone else. The immediate locality of Karrageen is peaceful and accessed along a single-track Devon lane (with plenty of passing places) leading down to the sea at the lost world of Hope Cove and its little village. After wandering through the sleepy rows of fishermen's cottages you'll think it eminently possible that this is still a place of clandestine meetings of pirates and smugglers, and that a raid from 'the revenue' isn't far off, such is the sense of detachment and timelessness in the air.

If you fancy breakfast by your tent, why not devour one of Karrageen's locally renowned (and oh so fresh) croissants. There are also a couple of pubs in the village serving decent food.

COOL FACTOR A simple site with enough space to spread out and relax.

WHO'S IN Tents, campervans, caravans, dogs – yes. Groups – no.

ON SITE Large grassy pitches, terraced and tree-lined, offering extra privacy, many with views across the valley. Plenty of electrical hook-ups. Facilities are excellent, with decent loos and 9 showers (4 women's, 4 men's, 1 family/disabled room equipped for baby-changing). The 20p shower charge is to preserve Karrageen's scarce spring-water supply. There are 50 hook-ups and campers have access to the freezer.

OFF SITE All the attractions of south Devon, including Torbay, are easily accessible from here, but locally – aside from walking the cliff paths – the boat trips on the rivers are the real treats: book a return sailing trip from Kingsbridge to Salcombe (01548 853607); or River Dart trip from Totnes to Dartmouth (01803 555872). Or take the sea tractor to Burgh Island.

FOOD & DRINK Posh nosh with a view can be found at the South Sands Hotel (01548 859000; southsands.com) in Salcombe, while in Hope the Sun Bay Hotel (01548 561371; sunbayhotel-hopecove.co.uk) does very good food, and the Hope and Anchor (01548 561295; hopeandanchor.co.uk) offers economical prices.

GETTING THERE From the A38 at Wrangaton take the A3121 south; left on to the B3196 to Kingsbridge and then the A381 towards Salcombe. At Malborough turn sharp right and then after ½ mile turn right again (signed Bolberry) and carry on down the lane for 1 mile, past the farm site. Karrageen reception is on the left.

OPEN Easter–end of September.

THE DAMAGE Tent, car + 2 adults and 2 children £15–£32 (depending on season and tent size) per night. Electric hook-up £3; dog £1.

hole station

Hole Station, Highampton, Beaworthy, Devon EX21 5JH 01409 231266 www.freewebs.com/holestationcampsite

Situated on the land of a former railway station in a sparsely populated part of Devon, this adult-only hideaway is a truly special place. We first heard about it in 2009, and it quickly became a favourite among *Cool Camping* readers, and we're pleased to say that it has retained all its rustic charm – along with its secluded woodland pitches, campfires and natural beauty.

Whether you bring your own tent or opt for a pre-erected Rent-A-Tent here, you're going to love your pitch. There are just 19 of them, spread about the place in woodland clearings. Each pitch bears its own number and offers privacy within a magical tree-filled setting. Each has a tarp strung up to one side, allowing some added all-weather protection and creating the perfect space to set up your own bush-craft kitchen.

The owners Greg and Liz eventually bought Hole Station after keeping their eyes on the property for years. They live in what was the old ticket office while their kids are residents of a renovated old railway carriage next door (think Annie and Clarabel-style from *Thomas The Tank Engine*) next door. Together they are slowly bringing the wood back to its former forest glory by coppicing and pollarding, which they do in winter, after the last of the season's campers has packed up and gone home.

The cut-down wood is used to create wildlife habitats and fuel for campfires. So feel a little smug, as you sit mesmerised by the licking flames of your fire at night, that you're forming a symbiotic relationship with the trees all around you. In fact, the clearing you're pitched in is helping to shed more life-giving light on the young oaks nearby,

enabling them to have a kick-start at growing into huge, majestic trees likely to outlive us for centuries to come.

It's not just the campfire culture, perfect pitches and woodland restoration that Liz, Greg and family have got right at Hole Station, though. The loos are of the compost variety and all rubbish (including food waste) is recycled or turned into compost wherever possible in order to give something back to this lovely corner of England.

Finally their resident pony Sanne is on hand to provide horse-and-trap rides and there are three goats – the preposterously named Dominar Rigel 16th, Kha'Dargo and Grace. Greg and Liz plan to re-launch their meadow as a centre for 'low-tech living' courses. Plus there's a signed Woodland Walk on which you half expect to encounter a fairy or two before reaching (handily labelled) The End – a top spot for watching the sunset. Evenings are peaceful wherever you are, with quiet time after 10pm.

So there you have it: Hole Station is as peaceful and bucolic as it gets, and about as refreshing and romantic a country getaway as you will find.

COOL FACTOR Camping in magical woodland clearings or meadow, with campfires, bush kitchens and a general atmosphere of true camping escapism.

WHO'S IN Tents – yes. Campervans, caravans, dogs, groups, kids, radios, TVs, musical instruments – no.

ON SITE Most pitches are situated in clearings in the woodland, with the remainder in the Culm meadow near to the facilities block. Campfires are permitted and you can sign up for a kit consisting of logs, kindling and firelighters. Park in the car park and transport gear using the wheelbarrows. The facilities block has covered washing-up stations with hot water, solar lighting, a freezer for cool blocks, electric showers and a charging station inside an old telephone box. Rent-A-Tent pitches feature fully equipped kitchens, cool boxes, grills, proper dining tables and chairs and washing-up stations.

OFF SITE Dartmoor is a 20-minute drive away and the beaches of Bude and Widemouth are a 35–40-minute drive in the opposite direction. You can be standing on a Dartmoor Tor in the morning, swimming in the Atlantic in the afternoon, enjoying dinner in a tucked-away country pub in the evening, and finishing the day sitting gazing into your campfire on site. If you fancy honing your Robin Hood skills, there's an archery centre just down the road: Arms of Old (01409 231171; armsofold.co.uk).

FOOD & DRINK Three pubs are within walking distance – the Golden Inn in Highampton (01409 231200), the Half Moon at Sheepwash (01409 231376; halfmoonsheepwash.co.uk) and the Torridge Inn in Black Torrington (01409 231243; thetorridgeinn.co.uk).

GETTING THERE M5 south, then A30 to Okehampton. Turn right (signposted Hatherleigh) when you reach the White Hart. Continue towards Hatherleigh then take the first exit at the roundabout (signed Highampton and Holsworthy). Go through Highampton village and, after 1 mile, turn left opposite the turnoff to Black Torrington. Hole Station is on the right.

OPEN April–late September.

THE DAMAGE £9 per person per night for BYO campers. Kitchen shelter, bench and firepit on every pitch. Rent-A-Tent for 2 adults £35 per night.

ocean pitch campsite

Ocean Pitch Campsite, Moor Lane, Croyde, Devon EX33 1NZ 07581024348 www.oceanpitch.co.uk

Thinking of Devon often evokes sepia-toned scenes of cream teas, chocolate-box cottages and rambling on wild Exmoor. Yet this genteel image of the county is only as true as you make it around these parts. Sure, there's the traditional charm of the sleepy village of Georgeham, not to mention the candy-floss 'n' kiss-me-quick chic of family resorts like Woolacombe. But if you've descended upon the North Devon coast with your tent on your back, your board under your arm and adventure on your mind, you've come to the right place – for Croyde Bay is undoubtedly England's surf capital.

Acres of sand, pounding surf, and bronzed lifeguards... welcome to the Gold Coast. It may be a tad cooler than the Aussie version but, more importantly, it is much nearer for us Poms. Okay, so our cousins down under might enjoy near perma-sunny skies, but on an early summer's morning, with the breeze just right, we'd take Croyde over Byron Bay any day of the week. With its lush green hills ravining down to blustery expanses of open beach, there's no disputing the beauty of Croyde Bay, a wide sweep of dune-backed sand right in the heart of the village gifting awesome waves to pros and beginners alike.

Anyone who was lucky enough to secure a pitch at legendary local campsite Mitchum's will know all about the spectacular views from this enviably elevated spot. Now that it's operating under the new moniker Ocean Pitch, newbies and veterans alike will be pleased to know that surfing is still big on the agenda. As new owners Benny and Lou are all too aware, surfers are an enthusiastic bunch (to put it mildly). Hours can pass as they scan the endless blue horizon for that elusive perfect wave. But from its priceless vantage point, Ocean Pitch is one of the few campsites in the area with direct beach views, meaning you can keep an eye on the surf from your... erm... ocean pitch, and race down with your board just as the waves are breaking. And if you're not here for the surf, it's just as great being able to wake up and see the ocean each morning before you cook your breakfast sausages. The stunning Croyde Bay provides a perfect canvas for this unparalleled campsite masterpiece, and the site is on the coastal path, so it's easy to reach the neighbouring beaches on foot.

COOL FACTOR Stunning views over Croyde Bay – the beach is a stone's throw away.

WHO'S IN Tents, campervans, well-behaved groups – yes. Caravans, dogs, stags, hens – no. Kids welcome but the owners prefer to limit the number of small children on site, so check when booking.

ON SITE 50 spacious pitches. Room for small and medium sized tents. Large tents can be accommodated at the top of the campsite. Hot showers, immaculately clean toilets, outside cold showers for washing wetsuits, washing-up basins, basic tent hire, Wi-Fi internet access, BBQ bricks, mobile phone charging at reception, cold drinks and snacks, friendly staff on site 24 hrs.

OFF SITE Book lessons on site with Lyndon Wake Surf School (01271 890078; lyndonwake.com) or visit the Museum of British Surfing (01271 815155; museumofbritishsurfing.org.uk) in Braunton. Take advantage of the stunning coast path with a walk to Baggy Point; or try horseriding on Croyde beach with Roylands Riding Holidays (01271 890898; northdevon-ridingholidays.com). Discover the area on two wheels by hopping on the Tarka Trail and exploring the beautiful coast and countryside. Bikes can be hired from Tarka Trail Cycle Hire (01271 813339; tarkabikes.co.uk) in Braunton.

FOOD & DRINK The Thatch (01271 890349; thethatchcroyde. com) pub is a lively surfers' hangout with decent food. The Blue Groove (01271 890111; blue-groove.co.uk) combines a beach-bum vibe with trippy artwork and an eclectic menu. In Georgeham, just inland, try the food and ales at The Rock Inn (01271 890322; therockgeorgeham.co.uk). For some of the best fish and chips on the North Devon coast, go to Squires (01271 815533; squiresfishrestaurant.co.uk) in Braunton.

GETTING THERE Follow the A361 to Braunton then the B3231 into Croyde. Turn left in the centre of the village then left again on to Moor Lane. The site is at the end of the lane.

PUBLIC TRANSPORT Train to Barnstaple then 10 minutes' walk to the bus station and bus 308 to Moor Lane. Benny and Lou also do shuttle runs for a small fee.

OPEN Mid Spring–end Summer.

THE DAMAGE £13–£15 per person per night; £3 per car per night. Kids under 12 years half price.

little meadow

Little Meadow, Watermouth, Ilfracombe, North Devon EX34 9SJ 01271 866862 www.littlemeadow.co.uk

The ancient South American tribes of Inca and Maya might have invented terracing to help with their crop cultivation, but seldom can they have done it so well as the folk have here at Little Meadow. By levelling off the land in a series of flat lawns, they've ensured that campers benefit from being plumb-line level with the well-tended soft grass for easy tent-pegging, while still enjoying views of the stunning North Devon coast. This Area of Outstanding Natural Beauty has everything: dramatic cliffs, wide sandy beaches and quaint little coves and harbours.

The terracing also helps create privacy – you'd never guess there are 50 pitches on this unassuming, environmentally friendly campsite, all set in a beautifully kept 100-acre organic farm. Part of this is down to their sensible policy on dwelling size, with the campsite owners actively discouraging mega-size tents or massive motorhomes. Everywhere you walk brings another unexpected delight, whether it's a rabbit hip-hopping across a nearby meadow or a set of swings for kids tucked away in a corner. There's also an outdoor table tennis table set up for use by all guests, and you can buy bats and balls at reception. While here, why not pick up some of the store's lovely regional products – from bacon, eggs and local meats to truly moreish homemade cakes. Bright splashes of flowers border the pitching areas, providing colourful framing to the views over Watermouth Bay, the Bristol Channel and the cliffs of Hangman Point. Its proximity to all things nautical is also in evidence, with huge old anchors, carved driftwood and colourful floats and buoys scattered around the reception area. It's a magnificent spot in which to settle comfortably into a deckchair, or one of the giant hammocks, and survey the scenery. You might even spy a seal or a basking shark if you're lucky (and in possession of a good pair of binoculars).

If you can drag yourself away, though, there are several must-dos in the area. A day trip to Lundy Island, by ferry from nearby Ilfracombe, offers outstanding views of England, Wales and the Atlantic. It might be just 11 miles from the mainland, but the sense of remoteness is incredible. There's no ferry between November and March, but well-heeled folk can always opt for the daily helicopter service (Monday–Friday). You should also consider taking a fishing trip from Ilfracombe to catch bass, pollack, whiting, cod and mackerel, which are all plentiful here. Gut them on the boat – under the tutelage of the skipper, of course – and you could have your breakfast, lunch and dinner sorted for the day. Alternatively, spend a day learning to ride the waves at one of the many surf schools in the area, at Woolacombe, Croyde or Saunton Sands; or take a beach horseriding lesson courtesy of Woolacombe Riding Stables. There's also Exmoor on your doorstep, of course, which is fabulous for walking. Plus it's not far from the site to the Hunter's Inn pub, from where there are any number of glorious treks you could do, including an easy stroll to the sea at Heddon's Mouth, after which you'll definitely have earned yourself a post-ramble pint.

COOL FACTOR Well-tended terraces providing magnificent ocean views.

WHO'S IN Tents, campervans, caravans, dogs (on leads) – yes. Groups, mega-size tents and huge motorhomes – no.

ON SITE Approximately 50 pitches plus an octagonal camping pod. The washblock has toilets, hot showers, washing machine and hairdryers. There's also ice-pack freezing and a basic shop selling essentials and local produce. Electric hook-ups are available. There's a small, wooded play area for kids, table tennis, Wi-Fi and a dog-exercising area. No campfires.

OFF SITE The closest attraction to the site is Watermouth Castle (01271 867474; watermouthcastle.com), a large stately home with old-fashioned exhibitions inside and a theme park behind. The other side of nearby Combe Martin, the Combe Martin Wildlife and Dinosaur Park (01271 882486; wildlifedinosaurpark.co.uk) is a zoo-cum-theme park with a dinosaur slant. In the opposite direction you can explore the rockpools at the unique Victorian Tunnels Beaches in Ilfracombe (01271 879882; tunnelsbeaches.co.uk).

FOOD & DRINK The onsite shop sells milk, cheese, eggs and home-made cakes. In Ilfracombe, Espresso (01271 855485; seafoodrestaurantilfracombe.co.uk) is a seafood restaurant famous for its crab and lobster dishes – all caught locally; and Brit-art wonderboy Damien Hirst's Number 11 The Quay (01271 868090; 11thequay.co.uk), flies the flag for modern British cuisine. Within walking distance, The Old Sawmill Inn (01271 882259; thesawmillinn.co.uk) is a serviceable family pub down the hill near Watermouth Bay.

GETTING THERE Little Meadow lies between Ilfracombe and Combe Martin. Leave the M5 at J27, take the A361 to Barnstaple. Just past the South Molton exit, turn right (signposted Combe Martin). Go through Combe Martin; the campsite is 500 metres past Watermouth Castle on the left.

PUBLIC TRANSPORT Train to Barnstaple then bus to the site.

OPEN Easter–late September.

THE DAMAGE Tent, 2 people and a car £14.50–£22 per night.

westland farm

Westland Farm, Bratton Fleming, Barnstaple, North Devon EX31 4SH 01598 763301 www.westlandfarm.co.uk

For city-dwelling campers especially, there are few things that bring the reality of camping home as much as taking a stroll through a dewy early morning field to use a shower block. Pausing to inhale the clear air – still scented with the smoky fragrance of last night's campfire – while watching the mist rising off the rolling fields, even the most jaded urbanite can't fail to be stirred.

Westland Farm is the perfect place for such epiphanies: a beautifully tranquil glampsite that looks out over a small lake surrounded by rolling, sheep-dotted hills. There's a variety of accommodation too, ranging from camping pitches in a lush, grassy field to a brilliant shepherd's hut set in a quiet corner at the top of the farm. Close to the loos and showers and nestled next to a babbling brook, the hut comes complete with a 5-ft double bed and small child bunk bed and airbed (if you need it) – perfect for a family of four. Then there's the giant yurt that comfortably sleeps six and a brand new, hand-built Drover Hut (also sleeping six) with a kitchen that houses a wood-fired oven and gas hob, in its own private corner of a field next to the stream. You can even snag a B&B room in the farmhouse if the outdoor life is not for you and, in case you're feeling lazy, they'll even cook you breakfast. A beautiful spot, and perfect for both a romantic getaway and an escape from the urban jungle.

COOL FACTOR Feeling like you're part of a working farm.

WHO'S IN Everyone, really. Tents, campervans, caravans, dogs (although not in the yurt), all kinds of groups – yes.

ON SITE Campfires allowed (in pits), 5 pitches, clean washrooms with 2 toilets and 2 showers, fridge-freezer, mobile charging point and fresh eggs available from the farm's hens. Kids can also help feed the horses or lambs.

OFF SITE Exmoor Zoo (01598 76335) is close by, and the beautiful towns of Ilfracombe, Woolacombe, Lynton and Lynemouth all offer plenty to explore.

FOOD & DRINK The Black Venus Inn (01598 763251; blackvenusinn.co.uk) in Challacombe, a 5-minute drive away, has superb home-cooked food in nice surroundings. The Old Station Inn (01598 763520; oldstationhouseinn.co.uk) at Blackmoor Gate is worth a look for its fine home-cooked food and atmospheric surroundings – good kids play area too. The New Inn at Goodleigh (01271 342488; thenew-inn.co.uk) also offers locally sourced products and excellent rural views from its beer garden. If you're looking to buy produce to cook, check out Barsntaple's famous indoor Pannier Market, which offers fresh local produce plus flowers, crafts, fashion and more.

GETTING THERE Head down the A39 in North Devon, setting the sat nav for EX31 4SH. Keep the speed down, because it's easy to miss the farm's sign when you're close.

OPEN All year.

THE DAMAGE Camping £8 per person per night; children half the adult fee. Under-4s free. Shepherd's hut from £75 per night, low season. Yurt £80–£85 per night for up to 4 people (extra people £7). Children cost half the adult fee. Under-4s free. Drover's Hut from £85 per night.

west middlewick farm

West Middlewick Farm, Nomansland, Tiverton, Devon EX16 8NP 01884 861235 www.westmiddlewick.co.uk

Ellie and her family are on their third visit to West Middlewick Farm this year. She's given her dad strict instructions to wake her up each morning in time to feed the lambs and help out with anything else in need of an enthusiastic pair of hands here. In fact, Ellie has become such an able farmhand she's even been given her own set of overalls. Because at this working dairy farm, just outside the sleepy hamlet of Nomansland near Tiverton, campers and their kids are encouraged to take an interest in what goes on around here.

The farm sits between the camping fields and the facilities block, so you'll inevitably wander past and find popping your head into one of the barn irresistible, with their welcoming labels and friendly residents. Getting to know the animals and helping with their care comes hoof-in-hoof with a stay at West Middlewick, and has done since 1933.

As Ellie's parents found out, this refreshing ethos is a huge hit with kids, with some actually begging their parents to leave the beach early so that they're back in time to watch the cows being milked and to help distribute the pig feed. Rabbits in hutches sit on the driveway, guinea pigs snuffle around, chickens roam freely by the barns and companionable cats prowl around on the hunt for attention.

The atmosphere is one of community and conviviality; adults chat cheerfully while their children race around together. And it's not just the kids who get caught up in the West Middlewick way; adults of all ages return year on year to fuss the animals and relax at this no-frills site... Watch out for Ellie and family when you arrive!

COOL FACTOR Lend a hand on a friendly farm.

WHO'S IN Tents, campervans, caravans, dogs (on leads and if good with other animals), groups (in the lower field) – yes.

ON SITE The site slopes down from the farm, and has hook-ups, water taps and a track for cycling round the edge. The more informal lower field has taps and hook-ups at the top. Facilities are a walk away from the site, near the farmhouse. One ladies' block – loos, basins, 2 hot showers (£1 for 10 minutes; 20p for 2 minutes), disabled loo/shower room with baby-changing. Around the corner are 2 washing-up sinks and a washing machine (£4). The gents' has loos and shower (also metred). There are 3 wooden cabins sleeping 6 in another field. No campfires, but BBQs off the ground are okay.

OFF SITE You can head to nearby Tiverton Castle (01884 253200; tivertoncastle.com), a compact castle that is informative as well as fun, or find out how honey is made and bees are kept at the excellent Quince Honey Farm (01769 572401; quincehoneyfarm.co.uk).

FOOD & DRINK The farm has a small shop selling local produce. There's also a freezer full of lovely Devon ice cream. The nearby Thelbridge Cross Inn (01884 860316; thelbridgexinn.co.uk) does cream teas, bar snacks and full meals. Slightly further afield, in Bickleigh, the Fisherman's Cot pub (01884 855237), on the banks of the river Exe, has fabulous views from its beer garden.

GETTING THERE Take the A361 towards Tiverton (off the M5). After 7 miles take the B3137 from the roundabout towards Witheridge, for 9 miles. A mile after Nomansland you'll see the farm on the right.

PUBLIC TRANSPORT Train to Tiverton, then bus no. 155 drops campers off at the farm.

OPEN All year.

THE DAMAGE Pitch + 2 adults from £9. May half-term extra £2 per night; July 20th–August 31st an extra £4 per night.

ENGLAND 61

petruth paddocks

Petruth Paddocks, Labourham Drove, Cheddar, Somerset BS27 3XW 07813 320870 www.petruthpaddocks.co.uk

Following its 2005 appearance in the television series *Seven Natural Wonders*, the craggy cliffs and dazzling caves of Cheddar Gorge were voted the second greatest natural wonder in the UK, and it doesn't take an expert to see why. As you follow the windy riverbed road along the former route of the Cheddar Yeo, steep green slopes carve ever deeper before you and you can't help but wonder how it looked with water thundering through. In fact, the river does still flow, now far beneath the surface, and its handy work has continued below ground, carving out spectacular caves and narrow limestone tunnels. It's not until you reach the village itself that the water reappears, winding away from the beautiful Mendip Hills.

It is here, on the doorstep of Cheddar Village, that you can find Petruth Paddocks, whose open grassy meadows beckon would-be campers inside. Down a track to the wooden gateway, campers, glampers and caravanners alike arrive directly into a large open field, fronted by a small white reception tent and a pair of picnic benches. After a chat with easy-going Jules, the site becomes your own and it's entirely up to you where you pitch. Chose from the plentiful space before you, with two pre-pitched tipis at the rear of the field, or head through a gate into the next-door meadow, aptly described as the 'chill-out field'. At its centre, a dilapidated Land Rover has become every child's playground, saddling up as they do in the driver's seat or clambering on the bonnet, while to one side a horse paddock nudges the edge of the campsite; another distraction for playful children.

The relaxed, pitch-where-you-like, attitude continues through the rest of the site, which rightfully prides itself on a laid-back philosophy and welcoming atmosphere for all. Music is welcome, balls can be kicked around and campfires are very much encouraged, with a quad bike humming around the site each evening offering more firewood and kindling to those in need. Don't be surprised when the trailer comes past with as many children as logs on the back – the quad is a popular ride with the little ones!

In the centre of the site, by the gate between the different fields, simple sanitary facilities are provided. Hot showers are housed in spacious cabins, so there's plenty of space to hang your clothes, with an adjacent toilet block on one side and washing-up sinks on the other. There are also a number of drinking water taps dotted around the site.

From your pitch, head by foot, bike or car into the surrounding area, stopping at reception to grab some info and brochures. On foot, it is Cheddar that beckons, with a collection of good eateries and the gateway back into the gorge. Those on two wheels should follow the Strawberry Line, an excellent cycle route that starts within metres of the campsite. Taking the car offers plenty to see and do, whether it be historic Wells' magnificent cathedral, Glastonbury Tor or the beautiful beaches of northern Somerset.

COOL FACTOR Easy-going camping for all, just a stroll away from Cheddar Gorge.

WHO'S IN Everyone! Caravans, campervans, motorhomes, tents, families, groups, couples, dogs...

ON SITE 400 pitches (15 with hook-ups). 12 hardstanding. A 6-berth and an 8-berth tipi also available for hire. There are toilet and shower blocks in the corner of the main field: 8 showers, 6 ladies, 4 gents plus urinals. Campfires are encouraged, with firewood delivered to your door every evening. Wi-Fi on site.

OFF SITE It's a 5-minute walk into Cheddar and a 15–20 minute walk to the start of the gorge (01934 742343; cheddargorge.co.uk), where activities include rock-climbing and abseiling, exploring the caves and Wookey Hole (01749 672243; wookey.co.uk) or learning about the history of this fascinating natural feature. Wells is close by and worth a visit, England's smallest city, with one of its most beautiful cathedrals.

FOOD & DRINK The White Hart (01934 741261; thewhitehartcheddar.co.uk) in the Gorge has a dog-friendly beer garden and offers discounts to Petruth Paddocks campers. The Rodney Stoke Inn (01749 870209; rodneystokeinn. co.uk) on the Wells Road has great views across The Levels, a large garden and play area. The Riverside (01934 742452; riversidecheddar.co.uk) is also a good choice, at the start of the Gorge road in Cheddar.

GETTING THERE From Wells you will pass Winchester Farm and Kart track on your left. This is immediately followed by a nasty S bend, then take the 1st left into Labourham Way. As soon as you've turned off the main road, take a left and then the middle road through the gates with the wooden Petruth Paddocks sign on your right. From the A38 Axbridge direction take the A371 through Cheddar village. Pass the football club and take the 1st right into Labourham Way, then a left and the middle road as above.

OPEN All year.

THE DAMAGE From £9 adults; £6 children; £3 dogs; £2 electric hook-up.

greenacres camping

Barrow Lane, North Wootton, nr Shepton Mallet, Somerset BA4 4HL 01749 890497 www.greenacres-camping.co.uk

Once upon a time, an enchanting couple created a peaceful outdoor living area that was both safe and comfortable for young families and lots of fun for children. They called this place Greenacres – a gigantic four-and-a-half-acre field with just 40 pitches spread around the perimeter. The entire central swathe is reserved for various dragon-slaying and spell-casting playtime activities, which are run by the Lazy Dayzee Crew. They pitch up here at weekends and during the week during school holidays – thereby giving mums and dads an opportunity to kick back without the little ones for an hour or so. When that's not happening, there's the occasional 30-a-side football match taking place in the field fit for Wembley, and perhaps a spot of ping-pong (aka wiff-waff), too. There's no visual electronic entertainment here, just a host of classic old-fashioned activities, such as see-saws, swings and bikes. There's also a very wide selection of books for both children and adults – who will have plenty of time for stress-free reading whilst the small darlings are busy exhausting themselves in the middle of the field.

Now, if all this has left you imagining a site full of noisy spellbound kids chaotically running among all the cars and tents, then relax. All the magic takes place in car- and tent-free zones. At sundown on summer evenings the lanes around the campsite come alive with magic beetles when the site hosts its ever-popular Glow Worm Safaris. And, to be honest, during school holidays at least this site is probably not best suited to quiet, reclusive couples looking for a bit of solitude. But outside of those times it's the perfect place to just turn up and do nothing, whatever age you happen to be. And in early September, when the *Cool Camping* operatives arrived, Greenacres was P&Q personified.

There's plenty of fun to be had in the environs of this fairy-tale campsite, as well. The moody Somerset Levels provide excellent walking opportunities or, if you fancy something that doesn't require wearing boots, there's the nearby cathedral city of Wells; the ancient market town of Shepton Mallet; and hippy-central Glastonbury is only three miles away. Just the spot for picking up a magic wand...

COOL FACTOR A spellbinding family campsite and, out of season, very quiet for the more mature camper.

WHO'S IN Tents, small campervans, groups – yes. Caravans, large motorhomes, dogs – no.

ON SITE 40 large grass pitches, 13 of which have 10-amp electric hook-up. Excellent, if slightly old-fashioned, toilet block. Facilities include toilets, showers, hot and cold water to wash basins, electric hook-ups and fridge-freezers. There are also bikes of all sizes for hire (£7.50 per day) and many toys provided free for the younger campers. Campfires and BBQs are allowed off the ground, with firepits to hire and logs for sale. Hut with local info and books to borrow.

OFF SITE Greenacres is close to the beautiful city of Wells, Glastonbury and the market town of Shepton Mallet. There's also a wealth of nearby attractions including Cheddar Gorge and Caves (01934 742343 cheddargorge.co.uk), Wookey Hole (01749 672243; wookey.co.uk) and Longleat Safari Park (01985 844400; longleat.co.uk).

FOOD & DRINK Ice creams, soft drinks, milk and eggs are available from reception, while fantastic local producers sell their wares here in high season. The family-friendly Lion (01749 890252; thelionatpennard.co.uk), a 20-minute walk away at West Pennard, offers hearty pub fare and some terrific ales. For a special dining treat you can't beat Goodfellows Seafood Restaurant (01749 673866; goodfellowswells.co.uk) 4 miles away in Wells, which does lovely set menus based on what's good that day.

GETTING THERE Greenacres is ¾ mile west of North Wootton village, at the centre of a triangle linking the towns of Wells, Shepton Mallet and Glastonbury. From the M5 take Exit 23 to Wells. The best approach is from the A39 Glastonbury/Wells road at Brownes Garden Centre. Follow the brown campsite signs. From Shepton Mallet take the A37 and A361 through Pilton, then turn right at Steanbow and follow the brown campsite signs (2 miles).

OPEN Start of May–late September.

THE DAMAGE Adults £9 per night; children (2–14) £4.50. Electric hook-up (10 amps) £4.50.

pitchperfect camping

Pitchperfect Camping, Woolverton, Nr Bath, Somerset BA2 7QU 01373 830 733 www.pitchperfectcamping.co.uk

Few campsites can better convey the draw of the Somerset countryside than Pitchperfect Camping – a site whose origins spring from evocative memories of the surrounding land. Yearning for a lifestyle back among the pastures, James and Emma gave up their jobs in bustling Brighton to craft their perfect campsite. With nothing but a dreamy image of sunsets, campfires and rolling hills, they bought an empty plot of land, rolled up their sleeves and set about creating what is now one of Somerset's most charming sites – a slice of rural bliss in a prime location.

Set in a grassy meadow, surrounded by a paddock where horses nose among the daisies, Pitchperfect has 42 tent-only pitches. There is ample space at each pitch and the abundance of toys and ride-on tractors make this a paradise for kids. Sparkly new facilities are kept immaculately clean and well maintained, while clever touches like the hairdryers or fridge-freezers show that Emma and James have really thought the place through.

Head to the onsite shop, which is well stocked with a bounty of local produce, and have a browse through the handy 'ideas board' where guests pin their recommendations. The colourfully scrawled tidbits will point you towards spots like Frome, with its yellow-stone cottages and attractive centre, or Longleat, one of the UK's most magnificent stately homes, joined improbably to a drive-through safari park.

The owner's enthusiasm is infectious and the only challenge is dragging the kids away from the onsite fun and games. The free-roaming chickens, sociable ponies and evening marshmallow sessions around the campfire make it an easy place to lose track of time. Not that it's a bad thing. There are few better places to kick back and enjoy being on holiday. Grab a local cider, fold out a chair and enjoy the tranquillity of this bucolic little bolthole.

COOL FACTOR A perfectly pitched campsite set in a beautiful location.

WHO'S IN Tents only. Dogs, families, groups by arrangement – yes. Campervans, trailer-tents, caravans – no.

ON SITE 2 bell tents for hire, 12 electrical hook-up pitches and 30 standard pitches. 6 showers, 5 men's toilets, 7 women's toilets and a family unit. The washing-up area has sinks, 2 fridge freezers, a kettle, microwave, book swap, kids toys, washing machine and tumble dryer. There's a trampoline, wooden pirate ship, swings, grass mound for kids to play on and ride-on tractors and scooters. There are small ponies in the top field, horses the other side of the fence and chickens and ducks roaming around. An onsite shop sells essentials, including local beers and wine.

OFF SITE Pitchperfect Camping is in an excellent location, with the local villages of Rode and Woolverton boasting 5 pubs between them. It's also a short drive into Frome, one of Somerset's most attractive towns. 14th-century Nunney Castle (08703 331181; EH) vies for your attention along with Longleat (01985 844400; longleat.co.uk), an Elizabethan stately home with a safari park in its extensive grounds (the campsite can offer discounts). Wardour Castle (01747 870487; EH) and Stonehenge (08703 331181; EH) border the historical city of Salisbury.

FOOD & DRINK The Red Lion in Woolverton (01373 830350; redlionwoolverton.co.uk) is a short walk away and serves excellent pub grub. The Mill (01373 831100; mill.butcombe.com) in Rode is another mile down the road and is great for families. There's also a good Indian restaurant at the end of the lane called The Bay Leaf (01373 474825).

GETTING THERE Taking the A36 from Bath towards Warminster you'll come to Woolverton; pass the Red Lion pub and take the 2nd right, towards Lullington. Pass Sleight Farm and the site is 300m further on the right. Coming from Frome, head north on the A361 towards Bath and you come to a series of roundabouts; head towards Bath until the Beckington roundabout. After the River Frome and Toll House, turn left towards Laverton. At the mini crossroad turn left, passing Sleight Farm; the site is 300m further on.

OPEN Easter–end September.

THE DAMAGE Standard pitch (includes 2 adults + 1 car) £19. Electrical pitch £23.

stowford manor farm

Stowford Manor Farm, Wingfield, Trowbridge, Wiltshire BA14 9LH 01225 752253 www.stowfordmanorfarm.co.uk

We can't all be to the manor born, but camping in the grounds of Stowford Manor – a delightfully relaxed campsite on the verdant Wiltshire–Somerset border – gets you close. A stunning 13th-century farmhouse with accompanying mill and assorted workshops provide the backdrop to two camping fields bisected by a stream, itself a great little spot for boating and paddling. If this seems like too much effort, afternoons at Stowford Manor can instead be whiled away in the garden, where sumptuous cream teas are served as you watch hens peck around the millpond and the gurgling River Frome. Bliss...

The facilities are good without being anything to write home about, but they are obviously well cared for. The site is overlooked by the assembled old buildings of Stowford Manor Farm, a perfect vision of a bygone England that has escaped any tasteless tarting-up and simply stands there, radiating dignity and elegance into the camping field.

Camping here isn't about being completely indolent, though. The local Swimming Club is a half-mile downstream; many wild-swimmers stay here, and campers are allowed to use the club for £1 a day. Alternatively, you can cycle along the canal to Bath, less than an hour away. Knowing what makes their campers tick, the Bryants have also printed a map of three pubs within walking distance, all of which have views and serve good ales and terrific food. What more could you want? Another cream tea? Oh, go on then...

COOL FACTOR Rural England at its finest. A peaceful site with river swimming, in a little-known but interesting part of England.

WHO'S IN Tents, campervans, caravans, dogs, groups – yes.

ON SITE 30 pitches with hook-ups spread across 2 fields. Campfires allowed off the ground. Washroom with 2 showers (50p coins), washbasins and washing-up area; plus 3 loos. Tea and scones served 3–6pm.

OFF SITE Farleigh Hungerford Castle (01225 754026; EH) is just up the road in Norton St Phillip, but if you fancy a spot of water-bound activity, head to the Kennet and Avon Canal (0800 1214679) in lovely Bradford-on-Avon, itself a sort of Bath in miniature. If you're going to get wet then do it in the river at Farleigh Hungerford Swimming Club (01225 752253) a few hundred metres downstream of the site.

FOOD & DRINK There are 3 super pubs (all with good food) in close proximity: the New Inn (01225 863123; thenewinnwestwood.co.uk), less than a steep mile's walk away in Westwood; Poplars Inn (01225 752426; poplarsinn.co.uk), in Wingfield; and the Hungerford Arms (01225 754949; hungerfordarms.co.uk) in Farleigh Hungerford. In Corsley, 4 miles up the road, the White Hart (01373 832805) dishes up gastropub nosh at decent prices. White Row Country Foods (01373 830708; whiterowfarm.co.uk) in Frome is famous for its high-quality foods and tea room. The nearest genuine farm shop is about 1 mile away from the site at Springleaze Farm (01225 720006).

GETTING THERE From Bath take the A36 south, then turn east on to the A366. The site can be found 3 miles west of Trowbridge, near Bath.

OPEN Easter–October.

THE DAMAGE Tent and 2 people £16 per night. Extra adult £6. Extra child £3. Electric hook-up £3.

thistledown farm

Thistledown Farm, Tinkley Lane, Nympsfield, Gloucestershire GL10 3UH 01453 860420 www.thistledown.org.uk

Thistledown is quite simply magical. More than just a beautiful campsite nestled among 70 acres of organic meadow and woodland, it is inspirational too. A dream realised by Richard Kelly, who has years of experience in environmental design and construction, as well as farming, Thistledown has been nurtured since 1993, when Richard began creating habitats for the wide range of local plants and wildlife. He now runs the site as an environmental learning centre with his son Ryan, and neither could be more helpful or enthusiastic about this camping environment.

It's easy to locate Thistledown: just head towards a majestic wind turbine located 300 metres from the entrance. The turbine was one of the first to be erected by the increasingly popular Ecotricity, the UK's first provider of mainstream electricity produced from renewable sources. It's a part of the genuine green vibe in this neck of the Gloucestershire woods, so if you've ever fancied living the sustainable *Good Life*, then this is probably the place in which to settle.

In the meantime you can camp in three main areas at Thistledown, with up to 80 pitches available in total. But don't for a minute think that you will be crowded out. The 70 acres take in trees, undulating pasture, glades of wild flowers, and space – everywhere. Even if there's a big group of noisy kids larking about in one of the pastures, with all the tree cover it's unlikely you'll even be aware of it.

The top site allows cars and offers camping on pitches individually mown into a pretty elderflower orchard, while the bottom two pastures are car free. Perfection. You can stretch out knowing nothing (save the odd startled deer) will drive into you. And for those with children, real freedom is a reality here. The pastures are flanked by woodland offering numerous opportunities for lengthy walks, nature watching or just some good old-fashioned hooning around.

Thistledown is a wildlife receptor site, which means species disturbed by developments in the area are rehomed here. Richard and Ryan often run talks, walks and events that are free for campers – from bird walks to bat evenings. At dusk you can actually wander down to a spot where badgers come out to feed and, as long as the wind is in the right direction (so they can't smell or hear you), you'll be able to stay transfixed for ages.

Most pitches have their own firepits and in the evening Richard whizzes by selling wood by the heaped barrowful. You can take your own, but are asked not to collect it from the woods as it provides shelter for the snakes and slow worms. Picnic tables are dotted around for campers – a perfect place to nibble baked goodies from the nearby village of Nailsworth while you enjoy the tranquil environment, stunning views and the nature trails on offer. Streams gurgle in the background and the rope swings near them offer excitement. But the really magical thing about Thistledown is its colour: the trees, grassland and all-round ethos. Pure Green.

COOL FACTOR Camping under the stars in an ancient valley surrounded by nothing but wildlife.

WHO'S IN Tents, groups, dogs (on leads) – yes. Campervans – yes (in elderflower orchard). Caravans – no.

ON SITE 80 unmarked pitches spread across 3 main camping areas: the elderflower orchard (20 pitches), where cars are allowed, and the car-free second (40) and third (20) pastures. The lower pastures are more sheltered and have composting toilets, hot showers and washing-up sinks. The elderflower orchard has events toilets only, but you can walk to facilities in the lower pastures. Campfires allowed in pre-dug firepits. The site has numerous walks, a lake and a birdwatching hide. Wood is available to buy by the barrowload (£10). A shop sells local produce.

OFF SITE A walk through the woods takes you to the fascinating Woodchester Mansion and Park (01453 861541; woodchestermansion.org.uk), a spooky unfinished Gothic manor. The Neolithic Nympsfield Long Barrow has spectacular views over the Severn Valley ` as well as internal burial chambers for viewing. Just along the ridge is the Uley Long Barrow – take a torch if you want to see inside.

FOOD & DRINK Foodie heaven Nailsworth is only 3 miles away, where Hobbs House Bakery sells sublime bread and William's Foodhall is an upmarket deli. Stroud Farmers' Market is open every Saturday 9am–2pm. Good local pubs offering food include the Old Spot Inn (01453 542870; oldspotinn. co.uk) at Dursley, with its own microbrewery, and the Black Horse (01453 872556) at Amberley. For a pub within walking distance, try Nympsfield's Rose & Crown (01453 860240).

GETTING THERE Take the A419 towards Stonehouse; after a mile take a right to Eastington and head on to Frocester. Go straight over the crossroads at the top of the hill and turn left after about 300m, towards Nympsfield. At the staggered junction go straight across, signposted Nailsworth. Thistledown is on your left.

OPEN Weather dependent, usually April–October.

THE DAMAGE Tent £10 per night + adult £7; child (over 4 years) £4; under-4s free. Dogs £2. Camping £5 in elderflower orchard if you arrive by foot, bike or public transport.

hook farm caravan and camping park

Hook Farm, Gore Lane, Uplyme, Lyme Regis, Dorset DT7 3UU 01297 442801 www.hookfarm-uplyme.co.uk

Island hopping dinosaurs were part of the scenery in these parts some 190 million years ago. Many lost their footing and fell into the sea, leaving their mark on what became known as the Jurassic Coast. Hunting down their fossils is a popular sport in the quaint harbour resort of Lyme Regis.

Picturesque and peaceful but within a stone's throw of the lively harbour town, Hook Farm offers the best of both rural and urban worlds. Tucked away in the small village of Uplyme, with views up the pretty Lym Valley, it's a lovely, leafy site that feels quite remote. And being in a designated Dark Valley, there's no light pollution at night – you can just lie back and watch the stars on a clear evening.

A few steps is all it takes to be warmly welcomed at reception, whisked past a section for caravans, and ushered into a beautiful terraced garden valley, where campers look like they're proudly privy to one of the best-kept camping secrets on the south coast. The site itself is well kept and welcoming, with pitches on several different levels, some spacious and open, others secluded and sheltered behind trees and bushes. Generous pitches allow you space to spread out with gazebos and blankets. A dozen are tucked beside various bushy nooks and crannies, offering a little more privacy. You could select your patch

according to your sleeping habits. Early risers should head west to enjoy the morning sun, and night owls looking for a lie-in can camp east, where the last rays of the day fall. Sunsets look best from the top of the hill, and the lower area is better shielded from the elements.

Friendly, quiet and gently undulating, it's a perfect spot for families. Children will enjoy the playground, complete with an old boat to clamber around, while their parents will appreciate the well-stocked shop selling fresh bread and croissants in the mornings and a village pub within easy strolling distance that serves local real ales and wholesome pub grub.

And if the peace and quiet of the countryside isn't enough, there's a great 45-minute walk down the valley, which runs alongside the River Lym and into Lyme Regis, with its bustling harbour, arty gift shops, beach and restaurants and cafés. You can either make it a circular walk and return via the coast path (the camp shop can provide details of the route) or, if you can't face the steep walk back uphill, call the resident tuktaxi, which will take you back to the campsite for about a fiver.

Fortunately for any young, eager fossil-hunters returning empty-handed from a day's beachcombing, plastic dinosaur eggs are sold in the campsite shop, which ought to lift spirits before the next outing.

COOL FACTOR Attractive terraced site in a prime location for fossil-hunting.

WHO'S IN Tents, campervans, caravans, dogs (only certain breeds), families, groups by appointment only – yes. Single-sex groups – no.

ON SITE 100 spacious tent pitches (58 with hook-ups), and 17 static caravans. Large, clean toilet blocks with solar-powered showers, freezers, a washing machine and dryer. Childrens' playground and a well-stocked shop selling local meat and eggs. No campfires, but off-ground BBQs okay.

OFF SITE Guided 3-hour fossil walks along the coastline, Saturday–Tuesday only (07854 377519). Dinosaurland Fossil Museum (01297 443541) in town opens daily. Great walks down the valley to Lyme Regis and along the coast path; fossil hunting beneath the local cliffs. Oh, and if the weather's good, you can just go to the beach.

FOOD & DRINK Hugh Fearnley-Whittingstall's River Cottage (01297 630302; rivercottage.net) is less than 2 miles away. Or take your pick of the many places in Lyme Regis, from Thai on the seafront at Largigi (01297 442432; largigi.com) to high-end cuisine at Hix Oyster and Fish House (01297 446910; hixoysterandfishhouse. co.uk) and the fantastically elaborate and delicious ice-cream sundaes at Rinky Tinks on the promenade.

GETTING THERE From Axminster, head south on the A35 then right on to the B3165 (Lyme Road). In Uplyme, turn right opposite the Talbot Arms pub into Gore Lane; the campsite's on the right.

PUBLIC TRANSPORT Train to Axminster, Dorchester, or Weymouth, then bus no. 31 to the Talbot Arms stop, and up the steep hill to the site.

OPEN March–October half-term.

THE DAMAGE Tent + 2 adults £15–£26 (depending on season and tent size) per night; child (5–16 years) £2.50; under-5s free. Hook-up £3.

rosewall camping

Rosewall Camping, East Farm Dairy, Osmington Mills, Weymouth, Dorset DT3 6HA 01305 832248
www.weymouthcamping.com

Dorset's coast has all the credentials for that perfect summer holiday. If the sun's shining, everyone's out paddling, playing and rockpooling. If it rains, the region is well prepared, with aquariums and oceanariums. With demanding tourists descending here in ever-greater numbers, it's no surprise that many of the campsites have progressed up the evolutionary chain. One such place is Rosewall Camping, which started life as a scrawny, scruffy field and has now developed into a highly polished, lovingly manicured camping ground with plenty of awards and accolades to prove it. Gradual, imperceptible, changes have occurred over the years. Apart from the grass, the amenities have been upgraded and expanded. The result is a highly evolved operation offering a comfortable, easy, hassle-free family holiday, with options to ride horses and fish the neighbouring lakes. If evolutionary pioneer Charles Darwin had been a camper, this is most probably where he would have stayed.

Such perfection won't suit all Cool Campers, but the cracking views and coastal location will. Anyway, those seeking a more rough-and-ready site will be around the corner at Eweleaze Farm. But for those looking for an easy holiday, Rosewall Camping is, as Darwin would say, the natural selection.

COOL FACTOR Coastal location, sea views, lots of onsite things to do.

WHO'S IN Tents, campervans, dogs – yes. Caravans – no.

ON SITE The main onsite attraction is horseriding; lessons/rides can be booked at reception (01305 833578). Facilities include two modern toilet blocks with showers, hairdryer points and washing-up facilities. The lower block has disabled facilities and a newly refurbished laundry room. There is a further laundry room next to the upper toilet block and shop. The shop is well stocked with basic provisions.

OFF SITE There is a small rocky beach about 200 metres from the site. It's fun for rockpooling or catching little crabs, but the main beach for swimming is the shingle beach at Ringstead Bay, about 5–7 minutes' drive. It's also accessible on foot via the coast path (30 minutes). The highly acclaimed Monkey World ape rescue centre (01929 450414; monkeyworld.org) is a 20-minute drive away.

FOOD & DRINK Head down the road at the Smuggler's Inn (01305 833125; smugglersinnosmingtonmills.co.uk), a cute country pub with a little stream running through a pleasant garden kitted out with swings and slides. The food is good-value pub fare and includes local seafood specials; kids' portions are available. For supplies to take back to camp, Craig's Farm Shop (01305 834591; craigsfarmdairy.co.uk) sells home-produced dairy products.

GETTING THERE Approaching from Wareham on the A352 Dorchester Road, turn left at the A353 Weymouth junction. At the Osmington Mills sign, turn left and follow the lane taking the first turning off on the right to the holiday park.

PUBLIC TRANSPORT Take a train to Weymouth, then a bus (X53) to Poole via Osmington village, or the 108 towards Wool via Osmington village, half a mile from the site.

OPEN Easter–end October.

THE DAMAGE Family of 4 costs up to £25, depending on season. Gazebos £5 in high season; pets £2.

white horse campsite

Whitehorse Farm, Osmington, Weymouth, Dorset DT3 6ED 01305 834314 www.whitehorsecampsite.co.uk

The Osmington White Horse was first etched into Dorset's rolling hills in 1808, a tribute to King George III, who frequented the area. Sat astride his 85-metre-long steed, Adonis, this beautiful limestone figure presides over the surrounding countryside, stretching southward to the Jurassic Coast. At the foot of the hill, in a swathe of grassy fields, lies the White Horse Campsite – a fleeting two-month campground beneath the galloping hooves of Adonis. Set in an Area of Outstanding Natural Beauty and less than two miles from the sea, White Horse is a countryside gem in a prime location. Made up of three huge meadows, the site is largely unadulterated grassland with no plastic playgrounds or concrete-clad receptions in sight. Flushing toilets and hot showers on site are conveniently located in two different areas, while a separate washing-up area is also provided for your dishes. Other than that you'll find only open space and a free rein on where to pitch. Tuck against the hedge-line or beneath the giant trees for extra protection, or nestle near the footpaths to give you a head-start when you wander to the pub.

Jan and Paul Critchell (the friendly site owners) will welcome you on arrival and offer up the chance to order some onsite goodies: home-baked croissants for the next morning or a fresh milk delivery for your cereal. Then an attentive but unobtrusive manner sees them return to their rounds on the campsite, a place they're rightfully proud of. Despite the site's vast size, the couple have thoughtfully restricted the campsite to just 30 pitches in each field, meaning campers will never feel short of space. Even a family group with a cluster of mansion-sized tents still have acres in which the kids can run wild.

There are few sites better located for activities on the south coast. Take one of the two footpaths that lead away from the meadows to Osmington and Sutton Poyntz (the latter has an excellent pub) or carry on towards the coast where you eventually join the South West Coast Path. Those in a car can head east to the unique delights of Durdle Door, Lulworth Cove and Kimmeridge Bay, or head west to the endless reach of pebbly Chesil Beach. If the weather has less seaside-friendly ideas, then historic Dorchester is also close at hand; an inland market town with plenty to keep campers occupied.

COOL FACTOR So much space but so few pitches. An easy-going campsite with loads of room, excellent views and the best of Dorset right on the doorstep.

WHO'S IN Tents, families, couples and dogs – yes. Campervans, caravans, motorhomes, noisy groups – no.

ON SITE 30 tent-only pitches in 3 fields. 2 toilet and shower blocks on site, with flushing loos, hot showers and plenty of dry space for changing – plus a separate washing-up area. Horses, sheep and cattle graze the surrounding fields and don't mind ogling children, while two footpaths also lead away from the campsite, one heading towards Osmington, the other to Sutton Poyntz.

OFF SITE The attractive town of Weymouth fronts a pleasant sandy beach, stretching at its end to the Isle of Portland. On the other side of the island, famous Chesil Beach reaches endlessly into the distance, trapping a pool of water behind it that hosts the Abbotsbury Swannery (01305 871858; abbotsbury-tourism. co.uk/swannery). Those who head in the opposite direction will discover Durdle Door and beautiful Lulworth Cove, unique coastal features that precede the crescent of Kimmeridge Bay. Inland, ruined Tyneham Village makes for an interesting and eerie visit. The Georgian town of Dorchester is a short drive away, inextricably linked with Thomas Hardy, whose former home (01305 262366; NT) sits on the outskirts of town.

FOOD & DRINK You can book a delivery of groceries from the farm on arrival. There are two pubs within 15 minutes' walking distance. The Springhead (01305 832117; thespringhead.co.uk) in Sutton Poyntz is closest, while The Sunray (01305 832148) in Osmington is also not far away.

GETTING THERE The campsite is directly underneath the White Horse – visible to your right if travelling from Warmwell Cross Roundabout on the A353. The entrance is situated immediately before the blue Weymouth Portland sign. Travelling from Weymouth, the entrance is visible on the left 100m after the Top Gear Weymouth garage.

OPEN 28 days in July and August.

THE DAMAGE Adults £10. Children under 14 free. Cars and dogs free.

woodyhyde

Woodyhyde, Valley Road, Corfe Castle, Isle of Purbeck, Dorset BH20 5HT 01929 480274 www.woodyhyde.co.uk

In a region full to bursting with wonderful campsites we've come across a real gem in Woodyhyde. Set among the iconic chalky downs of the Purbeck Hills, this traditional family-friendly site lies in Dorset's spiritual heart.

The campsite itself lies across three fields – a small field adjacent to the Swanage Steam Railway line, a spacious medium field, where you'll also find the main facilities block, and a large field with acres of room and broad countryside views. Wide-open spaces here are just crying out for rowdy ball games or a few flicks of a frisbee. Unmissable kiddy bliss.

The leafy countryside vista is the perfect backdrop for some early morning yoga, but don't be alarmed if your meditation is interrupted by a sudden woosh and parp – that'll be the Swanage Steam Railway. The old engines whistle and wheeze past the site between Swanage and Corfe Castle. It's just a pity it doesn't stop right here – the nearest station is at Harman's Cross, 10 minutes' walk away.

Being based on the Isle of Purbeck (in actual fact a peninsula, but we're not ones to quibble), you're just a stone's throw from some of the great beaches and coastal views that mark Dorset's famed Jurassic Coast. Be sure to take time to visit the iconic Durdle Door – a huge natural limestone sea arch and unmissable photo opportunity.

With refreshingly understated facilities, acres of space, easy access to some of the region's hidden coves and the obligatory steam train chugging gently past your tent, Woodyhyde is an utterly charming throwback to the camping of yesteryear. Sit back and relax as younger campers live out their own Blytonesque adventures.

COOL FACTOR Room to move, room to breathe, room to play.

WHO'S IN Tents, dogs, groups – yes. Caravans – no.

ON SITE Around 150 unmarked pitches on 3 fields across 13 acres, plus 66 pitches with electric hook-up and 25 hardstandings. Dogs are allowed in 2 fields; the largest field is dog-free. A brand new shower block houses 18 showers (including separate male and female disabled shower/toilet) and external washing-up facilities. A large shop at reception sells camping essentials, general supplies, ice pack re-freezing and gas bottle exchange. A selection of beers, ales and wine is also available.

OFF SITE There's no better way to explore the stunning Jurassic Coast than by ambling along the South West Coast Path. The long, sandy Blue-Flag beach at Studland Bay is just 10 minutes' drive from Woodyhyde, and the entire Jurassic Coast, including Lulworth Cove and Durdle Door, is within easy reach. Putlake Farm (01929 422917; putlakeadventurefarm. co.uk) at Langton Matravers, offers animal adventures. Or hop on the picturesque Swanage Steam Railway (01929 425800; swanagerailway.co.uk).

FOOD & DRINK Walk over Ballard Down, passing Old Harry Rocks and winding up at the award-winning Bankes Arms Country Inn (01929 450225; bankesarms.com). They serve food made with fresh local produce and a range of ales from small independent breweries, including their own.

GETTING THERE From the village of Corfe Castle, take the A351 towards Swanage. A mile outside Corfe, look out for the 'Woodyhyde' sign and turning on the right, then follow the track under the bridge and into the campsite.

PUBLIC TRANSPORT Train to Wareham, then bus no. #142 to Harman's Cross; the site is about 350m off the main road.

OPEN Beginning March–end October.

THE DAMAGE Adults £8; children (under 13) £4; a family of 4 £20; hook-up £5; D of E £6; shower tokens 50p.

downshay farm

Downshay Farm, Haycrafts Lane, Swanage, Dorset BH19 3EB 01929 480316 www.downshayfarm.co.uk

A trip to Downshay Farm is a little like embarking on a journey back in time. An ancient steam locomotive services the nearest train station to the campsite, huffing and puffing the six miles between Swanage and Norden. It's a fitting way to arrive, aboard a relic from the bygone era of romantic and memorable travel, a time when a large part of the thrill of the trip was the journey itself.

From Harman's Cross station it's a short uphill walk through narrow country lanes, where you may not even see a car nor any other sign of modern life, except in peak summer. Turning right into the farm and on past the old stone farmhouse, you'll find the camping field 100 metres up the track.

Campsites with sprawling views, wide-open spaces and big skies don't come much better than Downshay Farm. The hospitable owners – who live in the large Victorian farmhouse – have struck gold with their location, near to the historically rich Jurassic coastline in one direction and stunning Corfe Castle in the other. This is a campsite with stately views; the castle perches on the Purbeck Hills in sight of campers and looks spectacular shrouded in early morning mist.

The facilities, a mixture of modern pre-fab and older-style wooden blocks, are fantastically clean (guests must mop up after their own shower and it works: the cubicles are spotless) and the pitches are sheltered and un-numbered, bordered by tall trees. It's sloping in places, so finding a good pitch is key, as is pitching in a direction to ensure a good night's sleep on these challenging gradients. But sloping campsites are often on higher ground and higher ground often means views, and so we've arrived at the crux of our journey. The views from Downshay Farm stretch out across the Dorset countryside like an age-old landscape painting.

If the gradient across much of the camping area is a problem, flatter pitches can be found on the lower ground around the edge of the site, but the trade-off will be a lack of views. The large tent field offers about 90 unmarked pitches (there is no specific limit – the owner just brings out the 'full' sign when he thinks it's time) and the field is usually left empty in the centre for games of football or frisbee.

Walks across the Vale of Purbeck also run right by the campsite, including an unmissable – if energetic – day-trek to Studland Bay and Lulworth Cove. Sadly the site is only open for camping during the school holidays, and you have to be quick or lucky to grab a decent pitch at this wildly popular Dorset haven.

COOL FACTOR Stunning views across the Dorset countryside to Corfe Castle.

WHO'S IN Tents, small campervans, caravans (in a separate field), well-behaved groups, dogs (on leads) – yes. Transit vans, motorbikes – no.

ON SITE Room for about 90 tents. The caravan field has 12 pitches (all with hook-ups) and a separate facilities block. Each well-maintained block contains hot showers (5 women's, 4 men's, 2 unisex), and toilets. Hairdrying point; freezers for ice packs; washing-up areas. BBQs and off-ground firebowls are okay.

OFF SITE On sunny days head to Swanage, Studland or Shell Bay beaches, or take the ferry to Sandbanks. Or take a steam train ride on Swanage Railway (01929 425800; swanagerailway.co.uk) to the evocative ruin of Corfe Castle (01929 481294; NT). Trains depart regularly from Harman's Cross station, 5 minutes' walk from the campsite. Consider also a visit to the excellent Tank Museum in Bovington (01929 405096; tankmuseum.org).

FOOD & DRINK Corfe Castle's ice-cream shop – Box of Delights – sells Purbeck specialities and Dorset cream teas (01929 481060). The real ales, ciders and pasties at the Square & Compass (01929 439229; squareandcompasspub.co.uk) in Worth Matravers are worth seeking out, as is the pleasant garden at the Scott Arms (01929 480270; thescottarms.com) in Kingston. Both are a 10-minute drive from the site.

GETTING THERE From Wareham, take the A351 following signs to Corfe Castle. Continue past the castle on the A351 for 2 miles. At the crossroads at Harman's Cross, turn right into Haycrafts Lane. Continue on this road for 1 mile and look out for the signs on the right.

PUBLIC TRANSPORT From Wareham train station, catch the Swanage bus to Harman's Cross or Gallows Gore, from where it's a short walk.

OPEN For 10 days around Whitsun weekend, then again for school holidays (mid-July–early September).

THE DAMAGE Adults £5 per night; children (over–11) £2, (under 11) £1 + £2/£3/£4 for small/medium/large tent; cars £2. Minimum fee per night £10.

acton field

Acton Field, Langton Matravers, Swanage, Dorset BH19 3HS 01929 439424 www.actonfieldcampsite.co.uk

Hidden behind a discreet residential slip road in Langton Matravers, random tufts of wild flowers adorn the natural bumps and curves of Acton Field on the Purbeck Hills. The unspoilt – verging on wild – terrain comprises a wide, sloping, grassy campsite, where you can see Swanage Bay glistening in the distance. Arrive early in peak season to claim the best-sheltered and flattest spot you can find, as exposed parts can get very windy.

Booking is required from the last week in July to the end of August, and outside those dates campers need to be members of DEFRA-approved organisations such as the Camping and Caravanning Club. Don't let this put you off, though: the minimal effort it takes to join is rewarded with a beautifully rugged camping experience that not every man and his dog can overpopulate.

Essential day trips include the scenic cliff-top walk from the village to swim at the Dancing Ledge tidal rock pool and caves. In 40 minutes you can walk along Priests Way down to Swanage Bay for a fish-and-chip beach supper, or to the famous Square & Compass pub in Worth Matravers. Buy a pint of cider and a pasty through a hole in the wall before relaxing on the pub's very own little slope… it could be a long stagger back.

COOL FACTOR Expansive, no-frills camping with views of the sea on the horizon.

WHO'S IN Tents, campervans, caravans, dogs (on leads), groups – yes.

ON SITE An unlimited number of pitches on a sloping (sometimes steeply sloping) field. No hook-ups. Campfires are allowed at certain times (enquire with the owners). Basic but spotless hut with showers (2 ladies', 2 gent's; 20p for 3 minutes). Two washing-up sinks; freezer for ice packs only. A mobile grocer visits every morning with freshly baked bread, chocolate doughnuts, newspapers and milk.

OFF SITE Cliff-top walks to Dancing Ledge, Seacombe Cliff and Winspit. Or take a steam train ride on the Swanage Railway (see p.81) to Corfe Castle (see p.81).

FOOD & DRINK The garden of the Scott Arms in Kingston is always delightful (see p.81), as is the cider and the pasties at the Square & Compass (see p.81) in Worth Matravers.

GETTING THERE Take the A351 to Corfe Castle, then the B3069 through Kingston towards Langton Matravers. The campsite is on the right as you enter the village.

PUBLIC TRANSPORT Train to Wareham, then pick up one of the many buses to Swanage. Alight outside the campsite at the Capstan Field stop in Langton Matravers.

OPEN Spring Bank Holiday week, then late July–late August. Members of DEFRA-approved clubs can camp at Acton Field Easter–late October.

THE DAMAGE £8–14 per adult per night (price depending on tent size).

tom's field

Tom's Field Road, Langton Matravers, Swanage, Dorset BH19 3HN 01929 427110 www.tomsfieldcamping.co.uk

In an area of rural Dorset called the Isle of Purbeck, which isn't actually an island, it seems appropriate that Tom's Field isn't in fact Tom's. It was at one stage, but Tom has now pitched his tent in that great campsite in the sky, leaving his field to be loved and camped on by younger generations.

Even if it isn't Tom's any longer, it is at least a field. And a rather a nice field too, comprising just over four acres of gently rolling soft grass with old stone walling around much of its perimeter. It's divided into a flat lower field and a slightly more undulating higher field, which is compensated for by the outlook: if you're looking the right way, you can see a long view seaward across Swanage Bay, and on a clear day you might see the Isle of Wight.

With so many attractions around here it's difficult to know where to start. The pub is probably as good a place as any, and what a pub the Square & Compass in Worth Matravers is. This gem has become an attraction in its own right, with visitors making a special trip to Worth Matravers to taste the ales and pasties, sit by the fire and bang their heads on the low beams.

This stretch of coast – aka the Jurassic Coast – is now a UNESCO World Heritage Site due to the geologically significant rocks that date back more than 100 million years. With that accolade, it has joined the likes of the Great Barrier Reef and the Grand Canyon as one of the wonders of the natural world. Old Tom would be proud.

COOL FACTOR Relaxed campsite with views of Swanage Bay and the Isle of Wight.

WHO'S IN Tents, motorhomes, dogs (on leads) – yes. Tents with a diameter of over 8 metres, caravans – no.

ON SITE As well as toilets and showers, facilities include 2 extra family shower rooms, washing-up sinks and freezer pack storage. A mobile shop sells all the breakfast basics. Otherwise, as the owners themselves say, 'regulars seem to like things staying exactly as they are'.

OFF SITE Treat yourself to a boat trip along the Jurassic Coast from Swanage. Contact Marsh's Boats (01929 427659; marshsboats.co.uk), visit the National Trust beach at Studland Bay or get the car ferry across Poole Harbour to explore Poole and Bournemouth. No visit to the region would be complete without a trip to that ultimate of photo opportunities, the iconic Durdle Door.

FOOD & DRINK Stock up on local, organic and fair-trade produce, including bread and eggs, at the onsite shop. As well as the quaint Square & Compass (see p.81) in Worth Matravers (a 5-minute drive or a half-hour walk away), the excellent Scott Arms (see p.81) in Kingston has a garden and views of Corfe Castle.

GETTING THERE Leave the A35 on to the A351 or A352 (depending on direction) and proceed for 11 miles. Turn right on to Haycrafts Lane; after a mile turn left on to the B3069 and after another mile turn right on to Tom's Field Road.

PUBLIC TRANSPORT Take the train to Wareham and then the bus, which stops at the end of the road, a 3 minute walk away.

OPEN Mid March–end October.

THE DAMAGE From £14 for a small tent with 2 people and a car to £20 for an extra-large tent with up to 2 adults and 2 children. Walkers' Barn is £13 per person per night; the Stone Room £30 for up to 2 people only.

burnbake campsite

Burnbake Campsite, Rempstone, Corfe Castle, Wareham, Dorset BH20 5JH 01929 480570 www.burnbake.com

There are those rare occasions when you arrive at a site and within minutes know that you'd like to stay all season. Burnbake is one of those. Its many plus points quickly add up to create a vibe so agreeable that, before you know it, you're on the phone to the office negotiating a second week's stay. Children in particular will love being able to run free through the woods, swing on the rope tyre, climb in wooden boats or build dams in the stream.

There are no designated pitches among Burnbake's woodland site – 12 acres of secluded, level ground, complete with burbling stream – so have a nose around to find a suitable nook or cranny. During high summer it can be busy and, as a result, it's not the quietest site, but there are some more peaceful places to pitch away from the main circuit.

Twelve brand new wooden lodges have crafted one corner of the site into a self-catering haven – not quite the canvas camper's dream but ideal for anyone looking for a more well-equipped woodland hideout. The lodges are also open year round so those, like us, who long to return after a short summer break can turn up again in the depths of winter.

In low season it's quieter and at any time of year it's a prime location for the National Trust's Studland beaches and for exploring the Isle of Purbeck, particularly on bike or foot. You can also cycle to Swanage or Wareham avoiding the main roads, or indeed to Corfe Castle itself, which is an iconic and uplifting old ruin if there ever was one.

COOL FACTOR A fabulously relaxed vibe at this sylvanian campsite, just a cycle ride from Studland Bay.

WHO'S IN Tents, campervans, groups, hikers, cyclists, dogs – yes. Caravans – no.

ON SITE 108 pitches but no designated spots. 12 bespoke lodges also available. Campfires allowed in containers off the ground. 2 large wooden huts house showers plus a baby-changing room, 2 washing machines and outside washing-up sinks. A shop opens for 2 hours each morning and evening selling sweets, breakfast buns, camping food and equipment. There is a woodland play area with slide and swings.

OFF SITE Studland Bay is an hour's walk or a 20-minute cycle. Hire bikes from Cyclexperience in Wareham (01929 556601; cyclex.co.uk/wareham).

FOOD & DRINK The onsite yurt café is open 9–11am and 6–9pm and serves breakfasts, pizza, veggies and other wholesome options. The Greyhound Inn at Corfe Castle (01929 480205; greyhoundcorfe.co.uk) is a good spot, with sharing plates and Purbeck ice cream. Treat yourself to afternoon tea in the lovely garden at the Manor House Hotel, Studland Bay (01929 450288), an 18th-century property with views across the bay.

GETTING THERE From Wareham, take the A351 to Corfe Castle, turn left under the castle on to the Studland Road, taking the third left turn, signposted Rempstone. From the Sandbanks Ferry follow the road through Studland, continue towards Corfe Castle and take the turning right on the brow of a hill, signposted Rempstone. From there follow the campsite signs for a mile; Burnbake is on the right.

OPEN Easter–September; lodges year round.

THE DAMAGE £10–£12 per pitch per night. Extra adult £4–£6; extra child £2–£3; extra car, tent, gazebo or large tent £3–£4.

farrs meadow

Farrs Meadow, Farrs Lodge, Cowgrove Road, Wimborne, BH21 4EL 07913 838726 www.farrsmeadow.co.uk

Perched on a hill just outside the pretty market town of Wimborne, with far-reaching views across the Stour Valley, Farrs Meadow is a rural camping gem with a wonderfully relaxed atmosphere. It's a perfect choice for anyone looking for a touch of wilderness that's not too far from civilization.

The campsite is small and delightfully car-free, with a quad bike available to carry your tent and belongings to your pitch. Quirky showers have been imaginatively installed in upcycled old horseboxes, which are deceptively spacious and the perfect setting to listen to nature's chorus while you take your morning shower. More horseboxes dotted around the campsite host compost loos, and the washing-up area makes ingenious use of disused cattle troughs, converted into long, deep metal sinks. There is a separate paddock for campervans, or those looking for a bit of extra comfort can choose to stay in a yurt or the tastefully converted stable – both of which are comfortably furnished with a double bed, two single beds, fire pits and outdoor furniture.

The main field is enclosed by beautiful mature trees that give dappled shade in the sun and shelter in the rain. During the day buzzards circle overhead and in the surrounding woodland you can hear the drill of the woodpecker, while at night bats emerge from the trees and dart between the tents, feasting on moths that are attracted by the campfire and torchlight, and the long grass emits an LED-like glow from the glow worms.

Wimborne is only a 15-minute walk away from the site and is worth visiting for the famous Minster of St Cuthberga, one of the finest churches in Dorset; and it's just a short stroll down the hill to the picturesque meandering River Stour, where you can enjoy a wild swim under the Eye Bridge with just brown trout to keep you company. Wander a little further to try your hand at catching them, with fishing permits sold on site for angling both in the Stour and also in the adjoining River Allen, a celebrated chalk stream that's great for fly-fishing. When evening descends, however, you'll find the best policy is just to settle down on one of the giant logs encircling the campfire in the main meadow and toast a marshmallow or two on the open flames. And if the weather doesn't agree, then fear not – it's a 10-minute walk to one of the coolest little pubs around, the National Trust-owned Vine Inn – a unique Dorset bolthole with a tiny bar that seems to encapsulate everything that's great about camping here: a small, independent place ensconced in beautiful countryside.

COOL FACTOR A charming Dorset site a short stroll from a swim-friendly river in the beautiful Stour Valley.

WHO'S IN Tents and campervans are welcome, as are dogs. No cars beyond the carpark, but a quad bike helps bring stuff into the meadow.

ON SITE 25 tent pitches, 6 campervan pitches, 1 furnished yurt, and a restored stable hut. All furnished accommodation options sleep 4–5 people. There are 4 long drop loos, 3 hot showers, natural cooking on the firepit and BBQs. There are rope swings, woods to build dens, a pond and an orchard. Throughout the season goats and alpacas are on grass-mowing duty.

OFF SITE The river is a mere 5 minutes' walk from Farrs Meadow and offers some of the best wild swimming in England. There are plenty of great marked bicycle routes nearby and National Trust walking routes border the campsite. For the rainy days, Wimborne, with its famous Minster, is a 10-minute walk away.

FOOD & DRINK An onsite shop sells home-grown organic veg, eggs and camping essentials. There is also a wonderful wood-fired oven from which pizzas, hot dogs and fresh baked bread can be bought on certain nights. The National Trust-owned Vine Inn (01202 882259), a 10-minute walk across the fields, boasts the smallest public bar in the country. The Squash Court Shop & Cafe (01202 639249; thesquashcourt. org) is also recommended, and sells vintage clothes and homewares along with its teas and sandwiches. It's a charming place with a thoroughly child-friendly atmosphere.

GETTING THERE From Wimborne head towards Blanford Forum on Victoria Road (B3082). Turn left on to Cowgrove Road at the hospital. Keep going past the football club. Farrs Meadow is the 2nd on your right after Farrs House.

PUBLIC TRANSPORT Bus to Wimborne Minster and then a walk or taxi to the site.

OPEN April–mid October.

THE DAMAGE Pitch rentals £25 for a tent and 2 people; extra adults £10; children £5. Yurt £100 a night. Old Stable £130 a night. Firepits £5 a night.

riversidelakes

Riversidelakes, Slough Lane, Horton, Wimborne, Dorset BH21 7JL 01202 821212 www.riverside-lakes.co.uk

We've always believed this is one of the top campsites in the UK, but this utter gem has just been getting better and better since our last visit. The owners Maggie and Nigel are as affable as they are creative and they don't do anything by halves. At the beginning of summer 2010, the couple and their two sons took on this 25-acre site, along with the resident Chinese geese, duck, swan, cat, chickens – and an entire season's bookings. Since then, both their business and their animal farm have been booming. The wild flowers and rope-tyre swings have been swaying, new little piglets grunting and, most importantly of all, the punters are smiling.

The low-key signposting (if you hit Drusilla's Inn you've gone too far) does little to hint at the magic that lies ahead, where the pitches are spacious and the atmosphere is almost other-worldly, despite the site's convenient location not far from the M27. Once you're in, park up and head for reception, where you'll probably meet Maggie.

The camping area comprises 12 acres of dreamy natural meadow and woodland, with three lakes enclosed by circumferential paths and thick shrubbery. All of the pitches are accessible by car so you can drive and unload before parking in the car parks. Mown pathways separate the clusters of pitches and the long, wild grasses create walls in between, so that all that sedentary campers can see of their neighbours is the smoke rising from their braziers. At dusk the overall vista resembles the basecamp of an intrepid expedition into the wild unknown. There's a stillness in the air. Total enchantment.

Groups (quiet ones) really love it here, booking out entire pitch clusters, each of which bears its own helpful name, so you can choose your spot according to your needs – great lake views, proximity to the facilities, sheltered woodland, tree-lined and ridgeway pitches, and isolated individual hideaways. You choose.

The facilities are top-notch: a new shower room has been upgraded so the water is always hot and there's a sheltered area for recycling with plug points.

The area beyond is full of great pubs and restaurants, though you'll need a car to sample the fish and chips or the Chinese and Italian establishments at Verwood; failing that you can just dial for a takeaway – many leaflets can be found on site. The narrow country lane outside of the campsite isn't ideal for young children to walk or cycle along, but just a few miles up the road is the fabulous Moors Valley Country Park, which has cycle paths, tree-top walkways and scavenger hunt trails. A sandpit play area for the very young and a larger adventure park for older kids are the cherries on top. It's expensive to park there but a lot of the areas are free. Take a packed lunch to enjoy in the picnic area before jumping on a steam train for a ride through the woods.

Alternatively, you can just stay put on the site: many families bring bicycles so their charges can tear along the woodland paths. If they're not doing that they're climbing trees, playing on swings or watching their dads fish. As for everyone else, well, they're just kicking back and enjoying the magic.

COOL FACTOR Spacious, relaxing, comfortable, and easily accessible. Regulars already know they have to book in advance, so newbies will need to be quick off the mark.

WHO'S IN Tents, campervans, caravans, dogs, groups (not young or noisy ones) – yes.

ON SITE 55 pitches, no minimum stay, and room for 5 campervans or caravans with hook-ups. Campfires in firepits or borrowed braziers: Logs are £5 per tub. The shower block has 8 showers supplied with renewable energy, loos, hairdryers, a family bath and baby-changing facilities. There are 3 washing-up sinks, a freezer and microwave. Ice packs are available. Soul Pad bell tents come with camp kitchens, mattresses, wooden decking outside and a bench table. A communal area, 2 washing-up sinks, and an electric powerpoint face a huge communal firepit. Recycling bins include a swap shop, where you leave/pick up anything that campers might use.

OFF SITE Moors Valley Country Park (01425 470721; moors-valley.co.uk) is just down the road, and has picnic areas, cycling tracks, forest walks and high-wire tree-climbing. One of England's most magnificent country houses, Kingston Lacy, is just outside Wimborne Minster to the northwest (01202 883402; NT), plus there's the Iron Age fort of Badbury Rings, in what feels like a very wild and remote spot a mile or so further north.

FOOD & DRINK Drusilla's Inn (01258 840297; drusillasinn. co.uk) is a right-turn out of the campsite and serves a whole range of pub grub including Sunday roasts and kids' meals. Or try the White Hart in Wimborne (01202 886050), which does decent pub grub and has a small beer garden.

GETTING THERE Take the M27 west and then the A31. Just past Ringwood take the A338 for Bournemouth but at the top of the slip road turn right at the roundabout towards Moors Valley Country Park and Horton. Slough Lane is 3½ miles after the country park on the right, after 2 mini roundabouts.

OPEN May–September.

THE DAMAGE Adult £9–11 high season, child £6–7, under-5s free. Soul Pad bell tent £40–£90 per night. This is a Camping and Caravanning Club Certified site so annual membership is needed if you stay outside August – join on arrival.

aldridge hill

Aldridge Hill, Brockenhurst, Hampshire SO42 7QD 01590 623152
www.campingintheforest.co.uk/england/new-forest/aldridge-hill

If you're looking for a back-to-basics, traditional camping experience, then Aldridge Hill is for you. Set in a heathland clearing, bordered by Ober Water and the snaking Blackwater Stream (two of the New Forest's prettiest waterways), Aldridge Hill provides campers with the unique opportunity to live in the midst of nature, while experiencing everything the New Forest has to offer; from its famous free-roaming ponies to the numerous wild heaths and otherworldly woodlands that make this place so special.

Lets be clear from the start – if you're a glamper, don't bother reading any further. Aldridge Hill has no toilets, no showers and no power, so this really is back-to-basics which is of course, one of the site's main draws. Another plus point is the sheer variety of pitches on offer. Campers can opt for cosy woodlands, or the wonderful heathland, home to some unforgettable sunsets. And with 170 pitches, you're unlikely to be kept awake by your neighbours.

You can follow the Ober Water Trail from the site (1.5 miles), which is a great way to explore the forest. Starting at Whitefield Moor car park, the walk passes through a variety of habitats, including heathland, bogs, grassland, woodland and the stream itself. The paths are a variety of smooth gravelled surfaces and compacted grassy ground, with some gentle slopes and plenty of resting places.

Back at Aldridge Hill, keep your eyes peeled for the site's resident feathered friends: redstarts, woodpeckers, nuthatches, tree creepers and more can all be seen circling above or nesting among the ancient oak trees. You may even see a tawny owl swooping from its perch to seize its prey.

With all this nature right in front of you, who needs David Attenborough?

COOL FACTOR As close to wild camping as you can get in the heart of the New Forest.

WHO'S IN Tents, caravans, motorhomes, trailer tents and dogs – yes.

ON SITE 170 undefined pitches on which to put your tent, caravan or motorhome and space for one car. There are no toilets, showers or electricity at this campsite, but drinking water taps and rubbish bins are available.

OFF SITE Liberty's Owl Raptor Reptile Centre (01425 476487; libertyscentre.co.uk), 11 miles from site, has daily flying displays, plus a reptile house with snakes, lizards and more. Paultons Family Theme Park (02380 814442; paultonspark. co.uk) is a 15-minute drive away and has over 60 family rides and attractions, while perhaps the area's most popular attraction, Beaulieu (01590 612345; beaulieu.co.uk), has over 250 vehicles from every motoring era – a must-see for motoring enthusiasts.

FOOD & DRINK Brockenhurst is a short walk away, offering a fantastic range of eateries, including the Blaireau Bistro (01590 623032; leblaireau.co.uk), situated in the grounds of Careys Manor Hotel and Spa. Or, after a busy day out in the forest, treat yourself to a bag of fish and chips at Rainbow Fish Bar (01590 622747; rainbowfishbar.co.uk). The Foresters Arms (01590 623397), a 5-minute drive away, offers an extensive menu of home-cooked food, welcomes children and well-trained pets and has a fantastic beer garden.

GETTING THERE From Lyndhurst: take the A337 towards Brockenhurst. Turn right on to the B3055 (Grigg Lane) and carry straight on over the crossroads. Take the first right after the Esso garage into The Rise and, at the end of the road, turn right into Rhinefield Road. Stay on this road for approx 1½ miles, then turn right into the Forestry Commission Beachem Wood car park. Follow the signs to Forest Holiday's Aldridge Hill site.

PUBLIC TRANSPORT Brockenhurst railway station is 1.2 miles) from the site.

OPEN Season 1: 22 May–2 June. Season 2: 26 June–8 September.

THE DAMAGE Prices per pitch (per night) including 2 adults start at £11.50 during low season.

ashurst

Lyndhurst Road, Ashurst, Hampshire SO40 7AR 02380 292097
www.campingintheforest.co.uk/england/new-forest/ashurst

Ashurst might just be one of the most picturesque campsites in England. Set in an enchanting woodland glade, surrounded by ancient oak trees, open grasslands and free-roaming ponies, Ashurst offers some serious camping eye-candy. The phrase 'location, location, location' certainly rings true here as this well-run, family-friendly site is the perfect base from which to explore the walks and traffic-free cycling the New Forest has to offer.

Situated on the eastern side of the New Forest, Ashurst is run by Camping in the Forest, who manage several sites in some of the UK's finest woodlands. Life here is wonderfully simple: there's a relaxed, 'pitch where you like' approach, so visitors have the choice of camping in the secluded forest, by the bushes, on open grassland, or somewhere inbetween. Facilities here are of a good standard too (with the addition of a recently refurbished shower block).

The local area is a walker's paradise. Lasting a few hours, Matley Walk (under 5 miles) begins east of Lyndhurst (the unofficial capital of the New Forest), and gives walkers a great tour around this unique and unspoiled environment, passing ancient woodlands, open heathland, bogs and pine enclosures. In case you needed any more persuading, there are also several excellent pubs and restaurants nearby. But of course, it's the back-to-basics, woodland camping that sets this place apart. With that enchanting scenery and easy access to the glorious New Forest, Ashurst is a true gem.

COOL FACTOR Spacious camping in a top-notch location.

WHO'S IN Tents, campervans, caravans and groups – yes. Dogs (except guide dogs) – no.

ON SITE 280 undefined spots with ample space. Flushing toilets, showers, family shower room, washbasins, chemical disposal point, laundry and drinking water taps.

OFF SITE Longdown Activity Farm (02380 292837; longdownfarm.co.uk) is a short drive from the site, and welcomes guests to bottle-feed the calves and goats, feed the ducks, meet the pigs and cuddle the baby rabbits while exploring the farmyard buildings.

FOOD & DRINK Ashurst is a 5-minute walk away, and offers a range of eateries, including the excellent Asha Bangladeshi Cuisine (02380 292885; tottonindianrestaurant.co.uk) and Herb Pot Bistro (02380 293996; theherbpot.com), which serves fresh seasonal food in a relaxed environment, including a wide choice of veggie options. The Happy Cheese (02380 293929; happycheeseashurst.co.uk) is a minute's walk from the campsite and serves home-cooked food all day, including an extensive children's menu. Finally the Forest Inn (02380 293071; forest-inn.co.uk) is a traditional pub with stunning views of the forest from its family-friendly garden.

GETTING THERE Ashurst Campsite lies 2½ miles northeast of Lyndhurst on the A35. Leave the M27 at junction 3 on to the M271, signposted Southampton Docks. At Redbridge Roundabout take the 2nd exit on to the A35, in a south-westerly direction towards Totton. Continue over two roundabouts, heading towards Lyndhurst. Pass through Ashurst village and continue over the railway bridge; the campsite is signposted just after the New Forest Pub.

OPEN Mid April–end September.

THE DAMAGE Prices per pitch (per night) including 2 adults start at £16.50 during low season.

embers camping beaulieu

Embers Camping Beaulieu, Palace Lane, Beaulieu, Hampshire SO42 7YG 0845 257 2267 www.emberscamping.co.uk

Embers Camping is one for the purists. Acres of space, no electrical hook-ups and a strict tents-only policy are accompanied by a blissfully liberal attitude to campfires (they're positively encouraged, in case you didn't guess from the name). All in all, this bucolic bolthole offers an idyllic camping experience, harking back to days of old. Situated on the sprawling Home Farm, right beside the tranquil River Beaulieu, Embers' spacious informal pitches are lovingly scattered among soft grass and blooming trees. The adjoining field is ideal for games and exploration.

With the chocolate-box village of Beaulieu just beyond your tent flaps, you'll be surprised how many attractions are within walking distance. The magnificent Beaulieu Abbey, National Motor Museum and picturesque river all make for a pleasant excursion, while the footpaths and bike trails that criss-cross The New Forest couldn't be closer. Hop in the car for the sandy beaches of Bournemouth or enjoy the flora and fauna of the North Solent nature reserve, where estuary salt marshes attract diverse wildlife.

Embers Camping really does boast the best of all worlds. You'll find simplicity and escapism amid the greens and browns of the New Forest, while easy access to the surrounding countryside provides everything you need for a holiday in the New Forest.

COOL FACTOR A perfect spot for exploring the New Forest.

WHO'S IN Tent campers, groups – yes. Caravans, campervans, motorhomes, dogs – no.

ON SITE 25 pitches in the Orchard and the Big Field, each with their own campfire. no electrical hook-ups. Hot showers (in portable cabins), loos, 2 washing-up basins.

OFF SITE Beaulieu village is an attraction in itself. The National Motor Museum (01590 612345; beaulieu.co.uk) is a short stroll away, and in the same complex Beaulieu Abbey and Palace House boast beautiful gardens and ornate antiques and treasures. The picturesque Georgian hamlet of Bucklers Hard is a 2½ mile walk down the river.

FOOD & DRINK The onsite shop caters to all basic needs. The Turfcutters Arms (01590 612331; the-turfcutters-new-forest.co.uk) is a friendly New Forest pub with sprawling beer garden. They also do takeaway fish and chips every evening. A leisurely riverside stroll takes you to Montys Inn (01590 614986), housed in the Montagu Arms Hotel (01590 612324; montaguarmshotel.co.uk) – a gorgeous 17th-century coaching inn with Michelin-starred restaurant.

GETTING THERE Approaching Beaulieu on the B3054 travelling south, you will find the site is just before the village and Beaulieu river on the left-hand side of the road.

PUBLIC TRANSPORT Trains stop at Beaulieu Road station, form where you can walk or cycle (4 miles). Or go on to Brockenhurst station and hire an electric 'New Forest buggie' which seats two people.

OPEN Most weekends, Bank Holidays and school holidays during the spring and summer months.

THE DAMAGE £20–£22.50 per adult per night and £5–6 per child. Pitches are allocated on a first come first served basis.

abbotstone wood

Abbotstone Wood, Basingstoke Road, Abbotstone Down, Nr Alresford, Hampshire SO24 9TQ 07720 290229
www.abbotstonewoodcamping.co.uk

In Germany, a pillow is classed as a 'passive weapon' and hitting someone with it can lead to charges of assault. A pillow! Just imagine going camping and trying to smuggle one of those weapons into your tent. Head down, tent up, open the car door, then use the sleeping bag to shield the view as you slip a pillow or two inside. Or create a diversion. Send a runner into the woods making loud bird noises as you dive for cover, a pillow stuffed beneath your jumper... okay, well maybe we haven't gone quite that mad yet but in a world full of rules something as simple as having a quiet kip in your tent should always be easy. And no one agrees with that more than the good folk of Camping Unplugged.

Now popping up with their third campsite, in the fields and forest of Abbotstone Wood, Camping Unplugged are all about shedding the rules to provide campers with a wide variety of pitches so they can choose exactly where to go. Driving through the trees that line the entrance, visitors pass through the woods and out into a meadow surrounded on all sides. Past the reception, this large field extends beyond, opening into a wide space ideal for campers who want acres to kick a ball or play a game of cricket. If it's seclusion you prefer, retreat back into the trees where you can pick between woodland glades or smaller spots tucked between the branches.

The campsite is ideally suited for large groups and, with so much space, there is plenty of room for everyone to pitch without bothering their neighbours. In the main field there are hot showers and toilets in the sanitary block, while woodland showers and long drops are dotted around the rest of the site so those in the trees don't have to walk miles every time nature calls. And if you want that authentic 'survival' feel, then kindling a fire is probably the perfect place to start. Campfires are more than welcome here, with grills provided so you can boil a brew over the flames or have a makeshift barbecue. On Saturday afternoons and Sunday mornings, the site also welcomes bush-craft expert Shaun. A trained Greencraft Instructor, Shaun offers two-hour sessions to help you master woodcarving and bush cooking, among other skills.

Offsite it's just a couple of miles to New Alresford, a quaint old town where chalky streams run into the River Arle. A decent market is held here most Thursdays, while in the centre of town the southern terminal of the Watercress Line Heritage railway means visitors can hop aboard a steam train and chug off towards Jane Austen's old home in Alton. With a little culture done and some local produce in the bag you can head back to camp. Just remember to bring that pillow (man's most lethal weapon) in case you meet any beasts that go bump in the night!

COOL FACTOR Camping in the forest – made easy!

WHO'S IN Tents-only (except VW Campervans). The site specialises in large family groups of 30+ people. Dogs are welcome at no extra charge.

ON SITE 75 pitches spread across the field, with a scattering of woodland spots. No electric hook-ups. There are flushing toilets and hot showers by the main reception area. There are also long-drop toilets and hot, gas-powered showers dotted around the site. Campfire grills are available for cooking on open-wood fires. Kids have unrestricted access to woods to build, swing and play.

OFF SITE The site is a couple of miles from New Alresford, a charming little town that is home to the southern terminal of the Watercress Line Heritage railway (01962 733810; watercressline.co.uk) to Alton. The campsite is within easy walking distance of The Grange (08703 331181; EH), Northington, a huge neo-classical pile set in landscaped gardens. They run an opera season here during June and July. Along the road from the site is an ancient hill settlement known as Oliver's Battery. If it rains, head to the excellent Winchester Science Centre and Planetarium (01962 863791; winchestersciencecentre.org), 5 miles from Alresford on the Winchester road.

FOOD & DRINK The Woolpack Inn (0845 293 8066; thewoolpackinn.co.uk), a mile away at Totford, is ideal for a beer, Sunday lunch, or both and is a nice walk from the site.

GETTING THERE Leave the M3 at the Basingstoke junction following the signs for the A30 and Alton. As soon as you get on the road to Alton, take a right on the B3046 for Alresford. The entrance to the site is signed, about ¾ mile south of the village of Swarraton.

OPEN April–September.

THE DAMAGE Adults are £15, discounted to £12.50 if they are accompanied by their children. Children (3 and over) are £6 per night.

inwood camping

Inwood Camping, Farleigh Road, Farleigh Wallop, Basingstoke, Hampshire RG25 2HP 07720290229
www.inwoodcamping.co.uk

This may sound strange but the great thing about Inwood Camping is that the second you pitch your tent, you regret it. The problem is, the grass here is *always* greener. Pitch in the 'big field' and you start to stare with envy at those snuggled beneath the trees. Pitch there, though, and you later find another, smaller meadow that seems to beckon you over, or you discover the lanky, dark green pines that tower over yet more perfect patches. So before you down tools and pop up the tent, take time to wander among the trees to get a feel for the entire space. The moral of all this will quickly spread into every part of your holiday: take your time, don't rush, for Inwood is a campsite made for exploration.

Set within a large copse that once joined the rest of Hampshire in swathes of endless forest, Inwood Camping has pitches of all varieties. Large groups can stick to the meadow spaces, the biggest of which offers excellent far-reaching views over the North Wessex Downs, while those seeking a little more peace can find a quiet wooded glade to call their own. Scattered throughout there are water taps and long-drop toilets – far more sanitary then the portable-potty variety. One of the best features, though, are the gas-powered showers, similarly dotted at various points around the site. Rustic, unique and fully encompassing the wilderness feel of the site, they're wonderfully hot and powerful, as well as conveniently placed.

Back by the reception area, there are more commonplace facilities: flushing loos, showers and washing-up sinks accompany a handy little shop selling essentials. Here you can also hire a grill – a

vital bit of kit when you discover that cooking over a campfire is encouraged more than gambling in Las Vegas. It's easy to see why. The whole ethos of the place is based around providing that 'proper' camping experience. Pitch where you want, play where you want, light campfires, build dens, watch the stars, spot the wildlife… the two main rules at Inwood seem to be 'respect the forest' and 'enjoy yourself' – rules we are more than happy to live by.

From the far end of the site there is an excellent 40-minute ramble into Dummer, a small village with an excellent pub. You could also take the car into the heart of the Wessex Downs to join the scenic trails and cycle routes there. There are offsite options a-plenty, but many people are simply captivated by the woods, and have no intention of leaving. With more space at Inwood than you could ever need, the site is full of life while never even approaching overcrowded. Once you settle in, the days just seem to drift away. Just don't get jealous of other campers. You picked your spot. Now stick with it.

COOL FACTOR Woodlands, meadows and campfires abound at this Wessex Downs wonderland.

WHO'S IN Tents, groups, families, couples, pets – yes. Caravans, motorhomes, campervans – no.

ON SITE Tent-only pitches in a variety of spaces. No electric hook-ups. Drinking-water taps and long-drop toilets are dotted around, along with excellent gas-powered showers. Flushing loos, showers and washing-up sinks can be found next to reception. There's a well-stocked shop with camping essentials and logs/kindling to purchase (£5). Please respect the woods by not burning wood collected yourself. Campfire grills are also available to hire.

OFF SITE Inwood is not far from Jane Austen country; the author's house is in Alton, and open to the public (01420 83262; jane-austens-house-museum.org.uk), and the village is a good base for walks and tours of the local area. Old Basing, just the other side of Basingstoke, is surprisingly rural, has a historic ruined castle and wonderful canal walks.

FOOD & DRINK The nearest village, Cliddesden, hosts a decent local in the Jolly Farmer (01256 473073; jollyfarmercliddesden.co.uk), while just over a mile's hike away in Dummer The Queen Inn (01256 397367; thequeeninndummer.com) serves locally brewed real ales and traditional food. An alternative venue for a pint is the Farleigh Wallop Estate Club (01256 324747), where campers can purchase temporary membership for a quid or so. The beer is keenly priced, there is a pool table, a beer garden, and a decent TV showing sport, but they don't serve food.

GETTING THERE Leave the M3 at exit 6 and follow the signs for Basingstoke. At the first roundabout turn left towards Alton (A339), turning left at the next roundabout and following the road under the M3. Turn right immediately afterwards on to the B3046 towards Cliddesden. Go through Cliddesden, continue past the Farleigh Wallop Estate and, after a mile or so, you will see a sign for Inwood Camping on your right.

OPEN Mid April–end September.

THE DAMAGE Standard adult rate £15, reduced to £12.50 per adult and £6 per child for families.

grange farm brighstone bay

Grange Farm, Brighstone Bay, Isle of Wight PO30 4DA 01983 740296 www.grangefarmholidays.com

The ultra-green, festival-hosting Isle of Wight has reinvented itself as a hip little island offering something for everyone, with exceptional waves for surfers, kite-surfing and paragliding, and summer events that attract new crowds every year. The isle is shaped a bit like a front-on cow's head. At its temple is, fittingly, a town called Cowes. At its respective ears sit the towns of Yarmouth and Ryde, both of which have regular ferry services to the mainland. And perched atop tall cliffs, behind the beach at Brighstone (about midway down the left of the cow's jawline), sits the charming Grange Farm campsite.

It's a lovely, unspoiled site situated in a beautiful part of the island. Two flat, grassy fields go right to the edge of the cliff and there's an overflow field across the road, aptly christened the 'Cool Camping Field'. You'll need a sturdy tent to cope with the winds blowing across the top of these fields, but the reward is a panoramic view across the sea and an easy scramble down to the beach below. It's a family-run, family-friendly site left deliberately undeveloped. Kids will love its Noah's Ark of farm animals, including alpacas (named Wallace and Gromit), kune pigs, goats, water buffalo and a variety of poultry. Plus there is a play area for ball games and a children's playground, with stepping stones and rope bridges, in case the beach should lose its appeal. All in all, a friendly and wonderfully varied site that enjoys a marvellous location.

COOL FACTOR Cliff-top pitches with panoramic sea views.

WHO'S IN Tents, campervans, caravans, dogs (in caravans) – yes. Groups – sometimes, by arrangement.

ON SITE 2 fields with 60 pitches, most with hook-ups; extra Cool Camping Field only open for 28 days in July/August. Campfires allowed on the beach below. A heated block has 15 free showers, a coin-operated bath, toilets and washing-up sinks. The site also offers self-catering in a variety of barn conversions and static caravans.

OFF SITE Lots of water-bourne activities are available, or take it easy exploring nearby Newport, whose Roman remains can be supplemented by the Roman villa at Brading (01983 406223; bradingromanvilla.org.uk), which has a visitor centre and museum.

FOOD & DRINK The Blacksmiths Arms (01983 529263; blacksmiths-arms.co.uk), near Newport, serves food and has a pleasant beer garden. Check out also the local vino at Adgestone Vineyard (01983 402503; english-wine.co.uk) in Sandown, one of the oldest vineyards in the UK.

GETTING THERE From Fishbourne/Cowes follow signs to Newport then Carisbrooke. At Carisbrooke take the A3323 to Shorwell and Brighstone. Just before Brighstone, turn left by the church and follow New Road to the end. From Yarmouth, follow signs to Freshwater Bay, then the A3055 for 5 miles; Grange Farm is on the right.

PUBLIC TRANSPORT From Yarmouth/Newport, take bus no. #7 to Brighstone. Get off at the Three Bishops and walk.

OPEN March–November.

THE DAMAGE 2 people, car and tent £12–£14–£17 per night. Discounts on ferries to the island available with Wightlink or Redfunnel if booked through the campsite.

ninham country holidays

Ninham Country Holidays, Ninham, Shanklin, Isle of Wight PO37 7PL 01983 864243 www.ninham.co.uk

Located on the southeast of the aptly nicknamed 'Garden Isle', Ninham Country Holidays is a campsite with a secluded rural feel, yet one that remains a short distance from one of the nicest resorts on the coast. With its functional new town and quaint, thatched old town, Shanklin has been a popular part of the Isle of Wight since tourism began here. No sooner have you hopped, skipped and jumped into the green countryside beyond then Ninham appears, a family-run camping park that is ideal for exploring the island. Although admittedly a large site, Ninham Country Holidays thankfully has none of the commercial atmosphere that you might expect. This is a family-owned and family-focused site based around the original farm buildings. The site's 230 pitches are also divided across two separate fields, split by a wooded valley and surrounded by mature deciduous trees that provide shelter and shade on warmer days. This secluded countryside feel is accentuated by the long private drive, which separates the site from any road noise while also acting as a speedy cycle path back to the outside world.

Campers have a choice between two fields: 'Orchard', the larger of the two with ultra-modern eco-facilities that do clever things with solar and rainwater-harvesting technologies (and which happen to include an extremely handy family room with specialist showers and a baby bath), and 'Willow Brook', with its own separate facilities

that – although more basic – are functional and well kept. In both camping areas, pitches are kept mostly to the edges of the field, providing ample room in the centre and ensuring campers aren't crammed together in the 18 acres of space. Those still wanting more from their pitch can even ask for the 'XL' option, so motor homes, awnings, gazebos and cars can all easily be accommodated in one spot.

If the weather turns, seek out the centrally located movie room and games room with table tennis, pool table, air hockey and more, along with free Wi-Fi and space to relax with a coffee or ice cream, served on site. Outside, Ninham also boasts a sports area and kid-friendly heated swimming pool – ideal if the weather is a little too nippy to enjoy the sea at nearby Shanklin Beach.

The best way to explore the Isle of Wight is on two wheels. Surrounded by mature woodland and rolling countryside, there is a fabulous network of footpaths and cycle routes that leads directly from the campsite and spreads out to cover much of the island. Those who head south can link up with the Shanklin Chine, a twisting pathway with steps leading down into a mossy gorge enlivened by the sound of a cascading waterfall. Meanwhile, by car, the rest of the island beckons, its plethora of attractions and summer festivals providing all with an entertaining itinerary, whatever your taste.

COOL FACTOR A popular spot outside of Shanklin where space is never a commodity.

WHO'S IN Tents, touring caravans, motorhomes – all welcome. Cyclists or guests arriving on foot and/or by public transport do not pay a pitch fee. Families and couples only; groups at management's discretion. Dogs not permitted in 'Orchard' during the school summer holidays.

ON SITE 2 camping areas separated by a wooded valley. 140 pitches in 'Orchard' and 90 pitches in 'Willow Brook'. Each field has separate facilities. Orchard has 9 showers per gender, 10 WCs per gender and 90% electrical hook-ups. Willow Brook has 4 showers and 5 WCs per gender, plus 50% electrical hook-ups. There's a laundry, a heated swimming pool and a sports area with volleyball, badminton, *petanque* and table tennis. Recycling is obligatory: bags are supplied on arrival.

OFF SITE Numerous bridleways lead from the site, and the seaside resort of Shanklin has a nice old town overlooking a sandy beach. Shanklin Chine (01983 866432; shanklinchine.co.uk) is a luscious green ravine with a walkway down to a handful of attractions at the bottom, including chipmunks and a Victorian brine bath.

FOOD & DRINK Farmer Jack's farm shop (01983 527530; farmerjacks.co.uk), in Arreton is excellent. The Pointer Inn (01983 865202; pointernewchurch.co.uk), in Newchurch, is one of the oldest pubs around and still deserves its local fame. In Shanklin, head for the waterside Fisherman's Cottage (01983 863882), which serves some of the freshest fish on the island.

GETTING THERE Sat Nav should use postcode PO36 9PJ. From Cowes/Yarmouth, go past the park entrance to Morrisons supermarket roundabout, turn 180 degrees and return to filter off left. From Ryde/Fishbourne, take the A3055 and turn on to the A3056 at Lake. Continue for 1km, over the Morrisons roundabout, and the site is on the left.

OPEN May–September.

THE DAMAGE Tent + 2 adults £13–£17.50; electric tent/caravan/motorhome pitch + 2 adults £18.50–£25.75.

whitecliff bay

Whitecliff Bay, Hillway Road, Bembridge, Isle of Wight PO35 5PL 01983 872671 www.wight-holidays.com

Only a few miles off the Hampshire coast, the Isle of Wight does its best to bottle the classic British holiday. An ever-popular retreat for walkers, cyclists and the bucket-and-spade brigade since Queen Victoria's reign, the island's leading attractions are its countless outdoor activities, mild climate and dense green hills that roll down to over 20 miles of unspoilt beaches. The last decade has also seen a youthful buzz injecting life into the island's towns and villages, attracting a new generation of campers with fancy gastropubs, vintage antique shops and international music festivals.

Found on the island's picturesque east coast, Whitecliff Bay is a great spot for families and small groups. The site offers a wide range of accommodation, with over 400 pitches for traditional campers set on a gentle south-facing slope with stunning countryside views. A variety of glamping options can be found at 'Canvas Village', where a dozen bell tents and 'Canvas Cottages' are ideal for those who don't want to compromise on comfort. If you're a camper striving for solitude then Whitecliff Bay probably isn't going to be for you. But what the park lacks in intimacy it makes up for in facilities, with large outdoor and indoor heated pools, a secluded sandy beach (with café), two restaurants and a supermarket that sells all the essentials.

The Isle of Wight is only 23 miles by 13 miles, and much of it is designated an Area of Outstanding Natural Beauty. The east coast is lined with charming Victorian resorts (such as nearby Sandown), while the scenic west coast is less developed and home to the pretty port of Yarmouth and the Needles, pinnacles of chalk towering out of the sea. Perfect walking territory, the island is criss-crossed with 500 miles of footpaths. If you don't feel like tackling the 64-mile coast path, then try the Tennyson Trail. Named after former Poet Laureate Alfred Lord Tennyson, this picturesque walk starts at Carisbrooke Castle and continues over Brightstone Down towards Alum Bay. Keep your eyes peeled for the 'barrows' on Mottistone Down, a burial site that dates back 4,000 years.

Days certainly fly by on the Isle of Wight. Whichever way you turn you'll find spectacular views, a plethora of attractions and miles of untouched coastline. Back at Whitecliff Bay the evenings are lively too, with onsite entertainment that includes artists from the West End and, in the summer months, outdoor film screenings overlooking the bay. And even if the 'holiday park' feel isn't to your taste, you can just kick back, light up the barbecue and take in those countryside views. Fantastic.

COOL FACTOR A great seaside spot for families.

WHO'S IN Tents, caravans, glampers, families, groups and dogs (maximum 2 per pitch) – yes. Hen and stag parties – no.

ON SITE 400 pitches with a selection of grass, electric hook-ups and hardstanding. Plenty of spaces for tents, plus 11 'Canvas Cottages' and 12 bell tents. 2 shower blocks and laundry facilities. Small shop, bar (with free Wi-Fi). Full access to the indoor and outdoor pools, indoor and outdoor playgrounds and sports lounge. Daytime activities include everything from archery to paintball.

OFF SITE Carisbrooke Castle (01983 523112; EH), built in the 12th century, is best known as the place where King Charles I was imprisoned. Osborne House (01983 200022; EH) offers the chance to visit Queen Victoria's favourite royal palace and its gardens.

FOOD & DRINK There are 3 onsite dining options, and the nearby Culver Downs Café provides simple home-made goodies at a spectacular location. The Crab & Lobster Inn (01983 872244; crabandlobsterinn.co.uk) was crowned 'Isle of Wight Dining Pub of the Year 2010' – and deservedly so.

GETTING THERE Following the A3055 Ryde–Sandown road, take the Marshcombe Shute southeast turn-off to Bembridge by the Yarbridge Inn. Turn left on to the B3395 Sandown Road and follow this into Bembridge. Passing Bembridge Airport on the left, take a right after the Propeller Inn and then the first left on to Hillway Road.

PUBLIC TRANSPORT Southern Vectis bus no. #8 runs from Ryde bus station straight to the campsite.

OPEN Touring camping available March–November. Everything else available all year.

THE DAMAGE Standard pitch £4–£27; service pitch £5–£32; super pitch £8–£50.

knepp wildland safaris & camping

Knepp Wildlife Safaris & Camping, New Barn Farm, Swallows Lane, Dial Post, West Sussex RH13 8NN 01403 713230
www.kneppsafaris.co.uk

It all started with a vision. The sprawling grounds of the Knepp Estate – centred around the imposing John Nash-designed castle – had, for over 220 years, been devoted to traditional arable and dairy farming. But with the UK's number of farmland birds, insects and other rare species of plant life dwindling, the team behind the West Sussex manor house embarked upon an ambitious project to reintroduce native flora and fauna back to this bucolic corner of the county. With the clay-heavy soil being unsuitable for intensive agriculture, the novel idea of using grazing animals as conservation management was hit upon. Now, over a decade later, the largest privately-owned 'rewilding' project of its kind in Europe has transformed the Knepp Estate into a veritable Eden of biodiversity.

Herds of free-roaming horses, Exmoor ponies, Longhorn cattle, Tamworth pigs and even red and fallow deer rove the estate's 3,500 acres. This unique environment is a magnet for nightingales, purple emperor butterflies, owls, snakes and lizards. The Knepp Wildland Project's expert ecologists offer a range of guided safaris around the site. So if you're batty about bats, or bees make you buzz, you can choose the tour that suits you best. Or if you'd prefer a more bespoke experience, the dedicated team here are happy to accommodate. What could be more awe-inspiring than experiencing the wildlife up close? Camping here, that's what!

While the setting feels every bit as wildly exotic as the Serengeti, camping at the Knepp Estate is far from a primitive experience. There's a dizzying array of fabulous glamping abodes available, from shepherd's huts, yurts and bell tents of all shapes and sizes – think of it as wild camping, with a small 'w'. But we reckon for a true sense of getting back to nature, the off-grid camping pitches can't be beaten. And they allow campfires! Naturally, for key ingredients of that all-important campsite supper, you can't get more free-range than the livestock roaming this unspoiled hideaway, available to buy on site.

Waking up to the sounds of nature is one of the great joys of camping. But the early-morning call of the resident beasts at Knepp Estate offers an added thrill – knowing that you're camping in one of the England's great mini-wildernesses, where nature reigns supreme.

COOL FACTOR The ultimate wildlife campsite.

WHO'S IN Adults-only site – ideal for camping couples looking for a wild retreat. Glampers, groups (except for stag and hen dos) – yes. No dogs, caravans... or poachers.

ON SITE 10 off-grid camping pitches; 8 x 4m unfurnished bell tents to hire, plus 3 shepherd's huts, 1 yurt, 1 emperor bell, 1 x 5m bell, 1 x 6m bell (all furnished). A huge tipi is also coming soon. Proper flush loos and showers, with compost toilets and fire-heated bucket showers for the more adventurous. Wi-Fi and mobile phone/laptop charging in reception. Onsite communal camp kitchen includes gas cooker, 6-ring hob, fridge-freezer with ice packs, sinks, plates, cutlery, plus pots and pans all available to use. Pitch-your-own campers bring their own cooking equipment but have access to another off-grid kitchen and communal dining area.

OFF SITE You might find it impossible to tear yourself away, but should you venture forth, be sure to visit the charming medieval town of Arundel. The South Downs, England's newest national park, is a short drive away, with the Seven Sisters Country Park arguably its most scenic stretch.

FOOD & DRINK Look no further than the onsite shop selling organic Knepp Wild Range venison burgers, Tamworth bangers and longhorn steaks for the BBQ, free range eggs from the camp chickens, seasonal fruit and veg from the Victorian walled garden, home-made honey and a range of pickles and jams. Good local boozers include the Crown Inn (01403 710902; floatingcrown.co.uk) and the Countryman Inn (01403 741383; countrymanshipley.co.uk) near Shipley.

GETTING THERE Travelling south from Horsham on the A24, take the first right for Dial Post, then the first right on to Swallows Lane. New Barn Farm track is on the left. Travelling from Worthing, take the first turn for Dial Post on the left, pass the pub and then take the second left on Swallows lane. New Barn Farm track is on the left.

OPEN April–October.

THE DAMAGE Furnished tents and huts £70–£120 per night. camping pitches £15 per night; unfurnished bell tents for hire at £12 per night.

blackberry wood

Blackberry Wood, Streat Lane, Streat, Nr Ditchling, East Sussex BN6 8RS 01273 890035 www.blackberrywood.com

You can stay at Blackberry Wood any number of times, but each visit is likely to feel completely different, partly because the secluded woodland changes with the seasons, but mainly because owner Tim is so focused on expanding his unique range of glamping accommodation, that there's no knowing what weird and wonderful structures you might find each time.

Near the entrance to the campsite a small, flat field accommodates an odd assortment of permanent caravans, some of which are available to hire. The centre of the field is a large play area where Tim occasionally lights a big bonfire and maybe a barbecue, a warm focal point of entertainment and sociability on colder evenings.

But let's start with the 'proper' camping, which is the heritage of this site. Nestled in the foothills of the South Downs, this secluded campsite is almost lost in the native woodland. The sought- after woodland pitches can be found behind the small glamping field. Follow one of the footpaths leading into the rambling straggle of trees and thicket to find 20 individual clearings, each comprising a firepit, some rudimentary seating and enough space for a medium-sized tent. With trees all around, each spot feels gloriously secluded and, with so few pitches in this part of the site anyway, there's a rare and special kind of peace, enhanced each evening by the soporific soundtrack of campfires gently fizzing; logs are available at the house.

Each pitch has its own personality and most have been named by previous campers, including Fruity in the shade of a crab apple tree, Minty

with its gloriously fresh-smelling herbs, and the more eclectically christened Aroha ('love' in Maori, in case you're wondering).

Facilities-wise, environmentally minded Tim displays prominent notices requesting the responsible use of water, with a new wooden facilities block boasting a waterless urinal in addition to solar lighting. One of the recent developments at Blackberry Wood is the opening of another camping area during peak season, across the road from the main site. Again, it's woodland camping, but there's a 'no kids and no groups rule', so it's great for couples looking for a peaceful escape.

But no review of this site would be complete without a round-up of the glamping possibilities. A characterful 1960s caravan affectionately known as 'Bubble' and a brightly painted gypsy wagon are fairly standard offerings, but there is now also a red Routemaster bus equipped with a kitchen/diner downstairs and a kids' soft-play area upstairs which handily converts into a bedroom. There's also a helicopter (we kid you not), which sleeps four and comes with central heating. Even the reception was in a caravan at the time of writing, but we hear that NASA is selling off de-commissioned space shuttles, so next year's check-in experience might be quite different.

All in all, a tiny, unpretentious campsite that is one of the best in England – not least because it has the four essential elements that make up a truly great site – earth, fire, water and an exceptional local pub, the Jolly Sportsman in nearby East Chiltington.

COOL FACTOR Back-to-nature woodland camping with a pagan vibe.

WHO'S IN Tents, dogs (on leads at all times), well-behaved groups – yes. Motorhomes, caravans – no.

ON SITE Campfires allowed in the designated firepits; logs and BBQ coal are available from reception, as well as food essentials. 4 hot showers on the main site take 20p coins; there's also a fantastic al fresco shower on the adults-only side of the site. Plenty of toilets and washing-up sinks.

OFF SITE You can strike out across the Downs to discover miles of walking uninterrupted by roads or cars. Depending on which direction you take, a 45-minute walk can take you to the village of Ditchling or to the Black Cap viewpoint, a high point on the South Downs Way. Maps are available at reception marking all the walks, pubs and other attractions. Chilled-out Lewes is just 5 miles away, or it's 8 miles to the bright lights of Brighton.

FOOD & DRINK There's a truly great pub within walking distance, the Jolly Sportsman (01273 890400; thejollysportsman.com) in East Chiltington, which is snug and cosy and serves a changing menu of gastro delights.

GETTING THERE From the M23 continue south on to the A23 for 14 miles. Turn left on to the A273 for about a mile, then bear right on to B2112 New Road for 2 miles. Turn right on to the B2116 Lewes Road and turn left on to Streat Lane after 2 miles. You'll see the site signposted on the right.

OPEN All year.

THE DAMAGE Camping charges per night are £5 per tent + £5–£9 per adult (depending on the season); children (3–12) go half price. 2-night minimum stay at weekends and 3-night minimum at Bank Holidays. The Double Decker bus is £70 per night + adult and children seasonal camping charges. The gypsy caravan is £35 per night + seasonal camping charges. The retro caravan is £35 per night + seasonal camping charges.

housedean farm campsite

Housedean Farm, Brighton Road, Lewes, East Sussex BN7 3JW 07919668816 www.housedean.co.uk

Slap bang in the heart of the peaceful, undulating East Sussex Downs lies Housedean Farm, a 900-acre family-run place. Being right on the doorstep of some of rural England's loveliest scenery, this is a walker's dream, but if you don't come here specifically for a jaunty stroll, *Cool Camping* advises (especially on a bright blue summer's day) that you surrender to the irresistible draw of the South Downs Way and get walking. You won't regret it.

With-20-or-so spacious, well-kept pitches, two cosy bell tents (each sleeping six) and one newly installed shepherd's hut, Housedean campsite caters for well-schooled campers and novices alike. The recently-installed bathroom facilities (four toilets and three showers) are also worth mentioning: a modern yet simple block, always immaculately kept, with the open-air hot shower being a real highlight. Campers can lather, rinse and repeat while gazing up at the fluffy Sussex clouds.

One of Housedean's plus points has to be its close proximity to the public transport-friendly A27, allowing visitors to easily explore the local and wider area (including bohemian Brighton the charming hillside town of Lewes) without the prerequisite of a car. There is, in fact, a bus stop right outside the campsite, so car-less campers could make the trip from Brighton train station relatively easily. However, that may also be classed as a disadvantage for those wanting to completely 'get away from it all.' The background hum of the road can be heard, and while it's not too intrusive (the camping fields are located at the rear of the farm), it is definitely noticeable. That said, the campers here don't ever seem bothered by it; there's too much else to be distracted by.

After an exhilarating day exploring the winding trails, river valleys and Saxon churches of the South Downs Way you will no doubt be looking for a serene setting from which to watch the world go by. As luck would have it, Housedean Farm fits the bill perfectly. The site's welcoming owners have stuck to their roots and created a campsite that doesn't pretend to be anything it's not; it's a genuine, traditional working farm, and that's just how we like it.

COOL FACTOR Epic views of the South Downs, plus a true sense of rural isolation.

WHO'S IN Families, groups (if pre-arranged and well-behaved), dogs, horses – yes. Caravans – no.

ON SITE 26 large pitches, each with its own firepit, plus 2 bell tents (1 furnished, 1 not) and a shepherd's hut – fully furnished with a double bed, single bed and wood-burning stove. Kindling, firelighters, disposable BBQs and bags of logs can be purchased on site. Mountain-bike hire available.

OFF SITE You're pitched on the South Downs Way so it would be a sin not to explore it. Brighton and Lewes are only a couple of miles away and can be reached by local bus. Lewes, a beautiful market town, boasts quaint antique shops, lots of cafés and restaurants.

FOOD & DRINK The Half Moon in Plumpton (01273 890253; halfmoonplumpton.com) is a charming 200-year-old-country pub with a pleasant beer garden, a cellar full of local ales and a varied menu that changes with the seasons. Picturesque Ditchling (7 miles away) is home to the cosy Bull (01273 843147; thebullditchling.com) and the White Horse (01273 842006; whitehorseditchling.com), which serves affordable, tasty pub grub.

GETTING THERE Coming from the west on the A27, pass the University of Sussex on the left and the Amex stadium on the right and follow the road a further mile. Turn left immediately after the bridge into the lay-by and you will see Housedean Farm in front of you. If heading west on the A27, follow signs to Brighton; after passing the Ashcombe/Kingston roundabout you will see the Newmarket Inn on the left. After a further ½ mile, before the bridge over the A27, turn left into the lay-by (signposted Housedean Farm). Go over the bridge and follow the signs to the farm.

PUBLIC TRANSPORT Frequent buses from Brighton and Lewes stop right outside the site.

OPEN March–October.

THE DAMAGE Adults £11 per night; children (3–15 years old) £7 per night. Bell tents: unfurnished £65 per night; furnished £80 per night. Shepherd's Hut: £160 for 2 nights and £60 per subsequent night (7th night free).

spring barn farm

Spring Barn Farm Park, Kingston Road, Lewes, East Sussex BN7 3ND 01273 488450 www.springbarnfarm.com

Surely one of the prettiest towns in Sussex, with its mixture of medieval and 18th-century houses, Lewes is bursting at its timbered seams with history. Beer lovers will be delighted to know that Sussex's premier ale, Harveys, is brewed in town, and there are plenty of cosy pubs in which to sample it. Lewes is also famous for its Bonfire Night, which sees a cast of thousands parading through the streets in fancy dress with burning crosses before the *pièce de résistance*: effigies are burned in the nearby fields.

Located on the undulating South Downs, in a vista of buttery hills and widescreen skies, Spring Barn Farm is manna from heaven for kids, and perfect for campers who like a good walk. Let's start with the secluded campsite: it's basic – little more than a field with a nearby loo block – but the views are fantastic. Look out over the downs, peer into the adjacent *Children of the Corn* maize field, and hear the myriad calls of animals from the adjoining farm, part of which is open to the public as a 'farm park'. Kids love this, and the menagerie outside, and campers get in half-price. If goats, rabbits, and chickens are passé, then show them the cheeky Shetland ponies and South American alpacas with their *Thunderbird*-puppet lips. The maze is great fun, too: three acres of twisting turns in which to lose yourself.

COOL FACTOR History and great South Downs walks just beyond your tent flaps.

WHO'S IN Tents, small groups – yes. Campervans, caravans, dogs, big groups – no.

ON SITE A total of 32 grassy pitches; mains cold water; no electricity; toilet block. Campfire pits available and BBQs allowed off-ground. Kids will enjoy the indoor slides, zip wire, pedal go-kart track, trampoline, swings, sandpit, pirate play ship, soft-play area for under-5s, maze and menagerie of animals. Come in Easter to bottle-feed newborn lambs and meet chicks and rabbits. Campers get into the farm half price.

OFF SITE Lewes has its photogenic castle (01273 486290; EH) – built during the days of William the Conqueror – and just south of the town centre, historic Anne of Cleves House (01273 474610; EH) makes for an interesting visit. Divorced, beheaded, divorced... hmm? Time for a history lesson.

FOOD & DRINK The farmhouse kitchen is a cosy place to hole up for breakfast or a Sunday roast. In neighbouring Firle, the Ram Inn (01273 858222; raminn.co.uk) does wonderful traditional Sunday lunches and has a range of local draught beers, plus a pretty garden.

GETTING THERE Follow the A27 towards Lewes and, at the Kingston roundabout, take the exit for Kingston village. Drive through the village to the T-junction opposite Wyevale Garden Centre and turn left. Spring Barn Farm is on the left.

PUBLIC TRANSPORT Take a train to Lewes. There is a new cyclepath/footpath that can take you all the way to the farm from there. (Taxis are also available from the station.)

OPEN Late March–late September.

THE DAMAGE £10 per adult per night. £6 per child per night. Half-price day entry to Farm Park for campers (or get a 3-day campers Farm Park pass, which is even cheaper. Log bags (£6.95) and kindling packs (£1.75) available.

the secret campsite

Brickyard Farm, Town Littleworth, Barcombe, East Sussex BN8 4TD 01273 401100 www.thesecretcampsite.co.uk

The Secret Campsite is, of course, not really very secret at all. Nor does owner Tim want it to be. He wants people to know about it, to come and support his fledgling business and the rural economy nearby. The real secret is just how special this campsite is. After arriving and parking at the reception and amenities area of a now defunct garden nursery, visitors grab a wheelbarrow, load up their gear and follow the grassy path up and over an old brick railway bridge. The railway underneath has long gone, leaving a beautifully overgrown path for you to explore. Accessing the site from the bridge makes it feel isolated, secluded – and just that little bit secret. From this vantage point, it's easy to take in the features of this place: just 18 hugely spacious pitches cut into the long grass of a secluded meadow, interspersed with a scattering of recently planted saplings and all encircled with a backdrop of ancient oak and hornbeam trees. Wild flowers are bursting to show off their colours, while the woods beyond are ripe for exploration. In fact, the plan is for plants to be a big part of this site. Tim is a botanist and wants to turn this place into the UK's first 'edible campsite. A planting programme is underway, with an increasing array of berries, edible shrubs and flowers growing freely, ready for campers to pick fresh and add to the saucepan.

In the meantime, there's something else growing quickly – and that's the reputation of the Secret Campsite. Secret? It won't be for long!

COOL FACTOR A special hideaway, almost cut off from the world and only an hour from London.

WHO'S IN Tents – yes. Caravans, campervans, big groups, young groups, dogs – no.

ON SITE 12 large pitches in the main meadow; another 6 on the car-park side of the bridge. Campfires allowed. 3 showers in an old stable block along with new toilets; compost-loo shacks are nearer the pitches. Trolleys are available to transport your gear to the main meadow. No shop as such, but you can buy firewood at reception and there is a farm shop 5 minutes' walk away.

OFF SITE Don't overlook the delights of Lewes, a pretty market town nestled in the South Downs just 5 miles away and walkable from the site. The South Downs National Park is a 3-mile stroll to Offham. Finally, Middle Farm (01323 811411; middlefarm.com) and Drusilla's Park (01323 874100; drusillas.co.uk) are both great for kids.

FOOD & DRINK Tim knows all the best places to get fresh, local produce, including the Holmansbridge Farm Shop (01273 401964; holmansbridgefarm.com). Pubwise, the Horns Lodge (01273 400422; hornslodge.com) is a 20-minute walk, through Balneath Woods and Markstakes Common, and serves great beers and traditional pub food. If all country pubs could be as good as the Griffin at Fletchling (01825 722890; thegriffininn.co.uk), with its delightful garden and exceptional food, the world would be a happier place.

GETTING THERE Head north from Lewes on the A275 and half a mile after leaving Cooksbridge turn right on to Deadmantree Hill. Follow the road for 2 miles to Holmansbridge Farm Shop. The campsite is the fourth turning on the right after here and shares the driveway with a house called 'Woodside'.

OPEN Mid March–end October.

THE DAMAGE Adults £16; Children 5–16 years £8; under–5s get in for free.

kitts cottage campsite

Kitts Cottage Campsite, Freshfield Place Farm, Sloop Lane, Scaynes Hill, West Sussex RH17 7NP 07733 103309
www.kittscamp.co.uk

James, the manager of Kitts Cottage campsite, is a wry chap; he looks as if he might have been a highwayman or pirate in a former life, so we're not sure whether to believe him when he points to the campsite's eastern treeline and says there's a ghost of a lady who sometimes walks through there from the woods. Certainly it's an atmospheric spot, and on creepy nights, as the north wind wraps its teeth around your guy ropes and whistles at your door, you might wish that we'd never mentioned it. To be honest, though, there's nothing faintly spectral about Kitts Cottage – indeed the story (coupled with James himself) just adds to the site's charm.

Sandwiched between Lewes and Haywards Heath, the 18-acre site takes its name from a house that used to stand here hundreds of years ago. There are no style awards or glamping Brownie points being won here. Kitts is all about bowling up with your tent and doing all the hard stuff like pitching up and cracking open your cool box, as well as stoking the flames in one of the many designated firepits. Essentially it's a huge meadow bookended on two sides by alluringly ancient woods and bordered by sheep-grazing fields; there's an area for families shaded by mature oaks, a section for groups further away, and the remainder is left for couples and singles. The eastern treeline is always kept free and uninterrupted for aesthetic purposes – an arboreal canvas that could have come from the brush of John Constable.

James runs it this way to keep things in balance, just like the unspoken eco-agreement with the nearby forest critters. Your side of the bargain is not to gather wood, or any kindling whatsoever – it's provided to you on arrival. And, in return, the creatures leave you alone. Fires are positively encouraged, though, as part of the site's back-to-basics ethos.

The site sits on a slight elevation, giving great views from the top of the hill. Gazing across the woolly backs of sheep and rusted ploughs you have to pinch yourself when you remember you're less than an hour from London. The surrounding woodlands are criss-crossed with public footpaths, one of which leads directly to the much-celebrated Bluebell Railway, which provides a journey into yesteryear with a fully working steam railway system. With its old-fashioned stations peppered with nostalgic signs, elderly conductors, and steam billowing from *Thomas the Tank Engine* funnels, it's a delight for even the weariest cynics. The footpaths from the site are perfect for getting back to nature and, if you don't fancy walking, then bring your bike to explore the woody glades, sunburned fields and pretty hamlets.

Cyclists heading east, or towards the coast, should also try the wonderful Cuckoo Trail – 11 miles of disused railway track, choking on wildlife and woodland as it meanders gently through quiet hamlets, monuments and the best of Sussex countryside. It starts in Polegate and zigzags through Hailsham, Horam and Heathfield. There are plenty of places en route to stop for a cheeky cool pint or a snack, as well as various sculptures in wood and steel to look out for. In May, keep an eye out for the Orange-tip butterfly, and orchids growing near the path.

COOL FACTOR Back-to-basics, camping. Ditch the iPod speakers and lace up your walking boots.

WHO'S IN Tents, dogs (on leads), groups, all folk – yes. Caravans not welcome but it's prime turf for campervans.

ON SITE Pick up firewood on arrival, then James will direct you to a pitch that suits. Although Kitts is acutely eco-conscious, the old al fresco facilities have been replaced with proper flushing loos and showers, housed in the field barn, along with a new covered dish-washing area. There are no bins on site, so campers are requested to take rubbish away with them (recycling facilities can be found nearby).

OFF SITE Sheffield Park and Garden (01825 790231; NT) features 18th-century ornamental gardens laid out by Capability Brown, which are bursting with azaleas, rhododendrons and views to set the soul alight. 20 minutes' walk from Kitts, the Bluebell Railway (01825 720800; bluebell-railway.co.uk) is operated by some charming old boys who will take you back to another era as they doff their caps and guide you on to the glorious old carriages as if you were off to Hogwarts School.

FOOD & DRINK Find warming fare at the Sloop Inn (01444 831219), a welcoming gastropub with food made from local organic produce and prices to match the affable atmosphere. Also nearby, at the end of Ketches Lane, Trading Boundaries (01825 790200; tradingboundaries.com) is a cluster of shops and galleries grouped around an old courtyard, including the only permanent gallery devoted to Roger Dean, and a café selling food all day.

GETTING THERE Take the A22 through East Grinstead and Forest Row; 100m after the Wych crossroads, turn right on to the A275. At the church in Danehill, turn right, following signs to Freshfield. A mile after Brickworks you'll see the Sloop Inn on your left. After ½ a mile take the first left into Butterbox Lane. Kitt's is on the left.

OPEN April–late October.

THE DAMAGE Tent + adult £12.50 per night; children (under 13) £7.50 per night; infants camp free. Minimum stay of 2 nights at weekends.

wowo (wapsbourne manor farm)

Wapsbourne Manor Farm, Sheffield Park, East Sussex TN22 3QT 01825 723414 www.wowo.co.uk

Wapsbourne Manor Farm, or 'Wowo', as it's affectionately known by a growing band of regulars, is a rare and beautiful thing – a great campsite within just two hours' drive of London. It's light on unnecessary rules and regulations and big on fun and freedom. With smoky campfires (facilitated by a firewood delivery-man who appears at dusk on his little tractor), old rope swings and free camping for performing musicians, this is not a site for Nanny-State obsessives. But go with the flow and you will find this rural wonderland to be the perfect outdoor adventure.

This magical spot always seems to have something new to reveal: another field hidden behind the thicket, a secret pathway, a yurt nestled among the trees. And while the 40 pitches in the camping fields come with plenty of surrounding space, there's a whole separate site that you might not see unless you go looking for it: the premium woodland camping pitches, otherwise known as the Tipi Trail. These eight pitches (christened with such delightfully spacey names as 'Hobbit', 'Woodland' and 'Little Owl') are secreted away in their own exclusive woodland setting, ideal for celebrities and newlywed couples looking for seclusion. What's more, they offer a fairy-tale-like setting for games of hide-and-seek. Two new additions to the site are the fully equipped shepherd's huts and a couple of roomy bell tents.

There's always something fun going on during summer weekend evenings: soup suppers; pizza making; and plenty of mingling. Children's entertainment is strictly of the old-school variety: climbing trees, swinging on tyres and making camps in the undergrowth. In fact, the entire 150-acre site is a huge, natural playground extending well beyond the four main camping areas. Saturday night is music night, with free camping for musicians in return for sing-songs around the fire. It's a hippified rule alright, but perfect for bohemian Wowo.

Nearby, the Bluebell Railway steam train is a big draw, as is Sheffield Park, arguably one of the country's finest gardens, lovingly sculpted in the late 1700s by Capability Brown. In autumn, black tupelos blend with the rusty reds of the maple and oak. Spring brings a lively riot of daffodils and bluebells. In summer there are flashy splodges of pink rhododendrons. Cricket fans may also care to know that the park was the venue for the first ever home tie between England and Australia in 1884.

But then many weekend visitors don't get that far, happy to settle for the pleasures of exploring the grounds of Wowo for a few days. With the evening air scented with campfire smoke, the soft murmur of sociability and perhaps a musical soundtrack, this wonderful woodland hideaway just oozes back-to-basics appeal. Leave the rules at home. Let the kids roam free.

COOL FACTOR A chilled-out campsite complete with a fun, buzzy atmosphere.

WHO'S IN Tents, campervans, dogs – yes. Caravans, motorhomes, groups of unsupervised under-18s – no.

ON SITE 40 standard pitches, 8 'Tipi Trail' woodland pitches, 4 yurts, 2 shepherd's huts and 2 bell tents for hire with a covered cooking area. 8 flushing compost toilets, 1 with shower plus 1 single shower in Tipi Trail area; 4 flushing compost toilets, 1 accessible flushing compost toilet in Lower Moat field; 2 flushing compost toilets in Middle Brook; 2 flushing compost toilets in Lower Brook. 2 basic shower blocks plus 1 accessible family wet room. A communal barn has a ping-pong table and piano; fridges and freezers; Wi-Fi; an honesty bookshelf; and coin-operated laundry. Onsite shop stocks local food, baked goods, ales and cider. A particularly nice touch is the complimentary soup and fresh bread served on Saturday nights in the communal area.

OFF SITE With a station right next door to Wowo, the Bluebell Railway (see p.119) is perfect for a *Thomas the Tank Engine*-inspired day out. Wander the beautiful National Trust landscaped gardens at Sheffield Park and Garden (see p.119), just up the road, or stretch the legs further and try the picturesque 42-mile Ouse Valley Way.

FOOD & DRINK The family-friendly Sloop Inn is a 40-minute walk from the campsite through shady woodland (see p.119). There are also 2 excellent gastropubs: the Michelin-rated Coach and Horses in Danehill (01825 740369; coachandhorses.co) and the Griffin Inn in Fletching (01825 722890; thegriffininn.co.uk), which are both less than 10 minutes' drive or a scenic trek along the Ouse Valley Way.

GETTING THERE Exit the M25 at junction 6 and take the A22, following signs for the Bluebell Railway. Pass the railway on the right and Wowo is the second on the right. From the south take the A275 north. Over the A272 at Chailey and Wowo is 1 mile ahead on the left.

OPEN Tipi Trail and yurts all year; camping March–October.

THE DAMAGE Adult £10 per night; child £5; under-3s free. One-off charge for cars £5. Tipi Trail pitches an extra £10 per night except during winter. Yurts £112–£250 per 2-night stay. Minimum stay 2 nights.

firle camp

Firle Camp, Firle Estate, Heighton Street, East Sussex BN8 6NZ 07733 103309 www.firlecamp.co.uk

The South Downs National Park is the UK's newest national park, so it seems entirely fitting that a brand new campsite with a fresh approach has opened in one of its most beautiful areas. The owner, however, is far from new to this game – it's James from much-loved Sussex site Kitts Cottage Campsite (see pp.18–19).

Firle is James' latest venture, blazing a trial with a pop-up campsite that's open just on popular summer weekends. Proper service commenced here in 2013 with a modest shower block replacing the portable loos, but don't expect huge changes as the beauty of this site is in its back-to-basics simplicity.

A large, flat, hedge-edged field is hidden behind an 18th-century stone barn; other than the pillar box shower huts, that's it, there's not much else to say. Except, look around – immediately beyond the hedges are the rolling South Downs, tempting you to leave your tent and walk straight off to explore this beautiful landscape, and there's a cracking country pub nearby to reward those that do. The Firle Place Estate, with it's renowned collection of Old Master paintings, and Charleston Farmhouse, of Bloomsbury group fame, are both within easy walking distance.

There are no marked pitches at Firle Camp, but expect James to cluster families and non-families in separate groupings, each around the essential firepit, of course.

COOL FACTOR Beautiful green countryside, all around.

WHO'S IN Tents, campervans, groups, dogs on leads – yes. Caravans, noisy groups – no.

ON SITE Campfires allowed. Around 40 tents maximum. A couple of pillar box shower huts produce a surprising amount of hot water. Pressure can be a little iffy, though, so anyone expecting a power shower will be disappointed. A washing-up area has covered sinks and ample room for drying and stacking. There is no hot water on tap. More encouragingly, the water that comes to the campsite is from Firle's own Downland Spring. It filters through the South Downs chalk making it cleaner, purer and softer than nearly anywhere else. There's a small shop in Firle village and a top-notch farm shop at nearby Middle Farm (01323 811411; middlefarm.com).

OFF SITE You can access paths directly from the site and walk to Firle Beacon (1 mile), from where you can pick up the South Downs Way (southdownsway.co.uk). Nearby, Firle Place Estate (01273 858307; firle.com) offers history and some of the best views in the area. The lovely county town of Lewes (4 miles) is also an easy trip.

FOOD & DRINK There's a great pub 15 minutes' walk from the site: the Ram (01273 858222; raminn.co.uk), with a high-quality menu and a lovely garden. Families should try the Barley Mow (01323 811322) at Selmeston, which has a kids' play area.

GETTING THERE From the A27, 4 miles east of Lewes, turn on to Heighton Street, marked by a sign saying 'Ripe 3, Laughton 5'. Firle Camp is 300m further on the left.

OPEN April–October.

THE DAMAGE Adults/under–13s £10/£7.50 per night. Under–2's free. Minimum 2-night stay at weekends.

embers camping bentley

Embers Camping Bentley, Halland, East Sussex BN8 5AF 0845 257 2267 www.emberscamping.co.uk

Some 700 years ago, the pastoral parkland of Bentley belonged to the Archbishop of Canterbury, who later granted it to a local aristocrat. Perhaps he sprinkled a little holy water on the meadows because, when it comes to camping, this place is truly blessed. On the first day the Lord gaveth grassy fields and ageing oaks; on the second he sculpted tearooms, a museum and an adventure playground; and on the third he produced fire (and maybe a marshmallow or two). The Eden He created is a combination of simple tents–only camping with a host of walkable activities on the doorstep. A real camper's paradise.

Surrounded by woodland and hedgerows, this unpretentious site has no electric hook–ups and just 45 ample pitches despite is expansive grounds. Campfires, as you'll guess from the name, are an essential part of an evening beneath the stars. And when daylight returns, there's an endless list of things to do. Head across the field to the Bentley Estate, where you can visit the motor museum, hop aboard the miniature railway or wander through the wildfowl reserve – the most diverse private bird collection in Europe. After a relaxing cuppa in the tearooms, hop in the car for a speedy journey through the countryside – despite its rural seclusion, some of the best attractions in Sussex are just a short drive away. The Georgian town of Lewes straddles the River Ouse as it carves its way through the South Downs. To the east, the historic towns of Battle and Hastings are preceded by Herstmonceux Castle. Then, of course, there's the coast, a 25-minute drive away.

Embers Bentley is both a gateway to the treasures of East Sussex and a county jewel in its own right. The picturesque estate and quiet camping meadow is a prize pick for campers who want to escape the rush of everyday life, while still having every attraction nearby.

COOL FACTOR Simple camping in a blessed location.

WHO'S IN Tent campers, groups – yes. Caravans, campervans, dogs – no.

ON SITE 45 spacious, tents-only pitches with no electrical hook-ups. A wooden sanitary block contains 8 new showers (4 male and 4 female), 3 loos for each gender, 2 urinals and 4 washing-up basins. Each booking affords 1 complimentary adult ticket to gain access to the Bentley Estate (01825 840573) for the duration of the stay. The miniature railway, motor museum and adventure playground will keep the kids entertained, and the Estate also plays host to an abundance of rare wildfowl. There are spaces for games, pleasant local walks and, of course, the excellent tearooms next to the museum.

OFF SITE This part of Sussex is rich in history, with both Lewes Castle (01273 486290; EH) and Herstmonceaux Castle (01323 833816; herstmonceux-castle.com) nearby, and Battle just beyond. The South Downs National Park (southdowns. gov.uk), stretches down to the Sussex Heritage Coast, home to countless beaches and chalky cliffs. The National Park hosts a wealth of outdoor activities including horseriding, boating and canoeing along with excellent walking and cycle routes, most notably the South Downs Way (southdownsway.co.uk), just a few miles from the campsite.

FOOD & DRINK There is a shop selling milk, farm eggs, local sausages and bacon, along with other camping essentials such as ice cream, snacks and marshmallows. The nearest pubs are the Halfway House (01825 750382; halfwayhouseisfield.co.uk), the Laughing Fish (01825 750349; thelaughingfish.co.uk) and the Anchor Inn (01273 400414; anchorinnandboating.co.uk), all within 1 or 2 miles.

GETTING THERE The campsite is just off the A26 a few miles outside of Lewes. Numerous signs on the A26 and A22 direct you to the 'Bentley Wildfowl and Motor Museum' where the campsite is located. For Sat-Navs use BN8 5AF, which will take you to the Estate.

OPEN April–September. Most weekends, Bank Holidays and school holidays.

THE DAMAGE £22 per adult per night; £6 per child of 4 yrs or older.

st ives farm

St Ives Farm, Butcherfield Lane, Hartfield, East Sussex TN7 4JX 01892 770213 www.stivesfarm.co.uk

'Three Cheers for Pooh! (For who?) For Pooh! (Why, what did he do?) I thought you knew…' Of the many things that the great Winnie the Pooh did and didn't do, the most significant, as far as this little corner of East Sussex goes, is that he chose to spend his entire fictional life around the unassuming Surrey village of Hartfield. What's not known is if he ever chose to stay at St Ives Farm, a quiet, idyllic countryside campsite just outside Hartfield, the village where A A Milne penned the famous stories. Hartfield, a one-street hamlet with a tiny village green and ivy-covered pubs, is the centre of Pooh Country. The old sweetshop where Christopher Robin used to buy 'bull's eyes' survives to this day, re-named Pooh Corner, and now does a roaring trade in cream teas, pots of honey and general 'Pooh-phernalia'. You can also pick up a map that will direct you to all the haunts frequented by the loveable yellow bear himself, including 100 Acre Wood, Galleon's Leap and Poohsticks Bridge.

If you can bear to drag yourself away from all this nostalgia, St Ives Farm is to be found just a five-minute drive north of Hartfield. After following signs for St Ives Tea Rooms, you'll need to take a last-minute diversion across a farmer's field and circumnavigate some long-stay caravans before finding the small camping area, which offers about 20 tent pitches beside a picturesque fishing lake and surrounded by arable farmland. Be warned that, with a limited number of spaces, the site is usually booked out by regulars at weekends, so a midweek break may be the only realistic option in summer. Being so far from the road,

St Ives has an unusually peaceful ambience – an atmosphere enhanced by the fact that campfires are allowed, and scent the air with the fragrant smoke of sizzling sausages and melting marshmallows. The only activity on site is coarse fishing for carp and perch in the well-stocked pond. However, the St Ives Tea Rooms at the farm next door seem to have a mysterious power over visitors to this place, who gravitate helplessly towards the flower-filled tea gardens for scones and jam at least once in their trip. So, it's three cheers for Pooh and for St Ives Farm, too. (Why, what did they do?) I thought you knew…

COOL FACTOR Secluded countryside setting with the added bonus of campfires.

WHO'S IN Tents only. Dogs are welcome, and free to frolic in their very own designated dogwalking area.

ON SITE The basic facilities suit this rustic place; just 3 chemical loos and 6 showers. Other than making campfires, the only other on site activity is fishing. The lake is stocked with carp and perch and fishing there costs £5/£9 per day for children/adults. Almost onsite is the adjacent tea garden, which serves tasty cream teas and light lunch snacks against an Ashdown Forest backdrop.

OFF SITE Do as Winne the Pooh would do – eat honey, play Pooh Sticks and wander around in the woods. In Hartfield, the old sweetshop where Christopher Robin used to buy bulls' eyes survives to this day. And if you're not too Pooh-ped after all that, then you can go walking with llamas at the Ashdown Forest Llama Park (01825 712040; llamapark.co.uk) in Forest Row.

FOOD & DRINK For top-notch food with an emphasis on locally sourced, seasonal produce, head for The Hatch Inn (01342 822363; hatchinn.co.uk) at Colemans Hatch. It's a quaint little country pub on the edge of the Ashdown Forest, a 50-minute walk or 10-minute drive from St Ives Farm, and handy for Poohsticks Bridge. The ivy-covered Anchor Inn (01892 770424; anchorhartfield.com) in Hartfield is a 15th-century free house with an unusual, old-fashioned, flower-filled veranda, as well as a pleasant beer garden and a selection of local ales.

GETTING THERE Follow the A22 southbound through South Godstone. After Brindley Heath, take a left on to the B2029 (Ray Lane) towards Lingfield. The road turns into the B2028 (Race Course Road). Turn right when you reach Dormans Road, eventually becoming Hollow Lane and meeting the A264. Turn left on to the A264 for 1½ miles then right on to Cansiron Lane becoming Butcherfield Lane. The campsite is a little further on the right.

OPEN April–late October.

THE DAMAGE £10 for adults, £5 for children per night.

hidden spring

Hidden Spring, Vines Cross Road, Horam, East Sussex, TN21 0HG 01435 812640 www.hiddenspring.co.uk

Hidden Spring does exactly what it says on the tin: family camping *à la ferme*, squirrelled away in fields corduroyed by apple orchards. It's situated near the sleepy village of Horam, which has all you might need, from a café, newsagent, butchers and chippy, and there's a palpable sense of calm that slips over you as soon as you drive up the leafy track and catch your first view of the campsite.

It's basic, but good basic, and for a reason too – owners Tamzin and David want their visitors to experience a back-to-nature treat, a place where kids can make dens in the copse, run wild through the orchard, and play hide-and-seek in the woods.

There are two fields to choose from – a tents-only option and one for campervans and caravans. But don't worry: given the site's pursuit of aesthetics over rampant profit, there are only a select number of caravans allowed at any one time, so the views of the undulating fields and grass-munching horses are unbroken. There are firepits like witches' cauldrons in the campervan field. You can buy wood and firelighters from Hidden Spring's little shop (which operates an honesty tab) and do the Neanderthal thing.

Of an evening you can listen to the owls begin their calling while your flames turn a rich Hallowe'en orange and carbonise your burgers; it's a beautiful spot to sit back and chill. The endless vistas of hay fields, the soft chalky backdrop of the South Downs, and the first-class pubs of East Sussex make a trip here well worth it, and there are more local attractions than you could hope to cover in a weekend, from castles to stately homes.

COOL FACTOR Eco-camping on a gloriously pretty farm.

WHO'S IN Glampers, tents, campervans, caravans, dogs (on leads) – yes. Young, noisy, large groups – no.

ON SITE 2 camping areas: Oak Field (car-free) has fully-furnished yurts and pitches for tents. Apple Field (where caravans and campervans are permitted), has pitches with electric hook-up. The shower and loo block is spotlessly clean. Campfires are allowed in firepits. There are kids' swings; dens in the woods; and a farm shop selling its own apple juice, locally sourced meat, eggs, milk and logs.

OFF SITE Wilderness Wood (01825 830509; wildernesswood. org) is a family-run working woodland park in the Sussex Weald. There are trails, a café, and a play area. Drusilla's Park (see p.116) is a great place to entertain the kids. Cyclists should try the nearby Cuckoo Trail: built upon 11 miles of disused railway track, it weaves through woods, fields and the best of the Sussex countryside.

FOOD & DRINK Grilling locally produced meat under the stars makes for a perfect dinner. Otherwise, try the Brewer's Arms (01435 812435; thebrewersarmsvinescross.co.uk) in nearby Vines Cross, which offers shabby-chic decor, a great atmosphere and an earthy menu.

GETTING THERE From East Grinstead head to Uckfield on the A22, then take the B2102 to Cross In Hand. Take the A267, turning left for Horam and heading through the village before turning into Vines Cross Road.

PUBLIC TRANSPORT Bus 52 from Polgate station runs to Horam, which is a short stroll from the site.

OPEN Easter–early October.

THE DAMAGE Tent pitches £18 per night including 2 people. Extra adults (16 yrs +) £9 per night; children 3–15yrs: £5 per night; no charge for infants under 3 yrs. Caravans and campervans £20 per night, including 2 people.

dogwood cottage camping

Dogwood Cottage Caravan & Campsite, Cackle Street, Brede, Rye TN31 6DY 01424 883570 www.dogwoodcamping.co.uk

Flick through the Dogwood Cottage visitors book and you'll struggle to find words that haven't been penned before: 'so secluded', 'so quiet', 'so friendly', 'so close to the pub!' The bulging book reflects the charm of this small site that has grown its custom largely through word of mouth, every visitor leaving with high praise and a vow to return the next year. Pitch up for a night or two and, nestling into one of the 15 prized pitches available, you'll quickly work out what makes this place so special.

On the edge of Brede, a rural East Sussex village, this campsite is set in one of the countless grassy meadows that sweep across the High Weald Area of Outstanding Natural Beauty. The surrounding trees and hedgerows provide shelter, as well as somewhere for kids to build a den, while a woodland pond also attracts plentiful wildlife. Sanitary facilities are fairly basic, with two toilets, a hot shower and a washing-up sink, but they are faultlessly well-kept and, with just a handful of campers, these rustic necessities are all you'll need.

While the spacious pitches and secluded surroundings make for a winning campsite, the Dogwood Cottage experience really comes down to the friendly welcome you receive from Phil and Katy. These laid-back owners are helpful yet unobtrusive, and passionate about their local area. Stacks of handy information can be found in the onsite shop where you can pick up camping essentials, groceries and logs. Phil and Katy's friendliness is mirrored in the village beyond, where two walkable pubs boast excellent food and the warmest of atmospheres.

Despite its quiet countryside location, Dogwood Cottage is a short distance from a wealth of attractions, with Hastings and Battle just a short drive away and the nearest beach just 15 minutes by car, while expansive Camber Sands is five minutes further. The ancient town of Rye is just as close. Its half-timbered, skewed-roofed buildings clustered along cobbled streets are as quintessentially English as they come.

In the evenings, return to the campsite for some late-night stargazing. With the village free of streetlights, the unpolluted sky is crystal clear. So, when the clouds are at bay, why not toast marshmallows round the campfire and keep an eye trained for shooting stars?

COOL FACTOR Wonderfully uncommercial camping with a local feel.

WHO'S IN Tents, caravans, campervans, motorhomes and dogs – yes. Groups – no.

ON SITE 15 pitches, 5 of which have electric hook-ups. 2 toilets, 1 shower, an outside washing-up sink and chemical disposal point. At the entrance an information room and onsite shop sells camping essentials, food and logs. Fire bowls are also available to hire.

OFF SITE There are plenty of good walks in the local area but a stroll in Brede High Woods is a particular highlight – the stunning ancient trees are over 400 years old and home to an array of birdlife. Head south to numerous beaches within driving distance or stop at one of the coastal towns. Hastings is an excellent choice, not only for its historic old town but also for the fantastic seafood that can be found. Those hoping for something more walkable need look no further than wine-tasting in the Carr Taylor Vineyard (01424 751716; carr-taylor.co.uk) or Brede Steam Giants (01323 897310; bredesteamgiants.co.uk), a steam museum in the village with free entry.

FOOD & DRINK The Red Lion (01424 882188; redlionbrede. co.uk) pub is a short stroll across the fields, while the Rainbow Trout (01424 882031; rainbowtroutpub.co.uk) is a 15-minute walk towards Broad Oak, providing a wide-ranging menu as well as a sizeable beer garden. Both are dog friendly. If fresh veg from the onsite shop isn't enough, try Brede Farmers Market, which runs every Friday 10am–noon in the village hall.

GETTING THERE From the A21 towards Hastings, turn left on to the A268 at Flimwell, following on to the A28. The campsite is between Westfield and Broad Oak. Look for the white sign at the drive entrance. Go to the end and through a gate (approx. 150m).

PUBLIC TRANSPORT Buses run from Rye and Hastings, stopping just outside the campsite.

OPEN All year.

THE DAMAGE From £10–£24 a night.

forgewood

ForgeWood, Sham Farm Road, Danegate, Nr Tunbridge Wells, Kent TN3 9JD 07720 290229 www.forgewoodcamping.co.uk

One of a bright young generation of new campsites, ForgeWood in East Sussex has taken *Cool Camping* principles and applied them beautifully. The site opened fully in 2010 after a low-key try-out the previous season, and it has proved to be an instant hit, with that killer combination of campfires, woodland pitches, a tents-only rule (with the exception of the odd vintage campervan), and a laid-back approach.

ForgeWood is a solid example of a new breed of campsites, places that totally 'get' that people want to let their kids roam around woods making camps and dens and getting dirty. They understand the importance of a campfire, the importance of providing a generous hoard of chopped wood and plentiful marshmallows, and that people don't want needless rules. They also understand that a camping trip is about being out amid nature, immersed in the experience of the wild, and don't spoil it all by providing rows of electric hook-ups and concrete pitches.

What ForgeWood and others are doing so well is putting the unassuming tent camper back at the centre of things. With an attractive mix of ancient woodland and open fields, this site gives tenters space and freedom. But it's those pitches within the woodland that stand out – surrounded by a sprawling, undulating thicket, unkempt and scattered with fallen branches, left to the influences of weather, nature, and time. It's a beautiful place to camp although, if truth be told, it's not entirely untouched – a regular visit from the tree surgeon ensures that all potentially dangerous overhanging branches are removed before they fall on an unsuspecting camper's head. But don't let small details get in the way of the experience: if it looks untouched, and you feel like you're camping out in the wilds, then... hey... you are!

Such splendorous surroundings are a function of the fact that ForgeWood is situated in a quiet corner of the vast Eridge Park Estate, a 3,000-acre expanse of countryside and farmland incorporating Britain's oldest deer park. The countryside site has been preserved since the 11th century, when William the Conqueror gave the estate to his half-brother Odo, a man of vast wealth and questionable morals who ended up in prison for embezzlement. Today the Estate belongs to the Marquess of Abergavenny, and although it's not open to the public, there are rights of way that allow visitors to explore parts of this area. Venison from the estate is available on the site in the form of sausages, burgers and steaks – ideal for the campfire. Firewood and marshmallows are also available at reception, as are handy little campfire cooking thingamajigs, which allow you to use your pots and pans on the fire instead of on the gas burner.

In case this site needs anything else to recommend it (which it doesn't), then the fact that there's a pub and a station nearby would seem to top it all off nicely. So, for London-based campers, it's possible to get here from London Bridge in just over an hour, including a stop for a pint of Badger at the Huntsman.

COOL FACTOR Expansive ancient woodlands and a strong campfire culture.

WHO'S IN Tents, occasional vintage campervans, dogs – yes. Caravans, motorhomes, young groups – no.

ON SITE At weekends and in school holidays, they run forest craft workshops for kids. There are also art retreats and bush craft courses for adults. Portable cabins are used for the reception and facilities, which include showers, washing-up sinks, disabled facilities and ice-pack freezing. A shop sells all the basics, including milk, bread, eggs and meat from the Eridge Park Estate. Fire grills and cooking equipment are available to rent or buy; plus firewood, marshmallows and other bits and bobs. At the other side of the car park is a restaurant/tea room, which is open in summer.

OFF SITE Walks through the Eridge Park Estate start from the campsite; maps are available at reception, which will take you variously to historic ice caves, a Victorian folly and a Saxon fort. A trip to nearby Groombridge Place (01892 861444; groombridgeplace.com) is a worthwhile excursion, with its renowned formal gardens and the excellent Enchanted Forest attraction for kids.

FOOD & DRINK The Huntsman (01892 864258; thehuntsmanpub.com), next to Eridge station, has a pleasant beer garden, ales from the Badger Brewery, and a changing locally sourced menu. Head into Tunbridge Wells for more diverse options, where there is a farmers' market on the first and third Saturday of the month at the Pantiles.

GETTING THERE Eridge Park is situated between Tunbridge Wells and Crowborough, just off the A26. Take the turning on the south side of the A26 signposted Rotherfield and Mayfield. Follow for a mile and ForgeWood is on the left.

PUBLIC TRANSPORT From Eridge station it's 30 minutes on foot (about 2 miles), or 5 minutes in a taxi.

OPEN April–September.

THE DAMAGE Adult (over 16 yrs) £15 per night; for families rates are £12.50 adult/£6 child (3 yrs and over), under-3s free. Minimum 3-night stay on Bank Holidays and 2 nights during the weekends in June, July and August.

badgell's wood camping

Badgell's Wood Camping, Whitehorse Road, Meopham, Kent DA13 0UF 07528 609324 www.badgellswoodcamping.co.uk

It is almost a disservice to call Badgell's Wood 'a campsite'. It feels more like you've driven into the woods, found a tranquil coppice clearing and slept the night hidden from the rest of the world. Such is the seclusion and simplicity of this back-to-nature spot that you forget it's really a carefully managed woodland, crafted so that every camper can enjoy that authentic outdoors experience. In an ancient setting where campers play second fiddle to badgers, squirrels and chirping birdlife, Badgell's Wood is a dreamy woodland escape.

Set in the 30-acre corner of a sprawling 250-acre forest, the campsite has ample space for pitches, each in their own unique spot and varying in size. Whether you want to tuck yourself away with a two-man tent, or park up a campervan with a group of friends, there'll be a pitch to suit; and, with peace and quiet top of this campsite's agenda, you can guarantee you won't be disturbed. Instead, kick back in your pocket of woodland paradise, kindle the campfire and let your kids loose among the trees.

Badgell's Wood Camping is striped with concrete tracks and access is still easy by car. From the pitches themselves, trodden pathways weave through the bluebell-clad floor to a sanitary block (which is built of wood, naturally) that houses sinks for washing-up and brand new showers. The ablutions offer some everyday luxury amid the wilderness, while brand new compost loos are also dotted throughout the campsite.

Although a hop in the car can take you to famous castles, pristine gardens and a host of family attractions, Badgell's Wood Camping is a place to forget the modern world. It's connected to far larger Whitehorse Wood, a huge expanse of forest riddled with footpaths and crossed by both The North Downs Way and The Weald Way. Since the site was once a World War II training ground, old huts and tracks can still be glimpsed among the trees.

Actually, you could easily forget the car altogether. On weekends, bush craft courses are run by Simon and Steve, experienced experts who tailor the courses to all ages involved. Then the rest of the week can be spent refining your new skills, whittling around the campfire or building dens between the trees. Children will love the rope swings, hanging from branches here and there, while those in need of a stroll should take to one of the woods, many footpaths.

As the Badgell's team rightfully proclaim, 'if you prefer your campsite with mown lawns, plastic playgrounds and a swimming pool then we're probably not for you'. But those with a romantic yearning for an off-grid escape should head straight for the Kent Downs. Badgell's Wood Camping will certainly do the trick.

COOL FACTOR Proper woodland camping bursting with wildlife and adventure.

WHO'S IN Nature lovers, families, groups, tents and well-behaved dogs – yes. Groups with an average age under 21 – no. A limited number of campervans permitted.

ON SITE Pitches consist of small clearings connected by footpaths. A wooden area with corrugated plastic roofing houses washing-up sinks and shower facilities, while compost loos are dotted across the site. Campfires are permitted on site (in the firepits provided) with grills and Dutch ovens available to hire. The reception sells firewood and camping essentials. Foraging for wood is not allowed.

OFF SITE Stroll across the private parkland at the edge of the site to the top of the Kent Downs AONB (01303 815170; kentdowns.org.uk), which offers magnificent views, as does Trosley Country Park a little further on. History lovers should check out the megolithic Coldrum Stones (01732 810378; NT), a 20-minute walk from camp. They don't call Kent the Garden of England for nothing and Riverhill Himalayan Gardens (01732 459777; riverhillgardens.co.uk) comes highly recommended for families. You'll find it around 30-minutes away, near Sevenoaks.

FOOD & DRINK The nearest pubs are the Amazon & Tiger (01474 814705) in Harvel or the Green Man (01732 823575; greenmanpub.com) on Hodsoll Street. A bit further away, at the Nevill Bull (01732 843193; nevillbull.co.uk) in Birling, the gracious guvnors, Kate and Paul, will give you a warm welcome and make sure you're well fed.

GETTING THERE The site is 2½ miles from the turning off the A227, between Meopham and Wrotham. Turn on to Harvel Lane (signposed Vigo Harvel). Follow the road for 2 miles and you will pass a turning on your left to Harvel. Keep going for half a mile and the campsite is on the right.

OPEN From the Easter holidays–end of October.

THE DAMAGE Per person, per night: adults (over 16 yrs) £12.50 with a reduction for families of £10 per parent and £5 for each child over 3 yrs.

welsummer

Welsummer, Chalk House, Lenham Road, Kent ME17 1NQ 01622 843 051 www.welsummercamping.com

If you're one of those people who lie awake at night fretting over whether you prefer camping in a field or in a wood – there's no shame in it, there are millions of us out there – you'll be relieved to learn that there is a select posse of sites that offers both, one of which is Welsummer. When you arrive, the site appears quite conventional: a short track off a minor road leads up to two small, flat camping fields. However, go through an unobtrusive gate underneath a beech tree and you enter a dense, dark wood harbouring half a dozen additional pitches that can only be described as naturalistic – the owners, Laura and Med, may have to point them out to you before you realise where they are. This is quite deliberate, as Laura used to camp in these woods as a child and her aim is to offer others a taste of the joys she experienced back then.

Situated on a smallholding with chickens roaming around a copse, bees zipping in and out of hives and a miniature orchard containing native English apples, Welsummer is a laid-back campsite that wears its quirky touches lightly (rainbow-coloured windsock, anyone?). Prepare to make friends here, too. This is the sort of place where meals are shared with strangers, especially with those who make the schoolboy error of not lighting their fire early enough in the evening to cook their jacket potatoes by a reasonable hour, so end up stuffing themselves with that gem of al fresco cooking: the half-incinerated marshmallow.

COOL FACTOR Untainted rural camping in a quaint Kentish smallholding.

WHO'S IN Small and large tents - yes. Campervans, caravans – no.

ON SITE Family-sized grassy pitches and smaller-sized pitches in woodland. No electric hook-ups. Pre-erected bell tents (sleeping up to 6). Sleeping hut (sleeps 2). Most pitches have a firepit (firewood is for sale). Male and female bathrooms each with 2 loos, 2 basins and 2 showers. Small shop selling basic foodstuffs, camping supplies, the smallholding's own free-range eggs, organically grown vegetables, hot drinks and homemade snacks. Kids will love the trees to climb and places to hide. Acoustic instruments and fireside singing are positively encouraged, but radios and other electronica are frowned upon. No looting the woods for firewood. Dogs welcome by prior arrangement.

OFF SITE Leeds Castle has been called 'the world's loveiliest castle' and is only 3 miles away – sheer stone-fortress perfection (01622 765400; leeds-castle.com). Consider also a visit to Biddenden Vineyards (01580 291726; biddendenvineyards.com), with wine-tasting and 22 acres of vines to admire.

FOOD & DRINK The Pepperbox Inn (01622 842558; thepepperboxinn.co.uk), near Ulcombe, a mile away from the site, does excellent food and has a beer garden.

GETTING THERE Exit at Junction 8 of the M20 and follow the A20; turn right (from the west) or left (from the east) on to Chegworth Lane. At the junction turn left on the Lenham Road. Continue for 1.2 miles after which you will find the site on your right.

OPEN April–October.

THE DAMAGE Pitches: backpacker £15; small £20; family £30; bell tents £60–£80; Sleeping hut £70.

the sunny field

The Sunny Field, Maxted Street, Nr Elmstead, Canterbury, Kent CT4 6DJ 01233 750024 www.thesunnyfield.co.uk

It was less than a year ago that Sasha and Philip bought the 16 grassy acres of Little Pett Bottom Place, and it wasn't long before they were lured outside by the colourful wild flowers and fluttering garden birds. After camping amid the greenery of their private paddock with family and friends, they began to realise how much fun could be had by pitching a tent on their doorstep. Now they have unbolted the meadow gate, set down the basic facilities and opened up their pristine pastures to the everyday camper.

Nestled in the Kent Downs, surrounded by ancient trees, The Sunny Field boasts a hilltop position that's blessed with sunlight all day long, hence its name, which is chosen by Sasha and Philip's children. Your arrival is tinged with anticipation as you wind your way through narrow lanes, the banks overgrown with cow parsley and long grass, to this truly secluded spot in the Kentish countryside. As you pull through the gate, you're greeted with a generous open space for just 15 pitches and a car-free site perfect for kids.

It is fair to say that things are pretty basic in The Sunny Field. Ablutions consist of compost loos that are kept immaculately clean, and there are standing pipe taps dotted around the site that supply easy access to running water. Other than that, it's basically an unadulterated meadow and it's this simplicity that is the real charm of the site. It provides a rustic, traditional camping experience, with campfires at each pitch and dogs welcomed.

When you're done larking in the flowers or clambering among the trees, you can clean off with a short stroll down the hill to the main

house where you'll find a hot shower you can use free-of-charge.

Such seclusion need not cut you off entirely and those willing to re-emerge from their countryside cocoon will find themselves in a position to make the most of this corner of Kent. By car, the beaches of Dymchurch, Sandgate and Folkestone are less than half an hour away, while Canterbury is just a 15-minute drive. Then, of course, there are numerous quaint local villages with excellent pubs, and there are top walking and cycling routes on the doorstep too.

The Sunny Field is the working definition of 'simple but effective'. Sasha and Philip saw a space made for perfect camping and thought, 'if something ain't broke, don't fix it!' Wildlife still enlivens the hedgerows and tranquillity is still the word. This is rural camping at its best.

COOL FACTOR Aptly named and correctly billed, sunny summertime camping in an untouched field.

WHO'S IN Tents, campervans, families and dogs – yes. Caravans, groups – no.

ON SITE Pitches in the main meadow and in the field below. No electric hook-ups. Facilities are basic but clean. There are compost loos on site and mains taps dotted around the pitches. A 300-m walk to the house brings you to a shower. There is a swing in the oak tree, a pitch for rounders, and Speedy the pig who always welcomes visitors! Campfires are permitted.

OFF SITE One of England's most venerable cities, Canterbury, with its historic cathedral (01227 762862; canterbury-cathedral.org), is a short drive away. Heading south takes you to the coast and the Cinque Ports of Dover and Hythe. Closer to home, forget the car and enjoy The Kent Downs AONB (01303 815170; kentdowns.org.uk), which is perfect for cycling and walking, with the North Downs Way passing close to the campsite (northdownsway.co.uk).

FOOD & DRINK It is possible to pre-order bread, fish, meat and vegetables. There is a great village shop in Stelling Minnis and the local garage at the top of the lane has just about all the basics. Perry Court Farm Shop (01233 812408; perrycourtfarm.co.uk) serves amazing apple juice and veg, with fish fresh off the boats from the coast on Friday and Saturday. For a meal out, try the Tiger Inn (01303 862130; tigerinn.co.uk) in Stowting or the Five Bells (01303 813334; fivebellsinnbrabourne.com) in nearby Brabourne.

GETTING THERE From the M20, exit junction 11 and follow signs for Canterbury on the B2068. Continue for 4½ miles until you get to Six Mile Garage and take a left turn down a very narrow lane (sign says '6.6'). Follow this track until you come to a sharp corner. The entrance to The Sunny Field is the gate on this corner.

OPEN May–September.

THE DAMAGE Tents and campervans from £25 per night.

hurley riverside park

Hurley Riverside Park, Hurley, Berkshire SL6 5NE 01628 824493 www.hurleyriversidepark.co.uk

If the River Thames is a song whose sedate opening bars of its Kemble source belie its climactic, rousing sing-along chorus in the City before its fade-outro into the expanse of the Canvey estuary and beyond, then the Henley-Marlow stretch is the melodious first verse, for it is here that the river enjoys a slower pace of life. Pleasure boats abound, ensconced on either side by heavy, green willows shielding picturesque Berkshire villages. And along this tranquil stretch of one of the world's great rivers sits Hurley Riverside Park.

One of the first things you notice is that Hurley Riverside Park is not a small campsite. In fact, it's a worryingly huge 200-pitch site with a high percentage of caravans, large motorhomes and static holiday homes. Hedges are neatly trimmed, pitches are clearly marked and an automatic barrier needs to be negotiated on entry and exit, which, for some, may feel more 'airport car park' than 'back-to-basics campsite'. But get over it, people, because this is the gateway to a Thames-side camping paradise.

With direct access to the water, this site really is all about the river. You could either arrive by canoe or boat and camp, or you could bring a boat along and use the campsite's own slipway to launch. Better still, make a raft out of some plastic water bottles and string! (You'll obviously need someone to video it all for *You've Been Framed*.)

It must be said that the tent pitches themselves are not by the river but set back behind tall hedges in a separate camping space. The area between the river and the pitches is a long, semi-wild meadow that is perfect for playing games, running around, eating al fresco and choosing which of the passing boats you would buy if you won the lottery. It's a special spot indeed, with the lush green countryside of the Thames Valley all around, red kites circling above, and the river traffic gliding by. And, unbelievably, it's barely an hour from central London.

The park has been run by four generations of the same family for the last 40 years prior to which it was one of the region's loveliest working farms. This rural heritage and family-friendly atmosphere is plainly in evidence today with the resident llamas and pygmy goats. The park has also received accolades a-plenty, including the prestigious David Bellamy Gold Award for Conservation for the last 15 years. Hurley even has its own guided nature trail, which follows the length of the campsite.

With canoeing, kayaking, fishing and a whole host of other waterbound activities to enjoy, all just an easily-reachable drive from the capital, Hurley Riverside Park is a fantastic base for campers fleeing the frenzy of urban living. It's also a short distance from regal Windsor, the attractive riverside market town of Henley-on-Thames, and, further afield, the dreaming spires of Oxford, so there's no shortage of great day trips to be enjoyed either. Whether or not you'll get to these places on your home-made raft, however, is anyone's guess.

COOL FACTOR Larking around on the riverbanks just a paddle away from the attractions.

WHO'S IN Tents, caravans, dogs (maximum 2 per pitch) – yes. Large groups – no

ON SITE 60 pitches in 'Oak' meadow (tents only) – 7 electric pitches. 70 pitches in 'Chestnut' (tents and caravans) – all electric. 3 heated shower blocks, 1 with spacious family shower rooms. Laundrette, shop, disabled facilities, children's playground and a nature trail. The park also has llamas and pygmy goats nearby. Campfires are not permitted.

OFF SITE The Thames Path (thames-path.org.uk) and the Chilterns Cycleway (chilternsaonb.org/cycleway.html)are two of the best ways to explore the surrounding area. Legoland (0871 222 2001; legoland.co.uk) is just 11 miles away, in Windsor, and the site offers discounts for this as well as other local attractions. Well-heeled Henley-on-Thames, which is famous for its annual regatta, is just down the river. If you get the chance, drive up to Watlington Hill to spot red kites. The views over the Chilterns are breathtaking.

FOOD & DRINK The closest pub is the Rising Sun (01628 825733; risingsunhurley.co.uk), which is a cosy place that serves decent pub grub and local ales. For high-end food, the Hand & Flowers (01628 482277; thehandandflowers.co.uk) in Marlow is the UK's only Michelin-starred pub; be prepared to book months in advance.

GETTING THERE Leave the M4, at junction 8/9 and take the A404(M) towards High Wycombe and Henley. Turn off at the third junction on to the A4130 (to Henley), turn left and go straight across the Burchetts Green roundabout and up the hill. Ignore the turning into Hurley village and turn right ¾ mile into Shepherds Lane. Or leave the M40 at junction 4 and take the A404(M) towards Reading. Turn off on to the A4130, turn right at the Burchetts Green roundabout and proceed as above towards Hurley.

PUBLIC TRANSPORT The 239 bus from Henley-on-Thames or Maidenhead stops outside the park.

OPEN March–October.

THE DAMAGE Tent + 2 people £13–£27 depending on season and size of tent.

swiss farm

Swiss Farm, Marlow Road, Henley-on-Thames, Oxfordshire RG9 2HY 01491 573419 www.swissfarmcamping.co.uk

At first glance, Swiss Farm seems worryingly commercial and a little too large scale to feature in a *Cool Camping* book.

But first impressions can be deceptive, and once you've spied the spacious adventure playground, the outdoor swimming pool and the still waters of the willow-fringed fishing lake, your reservations will soon evaporate. Just outside the quintessentially English market town of Henley-on-Thames, this site is a great place to stay during the festivities of the summer's Royal Regatta, an annual event launched way back in 1839. In those days it was all about the rowing races, watched by moustachioed, straw boater-wearing Victorian gents, who stood on the river banks clapping genteelly. Nowadays the crowd is quite a bit more raucous, and the races seem to play second fiddle to days of riverside fun and frolics in the sun.

At quieter times of the year, Swiss Farm is simply a great place to come and relax by the lake, a base from which to explore Oxfordshire's countryside, hills and interesting towns. On the site itself you can splash about in the open-air swimming pool (open June–September) or relax at the picnic tables with a freshly made sandwich from the onsite café. And in the evenings it's a place to enjoy family barbecues in the dusky evening glow.

COOL FACTOR Packed full of fun for kids and all an oar's length from regatta-hotspot Henley-on-Thames.

WHO'S IN Tents, campervans, caravans – yes. Groups – no. Dogs – not during school holidays.

ON SITE 2 large facilities blocks; free hairdryers and baby-changing cubicles; laundry; Wi-Fi and hook-ups all available. There is an onsite café, a small playground in a spacious, rabbit-inhabited field, and a lake for fishing (£2 per child, £3 per adult for half a day) and duck-feeding.

OFF SITE Odds Farm Park (01628 520188; oddsfarm.co.uk) is a 25-minute drive away, and offers a fantastic family day of farmyard fun. There's hands-on bottle-feeding lambs, sheep-shearing and milking demonstrations, mini-golf and go-karting. If it rains, try the award-winning River and Rowing Museum (01491 415600; rrm.co.uk) in Henley, which is full of boats, as well as a fantastic *Wind in the Willows* gallery.

FOOD & DRINK Grab some of the fantastic meat available at Gabriel Machin (01491 574377; gabrielmachin.co.uk) for a smokin' BBQ back at the site.

GETTING THERE Exit the M4 at junction 8/9, taking the second exit at the roundabout on to the A404. After 2¼ miles take the Henley-on-Thames exit, which merges on to Henley Road (A4130). Follow this on to Henley Bridge. At the traffic lights, go straight on into Hart Street, then right on to Bell Street, then straight across the first of 2 mini roundabouts, and then left at the second on to Marlow Road. The campsite is on the left.

PUBLIC TRANSPORT Train to Henley-on-Thames and then a walk through the town to Marlow Road.

OPEN March–October.

THE DAMAGE A non-electric pitch for a family of 4 (kids aged 5–15) with 1 car costs between £13–£20. Prices during Regatta Week are £20–£40 per night. Dogs only permitted during low season.

cotswolds camping

Cotswolds Camping, Spelsbury Road, Charlbury, Chipping Norton, Oxfordshire OX7 3LL 01608 810810
www.cotswoldscamping.co.uk

Cotswolds Camping is run by two very hard-working friends (with a little help from their husbands). No one lives on the site, but a lot of work goes on in the background to ensure it's a well organised, extremely relaxed experience for everyone who stays.

The campsite is on the edge of the market town of Charlbury, with stunning views across the Evenlode Valley. It offers a couple of grass fields flanked by pine trees, with walks across open countryside accessible through a gate at the back. There's a bijou summerhouse for those seeking indoor space in inclement weather; the washing facilities are all housed in the yard next to the field; and there's even a small modern kitchen. So all in all it's a very civilised affair. Caravans aren't banned, but the simplicity of this site appeals far more to dedicated tenters. It's a perfect place to kick back, fill your lungs with fresh air, read the paper, and listen to the surrounding cows, sheep and chickens. Oh, and waking up to the sounds of resident wood pigeons is priceless.

As well as being a great springboard for visiting the surrounding Cotswolds villages, the site is also well located for food. Wander into Charlbury for its many pubs, or head to the little village of Chadlington for a great community-managed shop, and a coffee shop that sprawls out on to the pavement a few doors down. You're not in the middle of nowhere here, but it feels like it.

COOL FACTOR Simple Cotswolds site (a rarity in these parts).

WHO'S IN Tents, campervans, caravans, groups, well-behaved dogs – yes.

ON SITE 20 pitches across 3 distinct areas, most with access to hook-ups. Immaculate facilities include separate toilet blocks with free showers. Kitchen with use of a fridge, toaster, kettle, and washing-up sink; disabled/family shower room and outside washing-up area. There's a basketball hoop, a little wood for hide-and-seek, and access to miles of footpaths. No campfires, but BBQs allowed.

OFF SITE Chadlington village 2 miles away has an excellent wooden adventure playground. The stately home of Blenheim Palace in Woodstock is only 6 miles away (01993 810530; blenheimpalace.com) and the Cotswold Wildlife Park (01993 823006; cotswoldwildlifepark.co.uk), is not much further.

FOOD & DRINK Nearby Charlbury offers many shops, the Rose & Crown pub (01608 810103; roseandcrown.charlbury.com), and the Bull Inn (01608 810689; bullinn-charlbury.com) for excellent food. To really live the high life, head over to Daylesford Organic (01608 731700; daylesford.com) near Kingham for upmarket cream teas.

GETTING THERE From Charlbury go north on the B4026 towards Spelsbury. After about a mile, the site entrance is on a bend on the right.

PUBLIC TRANSPORT Train to Charlbury then bus X9 towards Chipping Norton will drop you at the gate.

OPEN Easter–October half term.

THE DAMAGE Tent + 2 adults £15–£18. Hook-ups £5. Minimum 2-night booking in July and August.

town farm

Town Farm, Icknield Way, Ivinghoe, Bedfordshire LU7 9EL 07906 265435 www.townfarmcamping.co.uk

From the top of Ivinghoe Beacon walkers will find one of the most commanding views in the Chilterns and, on particularly clear days, can see as far as the North Downs in faraway Kent – sweeping vistas of a rich agricultural landscape that mark the place out as beautiful camping country. Framed between golden wheat fields and sheep-dotted meadows is Town Farm. The resident Leach family has been tending the land here for nearly a century, but only recently unlatched their gates to campers. Quickly becoming a firm family favourite, the site has swapped lambs for prams, tractors for campervans and transformed old sheds into all you need for a weekend in the Chilterns.

The camping field is behind a barn and is vast. Tents can be pitched at the foot of the Beacon, ready for a sharp morning walk to its summit and along the famous Ridgeway, or pegged down on the campsite's edge, with stunning views over the Vale of Aylesbury. Ignore the pylon wire that runs along the right of the site, and turn left towards the Chilterns, passing a new, hip washing block with dark-brown chalet-style wood exterior and minimal white chic interior.

The added ablutions block, accompanying the existing facilities in converted farm buildings, is just one of a few recent changes here. Owner Charles, followed loyally by two amiable golden retrievers, is quick to point out that the atmosphere remains much the same. A well-equipped playground has replaced the old trampoline, Wi-Fi is readily accessible and new tent-renting options are available, but at its heart Town Farm is the same unpretentious

rural campsite. In the evening time the crackle of campfires is the only background noise and in the morning it's the peaceful chirp of birdsong, at least until the children are back in charge.

Frazzled parents looking for activities to wear out their brood have plenty of choice, both on and off site. Along with the playground, there is a football goal and tennis court, plus a pick-your-own farm that opens to the public in summer, while beyond, the pleasures of the Chilterns await, and endless cycling, walking and horse trails. Come night-time everyone will be sleeping soundly.

COOL FACTOR An ideal trial location for first-time campers and Londoners not wanting to stray too far from home.

WHO'S IN Tents, campervans, caravans, dogs (obedient ones that won't bother the sheep), groups – yes. Noisy groups – no.

ON SITE A total of 50 pitches, with 12 hook-ups for caravans/motorhomes only. Campfires allowed in the onsite firepits (rented for £5; wood bundle £6) and BBQs raised off the ground. The facility blocks have hot showers, disabled toilet and shower, washing-up sinks, a washing machine (£3.50), tumble-dryer (50p/8mins), freezer, Wi-Fi and electricity points. There is a chemical disposal point. There is a wooden playground with swings, slides and climbing frames and access to the farm's tennis court. The whole site is regularly tended by Charles and his family, who are ever-present yet unobtrusive. There is a distant murmur of local traffic.

OFF SITE Whipsnade Zoo (01582 872171; zsl.org/zsl-whipsnade-zoo) is just 10 miles away and makes a great day out. The Chilterns Cycleway (see p.141) details 170 miles of cycling routes in the area, while walkers inevitably head straight from Town Farm up to the top of Ivinghoe Beacon, which offers stunning views and the starting point for the famous Ridgeway long-distance footpath.

FOOD & DRINK Enjoy local produce fresh from the Mead's Farm Shop and Café (01442 828478; pemeadandsons.co.uk) at Wilstone or head to Leighton Buzzard farmers' market, which takes place every third Saturday.

GETTING THERE Town Farm is just off the B489 between Ivinghoe and Dunstable (on your right if travelling west).

PUBLIC TRANSPORT Train to Tring, then taxi (£10) or 45-minute walk along the Ridgeway Path.

OPEN All year.

THE DAMAGE Adult £8–£10 per night (depending on length of stay); child (4 to 18 years) £5; under-4s free; dogs £2. Group rate for Duke of Edinburgh Award.

twitey's tipis and camping

Twitey's Tipis & Camping Meadows, Lowe Farm, Hunscote Lane, Wellesbourne, Warwickshire CV35 9EX 07725 944204
www.twiteystipis.co.uk

Cross 14 acres of sprawling grass meadows, accommodating a maximum of 15 tents at any one time, with friendly owners who hold a relaxed, camp-where-you-like attitude, and you've got yourself one roomy place to pitch. Throw in some world-class Shakespearean sights, neighbouring medieval castles and countryside vistas that inspired some of the world's greatest literature, and you've stumbled upon Twitey's Tipis and Camping Meadows; 'A Midsummer Night's Dream' of a campsite.

'Peace and tranquillity is the order of the day,' says the site's owner Michael Twite, who's created a truly loveable, spacious campsite. Upon arrival, you'll be presented with a wheelbarrow to help move your kit. The flat, mown pitches are well spaced out and hidden in one of the two wild flower meadows, providing a sense of remoteness and seclusion. As the name suggests, tipis can also

be rented. The site's small 'Hamlet' of abodes (three in total) have been thoughtfully positioned to overlook the meadow, and come furnished with lanterns, kitchen utensils and logs ready for a sunset campfire.

Warwickshire may have been just another pleasant English county were it not for the birth of one rather gifted playwright. William Shakespeare was born and died in Stratford-upon-Avon (four miles away), and the sights linked to the great man's life there have become a magnet for tourists. You can also follow 'Shakespeare's Way', which replicates the 146-mile route the young writer took on his travels to and from London – the earliest section of which passes rolling hills, the weaving River Stour and honey-coloured Cotswold cottages. However, you may find there's quite enough at Twitey's to keep you busy and fulfilled. Active days, peaceful nights. Life's good at Twitey's...

meadows

COOL FACTOR Space and tranquillity nestled conveniently close to all the main Warwickshire attractions.

WHO'S IN Tents, glampers, kids and well-behaved groups – yes. Caravans, motorhomes and dogs – no.

ON SITE 15 mown pitches and 3 tipis (2 x 4 bed; 1 x 6 bed) in a meadow of long grass and wildflowers. All pitches have their own firepit, and tents are also available for hire. Showers, toilet block, washing-up area, small reception/shop, charging facilities, recycling and gas cylinders available.

OFF SITE Warwick is only 6 miles away and boasts one of the finest preserved castles in the country (01926 495421; warwick-castle.com). Grand Charlecote Park (01789 470277; NT) is only a mile away, surrounded by its own deer park, on the banks of the River Avon, where you can take a scenic cruise. Wellesbourne Mountford Airfield (01789 842007; wellesbourneairfield.com) is also right on your doorstep. Check out the underground WW2 museum as well as a resident Vulcan Bomber.

FOOD & DRINK The Kings Head (01789 840206), located in Wellesbourne, oozes rural charm and rustic character that provide the perfect backdrop for savouring their hearty pub food and the carefully nurtured cask ales. Located more centrally in the village, the Stags Head (01789 840266; stagshead-wellesbourne.co.uk) is more of a local; a family-run business for over 15 years that also does good pub food.

GETTING THERE Leaving the M40 at junction 15, head south on the A429 signposted Stow-on-the-Wold. Past the village of Barford, as you approach Wellesbourne, turn right, signposted Charlecote. Drive through the village until you reach a crossroads. Drive straight across on to Loxley Lane and, after a few hundred metres, turn right into Hunscote Lane. After approx. 100 metres turn right into a shared driveway signposted Lowe Farm. Please call half an hour before arriving.

OPEN Early April–late October.

THE DAMAGE 10m tent pitches (with firepit) £25 per night for 4 occupants. Extra occupants £5 per night. 10% discount for stays of 4 days and over available. Tipis start at £195 (minimum 2-night stay) for 4 people.

brook meadow

Brook Meadow Farm, Welford Road, Sibbertoft, Market Harborough, Leicestershire. LE16 9UJ 01858 880886
www.brookmeadow.co.uk

People seem to fall in love with Brook Meadow – particularly the staff! Fishing bailiff Mick had been coming to the site for years with his wife Pam before taking on his current role; and site manager Vanessa chose the campsite as the venue for her wedding reception before returning to work and live here with her family.

It does feel like a special place to camp. Perhaps it's the sunsets over the lake? The cattle grazing peacefully in the neighbouring fields? The hundreds of stars clearly visible on a cloud-free night? Or perhaps it's the philosophy of the owner-farmers Jasper and Mary, who want people to come and enjoy their land. This even extends to providing free camping for groups of youngsters working towards their D of E awards.

It's a peaceful, secluded site with 50 pitches over 15 acres and a five-acre fishing lake. Ducks waddle around and you might catch a glimpse of the resident wildlife – deer, hares, red kites – or hear owls hooting in the night. It feels very spacious. Some of the best pitches are around the fishing lake on the lower of the two fields (shared with three holiday chalets), although families with kids tend to opt for the top field for The Mound, which kids love to scramble on.

The site has a couple of high-adrenaline neighbours: Avalanche Adventures next door, where you can hire quad bikes or try your hand at clay pigeon shooting and other activities; and the Gliding Centre at Husbands Bosworth Airfield just down the road, where you can get a birds-eye view of the site as you drift by overhead.

COOL FACTOR A secluded campsite to fall in love with.

WHO'S IN Tents, campervans, caravans, dogs, groups (by arrangement) – yes.

ON SITE Around 50 pitches (including 17 hardstanding and 8 grass with hook-ups) with several next to the lake. Campfires allowed if contained and off the ground. A fishing lodge houses 2 unisex toilets and shower rooms, 2 washing-up sinks, a kettle, microwave and freezer, and a laundry room with washing machine and dryer, plus baby-changing facilities. Showers are free and solar-powered, and the fishing lodge facilities will soon be joined by a new toilet block. Fishing is £8 per day.

OFF SITE For outdoor activities there's Avalanche Adventures (01858 880613; avalancheadventure.co.uk) and the Gliding Centre at Husbands Bosworth Airfield (01858 880521; theglidingcentre.co.uk) both bookable in advance. More sedate alternatives include the lavish house and gardens at Cottesbrooke Hall (01604 505808; cottesbrooke.co.uk).

FOOD & DRINK The Red Lion in Sibbertoft (01858 880011; redlionwinepub.co.uk) does great food and is just a mile away. The CAMRA-recommended Wharf Inn at Welford (01858 575075; wharfinn.co.uk), can be reached by footpath from the site.

GETTING THERE Leave the M1 at junction 20 and follow the A4304 towards Husbands Bosworth. Midway between Husbands Bosworth and Welford on the A5199, turn off towards Sibbertoft. The farm entrance is 1½ miles on the left.

OPEN All year.

THE DAMAGE Flat rate of £14 per pitch per night, £17 with electricity. Free to D of E groups.

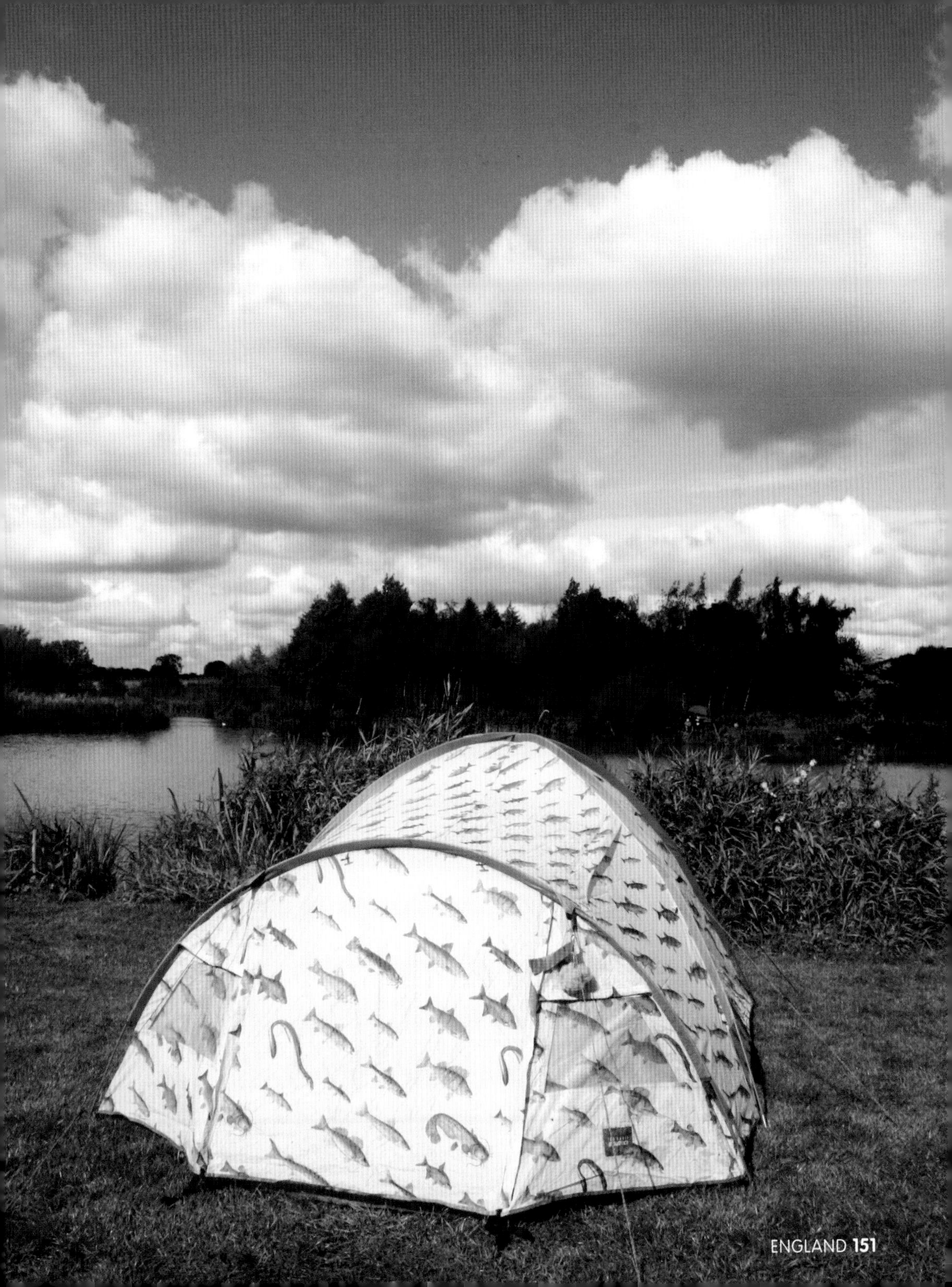

wing hall

Wing Hall Estate, Wing, Oakham, Rutland LE15 8RY 01572 737090 www.winghall.co.uk

The 100 acres of garden and fields surrounding the manor house at Wing Hall make for a wonderful place to camp. Sitting just outside the pretty Rutland village of Wing, the site overlooks a colourful collage of woods and rolling fields of wheat and rape, and just a mile down the road is the lovely 3,100-acre reservoir, Rutland Water. Created by flooding in 1974, the water and surrounding area now provide both a haven for wildlife and sport and leisure opportunities, with the 25-mile track around its perimeter making a beautiful cycle route. Surrounding the reservoir, a major nature reserve and wildfowl sanctuary spans some 1,000 acres and has several pairs of resident ospreys, which can sometimes be spied from one of more than 30 birdwatching hides dotted around the water.

Robin Curley's great-great-grandfather built Wing Hall in 1891, and she has lived here all her life, long before England's tiniest county, Rutland, regained its independence from Leicestershire in 1997. The campsite used to be a basic, fiver-a-night-type stop, but Robin and her five (now grown-up) children have created something more sophisticated here over recent years. Son Lyndon has transformed the onsite shop into a delectable deli, stocked with locally sourced organic produce, artisan breads and a wide selection of wines and ales alongside the usual campers' basics. The shop also has maps of local walks, onsite bike hire, and daughter Zia runs the Veranda Café, serving up breakfast, lunch, afternoon teas and evening meals, including local treats like local rib-eye steak and roasted goats' cheese with homemade salsa.

Enjoying one of Zia's cream teas on the lawn, you can easily forget you're on a campsite – it feels more like the grounds of a stately home.

The campsite has four camping fields with around 250 pitches across the whole site, of which 20 are for caravans. A large, flattish field on the left as you enter is for tents only. A second field on the right of the long, tree-lined entrance drive has wonderful views across the surrounding countryside and is for tents, caravans and mobile homes. A third field has a handful of pitches overlooking the valley and the resident free-range chickens, while a fourth field has swathes cut through wheat to provide more pitches and some of the best views. A short walk down through another wheat field takes you to the fishing lakes at the bottom of the estate. There's loads of space to play or cycle around the site, and a large tree in the middle of the second field, with a couple of swings slung from its branches, provides a focal point for kids.

Despite the campsite's wide range of facilities, the general ambience of this place is far away from the holiday-park atmosphere you might expect. And the no-music policy, which is particularly popular with families, helps to maintain a peaceful feel. As night falls, parents sweep up their offspring in compliance with one of the few onsite rules – unaccompanied kids back under supervision after dark – and tranquillity reigns. In any case, if splendid isolation is required, there are plenty of nooks and crannies and hideaway pitches to hole up in.

COOL FACTOR If you aren't to the manor born this is a great place in which to pretend you are.

WHO'S IN Tents, caravans, dogs (on leads) – yes. Groups of young people and single-sex groups – by arrangement only.

ON SITE 4 large camping fields spread over a large part of the 100-acre estate. 7 new showers join 5 older ones; there are 6 covered washing-up sinks and 3 blocks of toilets. Campfires are allowed in firepits – bring your own or rent them (£2 per night). The shop sells bags of firewood and opens from mid March to the end of September. Campers can fish (and birdwatch) from the 3 lakes at the bottom of the estate for a daily fee of £7. There's also onsite cycle hire that rents bikes for £15 per day or £10 for half a day.

OFF SITE At Rutland Water, Normanton Church Museum (01572 653026) charts the history of the reservoir, and the Rutland Belle (01572 787630; rutlandwatercruises.com) cruises around the shoreline from Whitwell. If you'd prefer to do it yourself, Rutland Water Sports hosts have-a-go sailing, windsurfing, kayaking and power-boating sessions (01780 460154).

FOOD & DRINK The Veranda Café opens all day at the weekend from April to September and from 11am to 5pm on spring and summer weekdays. If you want to venture off the site, the 17th-century Kings Arms (01572 737634; thekingsarms-wing.co.uk) in Wing is a short walk away and has real ales and excellent local seasonal food.

GETTING THERE From the A47 take the A6003 towards Oakham. At Preston, turn right after the village pub, signposted Wing. Follow the road up the hill to Wing and turn right into the campsite at the top.

PUBLIC TRANSPORT Train to Oakham then either the Rutland Flyer bus towards Corby, which passes through Wing once a day in one direction and twice in the other (Monday–Saturday), or a taxi (around £10).

OPEN All year.

THE DAMAGE Adult £7 per night; child (under 14) £3.50 per night.

karma farm
eco campsite

Karma Farm, 8 Fen Bank, Isleham, Ely, Cambridgeshire CB7 5SL 07900 961217 www.islehamfen.co.uk

Will Taylor bought the land here a generation ago and built his farmhouse from scratch: a carbon-neutral, turf-roofed dwelling that must have seemed quite revolutionary at the time. The low-impact eco-house sets the tone for the rest of Karma Farm, which straddles the Suffolk–Cambridgeshire border. The campsite occupies a pretty spot by the side of the River Lark, with 40 unmarked tent pitches – visitors can simply stroll around and choose the nook they most fancy. There is also a yurt and a tipi, both basic enough to challenge the use of the term 'glamping', and a better-equipped three-berth cabin.

In keeping with the rustic vibe, campfires are permitted, with wood available on site. There's a games field and covered shed for rainy days, plus decent-if-basic washroom facilities, including a large shower pod into which you could fit your whole family (or a very friendly group).

But perhaps the best thing about Karma Farm is its location right by the river. A track follows the river for seven miles to Prickwillow, while in the other direction a path takes you to the Jude's Ferry Inn about two miles away.

COOL FACTOR Farm camping at its eco-friendly best – in the heart of the Fens.

WHO'S IN Tents, campervans, caravans, groups, dogs – yes.

ON SITE Campfires allowed. Facilities include 2 toilets, 2 hot showers, 1 solar shower and 1 propane-powered shower pod plus a portable cabin with extra toilets and washbasins. Bikes available for use, for a donation.

OFF SITE As well as the walks and cycle rides along the river, and birdwatching on site, both the Wicken Fen nature reserve (01353 720274; NT) and the RSPB Lakenheath Fen nature reserve are a short drive away.

FOOD & DRINK The village of Isleham is a 20-minute walk and has shops and 2 pubs, the Griffin (01638 780447; thegriffinisleham.co.uk) and the Rising Sun (01638 780741), both of which do reasonable food. There's also a relatively upmarket restaurant, the Merry Monk (01638 780900; merry-monk.co.uk), which Will recommends. You can also walk to the Jude's Ferry pub (01638 712277; judesferry.com), a lovely 2-mile walk along the river.

GETTING THERE Take the A14/A11 and, roughly halfway between Newmarket and Barton Mills, take the B1085 north (signposted Freckenham) to Isleham. Drive through the village, bearing left down Sun Street past the post office, and make a left down Waterside; the site is a mile down the track.

OPEN April–October.

THE DAMAGE £6.50–£8.50 per person; children half price, and no charge for those under 6 years old. Yurts and wood-clad cabin £30 plus the per person charge.

swattesfield

Swattesfield Campsite, Gislingham Road, Thornham Magna, Suffolk IP23 8HH 01379 788558
www.swattesfieldcampsite.co.uk

Deep in the wilds of north Suffolk, keen camper Jonathan set up this seven-acre campsite with his dad in 2011. It's a simple site exuding the perfect *Cool Camping* vibe, with two grassy fields – one for camping, the other for glamping – separated by a small lake with some adjoining woodland to explore. What we like most about Swattesfield is that there's so little to actually do! It's in a thoroughly rural location in the glorious Waveney Valley and is a great place for a spot of serious navel-gazing, with few distractions apart from the bucolic strolls you can do across the well-marked paths and bridleways of Thornham Walks, on the next-door Thornham Estate. The Estate is also worth exploring for its historic Walled Gardens and other gentle activities, as well as a source of sustenance with outbuildings that have been converted to cafés, artisan shops and the like.

You can pitch your tent in the bottom field or the woodland beyond, or take up residence in one of three boutique bell tents, which comfortably sleep four; two Pixie Huts, which include a double bed and enough space to sleep smaller pixies; and a converted hay cart which also has a double bed and two kids' single beds. There are suspended firepits for campfire cooking, fuelled by the big bags of logs and kindling they sell at the shop, and some of Jonathan's mates recently built him a fabulous outdoor pizza oven out of recycled materials. Overall, this is lovely chilled-out site in a special Suffolk location that feels a long way from any madding crowds.

COOL FACTOR Wonderfully tranquil with not a jot to do but walk, cycle or just sit and think.

WHO'S IN Tents, small campervans, dogs – yes. Caravans, big groups, young groups – no.

ON SITE 6 unmarked, grassy camping pitches. 3 bell tents (sleeping 4/5), 2 Pixie Huts and converted hay cart (sleeping 2 adults and 2 children). Campfires allowed off the ground. No hook-ups. Simple but clean toilet block, with 2 showers, 6 sinks and 6 toilets. Communal fridge and freezer, plus food preparation area with double sink. Gislingham's village shop is a 15-minute walk away.

OFF SITE Thornham Walks (thornhamwalks.org) – 12 miles of waymarked footpaths – is accessible from the site (open daily 9am–6pm April–October; shorter hours in winter).

FOOD & DRINK A special greeting pack and breakfast, lunch or nibbles hamper can be provided on request. The Thornham Estate's Forge Tea Room (01379 783035; theforgetearooms.com), the Four Horseshoes Pub (01379 678777; thefourhorseshoes.net) and Thornham Coach House (01379 783373; thornhamcoachhouse.com) are a 15–20-minute walk away and serve lunch and dinner.

GETTING THERE From the A140, follow signs to Thornham Walks and continue past the Walks entrance for about a mile and turn right soon after the 'school' sign – the entrance to the site is on the right. Travelling from the opposite direction through Gislingham, exit the village towards Thornham Magna; the 'school' sign is about ½ mile out of the village.

OPEN Open from the first spring half-term until the last half-term of the year.

THE DAMAGE Tent pitches from £12, campervans from £17 per night; Pixie Huts from £195 per Mon–Fri or Fri–Mon; bell tents from £170 per Mon–Fri or Fri–Mon; Suffolk hay cart from £195 per Mon–Fri or Fri–Mon.

high house fruit farm

High House Fruit Farm, Sudbourne, Woodbridge, Suffolk IP12 2BL 01394 450263 www.high-house.co.uk

Too often campsites on farms give the impression of having been not just an afterthought, but a thought that has occurred long after the afterthought. If you could hear the farmers' thoughts, they would be thinking, 'Any scrap of land will do, no matter how unsuitable it may be for camping'. The reverse appears to have taken place at High House Fruit Farm, where the very best spot for camping has been selected: a small, flat field protected from the North Sea winds by attractive trees all round, and yet open to the sun. It's also just a hop and a step from the facilities, housed in a farm building. The trees are, in turn, surrounded by apple orchards, which somehow give the place a summery feel whatever the season or the weather.

The 110-acre farm is primarily one on which cattle graze, but there's still plenty of room for the apple trees as well as for the rhubarb, gooseberries, currants, loganberries, blackberries, cherries and plums, many of which you can harvest yourself (it's a pick-your-own farm too: punnets and measuring scales are available in the farm's tiny shop, where you'll also find bottles of homemade apple juice, preserves and a small selection of veg).

Peace and tranquillity are the order of the day here. The farm itself is far from anywhere in particular, and the maximum number of people allowed on the site is a mere 15, so there's always plenty of room to spread out. Please do note, however, that advance booking is mandatory, so don't just rock up here, empty punnet in hand, and hope.

COOL FACTOR Pure peace and quiet in a quaint, attractive ½-acre meadow.

WHO'S IN Tents, campervans, couples, and small groups – yes. Caravans, motorhomes and dogs – no.

ON SITE Room for a maximum of just 15 people in a flat, sheltered field. This is an off-grid campsite, so facilities are basic but clean. There are 2 toilets, a washing-up area and a kettle, but no showers.

OFF SITE Orford Castle (0870 3331181; EH) has fabulous views over Orford Ness (01728 648024; NT), a National Trust nature reserve which you can reach on daily ferries throughout the summer. Snape Maltings, (01728 688303; snapemaltings.co.uk) near Aldeburgh (5 miles from the site) is a former maltings rescued from dereliction by local composer Benjamin Britten that now incorporates a concert hall and a collection of shops and restaurants.

FOOD & DRINK There are several cracking options in Orford, 2 miles away, including Hotel Inspector Ruth Watson's excellent pub with rooms, the Crown & Castle (01394 450205; crownandcastle.co.uk), which does fabulous, moderately priced food using lots of locally sourced ingredients. Towards the Quay, the more traditional Jolly Sailor (01394 450243; jollysailororford.co.uk) also does delicious food, but perhaps Orford's most original choice is the restaurant of the Butley Oysterage on the main square (01394 450277; pinneysoforford.co.uk) which, as you might expect, does wonderful fresh fish and seafood.

GETTING THERE Follow the A12 and turn right at the Woodbridge/Orford turnoff (A1152), past Melton station and on to the B1084 towards Orford; turn left in Sudbourne, past the church and on to Ferry Road; follow this until you come to the right-turn on to High House Farm Road.

OPEN April–October.

THE DAMAGE Adults £7.50 per night; children £3.

whitlingham broad campsite

Whitlingham Broad Campsite, Whitlingham Lane, Norwich, Norfolk NR14 8TR 07794 401591
www.whitlinghambroadcampsite.com

A pebble's throw from a beautiful lake, this is a campsite with traditional and luxury accommodation, plus bundles of outdoor activities, and all just a leisurely stroll from one of England's prettiest cities – what more could you want?

Whitlingham Broad Campsite is a relatively new campsite in a county with no shortage of magnificent spots to pitch up. Situated in the spacious 80-acre Whitlingham Country Park, it is both a useful gateway to the Broads and a perfect base for exploring the medieval delights of Norfolk's county capital. The spacious grass pitches are spread over the upper and lower fields. You can park up tent-side in the lower field while the upper is a car-free haven, meaning there's plenty of room for a run and a play (pooches are welcome too!). There are also fully furnished bell tents, a yurt *and* two cute and cosy shepherd's huts, with views overlooking the Great Broad. The lure of the Broads is inescapable in this part of the world, with scores of visitors flocking to enjoy the wet and wild delights of Norfolk's many navigable rivers and waterways, and Whitlingham Broad Campsite is ideally situated to join in the fun. The park's award winning Outdoor Education Centre provides a host of activities, including kayaking, sailing and windsurfing. And if you'd rather keep your feet strictly on *terra firma*, there are countless scenic walks and bike rides to enjoy.

COOL FACTOR A scenic site with numerous water-borne activities on your doorstep.

WHO'S IN Tents, campervans, dogs – yes. Caravans – no.

ON SITE Grassy pitches, set over 2 fields (one of which is car free). 6 furnished bell tents, 2 shepherd's huts and 1 yurt also available. 3 ladies' loos and 2 gent's loos plus urinals. 2 shower rooms (1 male, 1 female), each with 3 showers and a communal changing area. Bell tents come with a BBQ for use. Campfires are allowed at all other pitches in raised firepits that are available to hire. The Whitlingham yurt includes a wood-burning stove, beds, soft furnishings, a gas BBQ and a hammock. The shepherd's huts include solar lighting, bedding, wood-burning stoves, a BBQ and a firepit.

OFF SITE The neighbouring Outdoor Education Centre offers plenty of broad-based aquatic activities including canoeing, paddle-board hire, sailing and windsurfing. The site is right on the Wherryman's Man and national Cycle Route 1.

FOOD AND DRINK There's a café at the nearby Visitor Centre though it's only open during the day. The Crown Point Tavern (01603 625689) in Trowse is a ten-minute walk and does food – plus plenty of places to eat and drink in central Norwich.

GETTING THERE From A47 exit on to the A146, signposted Norwich, Trowse. At the traffic lights, turn left and get in the right-hand lane. From here on follow brown signs to Ski Club and Country Park, leading you directly to the site.

PUBLIC TRANSPORT Norwich train station is approx. 35 minute walk away).

OPEN All year (pre-bookings only in the winter season).

THE DAMAGE Adult from £7; under-15s from £4; bell tents (sleep 6) from £65 a night; up to 4 nights in a yurt from £280; shepherd's huts from £50 a night.

clippesby hall

Clippesby Hall, Hall Lane, Clippesby, Norfolk NR29 3BL 01493 367800 www.clippesby.com

Set in the manicured grounds of John Lindsay's family manor house, this site forms its own little self-contained canvas village. The facilities are pretty extensive, with 120 pitches (many with electric hook-ups), a small outdoor swimming pool, two grass tennis courts, a football pitch, mini-golf, archery courses, two children's play areas – including a wooden adventure playground – a tree house in the woods, a games room, cycle trail, bike hire, shop, café, holiday cottages, pine lodges and even an onsite pub.

You might assume that this place is about as quiet and peaceful as a night spent on the hard shoulder of the A12. But somehow John and his family have managed to incorporate all of these amenities into the grounds of their delightful home, while still retaining its unique character and personality. The result is an exceptionally tasteful camping park with a relaxed, family atmosphere.

The site began life as a market garden, but campers have been coming here since the 1970s. It has gradually evolved at its own pace and today the pitches are divided across several discrete camping areas, each landscaped and spacious enough to avoid any feeling of overcrowding, and named according to their individual characters. Pine Woods is a dog-free space almost entirely surrounded by conifers, The Orchard has plenty of tree cover, while The Dell is hidden away in a quiet corner with woodland pitches just for tents. Rabbits Grove is a favourite among younger campers and the Cedar Lawn has pitches spread out over a gently sloping sweep of lawn beneath a huge cedar. There is plenty of space between pitches and some interesting little nooks and crannies mean that, even in busy periods, you can still find a relatively secluded space.

Clippesby Hall is also the perfect location from which to explore the Broads National Park, a network of rivers and lakes that forms Britain's largest protected wetland. True to form, John has organised a unique way of exploring the Broads. The CanoeMan (aka Mark Wilkinson), accompanied by his two springer spaniels, Mr Darcy and Uisce, takes you directly from the site for a peaceful nature-spotting canoe trail through beautiful waterways inaccessible to motor-powered boats. If you'd rather explore the local area by pedal power, Clippesby also hires out bikes, along with route maps, helmets, locks, child seats and other accessories.

Don't be surprised when you are personally guided to your pitch on arrival – this is all part of the service, along with the deliberate decision not to put large, obtrusive pitch markers and unnecessary signs everywhere. After all, this is John's home and garden. It's been in the family since his grandfather bought the hall back in 1945, and he doesn't want to ruin it by making it look like, well, a regular campsite. And that's the beauty of this unique place. It doesn't feel like a conventional, campsite. It's more like camping in the delightful grounds of a stately home.

COOL FACTOR Great facilities combined with a peaceful, family atmosphere in a beautiful rural location.

WHO'S IN Tents, campervans, caravans, dogs – yes. Big groups, young groups – no.

ON SITE 120 pitches, spread across 8 distinctive areas. All except The Dell have electricity. Onsite entertainment includes an outdoor heated swimming pool, grass tennis courts, mini-golf, archery, children's play areas, a games room, bike hire, shop, café and even an onsite pub. Facility blocks are dotted around the place and have modern showers, toilets, basins, a family room and washing-up sinks with draining boards outside. No campfires permitted.

OFF SITE Clippesby Hall's welcome pack includes a booklet all about discovering The Broads, including ideas for days out on foot, bike and boat. One of the best means of exploration is in a Canadian canoe with 'CanoeMan' Mark Wilkinson (0845 4969177), who runs all sorts of wildlife-spotting and bush craft tours. For something bigger, head for Potter Heigham, 4 miles north of the campsite. Here boatyards hire out all sorts of vessels by the hour or day, as well as pleasureboat trips.

FOOD & DRINK Susie's Coffee Shop serves hot drinks and croissants for breakfast, and sandwiches and cakes throughout the day. You can order freshly baked bread or pizza to take away. The campsite pub, the Muskett Arms, serves decent meals and local real ales and ciders. Off the site, try The Ferry Inn (01493 751096), right on the river in the pretty village of Stokesby – the perfect spot to down a pint of ale while checking out the traffic on the river.

GETTING THERE From the A47 between Norwich and Great Yarmouth, take the A1064 north at Acle. Take the first left at Clippesby on to the B1152 and follow the signs to 'Clippesby Hall'.

PUBLIC TRANSPORT Train to Acle, then a taxi or the owners can pick you up from Acle if you book in advance.

OPEN All year.

THE DAMAGE From £12.50 to £36 for a tent, car and 2 people. Extra adults cost £6.50, children £3, under-3s free; dogs £5, hook-ups £4.

the fire pit camp

The Fire Pit Camp, The Firs, Wendling, Norfolk NR19 2LT 07717 315199 www.thefirepitcamp.co.uk

If there is such a thing as the perfect campsite for families, The Fire Pit might just be it. Nestled on the fringes of the classic Norfolk village of Wendling, the site is a family-friendly camping extravaganza, inviting young and old alike to play, create and explore the surrounding wild beauty. With not a car or caravan in sight (leave your motor at the car park then trundle your gear over in the wheelbarrows), your little campers can run around the two big playing fields (conscientiously adorned with 420 sapling trees from the Woodland Trust) to their heart's content.

The camping meadow hosts 15 spacious camping pitches, with a communal firepit, a big natural playing area and a retro double-decker bus. The centrepiece is The Wren's Nest, a two-level Hazel Dome Bender tent crafted using recycled materials that sleeps eight in three doubles and two singles. There is also a communal cooking area with a couple of butlers sinks and a fridge and worktop, though a new onsite coffee and cocktail bar will keep you away from the kitchen! They serve barista coffees, freshly made cocktails, great campside breakfasts (the best fluffy organic pancakes in Norfolk!) and communal food if pre-ordered. The Fire Pit also does a popular sideline in exclusive site hire, including weddings and bespoke family camping parties.

Should you be able to tear yourself away from the site, there are a multitude of great days out just a short drive from the site, with the north Norfolk coast, the Broads and more all within easy reach.

COOL FACTOR Back-to-basics, sociable family camping at its best.

WHO'S IN Glampers, campers, families – yes. Dogs, caravans – no.

ON SITE 21 spacious tent pitches with a communal firepit. No electric hook-ups. Washing-up area with 2 butler's sinks and solid oak work-tops. Family sized shower room in converted old goat shed with hot water and 3 loos. Glamping available in the Wren's Nest, a Hazel Dome Bender tent which sleeps 8 and has a wood-burning stove and fully equipped kitchen area complete with 2-ring gas stove. Coffee and cocktail bar.

OFF SITE Nearby Gressenhall Farm & Workhouse museum (01362 869263) is a great mixture of historical attraction and working farm. The Green Britain Centre (01760 726100; greenbritaincentre.co.uk) in nearby Swaffham boasts the only climbable wind turbine in the world!

FOOD & DRINK The Greenbanks Hotel and Restaurant (01362 687742; greenbankshotel.co.uk) in nearby Great Fransham is worth a visit, as much for the setting as for the refined local cuisine. The Windmill in Necton (01760 722057; thenectonwindmill.co.uk) is a friendly place that serves well-above-average pub grub.

GETTING THERE Follow the signs to Wendling off the A47; the site entrance is on the main road through Wendling opposite a bus stop.

PUBLIC TRANSPORT Regular buses run to Wendling, Norwich, Kings Lynn and Peterborough from Dereham.

OPEN Individual camping only during school holidays, and July and August. Exclusive hire of site all year.

THE DAMAGE Tent pitches £15 per adult per night; £7.50 per child per night; under 2s free. Wren's Nest is £130 per night for up to 4 people, £12 per extra person. Exclusive hire available, see website for details.

deepdale backpackers and campers

Deepdale Backpackers & Campers, Burnham Deepdale, Norfolk PE31 8DD 01485 210256
www.deepdalebackpackers.co.uk

Come mid September, most people of sound mind put any thoughts of camping to rest. It's not just because the days start to turn colder but because there aren't that many campsites that stay open once the leaves begin to curl and drop. Nudging the north Norfolk coastline, Deepdale Farm in Burnham Deepdale is a rare exception.

Some believe there is no better time to visit Norfolk than autumn – the hedgerows are pregnant with blackberries and the county is a vision of russet-coloured forests and blush-coloured clouds – and this well-established North Norfolk coast site is a great place to come if you do, with around 80 pitches and six tipis and yurts. These are not tipis awash with Indian silks and ethnic blankets, but they don't need to be. They are well-maintained and equipped with a cast-iron chimenea for heat, including kindling and fuel for the fire, foldaway chairs, a barbecue and a lantern. Sleeping in the round, with the wind whispering softly above you, is enchantment enough.

There's often an enthusiastic programme of events at the farm, with everything from organised stargazing to cookery classes with local produce. But in any case there are diversions a-plenty in and around Burnham Deepdale. You are so near to the sea here that an excursion to the water's edge is a must, with wonderful beaches beckoning and great coastal walks in abundance.

COOL FACTOR A winter – and summer – wonderland.

WHO'S IN Tents, small campervans, dogs – yes. Caravans, big groups, young groups – no.

ON SITE There are 5 eco-friendly hot showers, 2 male toilets and 2 urinals, 3 female toilets, a unisex toilet block plus washing-up facilities. The water is heated by solar panels, with an oil burner back-up. Along with an onsite camping shop there is a handy café next door. No campfires.

OFF SITE Grab your wellies and revel in the muddy marshes and rockpools around the harbour at Brancaster Staithe. Or escape to the posh boutiques of Burnham Market. It's not called Chelsea-on-Sea for nothing. Further afield, there's the huge, pine-backed expanse of sand at Holkham Bay.

FOOD & DRINK The Deepdale Café next door serves everything from quality English breakfasts to chunky home-made soups (including evening meals in summer). The White Horse (01485 210262), a 5-minute walk west, is a buzzy gastropub serving local fish and shellfish.

GETTING THERE Take the A11, turn off to Swaffham and head northwest on the A1065 towards Fakenham. Take the first exit at the roundabout, then right on to the B1355, continuing to Burnham Market. Here there is a sharp left on to North Street before you need to turn right again, back on to the B1355 (Bellamy's Lane). A mile along the road turn left on to the A149, and the site is in front of you.

PUBLIC TRANSPORT Train to Cromer, Sheringham or King's Lynn, then the Coasthopper bus.

OPEN All year.

THE DAMAGE Tent camping is per person per night: adults £4.50–£9; children £2.50–£5. Tipis/yurts £40–£114/£50–£145 per night, depending on season and numbers.

penlan farm

Penlan Farm Caravan Park & Campsite, Brilley, Hay-on-Wye, Herefordshire HR3 6JW 01497 831485
www.penlancampsite.co.uk

The further west one ventures into Herefordshire the more it seems like a different country all of its own, lost in some distant time; the sort of place you could expect to turn a corner and bump into a buxom milkmaid shouldering a rustic yoke. It's no surprise, then, when the friendly owners at Penlan inform us that the 'modern' part of their stone and wooden farmhouse dates from the late 1600s (the rest of it being a good 100 years older).

A mere half-a-mile from the Welsh border and seemingly hundreds of miles from anywhere anyone might call home, Penlan Farm is a 50-acre organic smallholding where Peter and Margaret run a flock of sheep and a herd of cattle, and where an apple orchard blossoms majestically each spring. Whether the livestock appreciate the views or not is a matter for speculation. Visitors to the site, however, can hardly fail to do so. To the far southwest are the iconic Brecon Beacons, while next to them are the hulking Black Mountains, in contrast to the gentler Herefordshire hills to the east. Drop down a field or two (the owners encourage their guests to go for a wander) and look to the left and there are the Malvern Hills. On a clear day you can even pick out the village of Birdlip on the edge of the Cotswolds, some 60 miles away. The campsite here first started taking customers in the 1960s but was closed a decade later when the farm became the property of the National Trust (which also owns the exquisite Cwmmau Farm a few fields away and well worth the stroll). Peter and Margaret – both born and bred in the area

– decided in 1997 to reopen the site (which no longer belongs to the National Trust) and have been sharing its extraordinary peace and quiet with campers ever since.

The camping area is a small, gently sloping, cutlass-shaped swathe of lovingly tended greensward. The caravan pitches – eight of which are seasonal – are at the back, while campers get the pick of the front row seats and enjoy the additional advantage of the shelter afforded by a low beech hedge. The lane that runs directly behind the site is, happily, almost exclusively the domain of infrequent tractors. It's a pity that telegraph poles cross the field below, but in summer it does mean that the wires between them are lined with swallows and pied wagtails. Look higher up and you might be lucky enough to see a red kite riding the thermals, while closer to hand there are various species of tit that nest in the eight boxes dotted about the site. As evening draws on, just as the streets of Hereford light up in the valley below, the horseshoe bats living in the farm's ancient barns take flight. Finally, as night falls, the woods behind the campsite are haunted by the calls of tawny owls. For those who enjoy looking down once in a while, the good news is that not all the local wildlife is airborne: a pond on the farm is home to great crested newts.

All in all it's a blissful place to stay – for peace, for its wildlife, and for its unusually special position surrounded by some of the most beautiful countryside in England.

COOL FACTOR So perfectly bucolic it should be bottled.

WHO'S IN Tents, campervans, caravans, dogs (on leads) – yes. Groups – no.

ON SITE 10 touring pitches and 10 pitches for tents. Immaculately clean shower block with 2 electric showers; games shed, fridge-freezer and a PYO fruit area. No campfires but the owners have BBQs that can be borrowed . A giant Jenga set awaits children of all ages.

OFF SITE Hay-on-Wye, with its second-hand bookshops and famous literary festival, is just 7 miles away. Paddles Pedals in Hay (01497 820604; canoehire.co.uk) does bike and canoe hire for adventures along the River Wye (they'll pick you up from wherever you end up).

FOOD & DRINK The Sun Inn at Winforton (01544 327677; thesuninnwinforton.co.uk) is recommended for food (but do reserve a table). The Erwood Station Craft Centre and Gallery (01982 560674; erwood-station.co.uk) at Erwood has a good café. Connoisseurs of the fermented apple should head for the presses at Dunkertons Cider (01544 388653; dunkertons. co.uk) in Pembridge.

GETTING THERE Don't SatNav the postcode – you'll end up half a mile away and in a jam if you're coming with a caravan. From Leominster, follow the A44 west towards Rhayader until it swerves around Kington. One mile after the second roundabout, turn left (signposted Kington Town Centre, Hergest, Brilley). After ½ mile, take the second turn right (signposted Brilley). After 4 miles, look out for a National Trust signpost on the left. At the same junction, turn left into Apostles Lane. Penlan is the first farmhouse on the right.

OPEN Easter–end of October.

THE DAMAGE Advance booking only. Tents – adult £7.50; child (5–12 yrs) £4; under-5s free. Caravan/campervan £16. Electric hook-ups £3; dogs £1.50.

foxholes castle camping

Foxholes Castle Camping, Montgomery Road, Bishops Castle, Shropshire SY9 5HA 01588 638924
www.foxholes-castle.co.uk

To wake up feeling literally on top of the world, or on top of Shropshire, at least, makes a truly invigorating start to any morning, and that's the feeling you get when you greet the day at Foxholes, whose expansive grassy plateau is surrounded by far-reaching views of magnificent hills, which wistfully beckon campers deep into their bucolic embrace.

There can be few campsites in England that enjoy such a vista: the foothills of the Cambrian mountain range, the famous bulk of the Long Mynd, Stiperstones – in whose Roman lead mines Wild Edric is said to be buried with his soldiers, ready to fight should England ever be endangered – and a cornucopia of other bumps, knolls and mounds that make up part of the 139-mile loop that is the Shropshire Way. With an almost 360-degree panorama, it's as near to heaven as a 'hillophile' is ever likely to get.

Four sprawling, natural camping areas are spread out among 10 acres. A sloping field at the back accommodates tourers and caravans; a cosy half-acre enclave suits tents requiring shelter; above that is a field that feels like a hilltop Iron Age fort (only without the ramparts); and there's a further, more out-of-the-way field which has been largely left to meadow. Campers arrive and pitch up in all weathers, but less hardy souls can book the comfortable, clean bunkhouse in the farmyard that sleeps six and costs a bargain £10 per bed per night.

Owners Chris and Wendy bought the property in 2006 and opened for business the following year, and they are experienced, easy-going hosts – just as long as you don't attempt to throw anything away that can be recycled. How else would they be able to make their castellated-roof tin knight, plastic recycling bin guard or papier-mâché notice board? They will readily invite visiting conservationists and the occasional camper into their kitchen for a cuppa and a chat, and their eco-friendly stance affects everything they do, with new eco-facilities that feature solar-powered showers and loos that are flushed by rainwater.

Pass by the metal sculpture of a fox, down towards the path that leads to the nearest town, Bishop's Castle, to find a little Buddha under the trees, collecting coins for the local air ambulance (Shropshire's roads are too windy and narrow to receive emergency vehicles quickly). The town itself is a very pleasant place to have on your doorstep, but if you want to leave the crowds behind, get out to the hills on the Shropshire Way – which passes right through the site – the Offa's Dyke Path, Wild Edric's Way or the Kerry Ridgeway, which are all within striking distance, the last of these doubling as a cycle route if you're a peddler rather than a plodder. Meanwhile, at basecamp, wildlife is nurtured, and the hedgerows left to grow freely, which pleases the birds that thrive here, and adds to the morning welcome. Just pack earplugs!

COOL FACTOR Views, views, views (and wildlife).

WHO'S IN Tents, campervans, caravans, dogs ('must be well-behaved, but we love them'), big groups, (well-mannered) young groups – yes. Non-recyclers – no.

ON SITE Roughly 100 pitches, but the site is never allowed to get too busy. No hook-ups. Fires permitted in drums rented on site. There are separate family/accessible wet rooms. Additional toilet and shower block with 3 female, 3 male showers and 4 female, 3 male toilets; plus 9 solar-powered showers and 10 toilets using rainwater for flushing. A washing-up area and common room with fridge, freezer, books and sofas. 2 cabins also available, one sleeping 6, the other 8.

OFF SITE For a small town, Bishop's Castle is a happening place. Each year it plays host to a May Fair (weekend after the first May Bank Holiday); a walking festival (second week of June); a stone-skimming championships (last Sunday in June); a carnival (first Sunday in July); party in the park (third weekend of July) and a beer festival (weekend after the carnival). It's also a peasant town for a wander, with lots of quirky, indie shops, pubs and restaurants.

FOOD & DRINK The Castle Hotel (01588 638403; thecastlehotelbishopscastle.co.uk) in Bishop's Castle has a cosy restaurant serving excellent dishes using locally sourced produce. Also in Bishop's Castle, the Three Tuns (01588 638797; thethreetunsinn.co.uk) is a good local that serves its own real ales (brewed around the corner), along with decent food. There's a farmers' market in Bishop's Castle town hall every third Saturday of the month, and an ordinary fruit and veg market there every Friday.

GETTING THERE Approach Bishop's Castle along the A488 that runs just to the east of the town. Turn west along the B4384 (Schoolhouse Lane) and first right up the B4385 (Bull Lane). Foxholes Castle is about ½ mile along on the left.

PUBLIC TRANSPORT Either take the train to Church Stretton and shuttle bus to Bishop's Castle (April–September); or train to Shrewsbury and take bus no. #552/553 to Bishop's Castle.

OPEN All year.

THE DAMAGE Adults £7; children under 13 £3; dogs £1.

small batch campsite

Small Batch Campsite, Little Stretton, Church Stretton, Shropshire SY6 6PW 01694 723358
www.smallbatch-camping.co.uk

For the past 500 million years, the area now known as Shropshire has had it tough. It's been pushed south towards the Antarctic, spat out from the earth's crust, sunk under the sea, reinvented itself as a coral reef, spent time near the sub-tropical equator and finally settled in its current location, along a relatively quiet fault line. The upshot of all this geographical to-ing and fro-ing is a fantastically varied landscape – and one that you get to experience first-hand at Small Batch campsite.

A huge number of activities are available to get you acquainted with this hotbed of geological activity. Hang-gliding from Longmynd peak gives you a chance to see the area from a unique vantage point, as does paragliding, cycling and even playing a leisurely round of golf. And then there's the Longmynd hike. Every year at the beginning of October, a smallish group of extreme hikers takes to the Shropshire hills to attempt a crazy, boot-wearying 50-mile hike. The challenge is to leg it up (and down) eight of the region's summits in less than 24 hours.

If this level of energy-sapping activity is not what you signed up for, there are plenty of far more sedate walks in this designated Area of Outstanding Natural Beauty. One of these conveniently starts from the charming Small Batch campsite, nestled at the base of the Longmynd. It's a much less arduous seven-mile round-trip that conveniently deposits you in the local Green Dragon pub a mere four hours later, and within spitting distance of your tent.

The tranquil riverside location is perfect for walkers and twitchers alike. The site itself is secluded and small, which has its advantages but can mean you're a bit close to your neighbours when it's full. There also seem to be an awful lot of rules, which can feel a bit unnecessary and overbearing. The upside is that it's been in the current Prince family for 43 years, which is enough time for them to gather a wealth of knowledge about the various routes up the Longmynd and other ridges. Alternatively, the Shropshire Hills Shuttle takes you up hill and down dale via some jaw-dropping views, and requires no more energy than what it takes to push the shutter button on your camera. And if eating and drinking the local grub sounds more your sort of thing, then come in July for the town's annual cake and ale trail.

Whether you like your holiday fast-paced and activity-laden or charmingly chilled out, it's up to you how much moving around you do. There is enough activity here to warrant another shift in the earth's crust – but it's unlikely to happen again for another million years or so.

COOL FACTOR Fall out of your tent and start walking.

WHO'S IN Tents, campervans, dogs, groups – yes. Caravans, motorhomes – no.

ON SITE The 30 pitches are served by basic but good showers, toilets and a washing-up area. Electric hook-ups are available. Waste unit at main house. Some Wi-Fi available.

OFF SITE The friendly owners are the best bet for info on the walks, or try Church Stretton's Information Centre. For some high-altitude adventure, you can go paragliding off Longmynd peak with Beyond Extreme (01691 682640; beyondextremeparagliding.co.uk), who are based in Church Stretton. Or, for more sedate activity, follow the antiques trail at Stretton Antiques Market, Church Stretton (01694 723718) – a local institution.

FOOD & DRINK There are plenty of yummy farmer's markets stocking local organic goodies – in Church Stretton (2nd/4th Friday), Ludlow (2nd Thursday), Craven Arms (1st Saturday) and Bishops Castle (3rd Saturday). Two pubs within stumbling distance are the Green Dragon (01694 722925; greendragonlittlestretton.co.uk), which serves really good food, and the slightly more atmospheric Ragleth Inn (01694 722711; theraglethinn.co.uk), which also serves decent food. It's also worth the short journey to the Kangaroo Inn in Aston-on-Clun (01588 660263; thekangarooinn.co.uk, a proper local where the welcome is warm and they have pub quizzes and beer festivals, and also serve food.

GETTING THERE From the A49, follow signs to Shrewsbury/Church Stretton, and take the B5477 signed Little Stretton. Turn left beside the Ragleth Inn, opposite the hard-to-miss thatched church. Take the next right, then continue straight ahead through the ford to the campsite.

PUBLIC TRANSPORT Church Stretton (2 miles away) has a train station. Bus 435 (TESS; 01588 673888) goes via The Ragleth Inn every 2 hours. The handy Shropshire Hills Shuttle (www.shropshirehillsshuttles.co.uk) will also take you all or part of the way up every single peak on weekends/Bank Hols.

OPEN Easter–end of October.

THE DAMAGE From £10 per tent per night; £15 per caravan; £3 electric hook-up.

underhill farm

Underhill Farm, Underhill Lane, Pant, Shropshire SY10 9RB 07773 046111 www.underhillfarm.org

'Just because it's known, doesn't mean it's explored', proclaim the Evison family, proud owners of Underhill Farm. And it's fair to say they know a thing or two about adventure and discovery. Back in 2009, when they bought this deserted property, it had been left to wrack and ruin for over 30 years and was as overgrown within as was the weed-woven garden beyond. Over the years, however, alongside trips to the Himalayas, blister-busting ultra marathons and treks through the Alps, they have transformed the smallholding into a delightful family home. Yet through it all they have maintained that element of natural wilderness. And today Underhill Farm is the perfect site for those looking to truly engage with nature. Perfectly poised in the Shropshire countryside, a few hundred metres from the Welsh border, Underhill Farm is a wonderfully unique campsite with a clear ethos and a warm community feel.

Snazzy, gadget-laden glampers looking for sumptuously furnished yurts are not the focus here. It's those hoping to learn about and enjoy the natural environment that feel most at ease in the green meadow clearings. In the main paddock, enclosed by tall old trees, there is ample space for up to five tents to pitch. Nearby, a wooden bridge leads to the communal firepit, allowing campers to share stories in the evening as they toast a sticky marshmallow or two. Those travelling light can forego the tent in favour of other options: an authentic Mongolian yurt, a larger Welsh yurt and a traditional canvas tipi (all with beds, rugs and

a simple set of shelves). All come accompanied by a shared kitchen area with all the basics for preparing and cooking some camping cuisine.

Once you've settled in you can begin to take in the rest of the site – an eclectic mix of functional spaces and natural pockets of wilderness. Traditional wildgrass meadows are interspersed with a wooded copse, bendy basket willows and a small apple orchard, while a converted barn space provides somewhere to hide away in bad weather as well as an area for organised workshops to take place. Needless to say, these activities make use of materials on the doorstep, whether it's willow weaving, pottery, or wool and looming workshops. Such events echo the site's sustainability and ecological focus, while its position next to a nature reserve only helps to encourage the rich wildlife that flourishes here. Don't be surprised to see the swooping wingspan of buzzards and peregrines flying overhead.

The Evisons aren't kidding when they say there is plenty to explore right here. But if you leave your pond-side pitch and head elsewhere you'll also find more than enough to keep you occupied. Limestone cliffs, excellent for climbing and caving, are a short walk in one direction, while in the other the Montgomery Canal stretches into the countryside, ideal for those with bikes. Then there's Offa's Dyke, Llanymynech Golf Club and canoeing on the River Vyrnwy, to pick out the highlights. You'll just have to come back for another visit.

COOL FACTOR Ecological, sustainable camping with a relaxed atmosphere and a wilderness feel.

WHO'S IN Despite the yurts and tipis, this is *not* a glamping site. Tents, families, couples, dogs by arrangement – yes. Caravans, campervans, motorhomes – no.

ON SITE Up to 5 tents on site, 2 yurts, 1 tipi, a small cabin and a camping barn. No electric hook-ups. Yurts and tipis are authentic, not glamping. They include campbeds and rustic home-made furniture, while bedding can be hired. Group hire and yurt guests also have access to a communal kitchen with a gas cooker, kettle, microwave and toaster as well as pans, crockery and cutlery. Guests can also use the home-made pizza oven. There is a fridge-freezer and washing-up area. The camping and events barn is used in wet weather for families and bespoke activities (wood and wool craft, pottery, wicker weaving and so on). The barn also houses a ping-pong table, books and games. In the main barn near the courtyard area there is a flushing toilet, one hand-washing basin and a separate shower. There is a communal firepit and fires are allowed in certain areas.

OFF SITE The famous Offa's Dyke (nationaltrail.co.uk/offas-dyke-path) footpath runs right past. The Montgomery Canal stretches into the countryside and makes for a pleasant walk or bike ride.

FOOD & DRINK The Cross Guns Inn (01691 839631) is within walking distance in Pant, while the next village, Llanymynech, has 3 pubs: The Dolphin Inn (01691 839672; thedolphininn. co.uk), Cross Keys (01691 831585; crosskeyshotel.info) and The Bradford Arms (01691 830582; bradfordarmshotel.com).

GETTING THERE Entering Pant from the south, pass the Cross Guns pub. Watch for a 40mph sign on the right and a small brown sign for Llanymynech rocks. Turn here and follow the lane until the tarmac runs out. The campsite is on your left.

OPEN Yurt, tipi and camping from May–September. Other accommodation throughout the year.

THE DAMAGE £15 per tent per night (for up to a standard 4-man tent); £200 per yurt per week or £30 per night. £100 per tipi per week or £25 per night.

forestside farm

Forestside Farm, Marchington Cliff, Uttoxeter, Staffordshire ST14 8NA 01283 820353 www.forestsidefarm.co.uk

There are some campsites that merely aspire to views and others that have them in spades. Look north from Forestside, a 156-acre organic dairy farm, and you'll enjoy a 180-degree vista that takes in both the Weaver Hills and the Peak District's Dove Valley, and still has room for more around the edges. At night, all those distant parts that looked uninhabited suddenly switch on their lights, presumably for the benefit of those watching from the farm. The site consists of an upper and lower field with flat grassy pitches and a small patch of hardstandings. As the name suggests, the farm is right next to a wood (listen out for tawny owls in the evening) that rises steeply behind it up Marchington Cliff, giving some shelter to the south. A very upmarket shed houses the facilities, including four highly civilised shower rooms. There is a tourist information room with laminated maps of a short, circular farm walk to sharpen your appetite for dinner or to get the blood circulating in the morning.

As for the rest of your day, this part of Staffordshire is endowed with so many nearby attractions that it's hard to decide what to do, from horseracing at Uttoxeter (4¾ miles away) to a couple of impressive country houses and the heart-stoppingly beautiful Manifold Valley cycle trail – a relatively easy round-trip of 18 miles that takes in various natural attractions along the way, including Thor's Cave and the limestone crag of Beeston Tor. Don't mention it to the kids, but you're also just a dozen miles from Alton Towers.

COOL FACTOR Simple farm camping in a beautiful location.

WHO'S IN Tents, campervans, caravans, dogs (on leads) - yes.

ON SITE 17 pitches (5 hardstanding), and a maximum of 30 people. 8 electric hook-ups. 2 loos and 2 showers for men and the same again for women. 2 camping pods are available, sleeping up to 2 adults and 3 children. There is a washing-up area, fridge, kettle, microwave, tourist info, recycling and chemical disposal point. Coarse fishing passes can be obtained on site. Kids can watch the cows being milked under supervision. No open fires and BBQs must be off the grass.

OFF SITE The Sudbury Hall Museum of Childhood (01283 585305; NT) is a grand 17th-century mansion with a childhood museum and host of special events. Or try Tutbury Castle (01283 812129; tutburycastle.com) – a prison for Mary Queen of Scots, with plenty of history to get your teeth into. Alton Towers (0871 222 3330; altontowers.com) is half-an-hour's drive away. The Manifold Valley cycle trail (01335 350503; NT) is a fairly gentle affair, and you can take a break at the Wetton Mill Tearoom (01298 84838).

FOOD & DRINK The Dog & Partridge in nearby Marchington (01283 820394; dogandpartridgemarchington.co.uk) does good food and real ales and occasional live music. The Barn (01283 820367; barnindian.com) is an Indian restaurant 1 mile down the road towards Draycott in the Clay.

GETTING THERE Take the A518 from Stafford to Utoxeter, and pick up the A50 the other side of town, heading east towards Sudbury. Turn right on the B5017 (Station Road) and continue over the railway line and turn right onto Stubby Lane. The campsite is on the left.

PUBLIC TRANSPORT Train to Uttoxeter (5 miles away), from where bus #402 runs to Marchington Cliff.

OPEN All year.

THE DAMAGE Backpacker up to £15; couple up to £20; family over £20; pods from £35.

common end farm

Common End Farm, Swinscoe, Ashbourne, Derbyshire DE6 2BW 01335 210352 www.commonendfarmcampsite.co.uk

Alton Towers may be only a short drive away, but this is an unashamedly simple, un-commercial campsite – a family-run place with just 30 pitches across a flattish field and lovely open views over the Manifold Valley across to Dovedale and Thorpe Cloud. With plenty of space for the kids to run around and ride their bikes, you might even get the chance to sit back and enjoy the scenery before being roped in for a game of cricket.

The site is also a great base from which to strike out and explore the southern tip of the Peak District, so it's great for committed walkers, too. A two-mile network of footpaths leads you straight from the site down to Dovedale, with its iconic gorge and stepping stones. From here, you can climb up the distinctive, conical Thorpe Cloud hill, which rises up from the side of the river Dove. Or a two-and-a-half-mile round-trip takes you through the tranquil Victorian landscape and woodland at the National Trust's Ilam Park, where you can stop off for a cream tea on the lawn. The historic market town of Ashbourne and the Manifold Valley and Tissington cycle trails are all within three miles of the site. The Tissington Trail starts in Ashbourne and runs for 13 miles and, like a lot of such paths, follows the route of an old railway line. It's mostly flat, and it's well-surfaced enough to attract walkers, cyclists and equestrian folk – as well as being accessible for wheelchairs for much of its length. Enough to keep you occupied, then – assuming you can tear yourself away from that game of cricket.

COOL FACTOR Stuff Alton Towers – kids make their own entertainment here!

WHO'S IN Tents, caravans, dogs, groups (double-check any restrictions on groups) – yes.

ON SITE 30 pitches for tents and caravans across a 2-acre flattish field. 8 x 16 amp electric hook-up pitches. 8 x 6 amp electric hookup pitches, the rest non-electric pitches, plus there's an overflow field for non-electric pitches. A stone barn houses a modern shower and toilet block with free hot showers, and there are 3 outdoor sinks and a freezer for ice packs. Campfires allowed with firebaskets available to rent.

OFF SITE The White Peak Estate (01335 350503; NT), including Ilam Park, is the most obvious place to explore. Or, around 30 minutes away by car, Kedleston Hall (01332 842191; NT) is an 18th-century mansion that was the home of Lord Curzon and is full of treasures acquired when he was Viceroy of India. The Tissington Trail is a nice, easy walk or cycle from Ashbourne (derbyshire-peakdistrict.co.uk/tissingtontrail.htm). For the Manifold Valley trail, see p.176.

FOOD & DRINK Good food at the Dog & Partridge (01335 343183; dogandpartridge.co.uk), half a mile from the site, where dogs are also welcome. The Royal Oak (01335 300090; royaloakashbourne.co.uk) in Mayfield is another good local (with yummy puds), and the Cock Inn at Clifton (01335 342654; thecockinnatclifton.co.uk) has an open fire and serves traditional pub grub.

GETTING THERE From Ashbourne follow the A52 towards Leek and continue through Mayfield to Swinscoe. Pass the Dog & Partridge pub and look out for a green sign for the site on the right.

OPEN Easter–September.

THE DAMAGE From £16 for 2 people with a tent and car. Children 3–15 yrs £3 per night. Adults 16 yrs+ £5 per night. Dogs £2 per night. Hook-ups £2–£4.

royal oak

The Royal Oak, Hurdlow, Nr Buxton, Derbyshire SK17 9QJ 01298 83288 www.peakpub.co.uk

The biggest challenge for those staying at the Royal Oak isn't wrestling with a sloped camping field (it's mostly flat), being kept awake by traffic (it's not near a main road) or finding things to do (it's slap bang in the middle of the Peak District). No, it's chomping your way through one of the award-winning pies that they sell at the onsite pub. You could probably actually camp in one of these monsters – they're that big. Packed with fine ingredients, they make for a fine reward after a day's play in the Peaks, especially if accompanied by one of the excellent local draught ales.

There are two camping fields here, one sloping and one flat, with space for around 30 pitches in all (bring strong pegs for the rocky ground in the upper field), and there's a converted stone barn with comfortable bunks if the weather's wreaking havoc. Surrounded by over 100 acres of farmland, with the 13-mile Tissington Trail passing right next to it and the Limestone Way actually cutting through some of the site, this is a great base for those interested in walking and cycling – especially since Parsley Hay Cycle Hire is two miles away and has a range of bikes for adults and kids, including tandems.

Bakewell, Ashbourne and the spa town of Buxton are all just a short drive away, making this an accessible and friendly place to get up close and personal with the British countryside – and with its pies.

COOL FACTOR Who ate all the pies? We did.

WHO'S IN Tents, campervans – yes. Caravans – no. Dogs, groups – by arrangement.

ON SITE Small campfires are allowed if contained and off the ground. Two camping fields (the lower one is flatter) with good washing-up facilities, free hot showers, and toilets in an old but modern and clean inside barn. There's also a water tap and an outdoor washing line.

OFF SITE Bakewell (famous for its puddings) has the Pavilion Gardens and charming Opera House. Ashbourne and the spa town of Buxton are all short drives away. Monyash village has a great park for kids. Parsley Hay Cycle Hire (01298 84493; parsleyhay.co.uk) is two miles away and has a wide range of bikes that you can rent.

FOOD & DRINK The Royal Oak serves real ales, alarmingly large pies and other award-winning pub grub. The best fry-up in the area is available at Old Smithy Tea Rooms (01629 810190; oldsmithymonyash.co.uk) in Monyash. Piedaniels (01629 812687; piedaniels-restaurant.com) in Bakewell serves fine French and English cuisine. There's also a pleasant café at Parsley Hay (01298 84888; parsleyhay.co.uk), a 2-mile walk from the site.

GETTING THERE Head towards Ashbourne (from Buxton) on the A515, and after 5 miles, take the right turn signposted Hurdlow, Crowdecote, and Longnor. After just 400m the Royal Oak pub and campsite are on the right.

PUBLIC TRANSPORT The nearest station within walking/taxi distance is Buxton (6 miles). There's no direct bus service but the Hartington Bus goes along the A515 and will stop on the main road, ½ mile away.

OPEN All year.

THE DAMAGE £20 per pitch per night; £25 per large pitch.

Award Winning Pub

Locally Sourced, Homemade Food
12-9pm Daily

Award Winning Local Real Ales

Camping & Bunk Barn
Accommodation

Freshly Brewed Coffee

cotton star camping

Cotton Star Camping, Windy Bank, Low Bradfield, Peak District National Park, Sheffield, South Yorkshire S6 6LB
07872 169439 www.cottonstarcamping.co.uk

When the Peak District was christened Britain's first national park in 1951 it was put firmly on the map as a place of awe-inspiring natural beauty, and, moreover, a landscape to be preserved. The mist-shrouded gritstone peaks and windswept moorlands have become the UK's home for walkers, bikers and all outdoorsy types, attracted to the rural, untainted vastness of it all. Camping here needs to be a subtle, unobtrusive affair, then. No gleaming concrete laundry blocks or strips of static caravans. It's not about adding a mix of new facilities but about simply appreciating what is already there – the wildlife, the scenery and the empty open spaces. Tucked between the trees on the banks of the Agden Reservoir, there's a 1.6 acre meadow that perfectly fits this bill. From late autumn through to spring there is little going on here, save for the chirp of the birds and the sound of squirrels rummaging through the undergrowth. But come the summer this grassy woodland space is the scene for a charmingly simple campsite that appears fleetingly beneath the Yorkshire sunshine before disappearing like a squirrel back into its drey for winter.

Cotton Star Camping offers off-grid, authentic camping for those who are willing to forgo the luxuries of piping hot showers and whining hairdryers in favour of a smoky log fire and a pitch beneath the sparkling night sky. Campers certainly aren't stranded, with clean portable loos at one end of the meadow and a supply of drinking water tapped to the site. But in all other respects this is a true back-to-nature experience. Comforts come in the form of fresh bread, pasties and the day's newspaper, straight from the delightful local store and café beside the village green in Bradfield, a quintessentially English settlement half a mile away.

On site, Cotton Star runs a variety of themed camping events throughout the summer and booking a pitch for 'simply camping' is possible form April onwards, although it's always worth checking the website for the times available. Workshops include traditional drystone walling, family bush craft, bird-spotting, campfire cooking and fungi foraging. The kids are spoilt with acres of space in the meadow in which to charge around making friends. In the evening, the communal fire becomes the focal point of the site, a glowing bowl of warmth beneath the fabulously dark skies this part of England affords.

When the next morning dawns, shafts of light streak through the tree line on the eastern edge of the field. Through the gaps, you can see Agden Reservoir sparkling in the morning sun. The reservoir is circled by a pleasant four-mile walk. It is one of several nearby, and Damflask Resevoir, in particular, offers opportunities for sailing, canoeing and fishing, although this, of course, requires finding time between hiking the local peaks, the most popular activity around here for quite obvious reasons.

COOL FACTOR Off-grid camping amongst the tree-clad hills of the Peak District.

WHO'S IN Tents (with pre-erected tents onsite available to hire), couples, families, walkers and cyclists – yes. Campervans, caravans, motorhomes – no.

ON SITE 30 pitches for simply camping, up to 60 during events. The 1.6 acre grassy field is enclosed in the woods, though through the trees on one side you still get splintered views of Agden Reservoir. Toilets are currently in well-looked-after portables with planning permission pending for future changes. Lighting is provided by solar lamps, fairylights and lanterns. Pitches vary in size, but there is plenty of space and you can also book pre-erected furnished tents in advance. There is a communal campfire and a large wood-burning stove stack for use.

OFF SITE The walks around nearby Agden reservoir and the other reservoirs in the vicinity are the thing to do. Otherwise just make the most of the location in the heart of the Peak District National Park (peakdistrict.gov.uk).

FOOD & DRINK It is just over a half-mile walk to Bradfield, with a village shop, post office and café, and an upper, smaller, hamlet, overlooked by the church. The School Rooms' café, bistro and farm shop (0114 285 1920; theschoolroomssheffield.com) sells a smorgasbord of local produce and is an excellent place to sit in the sun with a cup of tea. Alternatively, a short but steep walk up the hill, The Old Horns Inn (0114 285 1207; theoldhorns.co.uk) is a traditional pub and restaurant serving great food. It is also well worth visiting the Bradfield Brewery (0114 285 1118), on the doorstep, to pick up some local ales.

GETTING THERE Take the A57 out of Sheffield to the Peak District National Park, turn right before Ladybower Reservoir, continue on to Mortimer Road, turn right on to Windy Bank, campsite on the right.

OPEN See website for details or contact campsite for exact opening times.

THE DAMAGE From £15 per night. Whole site hire also available for private camping events.

tattershall lakes

Tattershall Lakes Country Park, 57 Sleaford Road, Tattershall, Lincolnshire LN4 4LR 01526 348800
www.tattershall-lakes.com

Camping purists will say, 'all you need for a perfect getaway is canvas and a campfire'. Others, however, may want a little more luxury when it comes to facilities and creature comforts. Covering both bases is Tattershall Lakes; souped-up camping for the sociable, and an ideal destination for families and groups wanting to discover rural Lincolnshire.

The park is set over a large area dominated by dozens of lovely lakes. The site's 210 pitches are spread across a vast grassy space they call the 'Woodland Retreat', a secluded meadow surrounded by trees, with a separate area for touring vans looking for more sturdy hardstanding spots. Luxury bell tents are available and come equipped not only with beds, duvets and pillows, but also electric lights. In terms of site facilities, there's everything you need, with clean and modern shower blocks, a handy shop and a fully equipped launderette. Add to that a bar (with Wi-Fi access), children's adventure playground, an indoor swimming pool, spa, gym and even a lakeside beach, then you start to get an idea of just how much there is to keep you entertained.

Water sports enthusiasts will rejoice at the activities available on the 180-acre lake. There's a wakeboard park (complete with quarter pipe), jet- and water-skiing, and, for those who like to take it a bit easier, pedalo hire. There are also two well-stocked fishing lakes where carp, pike, bream or eel could be your catch of the day. Other onsite activities include golf, spa treatments, pool and snooker, archery, axe-throwing, paintball, crossbow, raft-building and pool kayaks, and the kids can enjoy panning for gold, pottery painting, badge making, balloon buddies, mask making, circus skills and more.

With all those activities and entertainment, you'll find time flies by at Tattershall, but it would be a shame to leave having not explored this special part of the country. Lincolnshire has a rich cultural heritage, long stretches of golden sands, and areas of unspoiled natural beauty. The many medieval castles and historic houses in the area offer you a momentary trip back in time, while the coastal nature reserves give you the chance to really get away from it all. If you're planning a winter visit, make sure you head to Donna Nook Nature Reserve where grey seals arrive in November and December to give birth to their pups. Bird lovers will enjoy a visit to Gibraltar Point where the salt marshes, lagoons and sand dunes are home to a huge variety of bird species.

This local area also has huge significance for the RAF and is where many of the country's airmen were stationed during World War II. You can take a hanger tour at the Battle of Britain Memorial Flight Visitors Centre (at RAF Coningsby), where you'll see Spitfires, a Hurricane and a Lancaster bomber up close and get a glimpse into the lives of the men who flew them.

COOL FACTOR Water sports heaven in historic Lincolnshire.

WHO'S IN Campers, caravans, glampers, groups, families, dogs (maximum 2 per pitch) – yes. Hen and stag parties – no.

ON SITE There are 210 spaces, some with electric hook-ups. Plenty of space for tents, plus bell tent hire for glamping. 3 shower blocks, laundry and washing-up facilities. Shop and 2 bars (with free Wi-Fi access). Guests have free access to the indoor swimming pool, beach, adventure playgrounds and evening entertainment.

OFF SITE Lincoln is worth a visit for its ancient centre, castle and especially its cathedral (01522 561600; lincolncathedral. com). Nearby Tattershall Castle (01526 342543; NT) boasts a classic tower and moat, and the coast is lovely, from Skegness to quieter spots like Sutton-on-Sea and Gibraltar Point nature reserve (lincstrust.org.uk/gibraltar-point).

FOOD & DRINK Accommodation comes fully equipped with everything you need to prepare your own meals and there's a choice of supermarkets and convenience stores nearby to stock up on supplies. The Boathouse Bar and Diner on site serves food through the day, including breakfast. The Bluebell Inn (01526 342206; bluebell-inn.com) is a quaint British pub in Tattershall, and serves delicious food. The Village Limits pub (01526 353312) in nearby Woodhall Spa is a good option for Sunday lunch.

GETTING THERE Take the A1 towards Grantham, then turn on to the A52 and follow the signs to Sleaford (A153). At Sleaford take the 3rd exit on the roundabout on to the A17 to Boston before turning left on to the A153 exit to Sleaford/Horncastle/ Skegness. Stay on the A153 and the campsite is on the right before Tattershall Castle.

PUBLIC TRANSPORT The nearest train station is at Metheringham, from where the no. #5 bus to Boston stops in Tattershall town, a 10-minute walk away.

OPEN All year. However entertainment and activities are only available from the end of March–October.

THE DAMAGE Standard pitch £4–£32, service pitch £5–£37; all prices per night (for up to 6 people) including entertainment passes.

three horseshoes

Three Horseshoes, Shoe Lane, Goulceby, Lincolnshire LN11 9WA 03334 561 221 www.the3horseshoes.com

Ian and Denise, the team behind the 'pop-up' summer site at Overstrand in Norfolk, have a permanent home for their latest venture – behind the Three Horseshoes pub in the village of Goulceby. It's situated right in the heart of a relatively unexplored Area of Outstanding Natural Beauty, the Lincolnshire Wolds, and has spaces for just seven tents alongside three fully equipped bell tents and a vintage caravan. It's a great spot for sitting and admiring the Wolds scenery and sunsets and, when you're ready for a little exercise, the 147-mile Viking Way passes by on its way from the Humber Bridge to Rutland Water.

This is definitely a traditional, get-away-from-it-all destination for campers, but their glamping options are also worth considering, including a retro 1970s caravan that's perfect for couples, and three large 'Lotus Belle' tents, comfortably equipped with a double and two single beds, wood stove, hob for cooking, electricity and a decking area outside.

Three Horseshoes is very much a site for doing nothing but if you do find yourself in need of some retail therapy, England's antiques capital, Horncastle, is about six miles away; or Louth (eight miles to the north) is the main hub of the Lincolnshire Wolds and was recently voted Britain's favourite market town, with independent shops and cafés galore. The quiet seaside town of Sutton-on-Sea, which comes with sandy beaches but without the kiss-me-quick atmosphere of the busier Lincolnshire resorts, is about a 40-minute drive away.

COOL FACTOR Small is beautiful – and so are the views.

WHO'S IN Tents, caravans, motorhomes, campervans, dogs and groups – yes, by prior arrangement.

ON SITE Campfires allowed. Seven pitches with hook-ups, three lotus belle tents and a retro caravan. Two unisex shower and toilet washrooms with free hot showers and more toilets in the pub.

OFF SITE Rand Farm Park (01673 858904; randfarmpark. com) is a working farm with animals to pet. The Lincolnshire coast is a short drive away, with relatively unspoilt resorts and big sandy beaches like the one at Sutton-on-Sea; nearby Mablethorpe has a seal sanctuary that is open to visitors (01507 473346; thesealsanctuary.com), plus the kiss-me-quick seaside town of Skegness is as bracing as it ever was – and also has a vast sandy beach. Further afield, to the south of Skeggie, Gibraltar Point Nature Reserve extends 3 miles along the coast (lincstrust.org.uk/gibraltar-point) and is a spectacular haven for birdlife that varies with the seasons.

FOOD & DRINK The Three Horseshoes does food and has an onsite shop. There's also the Bluebell Inn in Belchford (01507 533602; bluebellbelchford.co.uk), which does good food, and the excellent Melanie's Resturant in Louth (01507 609595), which has been called Lincolnshire's best place to eat.

GETTING THERE Heading north on the A153, turn left as the road bears right, just before Scamblesby and Cawkwell. Follow the road into Goulceby and turn left on to Shoe Lane.

PUBLIC TRANSPORT CallConnect services 6H (to Horncastle) and 51F (to Louth) stop 300m from the site.

OPEN All year.

THE DAMAGE From £15 per pitch for two people, tent and car. Belle tents from £49 a night; caravan from £35 a night.

wold farm campsite

Wold Farm Caravan and Camping Site, Bempton Lane, Flamborough Bridlington, East Yorkshire YO15 1AT 01262 850536
www.woldfarmcampsite.co.uk

Opened in 2008, this is a site for lovers of open fields and big skies. Three-quarters of a mile up a rough track, Wold Farmhouse stands in wondrous isolation on the great chalk promontory that is Flamborough Head. The small camping field enjoys uninterrupted views over the sheep-filled fields to both Flamborough lighthouses (the new one on the left, the old one on the right) with a sliver of sea to top it off. The place is an Eldorado for walkers and birdwatchers, and if you just can't be bothered to camp, their 'log pods' accommodate up to four people and have electricity and cooking facilities.

Take the campsite's private path through the rolling sheep-filled meadows to Bempton Cliffs, just 400 metres away, where you can see, smell and hear the 200,000 nesting sea birds, including puffins, gannets and guillemots. It's also a good place to link on to the circular six-mile walk of the entire headland: the best way to take in all the views. For those who enjoy beaches, Flamborough has four, two of which are sat at the feet of well-established nature reserves with trails along wooded ravines, rocky outcrops and wild flower meadows.

There are so many things to do in this corner of Yorkshire that the owners present campers with a welcome pack. It includes information on Sewerby Hall and Gardens three miles away which, in 2009 successfully defended its title as Britain's Best Picnic Spot. Take along a sandwich and a flask to find out what all the fuss is about.

COOL FACTOR A cliff-top paradise for birdlovers.

WHO'S IN Tents, campervans, caravans – yes.

ON SITE Two fairly flat fields with spacious pitches, some with electric hook-ups. Toilet and shower block, new for 2014. Drinking water and washing-up facilities. Exclusive to guests is a scenic path for gaining access to the cliffs. Quiet picnic area.

OFF SITE Sewerby Hall, Zoo & Gardens (01262 673769; sewerbyhall.co.uk) is a lovely spot, as is the RSPB reserve at Bempton Cliffs (rspb.org.uk). You should also consider taking the 'Puffin cruise', which leaves from North Pier in Bridlington 5 miles away, on which you can spot puffins from late May to mid July and Skuas in September; advance booking advised (01262 850959; yorkshire-belle.co.uk). Flamborough Head Lighthouse, 3 miles from the site, was built in 1806 and is still very flashy today (01262 673769; trinityhouse.co.uk). Try also the fairytale-like nature trails at Danes Dyke and South landing.

FOOD & DRINK There's a pub for every taste in Flamborough and a surprising number of them given its seemingly remote location, but the one with a reputation for decent food is the Seabirds, Tower Street (01262 850242; theseabirds.com).

GETTING THERE Take the Scarborough road out of Bridlington and turn left on to Marton Road/B1255. Follow this for a couple of miles, past Bridlington Bay golf course, to Flamborough, through the village and beyond.

PUBLIC TRANSPORT There is a train station at Bempton; bus no. #510 from Bridlington runs to Flamborough.

OPEN March–November.

THE DAMAGE Tents and caravans £12 per night, based on 2 people. Extra people £3. Electric hook-up £4. Log Pods £70 for 2 nights, based on 2 people; £5 per extra person; minimum 2-night stay.

crow's nest

Crow's Nest Caravan Park, Gristhorpe, Filey, North Yorkshire YO14 9PS 01723 582206 www.crowsnestcaravanpark.com

Crow's Nest is a tale of two campsites. The first is a large holiday park with a bar, café, fish and chip shop, indoor swimming pool, and row upon row of static caravans. Not exactly *Cool Camping*. But venture a little further and, in sharp contrast, you'll find a large tents-only field with panoramic views over the sea and across the Yorkshire Wolds and the Vale of Pickering. A children's playground forms a handy boundary between these two very different camping areas.

The tent field climbs up and then slopes gently down towards the cliff-top. There's room for around 200 tents (and the odd campervan) on a pitch-where-you-like basis. As you head up the hill you'll spy some secluded areas surrounded by hedges for small groups of tents and, the closer you get to the sea, the quieter and more peaceful the site becomes. Large family groups head for the serviced pitches near the playground, while a mixture of couples, groups and families are spread across the rest of the site. You can take the path down the cliffs to the shingle beach at Gristhorpe Bay and, if you're lucky, you might spot members of the local seal colony who live on and around the rocks here.

COOL FACTOR The best of both worlds – cool camping with lots of facilities.

WHO'S IN Tents, 1 or 2 campervans, dogs, groups – yes.

ON SITE Grassy pitches, with electric hook-ups available, and caravans for hire. Lots of space between pitches. Ablutions blocks are on the main site but there is a covered washing-up station on the camping field. A well-stocked shop joins the other facilities on the main holiday-park site, where you can refreeze cold packs and stock up on food and drink basics. About 12 electric hook-ups near the play area. No campfires.

OFF SITE The long-distance Cleveland Way (nationaltrail.co.uk/cleveland-way) runs along the cliff top in front of the site and you can follow it to Filey (around 2½ miles) in one direction, and Scarborough (5 miles) in the other.

FOOD & DRINK The restaurant at the Copper Horse (01723 862029; thecopperhorse.co.uk) in Seamer has a theatrical theme and serves award-winning food. For great fish and chips there is a takeaway on the park, or you could head to the excellent and locally renowned Inghams (01723 513320) on Belle Vue Street in Filey.

GETTING THERE The site is just off the A165 between Scarborough and Filey. A couple of miles north of Filey there's a roundabout with a Jet petrol station on the corner. Turn left here and Crow's Nest is the second caravan park on the left.

PUBLIC TRANSPORT Bus 120 runs between Scarborough, Filey and Bridlington, and Crow's Nest has its own bus stop at the bottom of the lane.

OPEN Early March–end October.

THE DAMAGE Tent (including up to 4 people) £15–£30 per night.

hooks house farm

Hooks House Farm, Whitby Road, Robin Hoods Bay, North Yorkshire YO22 4PE 01947 880283 www.hookshousefarm.co.uk

Robin Hoods Bay, near Whitby in North Yorkshire, is an area steeped in romance and intrigue. Its very name is a mystery: there's nothing to link this place with the infamous green-clad hero of Sherwood Forest, but the name stands as an inexplicable suggestion of some legendary past.

What's certain is that this was smuggler country. And, if you arrive at Hooks House Farm late on a clear evening under a full moon, you'll be able to picture the scenes from long ago, as the breathtaking sight of the wide sweep of the bay is laid out beneath you in the silvery moonlight... Step back a few centuries and you'd have spotted the shadowy figures as they emerged from small wooden boats and scuttled towards the shore clutching their booty... Even now, the charming town of Robin Hoods Bay has the feel of an age-old smugglers' den, with unfeasibly narrow streets and tight passageways – although these days you're more likely to stumble across a second-hand bookshop than hidden contraband. Ancient fishermen's cottages cling to the near-vertical slope as the cliff drops down to a little harbour at the water's edge. In addition to this older part of town there's a newer, Victorian enclave at the top. The well-ordered mansions are a world apart from the cobbled jumble below.

To shed some light on the town's past, the volunteer-run museum, reached via the narrow cobbled pathways and steps, has a model of a smuggler's house, showing how contraband could be concealed, as well as stories of shipwrecks and historic rescues.

Although the bay is picturesque, it doesn't have a beach to tempt sunbathers. The ground is dark and rocky – more suitable for bracing walks, rockpool explorations, and fossil hunting than lazing around. But the wide sweep of this bay is stunning and, at the friendly, family-run campsite at Hooks House Farm, high up on the hill above town, you couldn't wish for a better vantage point. The first-rate views really make this site: from its grassy field sloping gently down towards the sea you can watch the tide wash in and out over the whole sweep of shoreline, or gaze across a colourful patchwork of sheep- and cow-dotted fields, woods, rolling hills and moors.

If you're feeling energetic, the surrounding countryside (including the Yorkshire Moors) is perfect. The disused railway line that runs through here on its way from Scarborough to Whitby has been transformed into a popular walking and cycling path and forms part of the long-distance Moor-to-Sea path. Robin Hoods Bay also marks the eastern end of the classic Coast-to-Coast Walk, while the Cleveland Way, a 110-mile National Trail between Helmsley and Filey around the North Yorkshire Moors, also makes its way along the coast here. If you're after shorter walks, try the half-mile stretch from the site down to the town, where you'll find several cosy pubs – all great venues for discussing the demise of smuggling as a lucrative career and the possibility of finding fossils on the beach, or even for speculating on how Robin Hoods Bay may have found its name.

COOL FACTOR Panoramic views over sea and moor from a peaceful, low-key site.

WHO'S IN Tents, campervans, caravans, dogs – yes. Groups – no.

ON SITE Pitches for 50 tents and 20 campervans/caravans spread out across a gently sloping field. A second field serves as a family play area. Clean but basic facilities, with 3 showers, 5 basins, and 4 toilets in separate blocks for men and women. There's also a block with washing cubicles. A further block has 3 washing-up sinks, a kettle, microwave, fridge and freezers. The campsite vibe is peaceful, relaxed and low-key, with no organised entertainment and no long list of rules and regulations to adhere to. The owners, Jill and Gordon Halder, are famously attentive, ensuring that visitors have everything they need. No campfires.

OFF SITE Robin Hoods Bay's narrow streets are fun to explore and Whitby is only 6 miles up the coast; its abbey (01947 603568; EH) is a good place to take in views over the town and the coast before you head down the famous 199 steps into the bustling old town and harbour. Several boat trips leave from the harbour; between mid September and early November the Speksioneer and its sister boat, the Esk Belle II ('The Big Yellow Boat') set off in search of minke whales, porpoises, dolphins and seals.

FOOD & DRINK Pubs in the town include Ye Dolphin (01947 880337), which has a cosy, smugglers' feel, and the Bay Hotel (01947 880278; bayhotel.info), which has views of the bay from its quayside location. The Swell Café Bar (01947 880180; swellcafe.co.uk) serves good coffee, and Bramblewick restaurant (01947 880187; bramblewick.org) is a café by day, candlelit restaurant by night.

GETTING THERE Heading south from Whitby on the A171, take the B1447 signposted to Robin Hoods Bay. Hooks House Farm is on the right, ½ mile before the village.

PUBLIC TRANSPORT Arriva buses from Scarborough to Middlesbrough run through Robin Hoods Bay and Whitby. Bus no. #93 stops at the campsite year round.

OPEN Start of March–end October.

THE DAMAGE Adult £8–£10 per night; child (3–15 yrs) £3; electric hook-up £3–£4.

camp kátur

Camp Kátur, The Camphill Estate, Kirklington, Bedale, North Yorkshire DL8 2LS 01423 855900 www.campkatur.com

It's fair to say that losing your job in your late 20s would challenge most people. But when Kerry Roy was made redundant in 2012 she took it as a sign she should follow her dreams. Losing her job was the perfect boot up the backside to realise a long-held ambition. Along with her similarly well-travelled partner Dave, this enterprising Yorkshire lass took the plunge and decided to set up her own campsite. But this wasn't to be any ordinary pitchup plot. Taking her cue from the range of global influences she encountered upon her travels, Kerry's pan-global camping vision was finally realised in the simply marvellous Camp Kátur.

Named after the Icelandic word for 'happy', Camp Kátur is nestled within the sprawling 250 acre Camphill Estate just outside Bedale, North Yorkshire. Okay, it's cheating a bit because you can't just turn up here with a tent. But, sitting within a peaceful 15-acre meadow clearing, fringed by thick woodland, it's such a great off-grid glamping experience we thought we had to include it.

Camp Kátur brings together a wealth of authentic abodes, great outdoor activities, and, most importantly, the best eco-friendly facilities. Guests are well and truly spoiled for choice with accommodation options. The four Hobbit Pods sit amid the trees. These cosy cabins are ideal for groups of four, with the Romeo & Juliet pod perfect for glamping couples. The twin Safari Tents (named Zaniah and Jabbah) will happily sleep a party of eight, and come complete with a private toilet and shower area. Sat as they are

atop an expansive decked terrace, you can roll up the lightweight canvas porch for extra ventilation, just like in the Serengeti. Yurt-wise, three spacious abodes await in the lush grassland clearings while the Molimo Tipi and 'Tinker' bell sleep six and five respectively.

With such an array of accommodations onsite, you could be forgiven for thinking that things are a little cramped. But so vast is the site that each tent/yurt/pod sits in perfect seclusion. There are plenty of wonderfully quirky luxurious extras too, like the outdoor eco-spa with hot tub and sauna, or the Nordic barbecue cabin – if it can withstand a Scandinavian winter, a bit of North Yorks drizzle won't trouble your flame-grilled feast. And because Camp Kátur lies within the Camphill Estate, you have pick of some first-rate adventures, from water zorbing and segways to zip wires and quad-biking, plus a fully-licensed café/bar, making it a perfect venue for an action-packed hen or stag do.

Despite all the activities on offer and the little flourishes of luxury, this is still very much a 'Great Outdoors' experience, however, with 'back-to-nature' shower sheds, woodland walks and a communal campfire to wind down the day. The only astonishing thing is that Camp Kátur has only been operating since 2013. It's a welcoming, well-maintained site with a laid-back communal vibe that's summed up in the Camp Kátur mantra 'Discover Your Outdoor Happiness'. So, thanks to that big boss who gave Kerry her marching orders, you can now discover yours.

COOL FACTOR Iceland meets the Serengeti – in Yorkshire!

WHO'S IN Glampers, tent campers, dogs – yes. They also host weddings, stag and hen dos.

ON SITE 15 luxury accommodation options including Hobbit Pods, Safari Tents, yurts, bell tents, tipis and Unidomes including the UK's first 360 degree panoramic Unidome. Public toilets on the site and shower sheds in the glamping area. Communal kitchen hut with washing and cooking facilities. Woodland Eco Spa with wood-fired hot tub and sauna barrel. Children's toy shed, mini-library, board and garden games, plus a playground with shelter. Lots of onsite activities available including clay pigeon shooting, tree-top adventures and more. Café bar with live music and other events, and free Wi-Fi. No open fires allowed but there is a communal campfire area.

OFF SITE The ancient streets of Knaresborough are a good place to wander – it's one of the UK's prettiest towns and home to crumbling Knaresborough Castle (01423 556188) and the legendary Mother Shipton's Cave (01423 864600; mothershipton.co.uk). If you're visiting in June, be sure to attend the annual Great Knaresborough Bed Race (bedrace. co.uk) – a quirky local tradition that attracts thousands.

FOOD & DRINK On site, the Nordic BBQ cabin can seat up to 16 and comes equipped with all the utensils you need. The Orangery serves up decent breakfasts, burgers and salads. The award-winning Fox & Hounds Inn at Carthorpe (01845 567433; foxandhoundscarthorpe.co.uk) has been refreshing weary folk for centuries, as has the convivial Borough Bailiff (01423 862170), Knaresborough's oldest pub.

GETTING THERE Camp Hill Estate is just 5 minutes from the A1, in between the lovely Ripon and Bedale, and just 30 minutes from Harrogate.

PUBLIC TRANSPORT Nearest Train station is just 8 miles away in Thirsk.

OPEN Early April–mid November.

THE DAMAGE Hobbit pods from £35 per night; tipis and bells from £60; Unidome from £70; safari tents from £90. See website for full details.

masons campsite

Masons Campsite, Ainhams House, Appletreewick, Skipton, North Yorkshire BD23 6DD 01756 720275
www.masonscampsite.co.uk

In the heart of the Yorkshire Dales, by the banks of the Wharfe, down the road from two traditional pubs – Masons is so good that even the owners still camp here. When their favourite campsite in the Yorkshire Dales came up for sale, Georgie and Grant bought Masons and set about scrubbing up an already popular site.

You no longer have to walk a mile to the nearest shop, since their onsite airstream office-cum-shop sells goodies including fresh croissants, eggs and meat pre-ordered from the local butchers in Grassington. In the height of summer it's an unbeatable way to fill up your barbecue. There is lots of space to pitch in two camping fields; plus they have bell tents for rent as well as Airstream caravans. The wide and mainly shallow river runs at the bottom of the two camping fields. Try your hand at fly-fishing from the large, flat stones while the kids happily pass the time catching crayfish with a bucket and net.

The flat camping fields have plenty of space for kite-flying and ball games, and lots of families bring lilos and dinghies. Paddling and jumping in the river, crayfishing and tree climbing offer further activities, along with the onsite chickens and ducks, which are popular with younger children. Although the site has beautiful views of its own, Grant says that campers make straight for the steep hill over the road for an even better vista. Footpaths lead from the bottom of the site along the river to Burnsall, which is a popular picnicking and swimming spot, as well as to Appletreewick and Barden Bridge.

COOL FACTOR On the banks of a river, with views over the Dales, lots of space for games, and 2 great pubs nearby.

WHO'S IN Tents, campervans, caravans, dogs – yes.

ON SITE The main camping field caters for tents, campervans and tourers, with 40 hook-ups. In the second field, which is open most summer weekends, tents pitch up along the river bank, leaving plenty of space for ball games in the rest of the field. The washing-up room has 8 sinks. There are 10 showers (including one family/disabled room) and the toilet blocks each have 10 toilets and 10 hand basins. The campsite's well stocked onsite shop, housed in their vintage Airstream office, sells eggs, bread, croissants and camping equipment. 10 rent-a-tents of various sizes, VW van and Airstream hire also available.

OFF SITE The big attraction locally is Bolton Abbey (01756 432758; boltonabbey.com), with stepping stones over the river, walks, tea shops and the Embsay & Bolton Abbey Steam railway (01756 710614; embsayboltonabbeyrailway.org.uk).

FOOD & DRINK Both pubs in Appletreewick serve food and are family-friendly. The New Inn (01756 720252; the-new-inn-appletreewick.com) has a selection of quirky beers, while the 16th-century Craven Arms (01756 720270; craven-cruckbarn.co.uk) has log fires and gas lamps.

GETTING THERE From the A59 between Skipton and Harrogate, turn north on the B6160 at Bolton Abbey, signposted 'Grassington'. After about 3 miles take the first right after Barden Tower, signposted 'Appletreewick' and continue for around 2 miles to a T-junction. Then turn left into Appletreewick village and continue until you reach the site.

OPEN Mid March–end October.

THE DAMAGE A pitch starts at £20 including one car. Dogs £1 and must be kept under strict control. Bell tents and yurts from £69 a night, with a 2-night minimum stay; Airstream from £395 for weeks and £335 short breaks; Mon–Fri/Fri–Mon.

usha gap

Usha Gap Campsite, Muker, Richmond, North Yorkshire DL11 6DW 01748 886110 www.ushagap.co.uk

Ahhh, the Yorkshire Dales – 'God's Own Country', as any, dyed-in-the-wool Yorkshireman will tell you. For those of us not privileged enough to have visited this fabled corner of the country, such ardent civic pride can seem a little excessive. That is, until you get here and have laid eyes upon the acres of lush, undulating fields patchworked by miles of drystone walls, and gently flowing brooks. Only then will you see that they really do have a point.

Deep in the heart of this pastoral paradise lies the chocolate-box Swaledale village of Muker, home of Usha Gap. The Metcalfe family have been farming the land here for centuries and its 260 hectares host a prize herd of Swaledale sheep, Limousin Cross sucklers cattle... and some of the UK's luckiest campers.

For those seeking a traditional Dales camping experience, Usha Gap is pitch-up perfection. Philip, along with wife Louise and their two sons Ben and James, are hospitality personified. Facilities are basic, but then you haven't come here for an ayvuredic therapy tent and wood-fired saunas. In fact, you won't even get a phone signal. And as for Wi-Fi... forget it! But who needs the fripperies of modern media when you've got the tranquil River Swale flowing gently beside your tent?

For food and sustenance, there's a good pub in Muker Village, and on Friday evenings the famous Ramsey's mobile fish and chip van arrives in Muker just after 7.30pm. Also, no visit to the northern Dales would be complete without a visit to the Tan Hill Inn – Britain's highest inn, at 1,732ft above sea level, and just a short drive north.

The photo opportunity alone is worth the visit.

Overall, though, you don't need to go far to make the most of Usha Gap, which really is one of the most picturesque campsites in the country. This being the northernmost of Dales, the views are stunning; with the vista from Upper Swaledale, over bucolic hay meadows, 18th-century barns, and animals grazing lazily in the pastures below utterly idyllic. The site is also fantastically located some of northern England's greatest walks – the Pennine Way and the Coast-to-Coast being just the most well-known and most epic. For something a little more achievable (if vertical), the heather-scattered summit of Kisdon Hill offers wonderfully expansive views over Swinner Gill and the Buttertubs Pass. Enjoy the silence.

COOL FACTOR Simple, back-to-basics camping in the heart of God's Own Country.

WHO'S IN Tents, campervans, caravans, dogs – yes. Large groups by prior arrangement.

ON SITE Around 50 pitches (no electric hook-ups). New toilets and showers, drinking water tap plus a new washing-up area and a dryer. No open campfires or BBQs permitted. Fire pits (for a £10 returnable deposit) and logs for sale (£5 a bag). A bucket of kindling and newspaper is £1.

OFF SITE In case you haven't guessed from all the sheep, the region is renowned for its wool production. Swaledale Woollens (01748 886251; swaledalewoollens.co.uk) in Muker is your one-stop-shop for fleeces and sweaters. Over the hill in Hawes, the Wensleydale Creamery (01969 667664; wensleydale.co.uk) has a visitors centre and restaurant for all you cheese connoisseurs. For the littl'uns, the Forbidden Corner (01969 640638; theforbiddencorner.co.uk) in Middleham is an eccentric labyrinth of tunnels, follies, sculptures and secret gardens. Finally, in a region with no shortage of natural wonders, Aysgarth Falls and White Scar Caves take some beating.

FOOD & DRINK The Farmers Arms (01748 886 297; farmersarmsmuker.co.uk) in Muker is a cracking little pub, complete with stone-flagged floor, a roaring fireplace, and mammoth, filled Yorkshire puddings. The Muker Village Teashop and Stores (01748 886409; mukervillage.co.uk) is the best spot to go to for tea and scones. Further afield, the Kearton Country Hotel (01748 886277; keartoncountryhotel. co.uk) in Thwaite serves up imaginative cuisine and has a lovely beer garden.

GETTING THERE Follow the A684 form Sedbergh to the west and turn left in Hawes up Cliff Gate Road. The site is at the top.

OPEN All year.

THE DAMAGE Adult £8; child (under 15 yrs) £3; toddlers (under 5 yrs) free; car £3; motorbike £2.

low wray

Low Wray, nr Ambleside, Cumbria LA22 0JA 01539 432733 www.ntlakescampsites.org.uk

Low Wray sits on the quieter western shore of Lake Windermere, away from the fleshpots of Ambleside and Bowness and, if the weather holds, it can feel like the most relaxing place on earth. A night or two here, next to England's largest lake is, we think, simply unforgettable.

As you'd expect from a National Trust site, it's well organised with good facilities but not overly regimented. There are several camping areas, including a quiet patch in a clearing surrounded by trees, and – best of all – a spot right on the shore with sweeping views across the water. There's a surcharge for the lake-shore pitches (and a slightly longer walk from the car) but you'll go to sleep to twinkling stars and lights across the water and wake up with the promise of a bracing dip just steps from your tent. Glampers can also choose pods (book with the site) or yurts and tipis (outside providers), while children have the run of the woodland trails, an adventure playground and shallow lake-shore bays.

Aside from the great location next to the lake and the possibilities for sailing, kayaking and fishing, the campsite is well-positioned to take in some of the Lake District's 'dry' attractions. There are plenty of opportunities for walking and cycling, with paths leading directly from the campsite. This is also Beatrix Potter country, so a trip here wouldn't be complete without visiting either her home at Hill Top near Sawrey or the Beatrix Potter Gallery in Hawkshead, which exhibits her original paintings.

COOL FACTOR Unforgettable lakeside camping.

WHO'S IN Tents, small campervans, dogs, organised groups outside the main holidays – yes. Caravans, mobile homes – no.

ON SITE 130 tent pitches; 10 pods, 2 Berber tents and 9 campervan pitches (no hook-ups). Plentiful facilities in 3 blocks plus hot-water wash-up areas and laundry. Site shop, wood-fired pizza tent, kids' playground, bike rental, kayak hire. No campfires; off-ground BBQs okay. New camping pods (standard and family size now available).

OFF SITE A lakeshore path leads to Wray Castle (015394 33250; NT), which is great for families with a range of activities. Boats also go from there to the Lakes Visitor Centre at Brockhole (01539 446601; brockhole.co.uk), and the terrific Treetop Trek (01539 447186; treetoptrek.co.uk).

FOOD & DRINK The small campsite shop opens during reception hours and has all the basics, including fresh bread and pastries every morning. Off site, visit the foodie-fantastic world of Lucy's in Ambleside (01539 432288; lucysofambleside.co.uk) or the gastro heaven of the Drunken Duck (01539 436347; drunkenduckinn.co.uk) with its award-winning restaurant and ales.

GETTING THERE From Ambleside, take the A593 to Clappersgate then turn left on to the B5286. Turn left again at the sign for Wray. The site is less than a mile on the left.

PUBLIC TRANSPORT Bus no. #505 from Ambleside drops you at the Wray turn-off, a mile from the site.

OPEN Easter–October.

THE DAMAGE Pitch for 1 tent, 1 adult and 1 car from £8.50; extra adult £6; child £3; dog £1.50. Pods £40–£55. Campervans with one adult from £13.

great langdale

Great Langdale, Ambleside, Cumbria LA22 9JU 01539 432733 www.ntlakescampsites.org.uk

In this most spectacular of areas, where grand views lurk around every corner, it's possible to become blasé and complacent, to grow almost immune to the beauty of these great pyramids of rock and the vast, flat pools of water shimmering with the reflection of blue skies.

The perfect tonic for this complacency has to be an excursion into the serene valley of Great Langdale, where the attraction isn't lake-based, but a countryside dominated by two modest but distinctive peaks: the Langdale Pikes – Pike O'Stickle (709 metres) and its loftier neighbour Harrison Stickle (736 metres) – which are Lake District landmarks. Although by no means the tallest peaks in these parts, they're an attractive pair, joined at the shoulder almost like giant Siamese twins.

To get closer to the Pikes, leave the town of Ambleside to the west and, instead of following the traffic on the main road towards Coniston Water, take a right at Skelwith Bridge village to head straight down the Langdale Valley. There are noticeably fewer tourists in this valley as it isn't on the A-list of Lakeland destinations. Just as the twists and turns finish and the road looks as if it might taper off into a narrow footpath, you'll find Great Langdale Campsite – a glorious National Trust site set in a wooded glen at the head of the valley and consisting of several small, grassy camping areas around an undergrowth-shielded beck. Impressive peaks and slopes surround the site on all sides: you really feel like you're in the true heart of the Lake District here.

Great Langdale is a typical National Trust campsite: well-organised, efficiently run, with just the right level of facilities and set in some of England's finest scenery. Cars aren't allowed in the camping areas, but none of the pitches are far enough for that to be a problem. The wood-fronted shower blocks contain plenty of facilities in school-style rows of cubicles. There's also a drying room to stash rain-damp walking clothes and boots overnight – a very handy extra.

As you would expect, the walking from here is first-class. A map is available from reception outlining four easy walks around the valley, each between three and seven miles in length. But despite being tempted by these steady rambles, many visitors are keen to go for glory and conquer the Langdale Pikes themselves. The start and end point for the ascent is at the New Dungeon Ghyll pub off the main valley road, just a few minutes' walk from the campsite. It's named after Dungeon Ghyll, a deep cleft that dissects the pikes on the slopes above, creating a 100 foot waterfall and a protected area for alpine flowers to flourish. You'll pass it as you shin up the path on the nine-mile round-trip to the peaks.

It's also possible to walk to Scafell Pike from here and on to another *Cool Camping* site at Wasdale Head. Scafell may be the tallest and most brag-worthy peak to conquer in these fells, but the Langdales are just as rewarding. You also get two peaks for the price of one. Not a bad day's work, and definitely worth a pint or two later on at the Dungeon.

COOL FACTOR A truly tranquil treasure in the heart of some classic Lake District scenery.

WHO'S IN Tents, trailer-tents, campervans, organised groups, dogs – yes. Caravans, large parties – no.

ON SITE 175 tent pitches and 9 pods. 2 large shower-and-toilet blocks. Well-stocked shop; laundry facilities. Off-the-ground BBQs fine, but no campfires. Bread oven for freshly baked bread in the mornings.

OFF SITE Easy walks around the valley shown on a map available from reception, while many visitors conquer the Langdale Pikes – the starting-point for which is just a few minutes' walk from the campsite.

FOOD & DRINK There are three good pubs within 10 minutes' walk of the campsite. Our favourite is the Old Dungeon Ghyll (015394 37272; odg.co.uk), a legendary Lakeland pub famous for its hiker's bar, where a roaring fire and a fine selection of ales are perfect for weary walkers. They also do food. The slightly smarter Sticklebarn (01539 437356) is another excellent pick, owned and run by the National Trust with an aim to give something back to the surrounding countryside. A pint here is only contributing to the well-being of the lake district, or at least that's how you can justify your weekend beside the fire sipping some of their local brews on tap! The third pub is the New Dungeon Ghyll (015394 37213; dungeon-ghyll.co.uk), which also has a walker's bar and serves dinner from a fixed-price menu.

GETTING THERE Take the A593 from Ambleside. At Skelwith Bridge, turn right on to the B5343. The campsite is 6 miles down this road; look out for the sign on the left after the New Dungeon Ghyll Hotel.

PUBLIC TRANSPORT Take the train to Windermere, then the no. #599 bus to Ambleside, where you can pick up the Langdale Rambler. The no. #516 bus from Ambleside stops a 5-minute walk from the site.

OPEN All year.

THE DAMAGE Pitch for 1 tent, 1 adult, 1 one car from £8.50; extra adult £6; child £2.50–£3; dog £1.50. Pods £40–£57.50.

eskdale

Eskdale Camping and Caravanning Club Site, Boot, Holmrook, Cumbria CA19 1TH 01946 723253
www.campingandcaravanningclub.co.uk/eskdale

The Lake District is arguably the most beautiful corner of England. With a combination of picture-perfect villages, sensational lakes and glorious green valleys, this remarkable region is the perfect retreat for any camper. Wordsworth described it as 'The loveliest spot that man hath found', and it's hard to disagree with him, especially on a clear Cumbrian day.

Tucked away down a narrow country lane, Eskdale can be found in one of the Lake's more secluded pockets. Run by the ever-friendly Sara and Martyn, the eight acres of flat, well maintained grassland are backed by tall trees with a tranquil stream snaking past.

Upon arrival, you instantly realise that Eskdale's facilities have been created with hassle-free camping in mind. Pitch sizes are generous, facilities are well-maintained, and the fully-stocked shop is a life saver when you realise you've forgotten your toothbrush.

If you wish to get reacquainted with Mother Nature, then Eskdale's location couldn't be better. The site is ideally placed for reaching the impressive Wasdale fells or climbing England's highest mountain, Scafell Pike. Also on your doorstep is one of the most beautiful train lines in England, the Ravenglass and Eskdale Steam Railway, an historic, narrow-gauge railway that carries passengers along seven miles of spectacular scenery on an unforgettable 40-minute ride.

In short, Eskdale has a cosy, friendly atmosphere and is a genuinely lovely place to camp, with great facilities.

COOL FACTOR Away-from-it-all camping in one of England's most beautiful corners.

WHO'S IN Tents, trailer-tents, small motorhomes, campervans, groups (call before booking), and dogs – yes. Caravans – no.

ON SITE 100 grass pitches, 50 with electric hook-ups. 10 camping pods and a camping barn (sleeps up to 8). Shower/toilet block, laundry room, inside and outside dish-washing areas, pay phone, and drying room. Fully stocked shop selling local produce, camping equipment and essentials. Enclosed trampoline, swings, and a woodland adventure play area for the kids.

OFF SITE The Ravenglass and Eskdale Railway (01229 717171; ravenglass-railway.co.uk) is a wonderfully nostalgic way to take in the scenery. The small, scenic village of Boot is just a few minutes' walk away. Close by, you can visit one of few remaining 2-wheel water mills at the Eskdale Mill (01946 723335; eskdalemill.co.uk), while the secluded Japanese Garden at Eskdale Green is one of the shining jewels in Cumbria's horticultural crown.

FOOD & DRINK The Woolpack Inn (01946 723230; woolpack. co.uk) is a traditional Cumbrian pub with a sleek new eatery serving gourmet pizzas. The family-run Brook House Inn (01946 723288; brookhouseinn.co.uk) was once voted West Cumbria's pub of the year, and serves fine British food and a wide range of local ales.

GETTING THERE Exit the M6 at junction 36 and follow signs to Lakes/Windermere, then the A590, A5092 and A595 towards Boot.

OPEN Late February 2015 to 13th January 2016.

THE DAMAGE Touring pitches £7.70–£11.30 per person/per night (children half price). Camping pods £43.75 per pod/per night. Camping barn (sleeps 8) £135 per night.

fisherground campsite

Fisherground Campsite, Fellside Cottage, Eskdale, Holmrook, Cumbria CA19 1TF 01946 723349
www.fishergroundcampsite.co.uk

This is a great site for kids. It ticks all their campsite boxes and probably a few more besides. Campfires are not only allowed, but positively encouraged in selected areas, with bags of logs complete with kindling and firelighters sold on site each evening. Owner Mick takes a 'we like you to succeed' approach – just don't forget to pack the marshmallows. The first thing that meets you on arrival is the pond, fed by a stream and usually full of children playing on tyre rafts. There's also a playground that has everything your young outwardbounder could desire in the way of zip wires, climbing frames, tyre-ropeswings and adventure courses, as well as plenty of rocks and trees for climbing and plenty of space for ball games. And there's an added bonus that the site sits along the route of the Ravenglass and Eskdale steam railway line – a fab way to arrive if you're coming by public transport. So if you've walked into the nearby hamlet of Boot and there are some tired little legs as a result, hop on board for a scenic trip back to camp. For the adults, the site is in the heart of the Eskdale valley, a quieter part of the Lake District, far from its hustle and bustle. Rugged, bracken-clad fells, woods and grazing sheep provide a splendid backdrop to rest your eyes on when you do eventually find time to relax.

COOL FACTOR A children's paradise with scenery for the adults. And no tourers.

WHO'S IN Tents, campervans, D of E and school groups, dogs - yes. Caravans, single-sex groups – no.

ON SITE Unmarked pitches in 2 main areas: a larger field nearest to the children's playground, and a smaller, quieter field, with wheel rims for campfires. The recently refurbished toilet block has ample hand basins, showers and loos; all clean and well-kept. There is a washing machine, 3 tumble dryers, a boot-dryer and freezer. No shop on site, but you can buy logs, kindling and firelighters. Noise after 10.30pm is not allowed.

OFF SITE Go by steam train to Ravenglass, or make the short trip to Dalegarth. From here you can walk into Boot or up to Stanley Force, following the tumbling beck up to the waterfall. A short walk towards Eskdale Green takes you along the River Esk, where a shallow area by the bridge is a good spot for a quick, if chilly, dip. There are hundreds of good walks near to the site, or bring your bike along.

FOOD AND DRINK Try The Boot Inn (01946 723711), The Brook House (01946 723288) or The Bower House (01946 723244) in Eskdale – good value food and drink in all.

GETTING THERE Beware of using Sat-Nav if you want to avoid taking the white-knuckle ride over Hardknott and Wrynose Passes. From the south, leave the M6 at junction 36 and follow signs for Barrow then, 3 miles past Newby Bridge, turn right towards Workington on the A5092. Keep on this road for around 10 miles; beyond Broughton-in-Furness, turn right towards Ulpha. Turn left in Ulpha village to Eskdale and follow the fell road to the King George IV pub, then right to Boot. The campsite is 300m further on the left.

OPEN Early March–late October.

THE DAMAGE Adults £6.50; children £3.50; vehicles £2.50 and dogs £1.50 per night. Surcharge of £6 per night for 6-berth+ tents and £3 per night for 3-berth+ – only during school hols.

ravenglass

Ravenglass Camping and Caravanning Club, Ravenglass, Cumbria CA18 1SR 01229 717250
www.campingandcaravanningclub.co.uk/ravenglass

Within a mere 30 miles, 16 beautiful lakes are squeezed between England's tallest mountains. The landscape of tranquil water, impressive valleys and charming stone-built villages gives the area an almost alpine air. Welcome to the The Lake District – Britain's most hyped scenic area, but with good reason.

Set on the outskirts of Ravenglass, a pretty Roman fishing village on the Lake District's west coast, this Camping and Caravanning Club site combines modern facilities with old-school camping principles. The world's oldest camping club have taken care in creating a site, so that the facilities – a modern shower block and a well-stocked shop – don't come at the expense of its natural surroundings. And what surroundings! With six acres of mature woodland lying just 500 metres from the dramatic Cumbrian coast, this unique destination is a walker's paradise.

And who's welcome? Well, everyone really. Ravenglass accommodates up to 75 caravans, motorhomes, and canvas campers like us. In fact traditional tenters shouldn't be put off by the number of hulking caravans allowed; the camping area is found in a peaceful, tree-lined section of the site. Also located in another wooded area are three new camping pods. These cosy alternatives are made from locally-sourced timber and insulated with wool, providing warmth and shelter – perfect for those seeking a little extra comfort.

Given a few days you could easily see most of the Lake District's most popular sights from here. But it's right on your doorstep (and away from the crowds) that the Lakes really shine. The breathtaking valleys of Eskdale and Langdale are sure to delight, and the village of Ravenglass itself is the access point for the excellent Ravenglass and Eskdale Railway.

COOL FACTOR 6 acres of woodlands and only 500m from the sea.

WHO'S IN Tents, caravans, motorhomes, kids and dogs – yes. Large groups – no.

ON SITE 75 spaces for tents, caravans, motorhomes and trailer tents, 56 of which are hardstanding with electric hook-ups. 3 camping pods for hire. Showers, family shower room, flushing toilets, washbasins and electric shaver sockets. Dedicated accessible facilities, chemical toilet disposal point, dish-washing facilities and shop. Payphone, drinking water taps, washing machines, ice-pack freezing, gas cylinders and Wi-Fi.

OFF SITE The site sits on the edge of the picturesque village of Ravenglass and just a short stroll from the sea. Ravenglass is the only coastal village in the Lake District National Park, and stands at the meeting point of three rivers flowing from the Lakeland's most majestic fells. The Hadrian's Cycle Way starts here and the Cumbria Coastal Way passes right by the site. You can take a trip on the Ravenglass and Eskdale Railway through the stunning Eskdale Valley. Or just try a circuit of the prime sights of the Lakes, taking in Windermere, Ambleside and Bowness and Wordsworth's Dove Cottage in Grasmere.

FOOD & DRINK The licensed onsite shop sells local produce and ales. There are 3 pubs in Ravenglass, all within walking distance), they include the family-run Ratty Arms (01229 717676), which does wide selection of pub grub and hosts a weekly quiz and frequent music events.

GETTING THERE From the south, leave the M6 at South Lakes turn-off. At the roundabout take the first exit to Barrow on to the A590 for 20 miles. Turn right at the A5092 to Whitehaven and Workington for 30 miles (this road becomes the A595). Turn left towards Ravenglass and the site is well signposted to the left. From the north, leave the M6 at junction 40. Follow the A66 west to Workington for 34 miles. Take the A595 to Whitehaven and drive past Whitehaven, Egremont and Gosforth for 25 miles. Turn right towards Ravenglass and the site is on the left.

PUBLIC TRANSPORT Nearest bus stop: 500m from site entrance. Nearest train station: Ravenglass, 500m.

OPEN February–November. Plus open during the Christmas/New Year's holiday.

THE DAMAGE £7.70–£11.30 per person per night. Camping pods £43.75.

wasdale head

Wasdale Head, Seascale, Cumbria CA20 1EX 01539 432733 www.ntlakescampsites.org.uk

England's highest mountains may not be on the scale of the Alps, the Andes or the Himalayas, but they are impressive in their own understated way. They also have the advantage of being readily accessible, and in most seasons they can be conquered relatively easily with the help of a pair of decent walking boots, favourable weather and a thermos of hot tea.

Several of the country's highest mountains are clustered around the northern end of Wastwater in the Lake District, where the National Trust has thoughtfully sited a campsite at Wasdale Head. From here, you can lie in a sleeping bag, head poking out of your tent and, as the dawn mist clears, you're able to survey the surrounding slopes and plan your ascent on these high fells. Alternatively, you may want to reach for the camping stove and kettle, stay snug in your sleeping bag and enjoy this most vertical of views from where you are. Most visitors, however, come here to get a bit closer and Wasdale Head is a handy base for Scafell Pike, being the start of one of the shorter but steeper ascents on the rock-strewn summit.

Back at base camp, there's a small shop for walking maps, friendly advice and blister-shaped plasters. Aside from the shop and the tidy, wooden shower block, facilities are not over-extravagant. Three small fields scattered with mature and planted trees provide plenty of flat grass for pitching and, with cars restricted to the designated parking areas, it's a peaceful site. Definitely a high point on England's campsite circuit.

COOL FACTOR Top wilderness location for hiking and climbing; great views of the high fells.

WHO'S IN Tents, campervans, dogs (on leads at all times) – yes. Caravans, groups – no.

ON SITE 120 tent pitches (4 with hook-ups), 8 campervan pitches with hook-ups; 7 pods with electric heaters and lighting, and 2 tipis with electric and wood-burning stoves There is a timed barrier system for arrivals (8–11am; 5–8pm), though with an advance reservation you can get in any time between 8am and 9pm. Hot showers, flushing toilets, disabled facilities, washing machines and dryers are all available and a small shop sells food and camping essentials. No campfires, no disposable BBQs.

OFF SITE Treat yourself to some tea-room goodies or just a bag of flour at Muncaster Watermill (01229 717232), a traditional village mill that's been in operation since 1455. Visit the Roman port of Ravenglass, the only coastal town within the Lake District, or take a chance at nearby haunted Muncaster Castle (01229 717614; muncaster.co.uk).

FOOD & DRINK The Wasdale Head Inn (01946 726229; wasdale.com) is the hikers' and climbers' favourite and is reputedly home to the biggest liar in the world (take that with a pinch of salt). They also serve hearty, wholesome food for under a tenner. Otherwise it's the Strands Inn (01946 726237; thestrandsinn.com), 5 miles back down the road to Gosforth.

GETTING THERE Approaching from the south on the main A595, turn right at Holmrook for Santon Bridge and follow the signs up to Wasdale Head. Approaching from the north, turn left at Gosforth.

OPEN All year.

THE DAMAGE Pitch for 1 tent and 1 adult, 1 one car from £8.50; extra adult £6; child £3; dog £1.50. Electric hook-ups £5. Pods £40–£55.

lanefoot farm

Lanefoot Farm, Thornthwaite, Keswick, Cumbria CA12 5RZ 01768 778097 www.stayinthornthwaite.co.uk

There's a pitch to suit all tastes at Lanefoot Farm. Love views? Park yourself in the big open field with a stonking vista of Skiddaw. Taking the kids? Head for the cosy family field. Seen the weather forecast and fancy a bit of shelter? Pop into the back garden of the farmhouse and find yourself a quiet spot among the wild flowers and trees.

There's been a campsite in this little corner near Keswick since the 1960s but it had rather fallen into decline when wonderfully amiable owners Gareth and Helen took it over a few years ago and injected it with new life (and some free-range chickens).

The facilities (which are constantly being upgraded) are the sort you'd be happy to eat your dinner off; there's a little shop on site, chickens roaming free, and a friendly chatty atmosphere. Cyclists are well catered for – the site is bang on the C2C route and there are mountain-bike trails aplenty in the nearby Whinlatter Forest. And if you've turned up to discover you've forgotten to pack your tent (we've all done it!) there's a shepherd's hut for hire (replete with four mattresses), as well as a couple of tree-shaded pods. Finally, pub quiz devotees will be excited to learn that nearby Bassenthwaite Lake is home to the vendace, Britain's rarest fish. Next question please, landlord!

COOL FACTOR Brilliant views and wet-weather accommodation, too.

WHO'S IN Tents, campervans, caravans, dogs (on leads), family groups, young groups (activities) – yes.

ON SITE Grass pitches for tents and hardstanding pitches with electric hook-ups for campervans and caravans. Shepherd's hut and pods also available. Campfires allowed. Good clean loos (3 female, 3 male) and 3 bright showers, washing-up area, drying room. Tiny shop sells basics and meats. There is some traffic noise.

OFF SITE Walks include popular local routes up Grizedale Pike and Skiddaw, while there's mountain-bike rental and world-class trails at Whinlatter Forest (01768 778469; forestry.gov.uk/whinlatter).

FOOD & DRINK Try a mini pub/hotel crawl in Braithwaite village, taking in the venerable Royal Oak (01768 778533; royaloak-braithwaite.co.uk), the traditional Coledale Inn (01768 778272; coledale-inn.co.uk), and the relaxed Middle Ruddings (01768 778436; middle-ruddings.co.uk). All of them do food. There's also the General Store (01768 778157; braithwaitegeneralstore.co.uk) for basics, organics, and local beers. If you scrub up nicely enough, there's classy dining not far from the site at the Pheasant Inn, Bassenthwaite (01768 776234; the-pheasant.co.uk).

GETTING THERE From Keswick take the A66 west. Take a left turn north ½ mile after the B5292 turning for Braithwaite. Lanefoot Farm is on the left, after ½ mile.

PUBLIC TRANSPORT Take the train to Penrith then bus no. #X5 to just beyond Thornthwaite, from where it's a couple of minutes' walk to the site.

OPEN March–December (except Christmas week).

THE DAMAGE Adults £8–£9.50 per night; child £4. Shepherd's hut and pods £37–£48 per night.

sykeside camping park

Sykeside Camping Park, Brotherswater, Patterdale, Cumbria CA11 0NZ 01768 482239 www.sykeside.co.uk

Sykeside is one of those campsites that are all about the views. Situated in the midst and mists of the Lake District's Dovedale valley and surrounded by the fells of Dove Crag, Hart Crag and Fairfield, it offers glorious mountain panoramas wherever you decide to pitch. Not only that; the Lakes themselves are enticingly close by, with unsung Brothers Water a short walk and serpentine Ullswater four miles further down the road.

Innumerable campers have been enjoying Sykeside's friendly embrace for over 35 years now. The current owners have been running the place for more than a decade and know a thing or two about how to make things run efficiently. The valley campsite is hidden away down a private drive below the roadside Brotherswater Inn and is fastidiously cared for, with neatly trimmed and well-nourished grass. If it sounds too manicured, one look up at the encircling fells puts everything into perspective. There's still a reassuringly natural, outdoorsy vibe and, as tent pitches are unmarked, campers can choose their very own patch of grass on which to throw up their canvas when they arrive.

The best place to pitch is on the terrace on the left-hand side of the site. As it's higher up it gives better views and stays relatively dry all year round (it's the only part of the site that is open to tents in the winter months), and as you can't take cars up the bank it's often quieter there in summer. Otherwise, you'll be able to park where you pitch – though after heavy rain they prefer to keep cars off the grass.

There's a wider-than-usual range of facilities, though the showers are shared with walkers, small groups and families using the onsite bunkhouse. There's a well-stocked shop at reception and – best of all – the campsite's very own Barn End Bar (weekends and school holidays only). When the bar's not open you only have to walk up the drive to the Brotherswater Inn, a quintessential Lake District pub that offers decent grub, draught beer and B&B accommodation for non-tenters. Energetic kids get the use of an entire spare field (except during lambing season), allowing plenty of space for running around and football games.

There are excellent hiking routes starting straight from the site, from easy strolls around Brotherswater – which is a relatively small and unknown lake, yet a favourite of Dorothy Wordsworth, no less – to more challenging ascents up the likes of Fairfield, Helvellyn and High Street. It's also easy to pick up the Fairfield Horseshoe ridge walk, ramble to Priest's Hole cave or amble all the way to Ambleside. The road outside the site, meanwhile, goes in two directions – three miles up to the top of Kirkstone Pass (where you can enjoy a pint or afternoon tea at the agreeable inn there), or three miles down to the lake at Ullswater. Here you can catch a steamer to Howtown or Pooley Bridge and then stroll back along the lakeshore – secure in the knowledge that, on weekends at least, you can recuperate later with your very own 100-yard pub crawl, from the Barn End Bar to the Brotherswater Inn.

COOL FACTOR Panoramic mountain views and great hiking right in the middle of the Lakes.

WHO'S IN Tents, campervans, caravans, motorhomes and dogs – yes. Groups of more than 6 adults (D of E excepted) – no.

ON SITE Space for 80 tents, 19 motorhomes (with hook-ups) and 5 caravans (on a separate site). Toilets (6 women's, 4 men's) and showers (5 women's, 6 men's) are clean and heated but shared with the bunkhouse. There's also a laundry room, dish-washing area (with freezer for ice packs) a shop selling groceries and camping gear, the Barn End Bar on summer weekends and the Brotherswater Inn all year. Off-ground BBQs allowed, but no campfires.

OFF SITE Boat trips with Ullswater Steamers (01768 482229; ullswater-steamers.co.uk) from Glenridding run year-round. It's a 16-mile, 30-minute drive to the magnificent Lowther Castle and Gardens (01931 712192; lowthercastle.org), just south of the enjoyable market town of Penrith.

FOOD & DRINK The Brotherswater Inn serves generous portions of pub grub. Otherwise, the best place is Ambleside, 7 miles away, where the excellent Zefirellis (01539 433845; zeffirellis.com) is an Italian veggie pizza/pasta place with its own cinema and jazz bar. Just outside Penrith, the Gate Inn at Yanwath (01768 862386; yanwathgate.co.uk) is a renowned gastropub serving tasty food.

GETTING THERE From Windermere, take the A592 towards the Kirkstone Pass and Ullswater. Head over the pass and down the other side and you'll see the Brotherswater Inn on the left. Coming from the north on the A66, take the A592 towards Windermere and the Kirkstone Pass; pass Ullswater, drive through Glenridding, and the entrance to the campsite is about 2 miles beyond Patterdale.

PUBLIC TRANSPORT Trains run to Windermere (12 miles away), from where the Kirkstone Rambler bus no. #508 runs right past the campsite (at weekends from Easter until October, every day during the school summer holidays).

OPEN All year except Christmas Day.

THE DAMAGE Tent + 2 people and a car £13.50–£23.50 per night; campervan (including 2 adults) £17.50–£25 per night; bunkhouse from £14.50 per bed.

side farm

Side Farm Campsite, Patterdale, Penrith, Cumbria CA11 0NP 01768 482337 www.patterdale.org

Side Farm, on the eastern side of the Lake District, might just be one of the most scenically situated campsites on the planet, sandwiched as it is between the steep slopes of Place Fell to the rear and the sylvan shores of Ullswater at the front. The view across the lake to the Helvellyn Fells is one of the most compelling and beautiful sights in England and to be able to simply open the tent every morning on to this stunning scene is reason enough to stay.

For many, just to sit by the tent with a good book, soaking up the magnificence of the scenery, may be sufficient. Others arrive with canoes, spending their time paddling the length and breadth of Ullswater, the second largest and most enchanting of the region's lakes. The lake has a rigidly enforced 10-mph speed limit, making this a very safe environment well suited to more sedate waterborne craft.

But if the boating opportunities are superb – and they are – the amazing variety of places to explore on foot from Side Farm is nothing short of astounding. The site lies immediately next to the lakeside path from Howtown to Patterdale, described by Wainwright, the legendary fell walker and guidebook writer, as 'the most beautiful and rewarding in Lakeland'. This is probably the first place to direct your energies, and the most interesting way of completing the walk is said to be by boarding one of the old Ullswater steamers at Glenridding, sailing to Howtown, then strolling back to the site. Undoubtedly a great day out, the sailing out and walking back makes quite an appealing kind of expedition. Unfortunately, at weekends or in high summer, most of humanity seems to find the idea just as enticing. We may be exaggerating a little bit, but if you like wild and beautiful places to yourself then choose your time or season carefully.

In the end, however, after staring at the rocky giants across the lake for a few days, the mind will inevitably start to wander up the slopes of Helvellyn – quickly followed by the feet. There are several excellent routes up this most famous of fells from the campsite (enough to keep you busy for a full week on this monster alone), but the one that everybody should do at least once is the dance across the top of Striding Edge. Yes it's popular, and yes it can get scary when the wind is howling around the rocky crest, and yes the weather can change from summer to winter in an instant. But this walk is one of the most attention-grabbing and exhilarating in the whole of England.

As for the site itself, it has flat pitching and adequate facilities including toilets and showers. But luxurious they are not, and they can also be somewhat overwhelmed when the site is full. Nonetheless, with a pair of walking boots, and a canoe, the idyllic location will more than compensate for any minor niggles.

COOL FACTOR Perhaps the most scenically placed campsite in England, with an unbeatable selection of walks.

WHO'S IN Tents, campervans, small motorhomes, dogs – yes. Caravans, large groups (unless pre-arranged) – no.

ON SITE Roughly 70 pitches spread out across the lakeside grass. 1 toilet block, with separate women's/men's, and a shower block, plus a washing-up area, 2 washing machines and 2 dryers. You can get a cuppa and a cake at the onsite tearoom. BBQs allowed off the ground. No campfires. Quiet times 10:30pm–7am.

OFF SITE Lake cruises on Ullswater with Ullswater Steamers (01768 482229; ullswater-steamers.co.uk); the nearest pier is a mile or so up the road at Glenridding. Ullswater itself is ringed with attractions, from Aira Force waterfall (01768 482067; NT) to the stately mansion and gardens at Dalemain (01768 486450; dalemain.com). There is also bike and boat rental nearby at St Patrick's Boat Landings (01768 482393; stpatricksboatlandings.co.uk).

FOOD & DRINK If proper pub grub is what you're after then try the Travellers Rest pub (01768 482298) in Glenridding. The nearest pub to the farm (a 15-minute walk) is Patterdale's White Lion (01768 482214; the-whitelion. com), a straightforward hikers' pub. For something a bit more posh, try the Lake View restaurant at the Inn on the Lake hotel (01768 482444; lakedistricthotels.net/ innonthelake).

GETTING THERE From Junction 40 of the M6 take the A66 west, then the A592 along the shore of Ullswater through Glenridding. Directions to the farm appear along the lane off the lay-by between the school and the church in Patterdale.

PUBLIC TRANSPORT From Penrith train station you can catch the bus to Patterdale and then it's a short walk.

OPEN March–October.

THE DAMAGE Adult £8; child £4; car £3; no credit cards.

the quiet site

The Quiet Site, Ullswater, Cumbria CA11 0LS 07768 727016 www.thequietsite.co.uk

Despite its unusual name, the reality is that the Quiet Site isn't much quieter than your average campsite. But the name is enough to put off any rowdies or big groups, so it's certainly more peaceful than many of the more boisterous Lake District options.

Standing atop the fells of what many hold as the Lakes' finest stretch of water, the Quiet Site looks down to Ullswater's mist-shrouded surface. Up here, it's a peaceful escape from the hustle and bustle of Glenridding town; a sanctuary of calm from the Lakeland summer crowds.

The site is ideal for accessing the peace of some of the Lake District's best footpaths, with several passing close by. On arrival you'll get a handcrafted walking guide, with decent walks around the area popped into your hand. They've tailored the walks to all sorts of people and interests, so you should find one that suits you – whether it's a full-on lung workout up the fells or just an easy-going amble with the kids. And if you've had your fill of bi-ped pursuits, go amphibious to get a watery perspective of Ullswater, either from the famous Ullswater Steamer or from a rowing boat or motorboat, both easily hired at Watermillock or Glenridding marina.

Come the end of the day, you don't even have to make any effort to lay your hands on a well-earned pint. The Quiet Site has its own public house, simply named 'The Quiet Bar'. Housed in the farm's original stone barn, a roaring open hearth greets you along with the über-friendly hosts and a raft of local ales. Unfortunately, if you're looking to escape campsite cooking you'll be disappointed: they don't do food.

While the Quiet Site aims to please everyone, there's a huge family focus with a massive adventure playground and playrooms in The Quiet Bar that could even bring out the kid in the grown-up within your group. Up here you escape the ambient light pollution from the surrounding towns at night. You'll gaze skywards in awe at the dazzling Milky-Way-strewn skies – clouds permitting. But being so far from civilisation can have its drawbacks, too; you can get cabin fever.

If you're looking for some serenity, great walking or just want to kick back with the family, the Quiet Site delivers. With this place having a hardcore following and attracting more by the year, just try to keep it all a little hush-hush.

COOL FACTOR Starry nights under the Milky Way and quiet days away from everything.

WHO'S IN Tents, caravans, campervans, small motorhomes, dogs – yes. Large groups (unless pre-arranged) – no.

ON SITE There's an onsite pub, free hot showers, washing-up area and small shop with all the basics. There are bell tents, camping pods and underground hobbit holes also for rent. The Quiet Site is committed to sustainable tourism and all hot water and heating in the bar, shop, office, cottages and service block is sourced from renewables.

OFF SITE Catch the Ullswater Steamer from Glenridding to Pooley Bridge (see p.217) via Howton, or just enjoy the cruise around the lake. You can get off at either place and walk back if your legs are up to it, though the full round-lake cruise is a beauty, with the 3,000-ft peak of Helvellyn rising above the serene waters. History bods may want to explore nearby Dalemain House (see p.217).

FOOD & DRINK Treat yourself among 67 acres of Windermere's woodland at The Samling (01539 431922; thesamlinghotel.co.uk). Similarly, on the shores of Lake Ullswater, the Sharrow Bay Hotel (01768 486301; sharrowbay. co.uk) has a Michelin-starred restaurant. You can do lunch or dinner but they're famous for afternoon teas. The onsite pub serves a variety of local ales but no food, and if you're after a more workaday dinner then head to the Brackenrigg Inn (01768 486206; brackenrigginn.co.uk) overlooking Ullswater for some above-average pub grub.

GETTING THERE On the A66 to Keswick, take the A592 towards Glenridding, turning right at the Brackenrigg Inn. The site is 1¼ miles further on your right.

PUBLIC TRANSPORT Train to Penrith then a 106 bus towards Glenridding. Get off outside the Brackenrigg Inn and follow the lane that runs beside the inn; the site is 1¼ miles further along on your right.

OPEN March–mid January.

THE DAMAGE Flat pitches £15–£30 per night. Prices include 1 tent, 1 car and 2 adults. Children over 12 £5 per night and under-12s go free. Dogs are £12 a night.

herding hill farm

Herding Hill Farm, Shield Hill, Haltwhistle, Northumberland NE49 9NW 01434 320175 www.herdinghillfarm.co.uk

The blood-curdling cries of Celtic barbarians once echoed across this campsite, reverberating off Hadrian's 20-ft high wall. Roman centurions in red bristled helmets would trudge past today's petting farm, the glamping wigwams and luxury tipis up to their lookout post on the edge of the mighty Empire. They'd never know the luxury of Herding Hill Farm's eight-person sauna – not least because the 'no loud groups' policy means they'd never get in.

In fact, despite its most historic of locations, this campsite is far from ancient and, while well-equipped and soundly run, it started out as just 20 grass pitches in 2012 before flourishing to its current size. Friendly owners, Anne and Steve had always loved camping in Northumberland and exploring the Kielder Forest National Park. So when they stumbled across this 55-acre farm, a stone's throw from Hadrian's Wall, they couldn't help but take on the challenge. Word got around, people kept coming and the family gradually built ever more features and facilities to accommodate their growing number of guests.

The resulting campsite is a well-located, family-friendly mix of traditional camping with extra luxury options. At the far end is a grassy two-acre field without electric hook-ups for those who want a basic pitch and the best views. While, at the bottom of this plot, you'll also find the Tentipi village – four pre-pitched Nordic tipis complete inside with a wood-burning stove. Stepping closer to the amenities block, you'll find further luxury options – eight wooden wigwams

with comfy futon-style beds, fridge, microwave, heaters and tea-making facilities. In a range of different sizes, the wigwams offer a hideaway for small families or couples. Those wanting to really indulge can have their very own bubbling private hot tub next door. The rest of the site is a combination of hardstandings and open grassland, with all pitches a short walk from the amenities block – an immaculate facility with underfloor heating, disabled access and – yes we weren't telling porkies – an eight-person sauna that can be booked out for private use.

When you drag the kids from the fort playground and venture beyond the campsite, there's a plethora of attractions close at hand. Voted England's favourite market town by *Country Life Magazine*, Hexham is a short drive away, with its famous abbey at its centre. However, nothing really matches a clamber up to Hadrian's Wall with the magnificent Roman fort of Housesteads nearby.

Whether it's this rich history that draws you in, or the mountain biking on offer around Europe's largest man-made lake in Kielder Forest, or simply meeting the alpacas and animals that live at Herding Hill Farm, this campsite is difficult to match for location. It's a paradise for those who love the outdoors, with the glories of the national park on your doorstep and history in the form of Hadrian's Wall. And at the end of it all you can slope back to the campsite, grab a cold beer from the take-away bar and simply relax. You're on holiday, after all; it would be rude not to.

COOL FACTOR A family-run campsite in prime location, with the best parts of Hadrian's Wall and the Kielder Forest National Park just around the corner.

WHO'S IN Almost everyone! Tents, campervans, caravans, and glampers. Backpackers, families and small groups, plus all dogs welcome. No large groups.

ON SITE 60 tent pitches, 11 hardstandings, 8 wooden wigwams, 4 tipis, a 28-bed bunkhouse and a luxury holiday lodge. The reception is also the site of a small fully-licensed bar and a shop selling camping essentials. There's an amenities block with hot showers, toilets, sinks, plug sockets and underfloor heating, as well as an 8-person sauna. A disabled/family room is also attached with both a bath and shower. There's a drying room, laundry room and outdoor sinks for washing-up. Wigwams are fully equipped; 3 are en suites with a private outdoor hot tub. Tipis can sleep up to 4 people and are fitted with a wooden floor. You need to bring your own beds, bedding and other essentials. The bunkhouse sleeps 28 in 4 rooms with a lounge with wood-burning stove and fully equipped kitchen.

OFF SITE North of the campsite lies Kielder Forest (visitkielder.com) a huge expanse ideal for walking, cycling and water sports. Hadrian's Wall, is less than a mile from the campsite and is best experienced at Housesteads Roman Fort (01434 344363; EH).

FOOD & DRINK Licensed bar on site, serving takeaway food and home-made pizzas, plus a small shop which makes freshly baked French sticks and crusty bread rolls (seasonal opening hours). The Black Bull (01434 320463) is a decent dog-friendly village pub or try The Mile Castle Inn (01434 321372; milecastle-inn.co.uk), ½ mile away.

GETTING THERE Take the A69 to Haltwhistle and look out for the brown Herding Hill Campsite tourist signs.

PUBLIC TRANSPORT The AD122 bus runs between Newcastle and Carlisle and stops right at the campsite.

OPEN All year (except 2 weeks in early January).

THE DAMAGE Tents: £20–£24. Caravans: £24–£28. Wigwams £38–£48. Tipis £45–£55. Prices are per tent per night and include 2 people and 1 vehicle.

hadrian's wall caravan campsite

Hadrian's Wall Caravan Site, Melkridge Tilery, Nr Haltwhistle, Northumberland NE49 9PG 01434 320495
www.hadrianswallcampsite.co.uk

The 82 miles of Emperor Hadrian's monumental, Pict-proof stone wall is Northumberland's most famous landmark. Though its military barracks are in ruins, the historical structures remain impressively atmospheric. It's easy to imagine how the soldiers must have felt, keeping watch at the very outpost of the civilised world. By day scanning a horizon of rolling hummocks and wind-blown heathland, by night using the light of the moon in a sky that, to this day, remains one of the darkest spots in Europe. The wall is now a World Heritage Site, but you can still camp just a mile or so from one of the most complete and dramatic sections at Hadrian's Wall Campsite.

The site is terraced on four levels, each commanding amazing views over open countryside and to the wall itself. In the summer months, an extra 'wild camping' field is opened up, with oodles of space for large families and campfires by arrangement. Weary backpackers can also rejoice: there's a strip dedicated entirely to your aching bones – no need to book, just stagger up on the day – with a handy cookhouse to help speed the post-walk meal along. The campsite is well located for rambles along Hadrian's Wall Path, an 84-mile National Trail shadowing the line of the wall. The site-owners will even arrange transport to or from your start/finish points, leaving you free to enjoy your linear walk and the wall. Just keep an eye out for those Picts.

COOL FACTOR Less than a mile away from Hadrian's Wall.

WHO'S IN Tents, campervans, motorhomes, caravans, dogs, groups – yes.

ON SITE Terraced pitches; 7 hot showers, hairdryers, toilets, laundry (washing machine/tumble dryer), fridge-freezer and hook-ups. Basic groceries sold at reception. Bunk barn sleeping 10. Disposable BBQs and campfires permitted in the wild camping area by arrangement. Order the night before for a full English breakfast.

OFF SITE The site is right on the Hadrian's Wall Path (nationaltrail.co.uk/hadrians-wall-path). Housesteads Roman Fort and Museum (see p.221) is just down the road, as is the Vindolanda Roman Army museum (01434 344277; vindolanda.com).

FOOD & DRINK A small café/shop sells groceries and serves food including breakfast. Pizza can be delivered to your pitch; evening meals and packlunches can be arranged. Haltwhistle is also a short distance away and has plenty of shops and cafés. The Milecastle Inn (01434 321372; milecastle-inn.co.uk), a mile to the west, serves great food and has a beer garden, an open fire and a resident ghost.

GETTING THERE From the B6318 Military Road, take the turning to Melkridge. The site is 300m further on the left. From the A69, 1 mile east of Haltwhistle, there's a staggered crossroads at Melkridge village. Take the turning opposite the village and continue for 2 miles.

PUBLIC TRANSPORT The campsite owners can collect you from Haltwhistle train station or from nearby bus stops.

OPEN All year.

THE DAMAGE Backpackers from £10. Tent and car £10–£15. Campervan from £12. Motorhome and caravan from £15. Electric £3.

walkmill campsite

Walkmill Campsite, Near Guyzance, Warkworth, Northumberland NE65 9AJ 01665 710155 www.walkmillcampsite.co.uk

There's no denying Walkmill is a bit special. If ever a campsite fitted the *Cool Camping* criteria, then surely this hidden pocket of Northumberland is it. So how did we come to this conclusion? A good question, and it involves plenty of unquantifiable notional nonsense like 'atmosphere' and 'vibe'. Then there's the all-important location, and this is perhaps the most important box to be ticked. Thankfully Walkmill is set in 10 acres of beautiful countryside, surrounded by idyllic woodlands and the weaving River Coquet, where canvas companions fall asleep to the sound of its lazy, trickling flow. Interested? We thought so.

'We promote camping in a natural, non-commercial environment' is how owner Claire describes Walkmill; and given the site's pleasing lack of evening entertainment and plastic playgrounds, we think that's a fitting description. The site is divided into two sections. The riverside pitches have vast amounts of space, shared only with the lambs and sheep at selected times of the year, giving these spots a real sense of 'wild camping'. However if you don't fancy the midnight toilet trek, you can hire your own portaloo! The main facilities are always clean and tidy, with many enjoying a 'proper' bathroom, located in the site's mobile home, which also doubles up as an information centre.

And when you finally tire of Walkmill (if you ever do, that is), the wild and remote Northumberland coast is right on your doorstep. Stretching 64 miles north of Newcastle up to the Scottish border, this dramatic landscape is loaded with impressive sights. Here you'll find the Elizabethan ramparts surrounding picturesque Berwick-upon-Tweed, the sturdy fortresses at Bamburgh, Warkworth and Alnwick, and delightful villages strung along miles of wide, sandy beaches that you just might have all to yourself.

A real attraction is Walkmill's abundance of wildlife, both on land and in the river. Swans, otters, herons and kingfishers lounge lazily by the riverbank; kestrels, buzzards and owls dominate the skies; while sharp-eyed campers have also spotted the odd badger. But Walkmill's greatest asset may well be the space – not just the physical kind but that all important head-space too. This is a spot for a little camping freedom and it does a world of good for anyone looking to unwind.

COOL FACTOR Refreshingly understated private camping in the unspoilt Northumberland countryside.

WHO'S IN Tents, caravans, motorhomes, campervans, kids, and well-behaved dogs – yes.

ON SITE 10 x 50-ft tent spaces on a flat, grassy area beside the river at the bottom of a sloping field. 9 pitches (on the top level) available for caravans and motorhomes. Walkmill's static caravan acts as an info centre and bathroom, with a hot shower, bath and toilet. There are 2 further toilets located adjacent to the caravan. Use of the kitchen's sinks, microwave, fridge-freezer and kettle is permitted. Fishing day tickets are available for salmon and trout in the River Coquet.

OFF SITE From the top of the private farm track it's a pleasant 30-minute walk to Warkworth Castle and Hermitage (01665 711423; EH), home to the Percys of Alnwick. Alnwick Castle – of *Harry Potter*, and, more recently *Downton Abbey*, fame – is also only a 15-minute drive away (01665 511100; alnwickcastle.com). Bicycles can be hired from Adventure Northumberland (01665 602925; adventurenorthumberland. co.uk) in Alnwick.

FOOD & DRINK Pub grub is available at the Hermitage Inn (01665 711258; hermitageinn.co.uk) and the slightly posher Sun Hotel (01665 711259; thesunhotelwarkworth.co.uk) – both in Warkworth. Ice cream addicts will love Morwick Dairy's (01665 711210, royaldouble.com) range of flavours. Their working farm is just across the river from Walkmill.

GETTING THERE From Warkworth, take the first left, signposted for Shilbottle. Follow the road for approx. 1 mile, over a railway crossing, and turn left towards Guyzance Brotherwick. Drive past Brotherwick Farm and continue for another ½ mile. Turn left at the bend, up and over a small stone railway bridge, and turn immediately right on to the farm track to Walkmill.

OPEN March–October.

THE DAMAGE Tents for adults £6.50 per night, children (2–13 years) £2.50 and additional cars £1. Touring caravans (based on a maximum of 2 adults and 2 children per caravan), from £12 per night, Touring caravans from £13.00 per night.

wales

campsite locator

ISLE OF
ANGLESEY

Liverpool ▪

▪ Beaumaris

▪ Caernarfon

Betws-y-Coed
131 132 ▪ 134
130 133

128

129

127

Welshpool ▪

126 122

Aberystwyth ▪

121

125

Cardigan ▪

117 118 119

120

110 123
109
St David's
106 107
113
108
Carmarthen ▪

116

111

112

Tenby ▪

114

Swansea

115

Monmouth ▪

124

Cardiff ▪

campsites at a glance

porthclais farm campsite

Porthclais Farm, Porthclais, St Davids, Pembrokeshire SA62 6RR 01437 720616 www.porthclais-farm-campsite.co.uk

On arrival at Porthclais Farm, you're greeted by a five-day weather forecast. This is indicative of the outdoors life that you can lead here, as well as the helpful and informative approach of the owners. They know that people come here to enjoy everything that the Pembrokeshire coastline has to offer – from walking the coast path, surfing, sailing, fishing and rockpooling, to generally pottering around the coastline. The lower fields have only a gorse hedge between you and the coast path, and the pretty harbour of Porthclais is just at the bottom of the cliffs. Depending on your preferred outdoor pursuits you could easily ditch the car for the duration of your stay, as the cathedral city of St Davids is only about a 15-minute walk away – either back up the lane or, for a slightly longer route with a view, along the coast path.

This site has a lovely relaxed attitude, from where you pitch to what you pitch. In high season there is a lively mix of family frame tents, one person pop-ups, tipis, bell tents and volleyball/tennis nets. The only real 'rule' is to set up camp 20ft away from strangers and 10ft between friends, but that's just a bit of good old common sense. The ablutions facilities are very good, if a bit of a hike from the lower field. There are no electric hook-ups but you're welcome to bring your own generator or solar panels. So, all in all, a pretty perfect place to pitch.

COOL FACTOR A big but intimate site with 180-degree views of a cracking coastline.

WHO'S IN Tents, caravans, campervans, groups, dogs – yes.

ON SITE 5 fields covering 24 acres for tents and one field of 5 acres for 12 caravans and campervans. Phone charging. Freezer pack loans. Two shower/toilet blocks: For women 9 toilets, 6 showers; for men 6 toilets, 6 urinals, 4 showers. 8 outdoor covered washing-up sinks and wetsuit washing tub. No campfires, but BBQ stands can be hired.

OFF SITE The Pembrokeshire Coast Path (nt.pcnpa.org.uk) passes close by and is a great way to reach nearby beaches like Porthllisky – which is good for rock-pooling – or glorious Whitesands to the west. Or try a spot of pony trekking with the St Davids Trekking Centre (01437 720526).

FOOD & DRINK The campsite shop has daily fresh essentials including milk, bacon and Welsh cakes. St Davids has everything else you need, including a WI market on Thursday mornings. There are pubs and cafés to suit all tastes and budgets, from the friendly Farmer's Arms (01437 721666; farmersstdavids.co.uk) to the more upmarket Cwtch restaurant (01437 720491; cwtchrestaurant.co.uk).

GETTING THERE At St Davids square pass the chemist (on your left), and follow Goat Street. Stay on this road for about two miles and look out for the Porthclais campsite entrance on your left, before the harbour.

PUBLIC TRANSPORT Train to Haverfordwest or Fishguard and Richards Brothers (01239 613756) bus to St Davids. 'Celtic Coaster' buses run via St Davids and will stop on request at Porthclais Campsite between June and September.

OPEN Easter–end October.

THE DAMAGE Adults and teenagers £7 a night; children aged 5–12 inclusive £3 a night; under-5's free. Caravans and campervans £14–£21 a night for 2 people.

caerfai farm

Caerfai Farm, St Davids, Pembrokeshire SA62 6QT 01437 720548 www.caerfai.co.uk

Caerfai Farm is one of the original pioneers of low-carbon camping. Indeed this organic, family-run dairy farm has won awards a-plenty for its eco-initiatives; for example the landmark wind turbine you pass on your way down the lane. However, you don't have to join the sandals-and-sackcloth brigade to camp here – it's a welcome-all, traditional campsite, with the usual scattering of tents, the odd campervan, buckets and spades, wetsuits and surfboards.

There are four fields, three of which look out to sea, with the best views had by those in the 'cliff field' next to the coast path. Yes, you are camping virtually on top of the Pembrokeshire coast, with pretty little Caerfai beach just a five-minute stroll away. There are adequate washroom facilities here, with solar heating, and a fantastic farm shop that sells some outstanding local produce, including matured Caerfai Cheddar and Caerphilly cheese produced on the farm. The morning croissant queues are legendary, with kids and adults alike racing back across the grass clutching brown paper bags to enjoy the contents with their morning cuppa.

It's an easy hop into St Davids for all the local attractions and you're brilliantly placed to explore the beautiful beaches that North Pembrokeshire has to offer. Do remember, though, that the views come at a price in inclement weather. Being on the edge of Wales, glorious sunshine and pancake-flat seas can often be engulfed by howling winds and lashing rain. Regulars (of which there are many) tend to opt for sturdy tents and double-check their pegs and guy-ropes!

COOL FACTOR Low carbon, cliff-top camping with magnificent views and tasty croissants.

WHO'S IN Tents, campervans and dogs – yes. Caravans, groups – no.

ON SITE 4 fields, 1 with storm shelter. Water standpipes within 100m of each pitch. Men's and ladies' toilet blocks with 1 shower each. 3 additional single showers, plus 2 family showers. Dish-washing room. Laundry room at the farm (across the lane). No campfires. Onsite farm shop.

OFF SITE If you want an adrenaline rush or just a good soaking, try TYF Adventure (01437 721611; tyf.com) for coasteering, sea kayaking, rock climbing and other waterbound activities. Surfers should head to Whitesands beach and wannabes can take lessons with the Ma Simes crew (01437 720433; masimes.com).

FOOD & DRINK The farm shop sells essentials and organic produce. St Davids has everything else. The Sound Café (01437 721717) is popular with a surfy crowd and renowned for its great breakfasts and tapas in the evenings. For ice cream lovers, it doesn't get much better than the gelato at The Bench (01437 721778; bench-bar.co.uk), which is made from Caerfai organic milk. For a pub, try the Bishops (01437 720422; thebish.co.uk), which does food every day, often including excellent fresh fish specials.

GETTING THERE From Haverfordwest, take the A487 to St Davids. Look out for the Visitor Centre on the left when approaching St Davids and take the left just before it. After about ½ mile, Caerfai Farm is on the left.

PUBLIC TRANSPORT Bus to St Davids and then a walk or short bus ride.

OPEN Mid May–end September.

THE DAMAGE £7/£3.50 per adult/child (3-15 years old). Car-less adults £5. Electric hook-up charged at £4 a night; dogs £3 a night.

newgale

Newgale, Haverfordwest, Pembrokeshire SA62 6AR 01437 710253 www.newgalecampingsite.co.uk

About halfway along the stretch of road from Haverfordwest (Hwlffordd) to St Davids, the road takes a steep dive down to the coast, to the stunning beach that is Newgale (Niwgwl). Surfers, kayakers, windsurfers and kite-surfers dot the bright water, while families spread out on the sand. And the campsite where many of these people hang out is in a large field, 30 seconds across the road. With such proximity, the location is pure heaven on a hot sunny day. The campsite itself is basic – a largely flat, virtually treeless field; a low bank separates it from the adjoining A487. But there's a great vibe in the evenings – and if you don't have any of the surf kit and fancy a go, you can hire everything you need from the Newsurf Beach Shop next to the site. When the weather's fine and you can see the sea shimmering from your pitch, you can easily understand why people come back for more, year after year.

COOL FACTOR Camping next to one of Pembrokeshire's best surfing beaches.

WHO'S IN Tents, campervans, groups, motorhomes (must be at least 6m from neighbour) – yes. Caravans, young groups, dogs – no. Quiet non-family canoe clubs are also welcome but need to book in advance.

ON SITE The facilities block has 10 toilets and 8 hot showers (50p token for 5 minutes), with cold showers for wetsuits behind it; the dish-washing room is open from 8am–8pm; no laundry facilities; the Newsurf Beach Shop (01437 721398) next door sells essentials. No campfires but charcoal and gas BBQs are permitted.

OFF SITE The beach of course is the thing here, but if you fancy a smaller, safer stretch, with rockpools for the kids to poke around in, then the beach at Solva should suffice. For all the surfing kit and caboodle, Newsurf (01437 721398; newsurf.co.uk) next door have you covered. If you fancy horse-riding on the beach, contact Nolton Stables (01437 710360; noltonstables.com) who also oddly enough organise zorbing and Segways in the local area.

FOOD & DRINK The Duke of Edinburgh (01437 720586) pub is right next door to the site – nothing special but it has a popular outside terrace. For light bites and sweet treats, Sands Café (01437 729222) and the Pebbles Café and Beach Shop (01437 710444) do the job. Otherwise the harbour village of Solva, with its pubs and restaurants, is 4 miles north and home to the Ship Inn (01437 721247), a CAMRA-award-winning pub that also houses an Indian restaurant, the Spice Galley. The Cambrian Inn (01437 721210; thecambrianinn.co.uk), also in Solva, does a decent Sunday lunch. For a friendly bar with sea views and good home-cooked food, the quirky Druidstone Hotel (01437 781221) is worth the short drive.

GETTING THERE From Haverfordwest, take the A487 west for 8 miles towards St Davids; watch out for the beach (you can't miss it) and the campsite is on the right.

PUBLIC TRANSPORT Trains run frequently to Haverfordwest, from where the regular St Davids bus stops at Newgale.

OPEN March–end of September.

THE DAMAGE £7 per adult and children over 12, £3 children 4–11. No advance bookings accepted.

ty parke farm

Ty Parke Farm Camping & Yurt Holidays, Llanreithan, St. Davids, Pembrokeshire SA62 5LG 01348 837384 www.typarke.co.uk

After deciding they liked the idea of opening a campsite on their farm in the western wilds of Pembrokeshire, Gary and Annie Loch thought long and hard about what kind of campsite they themselves would wish to stay on. They realised they now had a golden opportunity – to create something new and perfect. That they have been so successful in such a short time kind of confirms that the original ideas were right for the sort of folk they hoped to attract.

Firstly, they were determined to create space for campers to breathe, both spiritually and physically, as an escape from the intense urban lifestyle most of us have to lead. And even though this was a brand new site, the experience had to reflect the original essence of camping – being more directly involved with the natural world. The impression you get is that Gary and Annie, possibly without realising it, have delved even deeper into man's camping past and are encouraging campers to feel just a little of what our prehistoric forebears must have felt when they were gathered around the fire at night: the mysterious gaze into the flames; the eerie sounds of the night, and the other creatures out there sharing their lives, but keeping their distance.

The effort to create this natural but comfortable camping experience has resulted in Ty Parke having just ten occupied pitches in a space where a hundred might take up residence on other campsites, and the provision of those 'sounds of the night' (very authentic they are, too) comes from their adjacent five-acre Nature Trail, which snakes for a mile and a half around the site, where badgers and foxes warily wander at night and, by day, you might see buzzards, owls, grazing sheep, lizards – and the friendly farm dog.

Ty Parke also offers four luxuriously appointed yurts for campers who wish to try something even more authentic or decadent, depending on how you view these things. Eventually – peaceful though it may be at Ty Parke, thoughts will turn to the outside world, and the Lochs are urging guests to bring their bikes with them and discover that there is enough entertainment to keep the family busy for the full week within an hour's bike ride. There are glorious beaches, quaint little harbours, adrenalin-rush boat trips, 'coasteering', pony trekking, big waves and even a cathedral; and all within reach on your push iron.

Ty Parke Farm is camping as it used to be, with the wilds pushing in around the edges, but without the hardships.

COOL FACTOR Immaculate facilities, a peaceful rural location and the feeling of space, which is provided by the limited number of pitches.

WHO'S IN Yurts, tents, campervans, small caravans, small groups, boats, surfboards – yes. Big groups, dogs – no.

ON SITE 8 pitches in the family camping meadow and 6 secluded pitches dotted around the farm. That's 14 in total, but only ever a total of 10 pitches at any one time. 4 luxury camping yurts also available. All spread out over a whopping 52 acres! Campfires allowed. Drinking water taps in all fields. 2 immaculate family washrooms with toilets and showers, laundry, 2 fridges, chest freezer and electric kettle. All the yurts also have their own compost loo and camp kitchen.

OFF SITE The Pembrokeshire Coast Path (see p. 232), is within 10 minutes' drive and gives access to some stunning beaches. Or hire a bike from Mike's Bikes in Haverfordwest (01437 760068; mikes-bikes.co.uk) and ride the cycle trail that runs close to the campsite. For adrenalin-rush activities (coasteering, surfing, kayaking), contact Preseli Venture (01348 837709; preseliventure.co.uk).

FOOD & DRINK There's a wood-fired pizza oven for weekly pizza nights up at the farmhouse. The Ship Inn (01348 831445; shipinntrefin.co.uk) at Trefin is a good village local and serves excellent food. The Sloop Inn at Porthgain (01348 831449; sloop.co.uk) is an evocative old pub located by the picturesque village harbour and worth visiting just for a drink, but it serves great food too.

GETTING THERE From Haverfordwest follow the B4330 towards Croesgoch for 10 miles and Ty Parke is on the right, or from Goodwick follow the A487 for 10 miles to Croesgoch. Turn left into B4330 towards Haverfordwest and the campsite is 4 miles further on the left. Pre-bookings only, so call for directions. The sign says 'PARKE' not 'TY PARKE'.

OPEN Early May–mid September.

THE DAMAGE Tent pitch £24 per night for a tent and 2 adults; children (5–14 years) £6; under-5s free. Yurts from £225 for a 3-night weekend break. Firewood £4 per very generous tub-load.

trellyn woodland

Trellyn Woodland, Abercastle, Haverfordwest, Pembrokeshire SA62 5HJ 01348 837762 www.trellyn.co.uk

There's a spot at Trellyn – as you stand on the rickety wooden bridge, looking upstream as water fizzles and licks at the flow-smoothed stones below – where the woodland canopy overhead is so thick with branches and leaves that, even on the brightest of days, the sunlight struggles to find a way in. The dappled yellow that does trickle its way through the trees lights the woodland with a mystical hue, sprinkling special magic about the place. You might expect fairies or elves to peek out from behind a tree, do a little dance and disappear again. And although on our last visit we didn't actually see any, it's impossible to rule it out completely. Trellyn is a magical place. It's calm and remote; a hidden woodland playground. And it's all down to two things – space and trees.

Across 16 acres of beautiful Pembrokeshire woodland, Trellyn stretches to just five camping pitches, three yurts and two geodomes. That's it. Even calling these spots 'pitches' is a gross misrepresentation. They're clearings, pockets of solitude carved out of the woodland and furnished with a picnic table and a covered campfire area with a grill. This is also a stroke of genius, allowing you to cook outside in all weathers instead of huddling over a tin of baked beans on a gas burner in your tent.

The domes are made from recycled bottles and timber, but rustic they are most definitely not. As for the yurts, they have raised wooden floors, sumptuous beds, wood-burners and rugs, cushions and sheepskins to add to the homely ambience.

The most ambitious yurt is actually three yurts in one: the 'Hobbit Yurt', with a main living area and two separate bedrooms on each side, reached through oak-panelled corridors just like a real Hobbit-hole. Set in its own landscaped 'Shire', it has solid oak floors, a wood-burner and hardwood furniture – all themed and influenced by Tolkien's stories. It really is like stepping in to your own bit of Middle Earth.

Two sociable additions to Trellyn are an outdoor pizza oven – lit when the campers all feel like a get-together – and a wood-fired sauna, for a really relaxing end to the day. There's also a basket of pre-cut wood and kindling ready and waiting for you when you arrive and – even better – when that runs out, you're free to grab the axe and raid the woodshed, chopping down the big old logs and pretending you're Ray Mears. The almost-coastal location of Trellyn means it's a perfect base from which to explore the attractions of Pembrokeshire. However, while there is plenty to do in the area, the best evening is to be had back on site, in your own special, cosy campfire area.

When *Cool Camping* first discovered this place in 2006, we wrote about how refreshing it was to find such a steadfastly uncommercial campsite, and how rare such beautiful, chilled-out woodland sites are. Since then, we've visited hundreds of other campsites and covered just about every inch of Wales hoping to find an equal to the Trellyn experience. We've failed. Trellyn wins. And very good luck to it.

COOL FACTOR Woodland, fires, space, and owners who care.

WHO'S IN Tents, glampers, groups, caravans, campervans –
yes. Dogs – no.

ON SITE Campfires allowed. 5 tent pitches, each nestled in
an open glade with a campfire, camp shelter, picnic table and
grill; 3 themed yurts and 2 geo-domes. Shared facilities are
immaculately clean, with solar-heated showers, washing-up
facilities, toilets, power supply for charging torches, etc, 2
communal freezers and 2 fridges with ice packs. There's also a
huge supply of beach equipment, including fishing nets, surfboards and wetsuits, lent out on a 'fair usage' basis. Electric
hook-up available. Bedding supplied in the yurts and domes.

OFF SITE Numerous beaches are just a short drive away and
Abercastle beach, with its low-tide sand and rockpools, is
100m from the campsite. For trips around Ramsey Island (for
seal, dolphin and bird spotting) take a large speedboat with
Voyages of Discovery (0800 854367; ramseyisland.co.uk).
Those keen on Welsh design should visit the Melin Tregwynt,
mill, shop and café (01348 891288; melintregwynt.co.uk).

FOOD & DRINK Kev and Claire often put out home-grown
veg (for a small donation) and their son Matt can provide
fresh, locally caught crab and lobster – and he'll even teach
you how to cook it. The Farmer's Arms (01348 831284;
farmersarmsmathry.co.uk) up the hill at Mathry is a good local
pub and serves food.

GETTING THERE From the A40 at Letterston, take the B4331
opposite the fish and chip shop and follow for 4 miles. At the
A487 crossroads, go straight across to Mathry; just after the
Farmer's Arms, turn right (signposted Abercastle) and after
2 miles the site is on the left.

PUBLIC TRANSPORT The Strumble Shuttle bus service
between Fishguard and St Davids stops at the campsite.

OPEN End May–early September (yurts, tipi, domes stay open
until end September).

THE DAMAGE Camping from £35 per night based on 2
sharing; tipi from £50 per night; dome from £60; yurt from
£70, all per night.

dale hill farm

Dale Hill Farm, Dale, Haverfordwest, Pembrokeshire SA62 3QX 01646 636359

Overlooking the mouth of the Pembrokeshire Heritage Coast is a regular field where you can pitch your trusty canvas home-from-home and enjoy the simple pleasures of life. The farmers here run a very relaxed ship and seem somewhat perplexed by campers' fascination with this spot. After all, it is only a large field, backed by a rocky outcrop with a few grazing sheep... oh, and did we mention the view?

In high season it's a wetsuit-drying mecca, littered with surfboards and dinghies, smoking barbecues, impromptu ball games and kids ducking in and out of the guy ropes. Sheer magic. Beware though: this site should really come with a warning. Camping at Dale Hill Farm could induce a certain smugness. Why? Well, not only are you on the closest campsite to coveted Dale, with its surfy, yachty gang, you also know that there's a short cut from the back of the site to equally surf-tastic West Dale. And, finally, you have a field 'with a view' (unless, of course, the sea mist has rolled in).

COOL FACTOR Stunning views; space by the bucket-load. Freedom. Surf.

WHO'S IN Tents, campervans, caravans and motorhomes families, dogs – yes.

ON SITE One huge field, where you can pitch wherever you want. It's best to set up your camp around the edge, so that everyone can roam free in the middle. There's a functional amenities block just outside the field gate in the farmyard. It's no oil painting, but offers 2 showers, 2 loos and a washing-up room with a fridge-freezer. Queuing is unavoidable in high season. As for activities, batting, balling and bicycling, tag and generally just hooning about are the order of the day on site.

OFF SITE Surfing is the thing here, but crabbing on the pontoon is another compulsory pleasure. Take a trip to the offshore island nature reserves of Skomer and Skokholm from the quay (01646 603110; dale-sailing.co.uk). Wander across to the stunning bay of West Dale for some surfing or boogie-boarding. The local surf shop (01646 636642) offers lessons (and hires out all the latest gear) for surfing, windsurfing, kayaking and catamarans.

FOOD & DRINK The Griffin Inn (01646 636227; griffininndale.co.uk) is a great place for pub grub, or just to watch the comings and goings in the estuary. The Boat House Café (01646 636929) is fantastic for everything from all-day breakfast to a crab platter.

GETTING THERE As you enter the outskirts of Dale (on the B4327) you'll see ponds and marshland on your left. Go over the hump-backed bridge and take the right-hand turn by the postbox. Go up the hill for ¼ mile and you're there.

OPEN May–October, but definitely worth ringing if you fancy visiting earlier.

THE DAMAGE A flat fee per night of £12 per tent.

dews lake farm

Dews Lake Farm, The Ridgeway, Lamphey, Pembroke, Pembrokeshire SA71 5PB 01646 672139
www.dewslakecamping.co.uk

First time campers? The family underwhelmed by the idea of a weekend camping in rural Wales? Then Dews Lake Farm might be the ideal choice for your first under-canvas foray. The site provides pitches for 'traditional campers' and 'glampers' alike on a friendly, authentic working farm teeming with wildlife and countryside character. Tucked away in sleepy Pembrokeshire, yet still conveniently close to the region's finest sights (including Manorbier Castle and Freshwater East Beach), Dews Lake Farm is the perfect choice for campers wanting to enjoy the wonders of Western Wales and its remarkably unspoilt landscapes.

The site's welcoming owner Bethan is also behind Cwtch Camping, a fabulous eco-pod retreat in nearby Rosemarket, so it's fair to say she knows a thing or two about running a successful campsite. On arrival you realise everything here is relaxed and pretty low-key. There are no designated pitches in the non-electric field; just rock up and choose your corner of tranquillity. You'll find decent facilities here too, with piping-hot showers, 16-amp electric hook-up points (for caravans) and handy phone charging stations.

Dews Lake's patch of grassy farmland is only six miles from the loveable bucket-and-spade town of Tenby. Literary greats such as Roald Dahl, Jane Austen and Beatrix Potter have taken inspiration from its elegant white Georgian mansions, glorious hilltop views and traditional fishing village feel. Today, Tenby is a postcard-maker's dream and delights visitors who stroll through its medieval streets lined with cosy pubs, quirky gift shops and tempting ice cream parlours.

As luck would have it, Dews Lake is also on the doorstep of one of Europe's finest beaches, Barafundle Bay. Reached after a short coastal drive, the immaculate, golden sands and turquoise waters give it an idyllic feel, and it often draws comparisons to the Caribbean. Out of season you often have the place to yourself apart from a few brave surfers who tackle the choppy Irish Sea.

From Barafundle, take a stroll to Bosherston lily ponds. The best time to visit them is in late spring or summer when the lilies are in full flower and the ponds are home to an eclectic array of wildlife, including otters, swans, herons, dragonflies and 'robbing' robins who won't hesitate to pinch food right out of your hands.

COOL FACTOR An authentic farm base to enjoy the wonders of Western Wales.

WHO'S IN Tents, caravans, campervans, groups, kids and well-behaved dogs – yes.

ON SITE 15 pitches with electric hook-ups and 20 without. 2 ablutions blocks have toilets and showers with individual shower and changing cubicles. A small kitchen area has a fridge, freezer, double electric hob and washing-up sink. 16-amp electric hook-up points (for caravans) and phone charging stations. Firepits can be hired and logs and kindling bought.

OFF SITE It is a 10-minute walk to the village of Lamphey, which is home to a ruined 13th-century Bishop's Palace. Manorbier Castle (01834 871394; manorbiercastle.co.uk) has a well-preserved 12th-century gatehouse; from there you can admire the view from the turret windows down to Manorbier's surfer-friendly beach.

FOOD & DRINK During summer there are regular pop-up local food vendors on site. The farm can also arrange outside catering for parties or guests hiring the entire site for a private do. The Dial Inn (01646 672426; dialinn.co.uk) is only ½ mile away and serves excellent homemade food and local ales. The Stackpole Inn (01646 672324; stackpoleinn.co.uk) is a great choice near Barafundle Bay and was recently crowned 'Best Gastropub in Wales'.

GETTING THERE Coming from Pembroke, take the second exit at the roundabout at the end of Main Street, (Station Road A4139) to Lamphey. Continue through the village on to The Ridgeway, and Dews Lake Farm is approx. ½ mile after the Dial Inn on the right. Coming from Tenby, take a slight right on Greenhill Road (A4139), on to Holloway Hill and continue on to The Ridgeway towards Lamphey. Before you reach Lamphey you will see the sign for Dews Lake Farm.

PUBLIC TRANSPORT There is a train station and bus stop in Lamphey 1 mile from the site.

OPEN March–November.

THE DAMAGE Caravan/campervan/large tent with electric hook-up is £14 per adult per night. Tent pitches without electric are £10 per adult. Kids are £4 per night; under-4s are free. No extra charge for dogs.

tir bach farm

Tir Bach Farm, Llanycefn, Clunderwen, Pembrokeshire SA66 7XT 01437 532362 www.tirbachfarm.co.uk

We sincerely hope you don't get lost in the snaking lanes that twist and turn their way towards the mellow spot that is Tir Bach Farm. But we promise that once you've finally found this farmland site, you'll be reluctant to leave.

Most people have dreams. Some people dream about winning the lottery or writing a best-selling novel. Living in Bristol, Ashley and Roze had a dream about moving to Wales to farm a smallholding and run a cute little family-friendly campsite. They heard about Tir Bach Farm which, appropriately, means 'small land'. And as soon as they visited this special little patch of Wales, they realised that their dream was right in front of them. They now have not only a campsite comprised of 24 tiered tent pitches, a family field and two comfy yurts, but also a grand collection of animals: kune kune pigs, goats, shetland ponies and a mule as well as geese, ducks, turkeys and the odd chicken scratching around the farmyard.

The farm is surrounded by the Preseli mountains and 12 acres of ancient woodland, with paths ripe for exploration and a small river, complete with a fallen tree-trunk bridge. With hardly any light pollution at night, stargazing is a must. One of the nicest things is that, at the end of a day out, you can return to the whispering stillness of Tir Bach Farm and just chill out. It's a mellow spot, because Roze and Ashley are mellow people. We think that you'll like it here so much that you might just start dreaming of moving to the Welsh countryside, yourself.

COOL FACTOR A pretty spot in lovely countryside run by a seriously special couple.

WHO'S IN Campers, glampers, dogs (on leads), groups (out of main season), campervans (no hook-ups) – yes. Caravans – no.

ON SITE There is a communal campfire in the main field or hire a fire pit. An old milking parlour houses 4 showers, toilets, a dish-washing area, washing machine and dryer. There is a large barn with BBQ, table tennis and the pizza oven, which is lit once a week during the school holidays. The yurts have their own kitchen with sink, water and gas hob plus all utensils, and a wood-burning stove, but bring your own bedding.

OFF SITE The nearest beach is at Newport (20 minutes' drive) while there are others less than an hour away, including Newgale (for water sports) and Dinas Head. You could easily spend a day touring the local castles, including Pembroke (01646 681510; pembroke-castle.co.uk).

FOOD & DRINK The Old Post Office (01437 532205) in Rosebush is good for home-made grub, including vegetarian options. The Tafarn Sinc Rosebush (01437 532214; tafarnsinc.co.uk) serves a menu of hearty, mainly meat dishes. The Bethesda Farm Shop (01437 563124; bethesdafarmshop.co.uk) is good for local produce.

GETTING THERE Turn right off the A40 on to the A478 and go through Llandissilio. Take a left-hand turn signposted 'Llanycefn'. Follow this until you come to a 5-road junction. Take the 3rd lane, keeping the yellow house to your right, and look for the 'Tir Bach' sign. Follow this until you see a thatched cottage on your left. Tir Bach is opposite.

PUBLIC TRANSPORT Take a train to Swansea, then another to Llandovery. The campsite is a 10-minute walk or there is a bus that stops at the supermarket 2 minutes from the site.

OPEN Easter–end September.

THE DAMAGE Adults £6.50–£7.50 per night; children £2.50–£3.50 (under-2s and dogs free). Yurt hire from £90 for 2 nights.

carreglwyd

Carreglwyd Caravan and Camping, Port Eynon, Swansea SA3 1NN 01792 390795 www.porteynon.com

The sleepy village of Port Eynon on the Gower Peninsula is dominated by campsites, and static caravan parks occupy various hillside fields above the town. But help is at hand at Carreglwyd, which has five camping fields, of which only the two closest to reception are favoured by caravans, with tents having the run of the place beyond. Pitches nearest the beach tuck in under the shelter of thick hedges, affording views of Port Eynon Bay from the higher ground.

All in all, it's a well-organised and well-equipped site, with modern showers that are both clean and free, plus a very good onsite launderette and a small shop at reception for the basics. But above all its direct access to the beach means that it's a perfect place for young families, with a half-mile crescent of calm, family-friendly waters and plenty of water sports opportunities that makes it kid-friendly heaven during summer.

Port Eynon is a relatively soulless spot beyond the beach, so if the sun is a no-show, head the other way out of the campsite, where a maze of paths explore the headland. This part of the coast is owned and managed by the National Trust, but it feels wild and untamed. Culver Hole is a mysterious four-storey building set into the rocks of the headland. Its origin may have been defensive, but it's highly probable that it has seen more use as a smugglers' hideout. Mewslade is a birdwatchers' paradise, while Fall Bay is the most unspoiled beach in the area; it's only accessible at low tide, but that doesn't stop many campers wading there or scrambling over the rocks to this idyllic bolthole. The coast path to Worm's Head and Rhossili is a spectacular five-mile walk, showcasing the most dramatic stretch of Gower coastline and possibly the best sunset in the UK – proof alone, if it were needed, of why Gower was selected as Britain's first official Area of Outstanding Natural Beauty.

COOL FACTOR The beach and location. Static caravan excess gives way to unspoiled National Trust coastline.

WHO'S IN Tents, campervans, caravans, dogs (on a lead at all times), families – yes. Big groups, young groups – no.

ON SITE 2 modern amenities blocks have toilets, hot showers, basins, a family room, laundry and washing-up facilities. Outdoor showers are available for wetsuits. An onsite shop sells groceries and camping accessories. Electric hook-ups and chemical disposal points also available. No campfires.

OFF SITE Gower Coast Adventures do boat trips from Port Eynon to Worm's Head (07866 250440; gowercoastadventures.co.uk), which are perfect for spotting gannets, guillemots and even puffins. For those after a water-based adrenalin kick, surfboards can be rented and lessons taken from Sam's Surf Shack in Rhossili (01792 350519; thebaybistro.co.uk).

FOOD & DRINK Among places to eat in Port Eynon, The Ship Inn (01792 390204) is recommended for its excellent food and lies just 2 minutes' walk from the site, while the Seafarer (01792 380879) serves decent fish and chips. In Rhossili the Bay Bistro (01792 390519; thebaybistro.co.uk) has lovely views and great home-cooked food ranging from breakfasts, soups and salads to hearty lunches and tea and cake. Also in Rhossili, the Worm's Head Hotel (01792 390512; thewormshead.co.uk) serves good food washed down with their very own ale. It's a stunning spot at sunset, and chef Kate Probert hosts day cookery courses at her home in Three Cliffs. 12 miles away, in Llanmadoc, you'll find the Britannia Inn (01792 386624; britanniainngower.co.uk) with estuary views and locally caught fresh fish on the menu.

GETTING THERE Getting to Carreglwyd is easy. Take the A4118 from Swansea (signposted Mumbles) and follow it all the way to the end. The entrance to Carreglwyd is just by the beach car park at Port Eynon.

PUBLIC TRANSPORT Regular buses run from Swansea directly to Port Eynon, stopping next to the campsite entrance.

OPEN All year.

THE DAMAGE £20 for 2 people, a car and tent, + £8 per extra person. Children 4–12 years £1, 13–17 years £2.

heritage coast campsite

Heritage Coast Campsite, Monknash, Vale of Glamorgan CF71 7QQ 01656 890399 www.heritagecoastcampsite.com

So you know about Snowdonia, the Gower and the Beacons, and the Pembrokeshire Coast needs little introduction. But how about the Glamorgan Heritage Coast Path? Starting from Cardiff Bay's regenerated waterfront and spanning 35 miles westwards to the seaside kitsch of Porthcawl, this stretch of Wales' recently opened national trail takes in some of the country's most spectacular scenery. The sweeping golden beaches of Whitmore Bay, the famous sand dunes of Merthyr Mawr, the innumerable charming cliff top villages – it's a wonder the area isn't positively overrun with holidaymakers year-round. But, hey, we're not complaining, and we know the perfect coastal campsite base to explore this magnificent region.

Glyn and Philippa George know a thing or two about hospitality. Having run their successful five-star B&B to much acclaim, the Georges decided to share their stunning corner of Monknash with the canvas contingent. When they opened up the adjoining brook-side paddock for a trial 28 days a couple of years back the response was so overwhelming that the ever-generous Glyn and Philippa realised it would be a shame to keep it to themselves. And so Heritage Coast Campsite was born.

This tents-only spot has space for just 30 privileged pitches spread across two paddocks on soft, level grass. With uninterrupted views of undulating Glamorgan hills and the sparkling Bristol Channel, you can almost hear the 'oo ar's from Devon on a clear day. Facilities are top-

notch, with a stables block housing immaculately clean facilities (and there are a few surprising extras, like a hot drinks machine and locally sourced meat available from reception). Heritage is a chilled-out, family-friendly site with views to savour, a brook to meditate beside and, of course, that breathtaking coast path to pick up. Pretty much ticks all boxes then, eh?

COOL FACTOR A simple, high-quality site in a beautiful undiscovered corner of South Wales.

WHO'S IN Tent campers, families, well-behaved dogs – yes. Groups allowed at owners discretion.

ON SITE 2 paddocks with space for 30 tents. New stable block houses gents' and ladies' facilities with 2 toilets, 2 showers, 2 sinks, handdryer, plus a hairdryer in the ladies. Unisex disabled bathroom with baby-changing facilities. Utility room with 2 basins, freezer and lockers. The Monk's Rest café is soon to open on site; a small shop with essential provisions and tourist information. Campers are not allowed to use disposable BBQs or bring their own logs but firepits are available to hire and logs and charcoal to buy.

OFF SITE Pick up the Glamorgan Heritage Coast Path and head north to Southerndown and Dunraven Bay – popular with surfers and just about everyone else in summer. Escape the crowds with a visit to the Heritage Coast Centre (01656 880157; glamorganheritagecoast.com). Nearby Merthyr Mawr Sand Dunes were the backdrop to the epic *Lawrence of Arabia* and the village still attracts the film industry today.

FOOD & DRINK In reception you'll find drinks, bottled water and milk, plus delicious Fablas Welsh Ice Cream. They also stock a limited amount of frozen local meats and bread. Just 300 metres from the site lies the excellent Plough & Harrow (01656 890209; ploughandharrow.org), with good ales, decent pub grub and live music on Saturday evenings.

GETTING THERE Follow the dual carriageway to Bridgend; at the 5th roundabout take the St Brides Major turn-off (B4265). About a mile beyond the village, take the right turn to Monknash and follow signs for the Plough & Harrow; right past the pub, and continue for 300 metres.

PUBLIC TRANSPORT Llantwit Major and Bridgend are the nearest train stations. The local bus service is the 145 Bridgend – Llantwit Major/X5 Llantwit Major – Cardiff.

OPEN Mid March–end September.

THE DAMAGE Standard pitch £16 per night, includes tent/vehicle and 2 people (parking on the pitch). Large pitch £20 per night, includes tent/vehicle and 2 people.

faerie thyme

Faerie Thyme, Crwbin, Kidwelly, Carmarthenshire SA17 5DR 01269 871774 www.faerie-thyme.co.uk

The Faerie Thyme founders had just two wishes: one was to create a campsite that they would like to go back to. The other Wish is one of the founders – a former Brighton-based interior designer who, with his wife, Irene, arrived at this three-acre smallholding in Crwbin over half a decade ago. Then began five years of sweat, toil and trouble to materialise a magical realm where imagination rules and – although children aren't allowed – everyone is encouraged to nurture their inner child. Have you walked the plank aboard the Jolly Roger recently? No, we didn't think so. Fun and games aside, Faerie Thyme is like the best part of any decent festival's green field - there's space to chill by giant dreamcatchers, an area to meditate by the stone circle or to get lost in a deep conversation around one of the site's many firepits. And like at Glastonbury, leylines snake back to a wizard heritage. The old quarry road, where druids would get their stones for nearby circles and the monuments placed around Myndd Llangyndeyrn, outside Carmarthen, is rumoured to be the birthplace of Merlin. If this all feels a bit 'far out', then bear in mind that Irene and Wish received numerous customer-feedback awards for the site – proof, if any were needed, that this place is as accessible and well-considered as it is unique and idiosyncratic. And although your hosts are hands on, they're also so open and friendly that it's impossible for anyone not to slip under their spell.

COOL FACTOR A truly magical place that will spirit you away from your usual troubles.

WHO'S IN Tents, campervans and caravans – yes. Dogs, children, big groups and young groups (under 25) – no.

ON SITE Campfires allowed in firepits and plenty of quiet places to chill. There are 6 electric hook-ups and 2 vintage caravans for those who want a comfortable and kitsch stay. There are 2 woodland pitches with firepits away from the main camping area. There is a shower wet room and toilets. There is also an onsite honesty shop to buy logs, kindling and Irene's handcrafted mementoes.

OFF SITE You'd be daft not to visit the impressive Myndd Llangyndeyrn standing stones, an ancient funerary monument which these days attracts an abundance of rare birds and uncommon invertebrates. Consider also a visit to the magnificent gardens and stately house at Aberglasney (01558 668998; aberglasney.org).

FOOD & DRINK Plans are afoot to start doing home-cooked meals, such as chillis and curries, which can easily be reheated over the fire (all pots and ladles supplied). Eggs, bacon and sausages are all available in the honesty shop. Carmarthen Market sells local cheeses and Carmarthen ham – a serious local rival to the Parma variety. For pubs, the New Inn (01269 871152) in Pontyberem serves good food and a wide range of ales, as does the Smiths Arms (01269 842213; thesmithsarms.co.uk) in Foelgastell.

GETTING THERE Follow the B4306 through to the top of Crwbin village. Faerie Thyme is clearly marked on a gate by a yellow bungalow, although it is not marked as a campsite from the road.

OPEN May–October.

THE DAMAGE Tent + 2 people from from £21.

the ceridwen centre

The Ceridwen Centre, Pen-y-Banc Farm, Drefach-Felindre, Llandysul, Carmarthenshire SA44 5XE 01559 370517
www.ceridwencentre.co.uk

To call the Ceridwen Centre a campsite is like saying Da Vinci was a bit handy with a paintbrush. For this purpose-built hillside hideaway is as adept at hosting workshops, retreats, courses and weddings as it is at hosting your glamping getaway. Nestled within 40 acres of lush (an adjective the locals are fond of) West Wales farmland, Ceridwen lies in the fabled Teifi Valley, which straddles the Ceredigion and Carmarthenshire borders. Helmed by the helpful host Simone, the site wears its green credentials proudly. There's a range of ingenious environmental features all over the farm including solar water heating, a biomass boiler and solar electricity. Little wonder it was awarded the Sustainable Tourism Gold Award for Carmarthenshire not so long ago.

Awards aside, there's plenty to tempt you to this spellbinding place. Undulating, verdant hills, gently flowing brooks, enchanting wooded glens, Ceridwen has views – and some. Then there's the accommodation. Besides several masterfully converted farm buildings (including a refurbished calving shed and über-luxurious central house), glamping guests have a choice of three hand-crafted Welsh yurts. Each sleep up to four, so are ideal for a small family. Sitting in sweet seclusion in a wild flower-strewn apple orchard, these fully furnished abodes are the very essence of 'getting away from it all'. For those with more amorous intentions, the gypsy Cwtch (Welsh for a heartfelt cuddle) is a lovingly restored 19th-century Romany wagon with views to die for. The Cwtch features all the antiquated charms of the traveller heritage – Welsh woollen blankets, china

collectables, a warming range stove. There have been more than a couple of marriage proposals made in this enviable spot – so don't be surprised if you find yourself returning a year hence for your own nuptials.

Whether you're here as part of a group or seeking solace and seclusion, Ceridwen radiates a peace and calm. You may chose to indulge in a few of the many varied workshops on offer, from yoga to creative writing – and there's no shortage of inspiration for purple prose. As you admire the red kites circling overhead you might like to consider that Ceridwen was the enchantress of Welsh medieval legend said to possess the cauldron of Poetic Inspiration – how apt a name for a setting whose charms you'll soon succumb to.

COOL FACTOR You'll soon be charmed by this legendary site.

WHO'S IN Tents, small campervans, dogs (under control) – yes. Parrots (not as crazy as this sounds!) – no.

ON SITE 3 yurts, gypsy wagon, Caban Bach (sheep's wool-insulated wooden eco-pod), Gardener's Lodge (converted caravan/log cabin), 5 tent pitches plus 2 hook-ups for campervans. Yurts furnished with traditional rugs, cushions and blankets, wood-burning stoves and proper beds. Cooking facilities shared in the summer house, with a 2-ring stove, utensils, sink and small fridge. There's a choice of toilet facilities – a compost loo close to the yurts, 2 conventional loos and showers down in the farmyard and a new hand-built eco-hut with 2 female loos and a female shower, 1 male loo, shower and urinal. Dining shelter by yurts. Table tennis in the big barn. Bike repair and hire on site.

OFF SITE Soak up this stunning corner of West Wales via the Teifi Valley Railway (01559 371077; teifivalleyrailway.org). The free-to-enter National Wool Museum (02920 573070; museumwales.ac.uk/wool) in Drefach Felindre offers a fascinating insight into Wales' industrial heritage.

FOOD & DRINK Simone is happy to whip up cakes for a special occasion, and groups can gorge themselves at regular summertime pizza nights. The centre also stocks plenty of local beer, cider and wine. The John y Gwas (01559 370469; johnygwas.co.uk) is a cracking little local just a mile down the hill. Or try the Daffodil (01559 370343) at Penrhiwllan, which serves stylish mains and decadent desserts.

GETTING THERE From Carmarthen take the A484 to Rhos, past the Lamb Inn and turn left past the white house on the right. Folllow the lane for a mile and the site is on the left.

OPEN All year. Yurts available from late March–October.

THE DAMAGE Tents £5 for the pitch per stay + £7.50 per camper per night. Campervans £6 for the pitch per stay + £8.50 per camper per night. Yurts from £122 for 2 nights. Caban Bach from £132 for 2 nights. Gardener's Lodge from £142 for 2 nights.

erwlon

Erwlon, Brecon Road, Llandovery, Carmarthenshire SA20 0RD 01550 721021 www.erwlon.co.uk

There is an element of camping that is all about surprises. The surprise, for example, of finding yourself eating crisps for breakfast. Or realising you haven't had a bath for a week. Or waking up to a priceless view of a Welsh valley. And because camping can sometimes be a bit unpredictable, it can be rather soothing to arrive at a campsite that does exactly what it says on the tin. And that's precisely what Erwlon does. There are no frills and no surprises to be had here, but it's a friendly, well-maintained and attractive site in the bosom of Wales' loveliest countryside. It strikes that all-important balance between being relatively unspoiled yet still featuring the sort of clean and cosy facilities that make camping more comfy.

All this should hardly come as a surprise as the Rees family have been running the site since the 1950s. Brothers Peter and Huw are now the third generation to be involved, so it's fair to say

that the Rees clan know a thing or two about running a successful, well-organised campsite. But Erwlon's real selling point has to be its location. Boasting 12 impressive castles, Carmarthenshire is fabulously littered with the evidence of successive cultures and kingdoms that have been swept away by one invader after another. This dizzyingly diverse county includes some of Britain's most scenic moments – towering peaks and lush, ancient woodlands – and never fails to cast a calming spell upon all that visit.

Erwlon is the sort of site that ticks many boxes. It works for those wanting to get away from it all, for those wanting the challenge of the Brecon Beacons, or for those wanting to discover some of Britain's finest castles, villages and coastline. You don't need to be eagle eyed to spot the charm of Carmarthenshire, and thankfully Erwlon provides the perfect base from which to go and explore it all.

COOL FACTOR A quiet little site snuggled up to the Brecon Beacons with more castles than you can shake a stick at.

WHO'S IN Everyone's welcome! Tents, caravans, campervans, groups and dogs – yes.

ON SITE 2 fields of 100 pitches, most with hook-ups. Laundry and dish-washing facilities, a drying-room and fridge-freezer. A play area with swings, and children are welcome to watch the cows being milked. You could eat your lunch off the floor of any of the 5 family rooms in the wash-block. Wi-Fi is available across the site.

OFFSITE There are also some major-league attractions within easy distance of the site. Carreg Cennen Castle (01558 822291; carregcennencastle.com) is a must-see. Big Pit National Coal Museum (02920 397951; museumwales. ac.uk/bigpit) is fab, as are the National Showcaves (01639 730284; showcaves.co.uk) at Dan-yr-Ogof, or you can take a thrilling trip to look for gold at the Dolaucothi Gold Mines (01558 825146; NT). The trails of Cwm Rhaeadr are also only a 20-minute cycle ride away, and make a fantastic place for a day out, with Bronze Age burial cairns and Iron Age hill forts. Finally, the biggest local attraction of all is the wonderful and very popular National Botanic Gardens (01558 668768; gardenofwales.org.uk).

FOOD & DRINK You can't visit Erwlon without a trip into Llandovery to the Penygawse Victorian Tea Rooms (01550 721727; penygawse.co.uk) where, beneath tinkling chandeliers, you can enjoy great lunches, excellent cream teas and the best coffee in Wales. For lip-smackingly good ice cream, head to Llanfaes (01874 625892; llanfaesdairy.com), where you can enjoy up to 50 flavours of locally made ice cream.

GETTING THERE Leave the M4 at junction 24 and head north along the A449 until you join the A40 at Raglan. Head west to Llandovery. The site is just off the A40, 1 mile east of Llandovery, on the road towards Brecon on the right-hand side.

PUBLIC TRANSPORT The no. #63 bus between Brecon and Swansea stops at the site's main gate.

OPEN All year.

THE DAMAGE £13 per night for a family of 4, £16 with electric hook-up.

camping at ynysfaen

Ynysfaen , Ynysfaen Cwmwysg, Trecastle, Brecon, Powys LD3 8YF 01874 636436 www.campingatynysfaen.co.uk

While most summer tourists from over the border descend westwards to the Pembrokeshire coast or north to the Snowdonian peaks, those in the know will tell you you're missing a trick in bypassing the rugged delights of the Brecon Beacons. In a land that's famed for mountains and valleys, the Brecon Beacons stand out for their beauty; and just outside the charming Brecon village of Trecastle lies the refreshingly no-frills campsite of Ynysfaen. Kids are free to run around the five acres of lush open space safely, unencumbered by cars and motorhomes at this tents-only site. A cosy two-person shepherd's hut is the only four-wheeled thing around here and it's travelling nowhere fast. While cars are not permitted in the camping field, guests can load their gear on to the colourful wheelbarrows provided. This low-impact ethos is in keeping with the site's enduring atmosphere of peace and tranquillity. While it's the perfect base camp for exploring the Beacons and the Black Mountains, Ynysfaen also offers a relaxing and bucolic retreat, soundtracked by tweeting birds and the gentle babbling of the River Usk.

Speaking of birds, the area has more than a few to keep the twitchers entertained. You can see red kites, redstarts, buzzards, kingfishers, herons, wild mallard and woodpeckers. You should also keep your eyes peeled for foxes, badgers and even the occasional otter, as they are known to have been spotted swooning around in the Usk.

Ynysfaen is also a great place for stargazing, as it is in the Brecon Beacons National Park 'Dark Skies Reserve', indeed the Usk Reservoir (a mile away) was named the 'darkest' place in the reserve.

Owner Jane is also a Dark Skies ambassador and knows her Orion from her Ryanair. She's happy to give a helping hand or some suggestions if you want tips on making the most of the experience. Just one of many strings to her bow, Jane can also claim to be a Brecon Beacons National Park Ambassador and a Fforest Fawr Geopark Ambassador, so has plenty of current and historic knowledge of the area and can keenly advise on where's best to go.

COOL FACTOR Star-spangled peace at this no-frills car-free camping gem.

WHO'S IN Tents, trailer-tents, well-behaved dogs – yes. Motorhomes, caravans, large groups – no.

ON SITE A maximum of 40 people with no measured-out pitches, so there is plenty of room. The large modern shower block includes hot electric showers (unisex, each in their own individual cubicle); 3 unisex toilets; 2 washbasins. There's a covered washing-up area with hot water. Maps of the local area are available. Campfires permitted in designated firepits (£5 to hire, fire baskets, logs and kindling provided). No electrical hook-ups. Shepherd's hut for adult couples only, with double bed, wood-burning stove and electrical sockets.

OFF SITE The Brecon Beacons National Park (breconbeacons. org) has a wealth of epic walks and outdoor pursuits. Just a mile from the site, the Usk Reservoir offers stunning views and fishing, while the Usk Reservoir Trail is a great way to explore the countryside on 2 wheels. Your lovely hosts can arrange pick-ups and drop-offs.

FOOD & DRINK The Castle Coaching Inn (01874 636354; castle-coaching-inn.co.uk), in Trescastle is a 3-star Georgian inn with a decent restaurant. Or, if you fancy going further, then both Llandovery (15 minutes' drive away) and Brecon (20 minutes' drive away) have numerous places to grab a lunchtime or evening meal. On site you can buy fresh free-range eggs laid by the farm's own chickens and seasonal home-grown fruit and vegetables.

GETTING THERE Follow the A40 Brecon–Llandovery road to Trecastle, past the Castle Coaching Inn, and turn left just before the antiques centre. The campsite is a mile or so up on the left. Watch out using Sat-Nav, as you may end up at one of the local farms!

OPEN March–October.

THE DAMAGE £10 per person per night – under-5s free. £1 per dog per night. Day visitors £2 per day.

pencelli castle

Pencelli Castle Caravan & Camping Park, Pencelli, Brecon, Powys LD3 7LX 01874 665451 www.pencelli-castle.co.uk

There used to be a castle on the site of this marvellously situated campsite, and although it may have been dismantled in the 1550s, chances are its battlements would be crammed full of flowers if it were still around. Not for nothing have the campsite's owners, the Rees family, won the 'Wales in Bloom' campsite category for over nine years now. Paying quiet attention to a camper's every need is what this dedicated family does so well, and the main reason why staying here is so special.

Pencelli is packed full of history but thankfully the bloody battles fought here up until the 1300s are now a thing of the distant past. The castle was around until the 1550s, when it was pulled to bits for local building material. But there are some shadowy reminders of its former grandeur all over the site – bits of the old walls, or the house itself, which was part of the chapel until 1583.

You can almost picture the castle as you pitch your tent in one of the three fields, which are ancient and spacious, with lots of shady, sheltered spots under big old oaks. Most pitches have a backdrop of stupendous heather-clad mountains and sheep-strewn, rolling hills. The Oaks field takes caravans, campervans and tents, the Meadows is tents only; and both lie in a horseshoe around the old moat, now part of the Monmouthshire Canal, which runs alongside the site. You can even launch your boat or canoe directly into the water from the camping field. Wooden picnic tables are scattered around and there are plenty of water points in all the fields. All in all, it's a well-organised and well-planned site, especially good for first-timers, with flat pitches, spotless facilities and even a castle-themed play area for the kids.

COOL FACTOR The views, canal-side situation and justified awards for 'Best Campsite in Wales'.

WHO'S IN Tents, campervans, children, caravans – yes. Big groups, young groups, dogs – no.

ON SITE No campfires, but BBQs welcome. With 80 pitches and 29 hook-ups over 3 fields, space is rarely an issue, and the facilities are spotless, with 10 showers, 2 family washrooms, a small laundry, fridge-freezer and washing-up facilities. A small shop stocks basics, and there's also a place to store and wash bikes and boots. There's a useful information room and you can order newspapers daily. Some pitches have disabled access and Wi-Fi. A play area, and a nature trail, which includes the red deer enclosure and vintage farm machinery, are great for kids.

OFF SITE The Brecon to Monmouthshire Canal (mbact.org. uk) runs directly past the site and you can take boat trips all year. You can also hire day boats for 4–8 people. Pen y Fan, the highest point in the Brecon Beacons, isn't far and is a great excursion. It can be reached by a combination of driving and walking and is well worth it for the magnificent views. The Taff Trail (01639 893661; tafftrail.org.uk), which criss-crosses this area, is a network of cycle paths running along the canal and through the villages.

FOOD & DRINK The Royal Oak pub (01874 665396) is 100m away, but the best food locally is served at the White Swan (01874 665276; whiteswanbrecon.co.uk) in Llanfrynach. There's a farm shop at Middle Wood, which is good for local meat. An onsite shop sells basic provisions, and if you order before 4.30pm you can have a delivery of milk and bread for the following morning.

GETTING THERE From Abergavenny take the A40 towards Brecon; 6 miles from Brecon turn left to Talybont-on-Usk. In the village turn right and the site is the first place you come to on the right.

PUBLIC TRANSPORT A train to Abergavenny, then bus no. #X43, which runs between Cardiff and Abergavenny, stopping near the Royal Oak pub.

OPEN Early February–late November.

THE DAMAGE £8–£10 per person; £4.50–£6 for 5–15-yr-olds, under-5s free.

fforest fields

Fforest Fields Caravan Park, Hundred House, Builth Wells, Powys LD1 5RT 01982 570406 www.fforestfields.co.uk

Ralph Waldo Emerson was not much of a camper. And although some of his Transcendentalist chums were never happier than in the great outdoors, it's doubtful many of them were big on camping. After all, equipment wasn't quite so advanced back then. Pop-up tents hadn't even been invented, let alone Cath Kidston floral patterns. But if they had ventured out (with giant tent in tow) some of their musings about the human spirit might just have waxed even more lyrical about the euphoric communion between Man and Nature.

It sounds a little on the wishy-washy side, but when you're by the long lake at Fforest Fields, looking up at the twinkling night sky, it's easy to see their point. The lake may be man-made, as is the campsite, its pathways, streams and flower beds, but it has been done with such care and taste that even Mother Nature herself would surely give it her blessing. And if you stand in the middle of this campsite and spin around, the natural scenery that greets the eye full circle is just breathtaking – rolling hills in every direction, forests thick with pine trees, grass, ferns, heather and crystal-clear streams... all the finest organic ingredients that make up a melting pot of countryside idyll. The best bit is that you're free to wander off in any one of these directions, because the land (all 550 acres of it) all belongs to Fforest Fields.

There is so much walking to be done here – over the hills, through the forests and across the moorland. Maps are available at reception to guide you and there's a six-mile waymarked walk to Aberedw village that's well worth doing, not least because it winds up at a terrific pub. Two fishing lakes allow for more sedate activity and the long lake's cool waters also make for refreshing swimming or canoeing in one of the site's kayaks. So the chance to commune with Nature is at an all-time high here. In fact, not far away, at Gigrin Farm in Rhayader, there's a red kite feeding centre, where you can get up close and personal with these majestic birds of prey.

The Transcendentalists would be even more thrilled by the opportunities for the human spirit to shine here, not just through tree-hugging and skipping barefoot across the grass, but also through old-fashioned trust. Campers are welcome to help themselves to locally produced food, wood and charcoal in reception and use the laundry facilities as long as they pay a contribution into an honesty box. Indeed, trust and honesty rule at this 100-pitch campsite – hopefully for years to come. Campers can also borrow home-made barbecue campfire structures to cook on in the evenings, and games and books to keep the entertainment flowing if it happens to rain.

A haven in the Mid-Wales countryside, it's not surprising that Fforest Fields entices people back year after year. One man loved it here so much that after his first visit he came back every year, always to the same pitch, until he reached the grand old age of 85 – a Cool Camper indeed! Once you've visited, though, it's easy to see why. The natural charms of this place work wonders on the soul and, as Emerson put it, 'In the presence of nature, a wild delight runs through... man.' He would've just loved it here.

COOL FACTOR The surroundings are stunning and the lake is a magical touch.

WHO'S IN Tents, caravans and dogs (on leads) – yes.

ON SITE A beautiful, timber-framed loo and shower building has underfloor heating, separate family rooms with baby-changing facilities, a laundry, washing-up room and a very popular drying room. 2 bell tents are available to hire, each sleeping up to 4 people and kitted out with their own separate kitchens. An information room has fridges, freezers and charging points. BBQs, wood, kindling and locally made charcoal are all available for toasting marshmallows. A small shop stocks local and organic produce and some of the essentials you might have left at home.

OFF SITE For something a bit different there's the National Cycle Collection (01597 825531; cyclemuseum.org.uk) at Llandrindod Wells – a bicycle museum with hundreds of different cycles, the oldest of which dates back to 1819. Those wanting to do a bit of biking themselves should head for Coed Trallwm mountain-biking centre at Aberwesyn, northwest of Builth Wells (01591 610546; coedtrallwm.co.uk), which has 3 graded trails of between 4km and 5km in length – though you'll need to bring your own bike.

FOOD & DRINK A tiny shop sells food essentials. The Hundred House Inn (01982 570231), ¼ mile away, has a nice atmosphere and decent food. Or head further and try the Fountain Inn (01982 553920) in Builth Wells – a decent boozer with a good choice of ales and an adjoining café.

GETTING THERE From the M5, take the A44 then the A481 towards Builth Wells. Fforest Fields is signposted and is on the left. From the M4, take the A40 then the A470 to Builth Wells, pass through the town, then at the roundabout take the third exit on to the A481. Fforest Fields is a few miles down the road on the right.

OPEN Easter–end October.

THE DAMAGE Pitches £4.50; adults £3.50; children (under 16) £2.50; babies free; hook-ups £2.50. Dogs are free, but must be kept on leads.

dol-llys caravan and camping

Dol-Llys Caravan and Camping, Trefeglwys Road, Llanidloes, Powys SY18 6JA 01686 412694
www.dolllyscaravancampsite.co.uk

Dol-Llys is camping as it used to be (and some would argue, still should be). This refreshingly understated site on the Evans family's working farm has been pulling in the punters for over 25 years. There are no bells and whistles; no guyrope gimmickry or fancy organised entertainment (unless you count the kiddies' play area). The beauty of Dol-Llys lies in its simplicity. And in this swathe of scenic Welsh countryside, that's really all you need.

This friendly site was crafted with families firmly in mind. There are no formal pitches, just seven acres of soft, level, well-kept grass with ample room for a scattering of 30–40 tents or so. Admittedly, some of Dol-Llys is given over to caravans (hence the tarmac paths), but we're pleased to report that these are in a separate area to the canvas contingent. Campers can pitch up by the facilities block for easy access to the more-than-adequate facilities, but the best spots are down by the idyllic river.

With anglers casting off for the plentiful trout and grayling, it's hard to believe the gently babbling brook snaking its way through Dol-Llys farm is one of the early stretches of the mighty River Severn. The source is a mere eight miles away at the foot of the Plynlimon mountain and the lively local town, Llanidloes is the first town on the river's course. More importantly, it has nine pubs. A 'watering hole' in every sense then…

COOL FACTOR Riverside simplicity at its best.

WHO'S IN Tents, groups, caravans, motorhomes, well-behaved dogs (on leads) – yes.

ON SITE Electric pitches, river pitches, secluded pitches, rough and rugged areas, and space for groups. Room for 30–40 tents. 20 caravan/motorhome pitches (18 of which are hardstanding). 5 unisex private shower/toilet rooms; 3 additional men's toilets and 1 shower; 3 ladies' toilets and 1 ladies' showers. Washing-up facilities. 'Campers Kitchen' with fridge-freezer, microwave, kettle and toaster. Campfires permitted by the river.

OFF SITE The Centre For Alternative Technology (01654 705950; cat.org.uk) in Machynlleth offers an educational and fun day out, demonstrating the cutting edge of sustainable technology. Check out the organic gardens and water-balanced cliff railway.

FOOD & DRINK The Red Lion (01686 430934) at Trefeglwys offers pub grub favourites. The Unicorn Hotel (01686 411171; unicornllanidloes.co.uk) in Llanidloes is a sleek café by day and a restaurant by night, offering refined regional faves such as Welsh lamb.

GETTING THERE Take the roundabout of the A470 into Llanidloes. Follow the road, passing the Texaco garage on your right. Take the 3rd exit off the roundabout over the bridge. Follow the road past the hospital and cemetery and take the next right, signposted Oakley Park (you'll see a brown campsite sign here). Follow the road for about ½ mile until you see the entrance on your right.

OPEN Early April–end October.

THE DAMAGE Pitch £7 per person per night; EHU £3 per night; children (4–15) £3 per night each; dogs £2 each.

llanthony priory

Llanthony Priory, Court Farm, Llanthony, Abergavenny, Monmouthshire NP7 7NN 01873 890359
www.llanthonycampsite.co.uk

Llanthony Priory resembles a mini Tintern Abbey but, being totally buried in a little-known spot in Wales amid the enormously gorgeous Black Mountains in the heart of the Brecon Beacon National Park, it's far less of a tourist trap. And unlike the great ruins of Tintern, it has its very own pub attached. Once you've persevered through the winding country lanes of the Ewyas valley and arrived at these antiquated ruins, it's hard to imagine how a small band of Augustinian monks managed to build such a majestic structure way back in the early 12th century. As you take in the glorious scenery it is, however, easy to see why they bothered.

As well as a public bar in the crypts of the abbey and a hotel occupying the Llanthony Priory's former lodgings, Court Farm – next door to the church opposite and the priory – has a field reserved for camping. The facilities are simple and thankfully the Passmore family who own the place are firm believers that Less is often in fact More. For example, rather than having a toilet block obscuring your view of the dramatic mountainside, the two-acre field has a cold-water tap with access to the public toilets in the nearby Priory car park. With no showers near this field, only hardcore campers are going to stay clean.

Bugle (pronounced Bew-glie) bridge is a well-known place to jump into the river on hot summer days, both to cool off and clean up. The bad news is that even on colder summer days the campsite doesn't allow fires. Never mind: if the chickens, who amble freely around the site, get around to laying, there are eggs available from the farm as well as home-made beefburgers and sausages to sizzle over barbecues. And the location, with the dramatic landscape framed by the arches of the priory's remaining window frames, really can't be beaten.

The campsite is rarely full, but because of its proximity to the abbey it remains popular all through the summer and much of the winter. Its other big draw is the omnipresent wall of the Black Mountains either side of the valley. Don't let the hardy climbers who often frequent the campsite put you off: once that initial climb is made, the ridge runs for miles without losing or gaining much height. All is not lost if you're not a hillwalker either: this valley holds a line of secretive paths and tracks along its entire length, which lead from one heavenly scene to another. The stroll to Cwmyoy, to view its mostly 13th-century parish church of St Martin, which leans improbably all over the place due to subsidence, will be one of life's little highlights. And leaving the confines of this Shangri-La to the north (ten miles as the crow flies or about 35 minutes of winding road) brings you to the bookish town of Hay-on-Wye (Y Gelli) right on the England–Wales border – a nice town in itself, but above all great for loading up on reading matter from its 30-odd second-hand bookshops before heading back to the site to read in perfect tranquillity.

COOL FACTOR A campsite framed by a ruined abbey and dramatic mountains – what more could you want?

WHO'S IN Tents, dogs, small campervans, big groups (if booked in advance) – yes. Large campervans, caravans – no.

ON SITE Facilities are few. Court Farm has a cold-water tap and there are public toilets (open 24 hours) at the Priory's car park. No campfires, but charcoal BBQs are allowed.

OFF SITE The countryside at Llanthony is stunning so you may not want to do much or move far once you're settled. A track leads up to join the Offa's Dyke long-distance footpath (nationaltrail.co.uk/offas-dyke-path). In Abergavenny, try the market that is on every Tuesday, Friday and Saturday.

FOOD & DRINK The Llanthony Priory Hotel bar (01873 890487; llanthonyprioryhotel.co.uk) – known locally as The Abbey – cooks up imaginative bar meals that are served in unforgettable surroundings. The Half Moon Inn (01873 890611; halfmoon-llanthony.co.uk) is a short stroll away and serves simple meals between 7pm and 9pm. The place is a real cullinary hotspot though, and among the best offerings are the Foxhunter Inn in Nantyderry (01873 881101; thefoxhunter.com), whose modern British cuisine is well worth the trip. The Hardwick (01873 854220; thehardwick.co.uk) closest to the site with a superb dinner menu (01873 854220; www.thehardwick.co.uk) and The Walnut Tree (01873 852797; thewalnuttreeinn.com), with a Michelin star to its name.

GETTING THERE From the south use the M4 and A449/A470 to Abergavenny; from the north and Midlands use the M5, M50, and A40, then the A465 towards Hereford. After 4 miles, turn left on to an unclassified road signposted to Llanthony Priory and follow the brown signs. The first campsite you come to is Lower Henllan Farm, after about 5 miles, then it's Maes-y-beran Farm and finally the Priory.

OPEN All year.

THE DAMAGE £3 per person with a discount for families. Children under school-age free.

castle knights

Castle Knights, Castle House, Usk, Monmouthshire NP15 1SD www.castleknights.co.uk

They say every Englishman's home is his castle. Well, what about the Welsh? We know of one Welshman for whom this old adage rings truer than most, for Tom Humphreys is the owner of Usk Castle in Monmouthshire. Built around 1120, this fantastically well-preserved Norman fortification overlooks the charming Mid-Wales market town, and beyond to the Black Mountains. It's a suitably atmospheric setting – the ancient ivy-clad walls, weathered gargoyles, an imposing round tower – history hued into every stone.

But, far from the cold-hearted overlord presiding over his medieval serfdom, Mr Humphreys has graciously opened up the castle grounds for a handful of lucky campers. Comprising four spacious, stripy pavilions (with additional space for around 10-or-so tents), Castle Knights offers guests the chance to indulge their most feather-plumed medieval fantasies.

Campers have the run of the castle grounds and the ruins are free to explore. Unsurprisingly, kids will adore this place, with medieval fancy dress, archery and bicycle jousting on offer. There's even a wooden watchtower from which your knee-high noblemen can plot their next defence of the realm. It's not all pitched battles, though. The setting is wonderfully peaceful. There's a magnificent sculpture trail by local artist Adam Humphreys (Tom's son), and the views over the undulating Monmouthshire hills are lovely. In short, this is the perfect setting for swaying lazily in the hammock.

Usk itself is steeped in history, and there's real pleasure to be had just strolling through this pretty town – the Victorian clock tower in Twyn Square, the cobbled pavements and the 17th-century houses are all presided over by the castle. Tom is a mine of local history too and his encyclopedic knowledge of the town's tempestuous past really brings this place to life.

COOL FACTOR Ancient ivy-clad walls, weathered gargoyles, an imposing round tower – there's history hued in every stone.

WHO'S IN Glampers, tent campers, dogs – yes. Groups (up to 20) can hire out the site exclusively. Stag and hen parties can also be arranged.

ON SITE 4 medieval pavilions (each sleeping 4–6) complete with 1 double and 2 single beds (plus extra singles if required). Additional space for up to 10 tents. Toilet and shower block with 3 toilets and 2 showers, plus fully equipped kitchen area with cutlery, fridge, freezer, gas hob and grill. 2 firepits and seating available.

OFF SITE There are spectacular walks in the area, not least in the stunning Black Mountains and Brecon Beacons National Park. The River Usk makes for excellent fishing, while summer sees young and old partaking in a spot of wild swimming. Usk is also on the National Cycle Route 42 from Glasbury to Gloucester for those wishing to explore Mid-Wales on two wheels. The famous Abergavenny Food Festival (01873 851643) is a must for foodies visiting at the end of September.

FOOD & DRINK The area is something of a gastro hot-spot.

There's the Michelin-starred Walnut Tree (01873 852797; thewalnuttreeinn.com), run by distinguished chef Shaun Hill, while the excellent Crown at Whitebrook (01600 860254; crownatwhitebrook.co.uk) offers a similarly sophisticated menu in a gorgeous Wye Valley setting. The Hardwick (01873 854220; thehardwick.co.uk) in Abergavenny is the favourite Welsh restaurant of a certain Michel Roux Jr. For something a little less grand but no less enticing, the Greyhound Inn Llantrissant (01291 672505; greyhound-inn.com) serves up pub grub favourites at reasonable prices.

GETTING THERE From M4 junction 24, take the A449 signposted Monmouth–Usk. The turn-off for Usk is the first exit, 7 miles on. Drive into Usk town centre, past the school, and turn right opposite the fire station. Follow this past Usk castle until you come to the campsite.

PUBLIC TRANSPORT Train to Newport and then bus no. #60 bus to Usk.

OPEN April–September.

THE DAMAGE From £60 (silver standard) to £100 (gold standard) per night. Rate reduction for multiple nights.

denmark farm eco campsite

Denmark Farm Eco Campsite, Betws Bledrws, Lampeter, Ceredigion SA48 8PB 01570 493358 www.denmarkfarm.org.uk

'There are dragons in there!' one young camper enthused as we made our way into the dark woodland adjoining the camping meadow at Denmark Farm. Fearing for our safety, the gallant squire grabbed his trusty sword (okay, so it was a long stick) and rushed past us with a chivalrous, 'And I'm going to get them'. Although we didn't encounter any dragons during the visit, their presence is eminently plausible at this Welsh conservation site, situated among the green humps and bumps of Celtic Ceredigion. You wouldn't blame the mystical creatures for sleeping off the effects of battling with medieval knights in a centuries-long hibernation somewhere within this 40-acre treasure trove of landscape. Encircling the camping meadow are woods, fields and ponds that have been slowly nursed back to life from the landowner's farming days. A commendable job has been carried out by Denmark Farm Conservation Centre in helping restore the site to nature, much to the joy of the local flora and fauna (dragonflies included). Pathways that lead through the woods beckon you towards fairy-tale adventures, one leading to a magical roundhouse, another to a spiky hide – is it a bird or a hedgehog? – by the long lake. Just be careful where you step; you wouldn't want to awaken any dragons – at least, not unless you have your own little St George on hand to fight them off.

COOL FACTOR 40 acres of natural, imagination-firing space.

WHO'S IN Tents, small groups, guide dogs – yes. Campervans, caravans, pets – no.

ON SITE No more than 10 tents, so booking in advance is necessary. 1 basically furnished yurt also available. Nature trails are waymarked across the site and the Centre runs 'Wild in the Woods' days for children, plus a variety of other workshops. In the woodland next to the yurt there's a well-equipped communal kitchen. A little further into the trees is the compost loo. There are no staff on site, and on booking campers are provided with detailed notes, including a helpful map and the code to use the showers and loos. There's another compost loo near the wildlife garden. Campfires are only permitted in hired firepits by prior arrangement.

OFF SITE Visit the wetlands at Cors Carons (01974 298480), about 7 miles away, which form a sanctuary for many species of bird and other wildlife, including otters. A circular walkway provides access.

FOOD & DRINK The Organic Fresh Food Company (01570 423099; organicfreshfoodcompany.co.uk) is just off the A485 and can deliver a fantastic array of produce to your door. For eating out, the Talbot Hotel in Tregaron (01974 298208; ytalbot.com) can't be beaten.

GETTING THERE From Lampeter take the A485 out of the town, signed Tregaron. After 2 miles take a left and continue up the lane. Keep going for another couple of miles and you'll see a sign for the farm, which is on the left.

OPEN April–October.

THE DAMAGE Adult £10 per night; child (aged 6–15) £5; under–6s free. Course participants £12 per night. Yurt hire £50 per night. Whole site hire £200 per night.

tyllwyd

Tyllwyd, Cwmystwyth, Aberystwyth, Ceredigion SY23 4AG 01974 282216 www.welshaccommodation.co.uk

If you need to get lost for some reason, then Tyllwyd is hard to beat. Squeezed in between the burbling waters of the River Ystwyth and an unclassified road, high in the hills at the top of Cwmystwyth, the site is about 20 miles inland from Aberystwyth. On the map it looks like the back of beyond, and in some ways it is – the nearest supermarket is in Aberystwyth, 20 miles away – but it doesn't always feel like it. Midweek and out of season, you could set your deckchair up in the middle of the road next to the site and not have to move it all day, but come a summer Sunday it can seem as though every motorcycle and classic car in the world is parading up and down this lonely strip of tarmac. This isn't actually the nuisance it might seem, happening as it does on just a single day. So, six days a week, those lucky folk camping at Tyllwyd have this lovely road at their exclusive disposal, the joyful sparkling stream of the River Ystwyth to splash about in outside the tent, an all-round view of the big green empty

hills of Mid Wales, and all laid out in a soothing, lush, green valley. In a nutshell: location, location, location.

Site facilities are good, too, though you have to cross the road to find them at the farmhouse which, once upon a time, was an inn catering for travellers on an important route across Wales. The present occupiers, the Raw family, are as welcoming as their valley is, though it should be noted that their midges offer a less friendly welcome at times.

The drive to Rhayader from the site, through the wastes of Wales, may be famously stunning, but the scenery in the other direction, downstream, is more rewarding and intimate. There are mountain-biking routes in the forest immediately to the north of Cwmystwyth and, about six miles from Tyllwyd, is Devil's Bridge, where you can climb aboard the train to Aberystwyth. The back of beyond? Maybe. But it also feels like the very centre of Wales.

COOL FACTOR Small, country campsite set in a scenic, riverside location.

WHO'S IN Tents, campervans, tourers, hikers, mountain bikers, dogs (1 per pitch) – yes. Big groups, party animals – no.

ON SITE 25–30 pitches, 16 hook-ups. Simple but immaculate separate male and female washrooms with hot and cold water, flushing loos, 1 hot shower (free). Small children's play area and sandpit plus paddling in the river. Ice packs frozen. There are some onsite farm walks with printed maps available to borrow from reception, providing a range of walks, from a short stroll before supper to a whole day spent wandering or pedalling over the farm's 3,000 acres and mountains. Open fires allowed in raised pits and BBQ facilities available alongside picnic tables. Watch out for the midges!

OFF SITE There is tonnes to do and see in the surrounding countryside. The nearby Hafod Estate (hafod.org) is fantastic, rugged walking country. Towards Aberystwyth, the Devil's Bridge Falls (01970 890233; devilsbridgefalls.co.uk) have been enticing visitors since the days of Wordsworth, who was inspired to write a poem about this great natural feature. There's also the Vale of Rheidol steam railway (01970 625819; rheidolrailway.co.uk), which runs from Devil's Bridge to Aberystwyth through stunning scenery.

FOOD & DRINK The Hafod Hotel (01970 890232; thehafodhotel.wordpress.com) at Devil's Bridge, 6 miles away, is a lively and attractive pub. New owners have transformed it into the village hub, with a tea room and restaurant as well as the pub.

GETTING THERE From Rhayader, follow the signposted road up through the Elan Valley for about 15 miles towards Aberystwyth; Tyllwyd is on the right. From Aberystwyth, follow the A4120 to Devil's Bridge, then the B4574 to Cwmystwyth, then the unclassified road signposted 'Rhayader'. The site is on the left after 3 miles.

OPEN Mid March–October.

THE DAMAGE Tent and car/campervan + 2 people £12. Children (5–15 years) £3. Extra adult £5. Tourer £13. Hook-up £3. Dogs free but must be on lead at all times.

graig wen

Graig Wen, Arthog, Nr Dolgellau, Gwynedd LL39 1YP 01341 250482 www.graigwen.co.uk

Only mad dogs and Englishmen go out in the rain, right? Well, where does that leave the Welsh? As anyone who's done their research will know, even in high summer the weather can be unpredictable in Wales. But see the lush, green valleys (lush, meaning attractive, is a word the Welsh adore) all around you? Their stunning looks are thanks to the beauty regime of a wet climate. Of course, the sun does come out in Wales, often within an hour of the rain, and there are days and days of dry spells. It's simply potluck. But whatever the weather, this campsite is an unmissable experience.

As befits one of the smartest operations in the book, everything the hosts do, they do to impress. When they first took over, the land was filled with old caravans, car batteries and monster conifers, so it's incredible that, just two years later, they had won the Green Snowdonia Award 2009 for Most Sustainable Campsite. Well-maintained facilities with hot showers are kept spick and span. Viewing benches overlooking Mawddach Estuary offer the best seat in the house at sunset o'clock, or step a little closer and test your animal spotting skills – owls, nightjars, glow-worms, badgers and kingfishers are all in residence here.

The pitches themselves are positioned to suit most tastes. Starting at the top: adjacent to the boutique-style B&B is space for ten tourers or tents. A parallel track leads to a couple of yurts (sleeping two and five respectively), plus a 'caban', an innovative new locally developed timber structure which has a rather Scandinavian feel and will sleep two; its glazed walls provide magnificent views. Isolated and sheltered among dense woodland, both the yurts and the caban offer total privacy. Back down the track you pass through a top gate and walk down a steep decline – not suitable for caravans or campervans. Career off through the hedgerow heather and bracken to some of their 'wild' camping spots. There are 18 of these tent-only spots, ranging from those with direct estuary views to pitches hidden in secret glades and a secluded hidden valley.

Intrepid explorers could tackle Cader Idris, the spectacular mountain right at the back of Graig Wen. It's a ten-minute drive to a cheap car park in a farmer's field, avoiding the crowds you get on the summit of Snowdon. And then there's the added challenge that, according to legend, if you spend the night on the top of Cader, you'll come down a poet, or yes, a madman...

You can cycle all the way to Fairbourne beach in Barmouth (which includes crossing the mouth of the estuary on a stunning bridge) without even seeing a road, and virtually the entire route to Dolgellau in the other direction is road-free, too. In addition to the cycle track, there's another family cycling path, plus a stack of more challenging trails at nearby Coed-y-Brenin, around five miles north of Dolgellau.

Back at camp after a hard day's cycling, it's time to light a campfire and, after burning rubber all day, burning a few marshmallows on sticks seems like an extremely well-earned treat.

COOL FACTOR Smooth access to walking, cycling, eating, sightseeing, swimming – and the beach.

WHO'S IN Everyone! Tents, campervans, caravans, glampers, dogs, cyclists/mountain bikers, walkers...

ON SITE 10 pitches with electric hook-up and 2 grass pitches for smaller tents on top field. 18 grass pitches in the lower fields (3 with parking). 2 yurts and a cabin for hire (Easter–October) and a bell tent (July/August). Arrive 2–4pm for lift to your pitch with quad or wheelbarrows provided to move your kit to lower field pitches. There's a steep hill-climb to the shower and toilet facilities. Campfires allowed on lower fields and communal campfire on top field. Bikes for hire.

OFF SITE Clambering Cader Idris (892m) is a great option and the family-friendly 'Pony Path' makes it manageable for all. Alternatively walk straight off the campsite along the stunning (and flat) waterside Mawddach Trail to Barmouth.

FOOD & DRINK The owners sell eggs, ice cream, marshmallows and breakfast hampers. Stock up on local produce and tasty treats in Dolgellau at the Thursday market. Good pub grub can be found at The George III Hotel (01341 422525; georgethethird.co.uk) 5 minutes' drive or an hour's walk along the estuary trail.

GETTING THERE Turn off the A470 Dolgellau bypass on to the A493, signposted Tywyn-Fairbourne. The campsite is 4½ miles further on the right. Head from Fairbourne on the A493, through Arthog, past the quarry and look for a sign saying 'Concealed entrance' on the left – that's it.

PUBLIC TRANSPORT Morfa Mawddach railway station is about 2 miles from the site, accessible by foot/cyclepath or bus. Buses run between Aberystwyth, Machynlleth and Dolgellau. Ask the driver to drop you off at Graig Wen.

OPEN Top field all year. Lower fields May–September.

THE DAMAGE Top field: £6–£9 per adult, £3–£4 children under 16; under-5s and well-behaved dogs on leads are free, Hook-ups £3.50/night. Tent camping fields: £10 one-off vehicle charge + adults £6–£9 per night; children £3–£4. Under-5s free. Back/bikepackers £6 all year. Yurts and eco-Caban/bell tent £160–£195 for 2 nights.

dinas – hideaway in the hills

Dinas Caravan Park, Hideaway in the Hills, Dinas, Llanbedr, Gwynedd LL45 2PH 01341 241585
www.hideaway-in-the-hills.com

With a name like 'Hideaway in the Hills' expectations of Dinas campsite were high. Thankfully, it didn't disappoint. Accessed by narrow roads and nestled in a picturesque Snowdonian valley, at Dinas you really do feel like you've stumbled upon a hidden gem.

Small, quiet and family-friendly, Dinas is on mostly level ground and split between the stream-side lower field and the upper field, which is surrounded by tall oak trees. Each pitch comes complete with its very own wooden picnic table and campfires are very much encouraged. For just a couple of quid you can hire a metal fire box, then you're good to go. Firewood is helpfully brought around each evening. Dinas is truly a place of peace and, as such, the owners ask that noise is kept to a minimum between the hours of 11pm and 7.30am, with loud music being a no-no. All this adds to the tranquil vibe and helps everyone get a good night's kip.

This truly is nature's playground – children will be entertained for hours building dens in the forest, creating dams in the stream or playing on the rope swings. The campsite also has its very own lake where you can hire a Canadian canoe and take to the water, or bring a blow-up dingy and enjoy splashing around.

If you like your camping a little more *luxe*, then Dinas also offers glamping in a pre-erected bell tent complete with double bed, duvet, pillows and... wait for it... your own wood-heated hot tub! Somewhere in-between this and a regular tent is the camping pod, which is also not too far removed from an authentic camping experience and feels a bit like sleeping in a snug den.

In truth you could quite happily spend your entire stay without venturing outside the boundary of the campsite, but then you would be missing out on some really special treats. The nearest beach is only three miles away and this section of coast boasts a plethora of unspoilt sandy stretches. Llandanwg is close by and has views across the peninsula and rock pools to explore. Shell Island (as the name suggests) is the place to head for some impressive additions to your crustacean collection. It also boasts some of the highest sand dunes in Wales. Morfa Dyffyn is another fantastic stretch of sand, and if you prefer to do your sunbathing in the buff, this is the place for you – just walk half a mile along and you'll spot the sign which declares naturists are permitted to disrobe.

Of course the best way to explore this area is on foot and the helpful folk at Dinas provide walking guides for leisurely strolls or more taxing rambles. There's also a little hill called Snowdon that's not too far away.

COOL FACTOR A peaceful, picturesque hideaway in a Snowdonian valley.

WHO'S IN Tents, glampers, families, couples and kids – yes. Dogs and large groups – no.

ON SITE 30 camping spaces, 1 glamping bell (with hot tub!) and a camping pod. Toilet block with free hot showers. Freezer ice-pack service. Each pitch has its own wooden picnic table. Pay phone available 24 hours. 6 electric hook-ups (lower field). Wi-Fi (upper field, paid-for). Coin operated tumble dryer. Canoe hire. Campfires in raised pits only.

OFF SITE The site gives direct access to the Ardudwy Way footpath (taithardudwyway.com), plus there are numerous walks in the Rhinogydd Mountains and, of course, the imposing challenge of Snowdon itself. Get on your bike and head to Coed y Brenin (forestry.gov.uk/coedybrenin) for some world-class mountain-biking trails through the forest, or Antur Stinlog (01766 832214; anturstiniog.com), which has downhill trails for every level. Nearby Harlech Castle is a UNESCO World Heritage Site, while the mock-Italianate Portmeirion village is an amazing attraction, made famous by the 1960s cult TV series, The Prisoner. There are also the steam trains of the Ffestiniog and Welsh Highland Railway (see p.289).

FOOD & DRINK The Victoria Inn (01341 241213; victoriainnllanbedr.co.uk) and Ty Mawr (01341 241440; tymawrhotel.com) in nearby Llanbedr are good places to refuel with decent pub food and good beer. Harlech has a wealth of tea rooms and cafés including the tasty Llew Glas Deli (01766 781095).

GETTING THERE Llanbedr village, 2.5 miles from the campsite, is situated between Barmouth and Harlech on the A496 coastal road.

OPEN All year.

THE DAMAGE Camping: £8 per adult per night. £3.50 per night for children over 3. Camping pods from £30 per night for 2 people. Glamping from £175 for two nights.

nant-y-big

Nant-y-Big, Cilan, Abersoch, Pwllheli, Gwynedd LL53 7DB 01758 712686 www.nantybig.co.uk

A campsite with a view. You've heard it all before, right? However, the unforgettable scenery greeting campers upon arrival at Nant-y-Bîg is much more than just a pleasant backdrop. This family-run, environmentally aware campsite is situated on the Llyn Peninsula, a remarkable region known as the 'Edge of Wales' – and if you like walking on the edge, you'll love Nant-y-Bîg. First question, where to camp? Guests have three options. There's a section for families only, with electric hook-ups (no coastline views here, but it's only a 10–15 minute walk to the beach); a second area with panoramic seaside views of Cardigan Bay; and a third spot set in the valley just above surf-friendly Porth Ceiriad beach. The majority of pitches are flat, well maintained and provide plenty of space for the kids to roam. Check the weather report upon arrival; if wind is predicted, ask for a sheltered spot. Nant-y-Big's cheerful owner Dylan displays the latest forecast in his tastefully converted reception area, which is housed in one of the old farm stables.

Facilities here are simple, well maintained and appropriate. There's a brand new shower block and the toilets are kept clean. Of course, ablution facilities aren't why campers visit this unique corner of Britain; they come for the sublime scenery and the opportunity to get reacquainted with nature at its glorious best. Despite this secluded location, the fact is Nant-y-Bîg isn't too far from civilisation. Abersoch (two miles away) comes alive in summer with an influx of surfers, boaties and beach bums. Fringed by lush green hills, the small town has a decent selection of pubs, cafés and restaurants, with some overlooking a pretty harbour.

If you enjoy coastal walking then Nant-y-Bîg is your Eden. The relationship between the Llyn Peninsula's steep hills and driving waters makes for intoxicating stuff. There's wildlife a plenty – keep your eyes peeled for the bay's famous dolphins and birdlife. But be warned: when Mother Nature gets herself in a bad mood, ramblers are a wee bit exposed, so make sure you bring a spare pair of socks and a waterproof jacket. However, the weather can change just as quickly, and when the sun reappears, illuminating the Irish Sea, you'll be so glad you came.

COOL FACTOR Cliff-top, back-to-basics camping, located slap bang on the Wales Coastal Path.

WHO'S IN Tents, campervans, motorhomes, caravans, dogs (on a lead at all times) – yes. Groups and noise after 11pm – no.

ON SITE Pitches spread across 3 large, separate fields (2 of which have sea views). The 'Family Field' is away from the sea but has the advantage of electric hook-ups and is very spacious. There are 4 showers, 6 toilets, 2 urinals and 8 washbasins. There is also an outdoor dish-washing area. If you're more about the views, then the 'Panoramic' or 'Near the Beach' areas are the better pick, with only 60 pitches over a whopping 9 acres of land. Facilities are basic but always clean. The toilet block for the 'Panoramic' area is down in the farmyard and has 7 toilets, 3 urinals and 4 washbasins. The 'Near the Beach' fields have a simple toilet block with 3 toilets, 3 washbasins and a urinal. BBQs are permitted off the ground but no open fires. Ice-pack freezing and Wi-Fi available.

OFF SITE The site is ideally located for easy access to the Wales Coast Path (walescoastpath.gov.uk). At the western tip of the Llyn Peninsula lies the pin-neat former fishing village of Aberdaron, home to the 5th-century church of St Hywyn (01758 760659).

FOOD & DRINK Best places in Abersoch are the Coconut Kitchen (01758 712250; thecoconutkitchen.co.uk) and the more pricey Venetia (01758 713354; venetiawales.com). Boasting breathtaking views across the sea, Yr Eifl and Snowdonia, Ty Coch Inn (01758 720498; tycoch.co.uk) is well worth the 30-minute drive and short walk.

GETTING THERE From Sarn Bach, head towards Cilan and after 600m you will see a small green metal shed on your left; the turning for Nant-y-Bîg is 30m up the road.

PUBLIC TRANSPORT Pwllheli railway station is less than 10 miles away, from where buses pass the end of the lane to Nant-y-Bîg 3 times a day.

OPEN April–October.

THE DAMAGE £9 per adult (16 years +), £3 for kids (3–15), free for children (under 3) and dogs £2. Electric hook-ups £3.50 per night.

aberafon

Aberafon, Gyrn Goch, Caernarfon, Gwynedd LL54 5PN 01286 660295 www.aberafon.co.uk

Let us not beat about the bush – this campsite scores on the old 'location, location, location' chestnut, in a beautiful spot sandwiched between the beach and the mountains on the Llyn Peninsula, 10 miles south of Caernarfon. Negotiating a steep, narrow lane to the site, past the bumbling stream by the amenities block, feels like you are descending into a secret valley within the mountains. Drive past a covered games room and the owners' lovely house, past upper fields and down to a joyous coastal 'Beach Field', a grassy patch so close to the sea as to be virtually in it. It can only be accessed by small vehicles and features 15 pitches with 10 electric hook-ups.

Both grassy tiers of the campsite sharply meet the rugged coastline and there is a tiny, partly sandy, wild beach full of rockpools to explore. Braver swimmers might attempt a quick dip – a little wild swimming is all part of Aberafon's package – but there are sandier swimming beaches along the peninsula. There is even a slipway to launch your boat from, should you happen to carry one with you. Co-owner Hugh is an extreme-sports fan, so he'll approve of anyone who wishes to canoe downstream, hike through Snowdonia or try wakeboarding at Glas Fryn Park, near Pwllheli. Hugh has regularly jumped off Gyrn Goch mountain, which overlooks the campsite, strapped to a paraglider. If you're feeling equally adventurous, sign up with the local paragliding school. So how best to describe the charm of Aberafon? Great location? Superb situation? Or how about astonishing situation in a wonderful location?

COOL FACTOR Fantastic seaside situation, with wonderful scenery and an away-from-it-all feel.

WHO'S IN Families, tents, campervans, caravans, dogs – yes. Groups – no.

ON SITE 65 pitches, for tents and tourers, 40 hook-ups. Campfires permitted on the beach; wood available to buy. Clean but basic facilities – 1 shower/toilet block, with 13 toilets, 6 showers and 4 urinals. Laundry facilities, dish-washer, ice-pack freezing, TV and pool room. Onsite shop for buying daily essentials, open in the summer holiday only. BBQs permitted off the ground.

OFF SITE All sorts happening near by, including the historic and rather quaint little town of Caernarfon, with its awesome castle (01286 677617; caernarfon-castle. co.uk). The atmospheric Llechwedd Slate Caverns (01766 83036; llechwedd-slate-caverns.co.uk) are a must-see, while Penrhyn Castle at Bangor (01248 353084; NT) is a more decadent affair. Cycle and walking tracks lead from the site to Clynnogfawr and Trefor, and bikes can be delivered (01753 798902; velovert.co.uk).

FOOD & DRINK Drive across the peninsula and treat yourself to some fine dining at the Plas Bodegroes (01758 612363; bodegroes.co.uk) in Pwllheli.

GETTING THERE Take the A487 from Caernarfon south towards Porthmadog for 4 miles, then the A499 towards Pwllheli for 7 miles, then sharp right into the very narrow lane at Gyrn Goch.

PUBLIC TRANSPORT Regular buses run within less than ½ mile of the site to/from Caernarfon, Porthmadog, Pwllheli, and Nefyn.

OPEN Easter–end October.

THE DAMAGE Adult £8; child £4; electric hook-up £3.50; boat on trailer £4.

bach wen farm

Bach Wen Farm & Cottages, Clynnog Fawr, Caernarfon, Gwynedd LL54 5NH 01286 660336 www.bachwen.co.uk

The Three Rivals mountain range splinters from the western edge of Snowdonia and drops towards the coast. In the foothills of the national park, where the slopes peter into tranquil countryside that then merges into beachy coast, Bach Wen Farm lies in an historic building with 7th-century origins. Tucked on this ribbon of land between mountains and sea, the farm has been transformed into a welcoming self-catering property. But with such a picture-perfect setting it's more earth-bound accommodation that boasts perhaps the best position, where owners Helen and Johnny have shaped an understated yet beautiful campsite – a peaceful destination for lovers of the great outdoors. Tucked in a secluded woodland glade a short walk from the farm buildings, tent pitches offer a quiet spot to relax on the seafront, while two newly finished glamping pods provide that little extra comfort. The pods boast electricity and a mini-fridge along with a toasty wood-burning stove that serves to keep the place warm during the colder winter months. The rusticity of the stove is echoed in the wooden cabinets and old lamps, while a fold-out futon acts as a cosy bed that gives extra space during the day. A private shower room and toilet make the place your own, as does a private area on the doorstep overlooking the sea; a dreamy spot in which to while away the twilight hours.

A recently renovated barn by the main buildings acts as a sociable space to shelter, where you can hang out with friends and download the day's activities. A few metres to the sea lands you on a beautiful stony beach, where shingle and rocks are washed by the waves before the tide recedes, revealing some softer sandy patches. It's a safe place for swimming and fishing, along with hopping among the rocks and sea life-spotting in the pools.

Campers shouldn't let the escapism of coastal living prevent them from heading elsewhere, though, since the surroundings of Bach Wen Farm are as pleasant as the site itself. Within walking distance the ancient burial chambers and historic church in Clynnog Fawr are the centrepieces of a charming village. A drive west along the Llyn Peninsula rewards you with further sandy beaches and a handful of quaint rural settlements. Hikers will, undoubtedly, head straight for the hills of Snowdonia National Park but it is also worth taking the time to explore parts of the longest coastal walk in the UK, which starts just next to the campsite in Clynnog Fawr.

Whether you traipse through the mountains or relax on the beach, Bach Wen Farm acts as the perfect base for exploring the northwest coast of Wales. Be sure to get back by bedtime, though, as the campsite is one of the best places from which to watch the sun set over the Irish Channel.

COOL FACTOR A tranquil campsite with stunning views in all directions.

WHO'S IN Tents, pod-bound glampers and dogs all welcome.

ON SITE Tent pitches in a beautiful secluded glade along with 2 glamping pods in a coastline spot with stunning views across Caernarfon Bay and Snowdonia. The site is 9 acres with access to a beach, where you can swim, fish and play. Camping pods come fully equipped with wood-burning stoves, mini fridge, electricity, futon and a private outside area overlooking the sea. Each pod has its own shower room. A recently renovated barn is accessible to all campers and has sofas and tables, books, games and a TV for all to use.

OFF SITE It's a short walk into the small local village of Clynnog Fawr, with the beautiful church of St Beuno, while Caernarfon Castle (see p.280) is within driving distance. Quaint Aberdaron is on the end of the peninsula, while Trefor (5 minutes' drive) is slightly nearer and has a quiet sandy beach. Alternatively, there is the Blue Flag-accredited beach at Dinas Dingle. Walkers should head to Snowdonia National Park (eryri-npa.gov.uk), which is best entered by a trek along The Nantlle Ridge.

FOOD & DRINK Clynnog Fawr is a 5-minute walk away. There is a shop selling basic commodities and a petrol station that stays open late, but no pubs in the village itself.

GETTING THERE From the M56, follow the A55 north and exit for Caernarfon. Drive through the town and follow the A487 towards Porthmadog. After 3 miles turn right on the roundabout to the A499 towards Pwllheli; after 7 miles you come to Clynnog Fawr. Continue past the church on your left and after 100m you will see a red sign for 'Bachwen Holiday Cottages' where you turn right.

OPEN All year.

THE DAMAGE Pods £50 per night. Camping £10 per adult per night; 5–15 year olds £5; under-5s free. Dogs free.

beddgelert

Beddgelert, Gwynedd LL55 4UU 01766 890288 www.campingintheforest.co.uk/beddgelert

Lovely little Beddgelert (meaning the grave of Gelert) is a quaint Welsh village made up of stone buildings, purple heather hills and the weaving River Glaslyn. Its name is said to refer to an old wife's tale (or should that be dog's tale?) regarding Llywelyn the Great, who believed his hound Gelert had savaged his baby boy. Llywelyn attacked the dog, and it soon fell to the ground gravely injured. However, moments later he heard a cry and stumbled through bushes to find his son snug in his cradle. Today, the 'grave' of Gelert is a popular tourist attraction, reached by one of the numerous riverside trails of the stunning Snowdonia National Park.

Situated in the heart of Wales' very first national park (established in 1951), Beddgelert is a charming, isolated campsite in a region brimming with dramatic foothills and lush forests. This unadorned site certainly harks back to traditional camping from days gone by. You'll find nothing fancy or flash here; pitches are large, flat and well laid out, while ablution facilities (showers, toilets and washbasins) are on the basic side but more than adequate. The site's friendly and informative wardens can be seen wandering the dense forest, and advise all campers to pack rock pegs, especially in the summer months.

The Snowdonia National Park is Wales' most notable (and most frequented) chunk of nature, with around 350,000 visitors choosing to climb, walk or ride the train to the summit each year. However, there's plenty more to discover than just Snowdon. Spanning almost 40 miles east to west

and over 50 miles north to south, it covers sandy beaches, craggy cliff tops and glorious estuaries. Thankfully, Beddgelert is located slap bang in the middle of this natural nirvana.

In these chaotic urban days, with alarm clocks beeping, computers glaring and headphones thumping, it may well be a blessing in disguise that there's no mobile phone coverage at Beddgelert. So why not take the opportunity to leave the modern world behind and escape to Snowdonia National Park, to camp by a serene stream and fairytale forest. Sounds tempting, right?

COOL FACTOR Peace and serenity in the heart of Snowdonia.

WHO'S IN Tents, caravans, motorhomes, trailer tents and dogs – yes.

ON SITE 195 spaces of various sizes. There are toilets, showers, a parent and baby room, electric razor sockets, washbasins, a payphone, recreation hall, children's play area, laundry facilities and drinking water taps. And a handy small shop selling groceries and camping equipment.

OFF SITE Sygun Copper Mine (01766 890595; syguncoppermine.co.uk) is a top family attraction, a 5-minute drive from Beddgelert. Above ground, ride the Snowdon Mountain Railway (0844 493 8120; snowdonrailway.co.uk), to the summit of the mountain, the highest peak in Wales, or take on the challenge of climbing it instead. For those after something less strenuous, mosey along the A498 leading to 2 of Wales' most beautiful lakes, Llyn Gwynant and Llyn Dinas, both providing excellent walking routes.

FOOD & DRINK Beddgelert Bistro (01766 890543; beddgelert-bistro.co.uk) offers tea, coffee and home-made cakes, and serves hot and cold meals. In a renovated chapel near the base of the Watkin Path, Caffi Gwynant (01766 890855; cafesnowdon.co.uk) is a great place for a drink or something to eat before, or after, a walk to the summit.

GETTING THERE From the M6 north and M62: follow the M56 west and join the M53; join the A55 and follow this until it joins the A487 towards Caernarfon. Follow the A487 to the A4085, and the campsite is on your right. From Birmingham and the south, follow the M6 and join the M54; take the A5 to Shrewsbury and join the A458 heading west to the A470 (NW) and then the A487 to Porthmadog. Join the A498 and turn right on to the A4085. The site is on your left.

PUBLIC TRANSPORT Buses S4 and 97, from Caernarfon and Porthmaodog respectively, stop at the site. The Welsh Highland Railway also stops at Beddgelert (see p.289).

OPEN All year round.

THE DAMAGE Prices per pitch (per night), including 2 adults, start at £13.50.

llyn gwynant campsite

Llyn Gwynant Campsite, Nantgwynant, Gwynedd LL55 4NW 01766 890302 www.gwynant.co.uk

Something about Llyn Gwynant needs to be explained right from the start – it can be a bit of a madhouse at times. Well, perhaps madhouse isn't quite the right word – though neither is it that wrong either. This large campsite can accommodate one hell of a lot of campers and, quite often, that is exactly how many can be found here. But it's only really a madhouse because everybody seems to be busy doing something, or about to do something, or recovering from having just done it. 'Frenetic' may be more accurate. 'Hyperactive' may be going a little too far, but by now the message must be sinking in: if you want outdoor action combined with your camping then Llyn Gwynant is probably *the* place to come to.

The list of activities taking place on, near or from the site on the late May Bank Holiday weekend, when the *Cool Camping* crew pitched up, reads as follows: canoeing, sailing, rafting, walking, rock climbing, abseiling, boateering, gorge scrambling and the presently trendy activity of coasteering. Not to mention just sitting here, wide-eyed, watching it all happen. With all this going on and the waters of Llyn Gwynant so handy for just messing about in, an active family holiday here offers an opportunity for everyone to be completely cream-crackered by the end of the day.

The variety and scale of the attractions on offer during school holidays does mean that a large number of young folk of all ages are actively encouraged to come here, but with careful management; in all the years the site has been operating, the incidence of noisy or unruly behaviour has been almost non-existent. Campfire enthusiasts can indulge themselves at Llyn Gwynant with 250 fire grates provided free for campers' use. All that they ask is that you only use wood purchased on site, and that you don't take it home with you, of course.

Llyn Gwynant is probably the top campsite in Britain for an activity-based family holiday, but outside of school holidays it's also a staggeringly scenic campsite in itself, and indeed can be one of the best places in Britain for the more reclusive camper: the kind of camper who just wants to immerse themselves in the natural beauty right in the heart of Snowdonia, bring the tent for a few days of peak-bagging in the surrounding mountains or just lazily paddle about untroubled in the crystal-clear waters of Llyn Gwynant.

For whiling away the wetter days there is even a railway that crawls its way to the top of Snowdon from Llanberis, which is just over the hill. However, *Cool Camping*'s man on the spot reckons walking up (and especially down) is the less scary option. So which Llyn Gwynant do you want to camp at? The mad, frantic outdoor activity-led campsite during the school holidays, or that peaceful near-empty hideaway in the mountains? It's just a matter of timing.

COOL FACTOR Staggeringly scenic location and an even more staggering array of outdoor activities on offer during the school holidays.

WHO'S IN Everyone! Tents, campervans, caravans, couples, families, groups, active campers – yes.

ON SITE Modern, well-maintained block with toilets and showers. A variety of camping spaces, some by the river and others overlooking the lake, though the immediate lake shore is kept for everyone to enjoy. You can park near your car at most pitches, though there are fields with a short walk to your pitch. Larger areas can be reserved for big groups.

OFF SITE Bodnant Gardens (01492 650460; NT) near Conwy is especially stunning in late May or early June. Penrhyn Castle, (see p.280) Bangor, is decadence on a huge scale, while Conwy Castle (01492 592358; conwy.com) in Conwy is equally special, particularly when you visit in conjunction with the old town walls.

FOOD & DRINK The Pen-Y-Gwryd Hotel (01286 870211; pyg. co.uk) is 2 miles away along an old Roman road, and is where the 1953 Everest team stayed while training, so is now the haunt of hill folk. Traditional atmosphere and excellent food.

GETTING THERE Follow the A5 from Betws-y-Coed to Capel Curig, turn left along the A4086 for 5 miles to Pen-y-Gwryd, then take the A498 for 2½ miles and the site is on the right at the head of the lake.

PUBLIC TRANSPORT Regular bus service passing the site to Caernarfon and Beddgelert.

OPEN Early March–early December.

THE DAMAGE Adults £9–£10 per night (high season), £11 August Bank Holiday; children (5–15 years) £5; under-5s free; dogs £1; firewood £5 per bag; refundable noise bond of £20 per person for groups of more than 4 people may be requested.

rynys farm

Rynys Farm, Nr Betwys-y-Coed, Snowdonia, Conwy LL26 0RU 01690 710218 www.rynys-camping.co.uk

Decisions, decisions. Everywhere you turn there are choices to be made, people pressing you for an answer, offering you options: three dozen digital TV channels; a thousand mobile phone tariffs; the bargain bucket or the supersize with fizzy and fries? Press the red button now. Please hold while we try to connect you... On the other other hand, Rynys Farm is a no-nonsense campsite run by Carol Williams, a no-nonsense woman, who gives you two choices. Do you want to pitch in the upper field (spectacular but windy) or the lower field (spacious and secluded)? Simple, done. Enjoy your stay.

The site is on a working farm nestled in a cleft of soft, green hill above the town of Betws-y-Coed to the west of the mighty Snowdon. The views are the kind you get in fabric softener ads: gentle, soft and comforting. But then there's the odd tractor and a bleating sheep to remind you that this isn't really an advertiser's stage set but real, live countryside. Nearby Betws-y-Coed is great if you like craft shops, outdoor wear and ice cream and was probably a real gem before the invention of the internal combustion engine. Now it suffers from having the A5 and its 18-wheelers rumbling through the middle of town. Still, it's a good base from which to explore the surrounding area and great for a cuppa if it rains.

As attractions go, the birthplace of the first man to translate the Bible into Welsh might not rank all that highly on your list. But old Bishop William Morgan's house at Ty Mawr Wybrnant, restored to its 16th-century glory, is a bit of a treasure trove of rural Welsh life. And even if you

don't fancy going in, there's an adventure to be had just getting there. It's in the southern part of the Gwydyr Forest Park and has a single-track road leading to it from Penmachno. If you pass by the Bishop's House and carry on, through a gate, the road sprouts a thin Brazilian of grass, which grows ever more unkempt, until you're driving on little more than two ruts on either side of shin-high grass that tickles the underside of your car. Then the bracken closes in and the tarmac breaks up and you're into the real wild stuff. It's not for the fainthearted, but if you keep at it the road does eventually bring you back out by Conwy Falls. And if it's a bit too hairy to do by car, it makes a great semi-offroad bike trail.

For a more sedate time, Rynys Farm is plenty big enough to spread out and relax in. Both fields catch the morning rays, bask in the warmth (with occasional showers) during the day and, as evening sets in, are raked by the sun setting slowly somewhere by Snowdon. It's all pretty simple, really, and the last decision of the day is only whether you'll want to stay here again tomorrow.

COOL FACTOR A site located above the tourist fray with fabric-softener views.

ON SITE An old stone building above the lower field has the WCs and showers (2 of each) and a kitchen and washing room. By the upper field there's a male and female WC. It's all kept clean and tidy, but the hot showers are 10p for 2 minutes or £3 an hour if you've had a hard day. Shepherd's Hut available all year and sleeps 2 people; includes a fridge, stove and all cooking utensils. Beautiful view in a secluded part of the site. Yurt sleeps 2 adults, 2 children and has mattresses, wood-burning stove, 2-ring gas stove and oven.

OFF SITE This part of Wales is criss-crossed by little steam railways. There's the famous one up to the top of Snowdon (see p.285) and the Conwy Valley Railway running out of Betwys-y-Coed (01690 710568 ;conwyrailwaymuseum.co.uk). There's also the 2-line Ffestiniog and Welsh Highland Railway (01766 516000; festrail.co.uk), linking Porthmadog, Caernarfon and Blaenau Ffestiniog.

FOOD & DRINK Betwys-y-Coed is the place to go for an enjoyable local meal. There is plenty of choice to suit all pockets and taste including The Old Ship (01492 640013; the-old-ship.co.uk) a traditional inn serving hearty food.

GETTING THERE A few miles short of Betws-y- Coed, past Rhydlanfair on the A5, and there's a sign 50m before the campsite. Turn right and follow the road up a steep single-track road and you're there. If you're coming from Betwys-y-Coed, the entrance is 50m past the Conwy Falls Café.

PUBLIC TRANSPORT There are reasonably frequent trains to Betwys-y-Coed and the Llangollen bus service stops near the Conwy Falls Café, from which it's a steep walk up to the site.

OPEN The site is open for tents all year, but caravans and campervans are only allowed between Easter and October.

THE DAMAGE Adults are £8, children £2.50, per night. It's £2 for a caravan and a dog is 50p (on a lead). Shepherd's hut is £45 per night. Electric hook-up £4 per night. Yurt £50 per night.

scotland

campsite locator

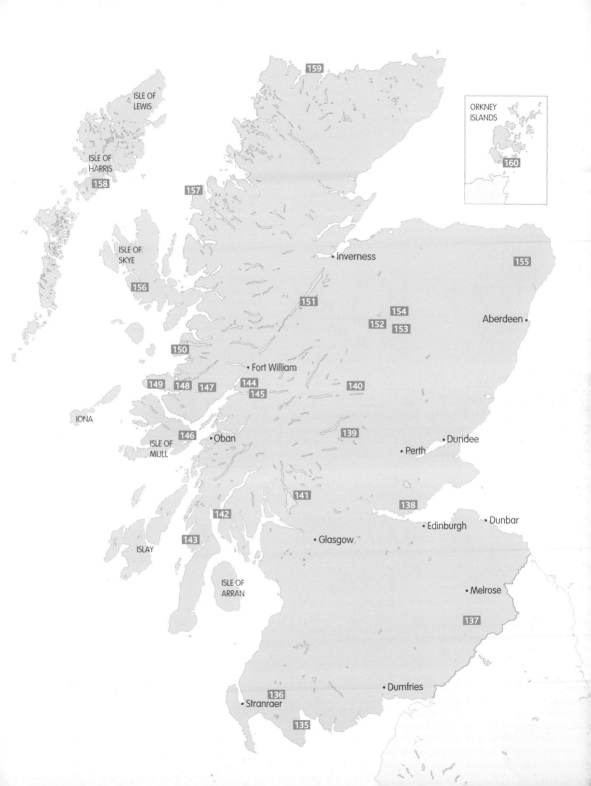

ISLE OF
LEWIS

ISLE OF
HARRIS
158

157

ORKNEY
ISLANDS

160

ISLE OF
SKYE
156

159

•Inverness

155

151

154
152 153

Aberdeen •

150

Fort William

149 148 147

144
145

140

IONA

146 •Oban

139

•Dundee

•Perth

ISLE OF
MULL

141

138

142

•Edinburgh

•Dunbar

ISLAY

143

•Glasgow

ISLE OF
ARRAN

•Melrose

137

•Dumfries

136

•Stranraer

135

campsites at a glance

drumroamin farm

Drumroamin Farm, 1 South Balfern, Kirkinner Newton Stewart, Wigtownshire, Dumfries and Galloway DG8 9DB
01988 840613 www.drumroamin.co.uk

A single lane, one-mile road leads campers down to Drumroamin Farm, with passing spaces on either side. Should you meet another car or caravan, the driver's face may tell a tale. Some, laden high with bags, tents and bicycles, will have children in the back, peering out of the windows, already half asleep from their weekend away. Others, caravans prim and clean, bimble down the lane with passengers bouncing from another fun weekend away or downcast at the thought of heading home. Whatever you see in the faces of those leaving, it will not be regret. Drumroamin Farm, it seems, is a place that leaves no one disappointed. Small, welcoming and unpretentious, the campsite has built a reputation as one of the friendliest in the Lowlands and it's safe to say that isn't set to change.

Poised a mile inland from Wigtown Bay, and with views across the surrounding countryside, Drumroamin Farm is a traditional site with very few frilly bells and whistles yet everything required for an excellent camping experience. Fields come no flatter than the grassy camping paddocks here, divided by wooden fences and low hedges to provide some extra shelter. A large, modern sanitary block has hot showers and is immaculately well kept. No sooner have you left your morning dewy footprints in the spacious cubicles, then they are wiped away, returning to the impeccable cleanliness you will find across the site, including the wood-floored communal space next door. Here a pool table and television are ideal for kids on a rainy afternoon, while a collection of books and a stash of brochures allow you to sit around and plan the next couple of days.

Outside, a covered sandpit and play area become a social point for little ones, who make friends with other campers before they take to playing ball games in the grassy space provided. Adults will also find a host of things to do in the vicinity and those who enjoy wildlife will be in their element. With views across a designated RSPB nature reserve, there's plenty to keep the twitchers occupied, including golden plover, pink-footed geese, ospreys and lapwings. Those willing to take a longer walk can also head to Garlieston, with its sleepy beach and working harbour.

Campers with a car will find a host of attractions further afield. Nearby Wigtown – Scotland's 'National Book Town' – boasts a cluster of second-hand bookshops and a pleasant main square. For many, however, a key attraction is not discovered by day but by night, when darkness falls in this quiet part of south west Scotland. Renowned for being one of the darkest areas in Europe, Drumroamin Farm enjoys spectacular skies and, on a clear night, campers can sit back and enjoy the twinkling blanket of the Milky Way.

COOL FACTOR Peace, quiet and pristine night skies.

WHO'S IN Tents, campervans, caravans, couples, families and well-behaved dogs – yes. Noisy groups – no.

ON SITE 20 electric hook-ups and 30 non-electric pitches. The site is at the end of a 1-mile-long lane with no passing traffic and surrounded by farmland. A modern shower block features a disabled shower room and a dish-washing area, equipped with 2 washing machines, a dryer and a large freezer. In a separate room there is a seating area with tables, chairs, a pool table and a TV for rainy evenings. There is also a small outdoor play area with a sandpit and loads of room for children to let off steam.

OFF SITE The neighbouring Wigtown Bay RSPB reserve (01988 402130) is within walking distance of the site, and there are plenty of other good walks from the campsite. Information and brochures on such routes can be found in the games room and, if you get chatting to Lesley and Ralph, they may have some local OS maps you can borrow. Garlieston is worth a brief stop for its beach and pleasant seafront and, just beyond, Galloway House Gardens (01988 600680; gallowayhousegardens.co.uk) is an exotic seaside gardens that's especially lovely in spring. St Ninian's Cave and St Ninian's Chapel, slightly further south (whithorn.com), have been sights of pilgrimage for centuries. Inland, head to Wigtown – Scotland's National Book Town, which has a host of good shops and eateries.

FOOD & DRINK For a meal out, try the Bladnoch Inn (01988 402200; bladnochinn.co.uk), about 2½ miles away. The food is delicious and reasonably priced.

GETTING THERE The campsite is a 20-minute drive from the A75 Newton Stewart roundabout. Take the A714 to Wigtown and after 5 miles turn right on to the B7005 and keep straight on to then rejoin the A714 at Bladnoch, heading towards Braehead and then Kirkinner (A746). Shortly after leaving Kirkinner take a left towards Garlieston on the B7004. Take the second turning on your left by the sign for Drumroamin.

OPEN All year.

THE DAMAGE £7 tent/caravan/motorhome, £3 electric hook-up, £4 per adult. £2 per child (under 16).

balloch o' dee

Balloch O' Dee Campsite, Kirkcowan, Newton Stewart, Wigtownshire, Dumfries and Galloway DG8 0ET 01671 830708
www.ballochodee.com

Balloch O' Dee's farm campsite is located in one of the Lowlands' most stunning areas – right on the edge of fir-cloaked Galloway Forest Park, with its clear night skies (it's the only European designated Dark Skies forest). James and Hazel bought the place in 2010 and, just 12 months later, opened its gates to campers in search of a rural retreat. Their hard work has paid off, as the campsite is fast becoming a family favourite. Back when we first visited in those early days it was the stark rusticity of the place, tucked away amid inspiring landscapes and boasting ancient stone farm buildings, that made it really stand out. Years later, with the addition of electricity, toilets and showers, there has been a change, yet the subtlety with which James and Hazel have shaped their campsite means the same unpretentious, rural-camping character still shines through.

There's plenty of space (15 acres to be exact) and the large camping field offers spectacular views across the surrounding countryside.

The atmosphere is relaxed and informal; kids can often be found paddling or trying to catch crayfish in the farm's tinkling burn before dragonflies appear at dusk. Communal campfires accompanied by evening sing-songs are commonplace while, in the morning, campers are woken by the dawn chorus and get to throw open their tent doors to the sight of Culvennan Fell, framed in the morning mist…

The aforementioned stone buildings have now been tastefully converted, with a barn space acting as a cosy sanitary block. Large 'rainfall' showers provide the perfect way to warm up if bad weather caught you out on a fell walk, while thoughtful touches like free, hand-made soaps and scented candles show the owners care as much for the site now as they did when they first unlatched the gates all those years ago.

The same thoughtfulness can be seen in their newest additions: a bunk-house Bothy in the old cowshed, and the wooden roundhouse, at the bottom of the field, each with fire-fed range ovens and an unbeatably snug interior.

Adjacent to the campsite are Balloch O' Dee's stables, where little campers can help out with the grooming and, if you're lucky, enjoy a brief ride around the site. Propped on the horse's rump, kids can marvel at wonderful views across the surrounding countryside and, by night, they can keep their eyes peeled for shooting stars as they ponder what sort of fun other campers might be having in another galaxy far, far away.

COOL FACTOR Set in a stunning location at the foot of Culvennan Fell and on the edge of Galloway Forest Park.

WHO'S IN Everyone! Tents, campervans, caravans, motorhomes, groups, dogs – yes.

ON SITE 30–40 pitches in the large camping field, with some hook-ups available. The Bothy sleeps 5–7, as does The Roundhouse. A converted barn serves as a comfortable shower room with toilets, washbasins and washing-up sinks. You can also use this room to dry clothes. Stone-built BBQs are dotted around the site. Rare-breed hens roam freely around the site and the challenge for the kids is to find and collect their eggs each morning. Campfires are permitted in previously used spots. The Bothy and the roundhouse are wonderfully snug glamping hideouts.

OFF SITE Children are welcome to visit the neighbouring stables for the day to groom the horses and help with mucking them out if they so choose (bring wellies and waterproofs!). Three Lochs Holiday Park (01671 830304; 3lochs.co.uk), a couple of miles down the road, hosts activities ranging from archery to mountain biking. You can book fishing at Loch Heron and Loch Ronald at the park's reception.

FOOD & DRINK The House o' Hill Hotel at Glentrool (01671 840243; houseohill.co.uk) has a fabulous location at the edge of Galloway Forest and a menu crammed full of local produce to match.

GETTING THERE Leave the M6, signposted for Stranraer (A75) and continue west past Newton Stewart and on for a further 6 miles. Here you'll see a right turn for 'The Three Lochs'. Balloch O' Dee is approx. 1½ miles along this road, on the right.

PUBLIC TRANSPORT There is no direct public transport service to the site, but if campers can make their way via bus to Newton Stewart, then the owners will be happy to arrange collection.

OPEN All year.

THE DAMAGE Tents £10 per night, caravans/campervans £12 per night. Per person £2.50 per night. Electric hook-up £3 per night. Kids and dogs free. The Bothy £45 per night; the Roundhouse £40 per night.

ruberslaw wild woods camping

Ruberslaw Wild Woods Camping, Spital Tower, Nr Denholm, Hawick, Scottish Borders TD9 8TB 01450 870092
www.ruberslaw.co.uk

Dark Ruberslaw, that lifts his head sublime, Rugged and hoary with the wrecks of time; On his broad misty front the giant wears. The horrid furrows of ten thousand years.

So wrote 18th-century naturalist and native son John Leyden, born in nearby Denholm village, of the imposing summit from which this magnificent Scottish Borders campsite takes its name, and it's true that pitching your tent on the slopes of the hill can't help but stir the soul. The Bailey family's scenic 500 acres of unspoilt Borders upland is the perfect setting for contemplative campers with a love of the rolling, enchanting landscape of the Cheviot hills and the healthy, varied local wildlife.

The beauty of this site is the sheer variety of tailored pitches to cater to the whims of all campers – from the intrepid pitch-your-own wild campers and remote safari tents, to the more sociable atmosphere of the Edwardian Walled Garden. With caravans turned away at the gate, Ruberslaw Wild Woods is a veritable canvas-connoiseur's paradise.

For campers, the Edwardian Walled Garden exudes an inclusive and welcoming atmosphere. Seek out your spot on the terraced pitches and mingle freely in The Hub, a large barn with a seating area centred on a huge fireplace where guests can eat, socialise or find shelter if it rains (not uncommon in this part of the world). It's a great place to make amends with fellow campers but should you want a bit of 'me time', head to the Edwardian glasshouse in the vinery with a book and relax beside the wood-fired stove. For something a bit more active, have a go at croquet, boules, volleyball or garden jenga on the recreational lawn.

The facilities are more than adequate and are kept pristine, with free hot showers, underfloor heating for the cooler months, free Wi-Fi, a fully equipped kitchen, a small shop and even a well considered boot-wash station.

If glamping attracts you, the safari tents hidden away in the woods are a must. Leave your car at The Hub and take only your food, toothbrush and a change of clothes – all the rest is provided. With a minimum separation of 300m between each pitch, you're unlikely to be kept awake by your neighbours.

One of the main draws to Ruberslaw is undoubtedly the surrounding wildlife. Keep your eyes peeled for red squirrels, owls, roe deer, foxes, elusive badgers and various birds of prey, including buzzards, sparrowhawks, goshawks and perhaps even a honey buzzard. Then as you recline back at your chosen corner of this enchanting space, cooking up something delicious over the crackling flames of the fire bowls provided, you can work out who won the game of animal i-spy in this most intriguing of Scottish regions.

COOL FACTOR Enchanting woodland campsite with some of the Scottish Borders' most stunning views.

WHO'S IN Tents, groups, D of E students and dogs – yes. Caravans, campervans motorhomes – no.

ON SITE 30 pitches within the Edwardian walled garden and orchard. Extra 'pitch-your-own' spots on the hillside (either single remote pitches or woodland areas where friends can camp in groups). 4 safari tents on the wooded slopes of Ruberslaw. Campfires permitted in the raised firebowls; campfire kits can be purchased at reception. There are 4 clean showers with changing facilities and underfloor heating, separate toilets with washbasins, disabled and baby-changing facilities and laundry facilities. The kitchen area comes fully equipped with fridge, cooker, microwave, kettle, washing-up sinks and a veg sink. Safari Tents come equipped with everything you need.

OFF SITE The site is located at the foot of the famous Ruberslaw Hill – no visit to the region would complete without scaling its slopes. It also allows easy access to the Borders Abbeys Way (bordersabbeysway.com), which takes in Kelso, Jedburgh, Melrose and Dryburgh. There are several castles and stately homes to visit, including Smailholm Tower, Bowhill House (01750 22204; bowhillhouse.co.uk) and Abbotsford (01896 752043; scottsabbotsford.com), the former home of Sir Walter Scott.

FOOD & DRINK The neighbouring village of Denholm is a 20–25 minute walk over the hill (or 5 minutes' drive). It is home to two splendid pubs: the Fox & Hounds (01450 870247) dishes up some fine hearty pub grub, and the Auld Cross Keys (01450 870305; crosskeysdenholm.co.uk) which has great ales, a coffee shop and an Italian restaurant.

GETTING THERE The site is well-signposted off the A6908, or the A6088 at Bonchester Bridge.

PUBLIC TRANSPORT There are buses from Hawick and Jedburgh to Denholm, or the owner may be able to collect you if called in advance.

OPEN March–first week in November.

THE DAMAGE From £6 per night for a small tent + a small charge per head, including dogs. Safari tents from £100 a night for 4 people.

gimme shelter

Gimme Shelter, 2 Dales Farm Cottage, Duloch, Nr Dunfermline, Fife KY11 7HR 07957 264805
www.camping-fife-near-edinburgh.blogspot.co.uk

Many campsites talk a good environmentally friendly game, but few put it into practice quite as well as Gimme Shelter, situated amid the meadows and hills just a few miles from the Forth Bridge. Recycling is practised throughout, there are no showers or hot water and toilets are of the sawdust-composting variety – not trendy off-the-peg numbers but, like most things here, self-built and brilliantly improvised. Rainwater is collected in various systems, including an old wine barrel, while a wood-burning stove has been made from a cleverly rejuvenated gas bottle. Rat-race escapees Chris and Yvonne Barley may have been dubbed hippies a decade ago, but really they were one step ahead of the eco-friendly game, banging a drum that is only now being heard by the rest of the world.

Over the years, Chris and Yvonne have managed to extend the property to include a couple of cottages and, ultimately, the hilly woodland that forms the campsite. Gimme Shelter's DIY style is undeniably impressive, from the handcarved wooden furniture that adorns every pitch to the funky but solid 'camping shack' made of oak and fir beams salvaged from the nearby dockyard, which boasts a large living space and two balconies that are ideal for sundowners.

It's all surprisingly quiet and secluded given its position in prime commuting territory for Edinburgh. Admittedly you can just hear the M90 from some of the pitches, but elsewhere it's the Pinkerton Burn tumbling through the site that makes the most noise.

The camping fields, like the site itself, give away the Barleys' tastes in music – choose between 'Strawberry Fields' and 'Rising Sun'. In the site's upper pitches, out in the open and exposed to the blistering Fife sun, there's drinking water available in containers. Then in the lower pitches, which tend to be secluded arbours within the shade of all the trees, there's cold-running mains water. All pitches have their own campfires and are set amid rich woodland.

So mazy is the wood, with some of the pitches accessible only through narrow grassy strips fringed with encroaching woodland, that there's a real feeling of seclusion, making it great for kids. Unless they're planning to machete their way through the woodland, the only way out is past their parents' tent. Gimme Shelter's other stab at glamping is a brilliantly reinvented caravan: it does give shelter, but very much in the Gimme Shelter style, where less is definitely more.

When it's time to go exploring away from the site, Inverkeithing is less than a half-hour train ride from Edinburgh across the famous Forth Rail Bridge. Or if you fancy something a little less busy, take a trip up the Fife Coastal Road. And if you want to go the whole hog, you can swing back through Dunfermline, another of Scotland's former capitals and the proud birthplace of Andrew Carnegie (once the world's wealthiest man) and, indeed, Gordon Brown.

COOL FACTOR Proper woodland camping with real wood campfires.

WHO'S IN Tents – yes. Caravans, campervans, groups, dogs – no.

ON SITE 24 woodland and meadow pitches, all with a campfire. No hook-ups. Cold water but no showers (though there are some available at a nearby leisure centre). Fire-starting essentials are available to buy. Basic compost toilets, drinking water, but not much else. It can get muddy in wet weather, though Chris and Yvonne have laid strips of an old tennis court down as paths. Two new additions to the site include the off-grid camping shacks (sleeping 4) and fully equipped classic Castleton caravan (sleeping 2).

OFF SITE Wee ones love nearby Deep Sea World (01383 411880; deepseaworld.com). Alternatively, take the train towards Edinburgh and hop off at Dalmen to explore historic South Queensferry – on the outskirts of which Hopetoun House (01313 312451; hopetoun.co.uk) has been described as 'Scotland's Versailles'.

FOOD & DRINK Inverkeithing is within walking distance for basic supplies and good ale at the Burgh Arms (01383 410384). The Compass (01383 821795; thecompass-dalgetybay.co.uk) in Dalgety Bay is the place to go for good fish and chips, or try the Albert Hotel (01383 413562; alberthotel-scotland.com), which serves excellent food and was said to be a favourite of the late Iain Banks.

GETTING THERE Take the first exit after crossing the Forth Bridge and follow signs to Inverkeithing; go through the town, past the station and on to Old North Road (B981) and follow the road for nearly a mile. The site is on the left.

PUBLIC TRANSPORT Train or bus from Edinburgh to Inverkeithing, then a mile's walk to the site.

OPEN All year by appointment.

THE DAMAGE £6 per person (all ages) per night; £6 per car for first night only, subsequent nights half price for children and under-2s.

comrie croft

Comrie Croft, Braincroft, Crieff, Perthshire PH7 4JZ 01764 670140 www.comriecroft.com

Before the Act of Union and the birth of the modern British state many Scots lived on crofts – smallholdings of land where communal living was the norm. In the heart of deepest Highland Perthshire, this 'all-in-it-together' ethic has been re-created at Comrie Croft. Run by a co-operative of likeminded, environmentally aware individuals, this is no mere campsite. Yes they take tents, but they've also got Nordic katas, an onsite Tea Garden and a superb bike shop, the latter handy for exploring the network of trails that snake off up the Croft's wooded hillside.

First-timers might feel most secure down in the low meadow by all the facilities, but more adventurous souls will want to push on up into the forest where secluded pitches await, each with its own campfire. Four of the five katas are up here too, a sort of Swedish tipi complete with a wood-burning stove and a large sleeping area strewn with animal skins. Not exactly super-chic glamping, but supremely cosy.

There is little need to leave the Croft. Down by the car park is a superb camp store which sells everything from fluorescent camping pegs to free-range eggs and local meat. Up the hill are those trails. You can walk them, but biking provides a much better way of exploring the hillside. You can brush up on your technique first at their skills park. On a busy day – and most weekends are busy – Comrie Croft buzzes with life, just as the traditional crofts once did in this charmingly scenic corner of Highland Perthshire.

COOL FACTOR Communal eco-aware living under canvas in charming Highland Perthshire.

WHO'S IN Tents, dogs (main camping field only), groups, young groups (with meadow exclusive use only) – yes. Caravans, campervans – no.

ON SITE 32 camping pitches. 5 katas tents. Campfires allowed. Solar and wind–powered amenities block with toilets and showers (including disabled access). With extra turf-roofed compost toilets and showers serving the High Meadow and some woodland pitches. Excellent camping store. Blue and red mountain bike trails and skills park with bike hire and helmets available. Network of marked walking trails and picnic areas.

OFF SITE The high land beyond the boundaries of the Croft is tough-going but opens up sweeping views of Strathearn for adventurous, well-equipped hikers and bikers. A map of local routes is posted up and available for sale in the store. The Auchingarrich Wildlife Park (01764 679469; auchingarrich.co.uk) is a handy family attraction just south of Comrie.

FOOD & DRINK The onsite Tea Room serves croissants and bacon rolls for breakfast, light lunches and home-made cakes. Comrie has a reasonable chippie (07514 678833) and the Royal Hotel (01764 679200; royalhotel.co.uk), which has a characterful hunting lodge-style bar and a decent restaurant.

GETTING THERE The site is two miles out of Comrie on the Crieff road heading east, well signposted on the left.

PUBLIC TRANSPORT The new Breadalbane Explorer (breadalbane.org) is a seasonal bus that takes mountain bikes and links a number of sights in Perthshire, stopping at Comrie Croft. The site is also served by the no. 15 bus from Perth.

OPEN All year.

THE DAMAGE Tents from £8 per adult, £4 under-18s. Pre-school free. Katas from £50 per night. 10% off accommodation bill if you arrive without a vehicle.

ardgualich farm

Ardgualich Farm, Ardgualich, By Pitlochry, Perthshire PH16 5NS 01796 472825

Ardgualich Farm is one of those rough-around-the-edges anachronisms you cannot help but like. The simple site has been run by the same family since the Second World War came to an end and has somehow managed to rumble on into the 21st century, still enjoying the epic scenery that first lured Queen Victoria to Loch Tummel back in the 19th century.

Queen Victoria fell in love with Loch Tummel to such an extent that she would scarcely let a trip to her beloved Scotland pass by without visiting at least once. Today, the spot where she used to regally perch and survey the silvery shadow of the loch is fittingly dubbed the 'Queen's View' - though not, as you may think, for Victoria, but probably for Robert the Bruce's wife, Queen Isabella, who used to rest in nearby woods when she was out and about.

With numerous whisky distilleries nearby, world-class salmon and succulent local beef all wrapped around heather-clad hills and mountains, it is easy to see why any queen in any century with a penchant for living the good life was drawn here.

The old farm has been joined by a collage of caravans and some static homes, but there is still some room for campers. There is a family-orientated field near the reception, but head right down the hill for the best spots. You can pitch your tent in the soft verges that fringe Loch Tummel, with only the sinewy sandy beaches and the lapping waves for company.

While simply sitting by the water's edge is enough for some, others choose to get in or on the water. Campers can bring their own small boats or canoes, though jet skis are mercifully banned. There is no launch charge at Ardgualich, leaving you free to explore the nooks and crannies of Loch Tummel at your own pace. Campers can also enjoy a free fishing permit. After a day spent reeling them in, you can explore your primitive hunter-gatherer instincts and feast on freshly caught barbecued fish.

Some of Loch Tummel's most famous inhabitants can be found above it rather than in it. Ospreys are now thriving around the shores of the loch after years of decline. Other flourishing residents you are likely to encounter include roe deer, who have been known to slip into the site and startle campers by nosing around in their breakfast supplies.

Today Ardgualich Farm may not exactly have all the luxuries fit for a queen – and some tent campers may roll their eyes at the surrounding static caravans and the unattractive road barrier at the edge of the campsite. But what this place does offer, if you bag one of the loch-side pitches, is a stripped-down camping experience with regal loch views. You can get back to basics and barbecue your own fish as you idle your time away admiring the scenery and the wildlife. Queen Victoria's ghost, as it wistfully haunts the hills above, will be ever-so-slightly jealous.

COOL FACTOR A queen's view for considerably less than a king's ransom.

WHO'S IN Tents, campervans, caravans, motorhomes, dogs (on a lead) – yes.

ON SITE Grass pitches for tents, some with electrical hook-ups; caravans and campers have hardstandings with electrical hook-ups. There is a new toilet block with hot showers in a portable cabin, including facilities for the disabled. It's serviced regularly and is kept reasonably clean. This is also where you'll find the washing-up sinks and a chemical disposal point.

OFF SITE If it rains, pop into the Queen's View Visitor Centre (01350 727284) to watch the short film about the area and enjoy a pot of tea. Afterwards follow one of two paths through the Allean Forest, part of the Tay Forest Park, to discover the ruins of a Pictish fort and a remote 18th-century homestead.

FOOD & DRINK The Loch Tummel Inn (01882 634272; lochtummelinn.co.uk) is an old-fashioned pub with a beer garden that overlooks the loch. Choose from the informal bar or loch-view restaurant. The homemade beef burgers and seared Shetland salmon are highly recommended. It also serves a range of good ales and whiskies.

GETTING THERE Heading north on the A9 from Perth towards Inverness, take the B8019 exit towards Killiecrankie. Turn left for Tummel Bridge (you're still on the B8019) and follow the road for 6 miles. The entrance to the campsite is on the left.

PUBLIC TRANSPORT The Pitlochry to Kinloch Rannoch bus goes past the campsite 3 times a day (4 times on a Saturday).

OPEN March–October.

THE DAMAGE £15 for a standard tent + 50p for each extra person. Extra-large tents £18. Electric hook-ups £3 per night. Dogs are welcome as long as they are kept on a lead.

cashel

Cashel Campsite, Loch Lomond, Rowardennan, Dunbartonshire, G63 0AW 01360 870234
www.campingintheforest.co.uk/cashel

The 'bonnie banks' of Loch Lomond have been Scotland's rural retreat for many a year. Teeming with dramatic hills, serene lochs and the freshest of fresh air, the region's popularity shows no sign of dwindling – and rightly so. Activities for the lively are bountiful, as are interesting places to try some traditional food, knock back a dram of whisky or experience one of Scotland's standout strolls, along the West Highland Way. Located right on the peaceful shores of Loch Lomond is Cashel, a welcoming, harmonious campsite with one hell of a view.

Cashel is very large but, despite having over 160 camping spaces, it's not hard to find a pitch with unobstructed loch views, although to guarantee this we suggest you book a premier pitch. The onsite facilities cover most needs and are clean, well maintained, and include one of the strongest showers you're ever likely to encounter while camping. There's also a small shop which sells all the things you may have forgotten (groceries and camping essentials), while the onsite takeaway provides campers with a much-needed pre-hike caffeine boost.

Loch Lomond (Britain's largest freshwater lake) was recognised back in 2002 when it became the focal point of the Loch Lomond & Trossachs National Park, the country's very first national park. Scotland's second most famous loch (after Ness, of course!) extends from Balloch in the south up to Killin, and Callander west to the dense forests of Cowal. Ben Lomond is the most popular mountain for hill-walking in the area. Superb views across rolling hills and tranquil water are your reward for the effort required to reach the summit.

'So, any negatives?' we hear you enquire. Well, touring caravans, motorhomes and trailer tents are all welcomed at Cashel, a fact that may raise a few eyebrows in the traditional camping community. But as you pitch next to the beautiful, lush surroundings of Loch Lomond and the Queen Elizabeth Forest Park, you soon realise that, despite initial worries, Cashel is most definitely a cool place to camp.

COOL FACTOR Pitch up on the banks of Loch Lomond, Britain's longest stretch of fresh water.

WHO'S IN Tents, caravans, motorhomes, trailer tents and dogs – yes.

ON SITE 168 pitches of standard, premium and select types. Flushing toilets, showers, family shower room, washbasins, chemical disposal point, laundry and drinking-water taps. Dish-washing facilities, children's play area and separate disabled facilities. Shop offers camping essentials.

OFF SITE The national park (lochlomond-trossachs.org) is perhaps the main event hereabouts. At Loch Lomond Shores (01389 751031; lochlomondshores.com), a 30-minute drive away, you can take in the beautiful surroundings or enjoy the stunning views of Ben Lomond from your own canoe, kayak or pedal boat. Loch Lomond Sea Life (01389 721500; visitsealife. com/loch-lomond) allows you to get up close to many endangered sea creatures that have been rescued but can't be released back into the wild.

FOOD & DRINK The Clachan Inn (01360 660824; clachaninndrymen.co.uk), 8 miles away in the pretty village of Drymen, is the oldest licensed pub in Scotland and offers delicious lunch and dinner menus in both the bar and restaurant. Closer, in Balmaha, the Oak Tree Inn (01360 870357; theoaktreeinn.co.uk) serves traditional Scottish food and ales.

GETTING THERE From the south, take the M8 to Glasgow and follow signs for Greenock. Take junction 30 on to the M898 and follow signs for the A82 Dunbarton, Loch Lomand, Trossachs. At the 4th roundabout follow the A811 for Stirling. At Drymen take the B837 to Balmaha Rowardennan. Cashel is on the left 3 miles after Balmaha. From the east and northeast, take the M9 to Stirling, junction 10, and follow signs for the A811 Erskin Bridge into Drymen; then as above.

PUBLIC TRANSPORT Train to Balloch and then bus no. #309.

OPEN March–October.

THE DAMAGE Prices per pitch per night including 2 adults start at £13.50.

glendaruel

Glendaruel, By Colintraive, Argyll PA22 3AB 01369 820267 www.glendaruelcaravanpark.com

Trees, trees and yet more glorious life-affirming, oxygen-pumping trees are the main attraction at this remote, 22-acre escape on Argyll's sleepy Cowal Peninsula. Glendaruel sits in a hollow at the foot of its eponymous glen, shrouded by woodland. There are only 10 pitches for tents, most set in a generously sized grassy field away from the caravans and statics, and red squirrels and rabbits often outnumber campers. A recent arrival has been the Little Camping Lodge: a cosy wooden bolthole that can sleep up to four and is a great wet-weather option, with the owners planning to pop up another couple of lodges over the next few years. More conventional campers can use the campers' kitchen-cum-dining shelter.

A variety of paths snake their way into the thick web of surrounding forests, with a large grass field also on hand for wee ones to run around in, and a couple of swings and a bijou playground. Cowal itself is not well known, even among most Scots, so its quiet roads tend to be ideal for cycling and hiking, while the surrounding waters dish up a rich bounty of seafood that can be enjoyed in the local restaurants and pubs.

COOL FACTOR The magnificent collection of mature trees and wildlife, family-friendly facilities and a glorious location.

WHO'S IN Tents, campervans, dogs, caravans, young groups – yes. Big groups – no.

ON SITE 10 pitches. Basic toilet block, shower and laundry. Campers' kitchen and dining shelter. Small shop selling a few essentials, plus a kid's swing and playground. Wi-Fi available.

OFF SITE Walking trails snake off into the towering forests while a variety of circular cycle routes await around the Cowal Peninsula. The Cowal Way (cowalway.co.uk) is a glorious 57-mile walking trail that rumbles right through Glendaruel. The impressive Kilmodan Carved Stones are just a few miles south. Dunoon, 18 miles away, has a swimming pool, leisure centre, museum, golf course and cinema. A little nearer, and continuing the tree theme, the Benmore Botanic Garden (01369 706261; rbge.org.uk/the-gardens/benmore) contains almost every tree it is possible to grow in the mild climate of western Scotland, so is an essential place for tree-huggers; or emerse yourself in nature more closely with a canoe-based wildlife tour, run by a friend of the campsite owners (07765 016543; argyllvoyageurcanoes.co.uk).

FOOD & DRINK Creggans Inn (01369 860279; creggans-inn. co.uk) is an atmospheric old place on the shores of Loch Fyne – enjoy a traditional ale from the Loch Fyne Brewery to go with your oysters. Inver Cottage (01369 860537; invercottage. com) is a friendly restaurant bursting with local produce, such as hand-plucked scallops.

GETTING THERE Ferries to Cowal from Gourock to Dunoon are frequent. Then follow the A815 north for 3 miles, the B836 west for 12 miles then the A886 north to the site.

OPEN April–October.

THE DAMAGE Tents/caravans/campervans £9–£12 per night, + adults £5.50; children £2, under-3s free; backpacker with small tent £7. Dogs are free.

port bàn

Port Bàn Holiday Park, Kilberry, Tarbert, Argyll PA29 6YD 01880 770224 www.portban.com

Have you ever felt like you've camped at the edge of the earth? No? Then come to Port Bàn. This tiny community near Kilberry, on the beautifully unspoiled western coast of the Knapdale Peninsula, may look like the last stop in Scotland but, of course, that's its attraction. The sheer beauty of this primitive landscape, coupled with its rich diversity of wildlife, makes Port Bàn a fascinating, remarkable retreat for any intrepid camper. Port Bàn also caters for caravans and motorhomes. However, they are in separate fields, with campers enjoying flat, well-maintained pitches and truly idyllic views across the North Atlantic to Islay and Jura islands.

This corner of the world possesses a real sense of the epic. Separated for centuries from the rest of Scotland by lochs and mountains, the Knapdale Peninsula remains secluded and sparsely populated. For lovers of history, there's an exceptional range of historic sites, including monuments, castles, historic houses and museums. Take to the seas and explore the wild and unspoiled coast of Argyll, or unwind on a more placid, serene cruise on one of Scotland's most famous lochs.

Despite the undeniably peaceful atmosphere, approachable owners and large list of onsite facilities (especially for the kids), the real highlight of Port Bàn has to be its jaw-dropping sunsets. There is little point trying to describe it; you really must experience this for yourself, preferably from around a campfire. Suffice to say, Port Bàn really is Scotland's west at its very best.

COOL FACTOR Glorious isolation, great facilities and memorable sunsets.

WHO'S IN Tents, caravans, motorhomes and dogs – yes.

ON SITE 30 pitches with electric hook-ups. Facilities (hot showers, flushing toilets, disabled access and large sinks) are clean and more than adequate. Launderette and a telephone box. Shop, café, restaurant and daytime lounge. Children's playground, games hall with pool and table tennis, tennis, crazy golf, volleyball and a beach. Campfires permitted on the beach. Bikes for hire.

OFF SITE The site is well placed on several cycle routes, including Sustrans Route 78 (Campbeltown–Oban) and a network of Forestry Commission roads ideal for mountain bikes. Visit the beavers in the Scottish Beaver Trial (scottishbeavers.org.uk), a project to introduce beavers back into Scotland. There's also the Kilmartin House Museum, (01546 510278; kilmartin.org), of local archeology.

FOOD & DRINK On site, the campsite shop sells essentials, Seaview Café coffee and light meals, and the Sunset Restaurant serves evening meals. Off site, the Seafood Cabin (01880 760207; skipnessseafoodcabin.co.uk) at Skipness will have seafood fans salivating.

GETTING THERE Take the M8 west, leaving at signs for Erskine Bridge. Go over the bridge and head towards the A82 (to Campbeltown.) Head up the side of Loch Lomond to Tarbet and the road becomes the A83. Continue on to Lochgilphead, where you turn left to Campbeltown. Continue through Ardrishaig, then a right turn (to Kilberry) takes you to the single track B8024 road. A further 15 miles and Port Bàn is signposted on the right.

OPEN April–October.

THE DAMAGE Standard pitches £11–£13; large pitches £14–£16. Extra adults £4; youngsters (6–15) £2, and dogs £1.

red squirrel

Red Squirrel, Glencoe, Argyll PH49 4HX 01855 811256 www.campsiteinscotland.com

Some people come to Scotland to delve deep into the country's rich history; others to traverse and climb its spectacular mountains – many of which are some of Europe's finest; while still more come just to enjoy a wee dram in the place where whisky began. If you fall into any of these categories, or even all three, then Red Squirrel campsite is the place for you. It's a cosy spot, dwarfed by a phalanx of towering highland peaks in a glen draped in bloody history and home to one of Scotland's most famous pubs, where whisky-drinking is practically obligatory.

The Red Squirrel lies in Glencoe, which is many a Scots' favourite glen – praise indeed in a country that overflows with dramatic scenery. From the moment you begin the descent from the barren wastelands of Rannoch Moor, it's clear you're approaching somewhere special, as the road dips to acknowledge huge glacial massifs on either flank. If you're not an experienced walker, then this is foreboding stuff. The visitor centre in the glen organises walks for those not keen on heading out on their own; but if you have the right gear, knowledge and experience, and remember to check the weather forecast, you can just set off on one of many hikes and climbs that break off in every direction.

The campsite is also perfect for those who enjoy mountains from a purely sedentary position. On a sunny day you can just laze around this grassy site, which spreads across 20 acres of meadow and woodland with a couple of burns snaking through it. The Red Squirrel describes itself as a 'casual farm site' and casual it is indeed,

with no official pitches. Push through to the end of the camp and follow the overgrown trail (you'll think you have gone the wrong way) and you can pitch on an isolated island with great views. Elsewhere, a freshwater pool sits invitingly, awaiting any camper brave enough to take the plunge and enjoy an invigorating swim. Another plus is that the site allows open fires in specific areas, though not after 11pm, when a silence rule descends on the camp.

After a hard day walking in the hills, or a sombre one visiting the massacre memorial and visitor centre that illuminates the glen's history, most campers seek refuge in the welcoming arms of the legendary Clachaig Inn. A sign at the door bans 'Hawkers and Campbells', and this is deadly serious; history in this part of the world is strictly of the living variety. All other visitors, though, are welcomed into the bar like long-lost cousins and soon enveloped in a world of tall stories, live music and one or two wee drams.

COOL FACTOR Epic mountain scenery that is laced with human drama.

WHO'S IN Tents, dogs, small groups – yes. Caravans, campervans – no. Large groups by appointment.

ON SITE New facilities blocks, water taps dotted around the site and a small information booth. Further toilets are scattered around the site, but you need to ask for them to be opened. There's a designated family area so kid campers can get to know one another and head off for adventures among the trees.

OFF SITE Naturally, there are plenty of spectacular walking routes to pick up just a stone's throw from the campsite. The Signal Rock walk is doable for the novices and takes in the enchanting An Tor woodland and The Clachaig Flats. Learn about the nature and history of one of the most spectacular glens in Scotland at the Glencoe Visitor Centre (08444 932222).

FOOD & DRINK The home-baked cakes on sale in the coffee shop are divine. The Clachaig Inn (01855 811252) is staggering distance up the road back towards Glencoe. The Boots Bar is the place to be if you've just come off the hills covered head to foot in mud. The main lounge bar is a more comfortable spot, with views out of the large windows; both serve hearty walker-friendly food like wild boar burgers, with regular music on Friday and Saturday nights throughout the summer season.

GETTING THERE Head north on the A82 from Stirling towards Fort William. About three-quarters of the way down Glencoe a right turn is signposted 'Clachaig Inn'. Follow this single track down past the inn to the campsite.

PUBLIC TRANSPORT Scottish Citylink (08705 505050) services from Glasgow (either bus no. 914 or 915, depending on when you're travelling) stop at the Glencoe Visitor Centre.

OPEN All year.

THE DAMAGE £10 per person, per night (inclusive of showers). Children under 12 cost £1.

caolasnacon caravan & camping park

Caolasnacon Caravan & Camping Park, Kinlochleven, Argyll PH50 4RJ 01855 831279 www.kinlochlevencaravans.com

Some Scottish campsites enjoy a scenic setting shrouded by mountains, others sit by an ice-blue loch or a wee burn that ripples through the heart of the site. Caolasnacon boasts all three, as well as catatonically relaxed owners who let campers pitch where they want and light campfires too. Yes, they take caravans and have some statics, but they also treat campers with respect and nothing really detracts from what is definitely the most appealing campsite in the area.

The pitches by the loch are ideal for kayakers and canoeists, who can just launch out into Loch Leven, while walkers will want to pitch further inland for the easiest access to the mountains – the Mamores across the water to the north, and Glen Coe's epic mountainscapes to the south.

A glorious scene, then, and you would assume that life really couldn't get any better – but it can, and has. During one of our *Cool Camping* stays here – at that gloriously still point in the evening when shadows began lengthening as the sun slips away – a family of otters emerged from the seaweed and undergrowth on the margins of the loch. We had to rub the disbelief from our eyes before watching them play happily in the shallows for over an hour, barely 10 metres from us.

These squeak-emitting little web-toed critters aren't the only wildlife to be spotted around the site, though. Come morning and the sky is alive with buzzards soaring across the loch, while resident golden eagles patrol the mountain slopes behind the site. The usual signs of human activity feel a safe distance away. With all this surrounding natural beauty, you could be forgiven for thinking that Caolasnacon is buried away hundreds of miles from anywhere else and therefore near-impossible to reach, but it isn't; the main road from Glasgow to Fort William is handily just three miles away, at Glencoe.

More sedentary souls can take a trip on one of the world's great railway journeys, the West Highland Line, from the bustling nearby tourist hub of Fort William. Many new arrivals soon ditch their grand touring plans, though, and just idle by the loch soaking up the epic views and scanning the water, wild hillsides and big skies.

Caolasnacon provides a unique opportunity to get away from it all, among some of the most appealing and least spoiled scenery in the land, but, amazingly, it remains within easy reach of all those modern conveniences that make camping life enjoyable, whatever the weather has in store.

COOL FACTOR A lovely lochside location set against a backdrop of classic Highland scenery.

WHO'S IN Tents, campervans, dogs, caravans, big groups, young groups – yes.

ON SITE 50 pitches. Those near the loch can be windy, but it does give some protection against the midges. Campfires allowed. Clean and efficient washrooms with decent showers, free hot water, toilets, washbasins, washing-up sinks, laundry and electric hook-ups. Gas can be obtained at the farm. Undercover chemical disposal point.

OFF SITE You can canoe on Loch Leven and there's world-class walking and climbing available in Glen Coe (0844 4932222). Ice Factor (01855 831100; ice-factor.co.uk) in Kinlochleven offers ice climbing and winter skills training. The ferries to Gigha, Islay, Colonsay, Arran and Jura (which are run by Caledonian MacBrayne ferries; calmac.co.uk) provide days out with a difference.

FOOD & DRINK The legendary Clachaig Inn (01855 811252) may infamously refuse to serve Campbells but otherwise it's a welcoming pub amid epic mountain scenery. On the opposite shores of the loch, the Lochleven Seafood Café (01855 821048; lochlevenseafoodcafe.co.uk) Kinlochleven, 3 miles away, serves local shellfish to savour. Also in Kinlochleven, the Bothan Bar (01855 831100) open from 4pm in the Ice Factor, is quite trendy and does food; the MacDonald hotel (01855 831539), not to be confused with the fast-food joint, offers traditional hotel fare as well as packed lunches for walks; and the Tail Race Inn (01855 831777; tailraceinn.com) is a simple pub doing simple food.

GETTING THERE From the A82 (Glasgow–Fort William road), take the B863 (right) in Glencoe, signposted to Kinlochleven. The site is 3 miles further on the left.

PUBLIC TRANSPORT Stagecoach's (01463 233371) no. #44 bus runs between Fort William and Kinlochleven.

OPEN April–October inclusive (or from Easter, if earlier).

THE DAMAGE From £11 per night for a small tent and 2 people to £21 for a large tent. If you stay 6 nights you get the 7th night free!

the shielings

Shieling Holidays, Craignure, Isle of Mull PA65 6AY 01680 812496 www.shielingholidays.co.uk

Long before the word glamping had ever come into the camping lexicon, Isle of Mull-based Shieling Holidays (the brainchild of David and Moira Gracie) were offering nights under canvas for those not keen on pitching their own tents. Their 16 starched white shielings may not be quite as glamorous as some places these days, but they are supremely flexible, and eight en suite shielings are also available with their own toilet and hot shower. Designed for a maximum of six inhabitants, they also boast cookers, worktops, electric lighting and gas heaters. You can either bring your own bedding, crockery, cutlery and kitchenware or hire it. For those without en suite arrangements, the site facilities are excellent, so there's no need to rough it here. One large Shieling also houses a common room where you can cook, wash dishes and sit by the multifuel stove. Or light the campfire outside and enjoy the spectacular view.

There are camping pitches, too, for those who prefer to put up their own tent, and the location could not be more dramatic. The waterfront site sits right on the strategic Sound of Mull, guarding the gateway to the Hebrides. Just across the water lies Morvern, while in the distance a flurry of mountain peaks vie for attention, including Ben Nevis. Otters are resident on the rocky foreshore and porpoises and dolphins regularly make an appearance. Many visitors just recline and watch the wildlife and the ferries travelling between the mainland and the isles.

If you've brought along a canoe or two, or even a boat, these can be launched at the front of the site where there's a handy slip road straight into the Sound of Mull. Behind the Shielings, climb the Hill of the Two Winds, a fine ridge with views made in heaven.

Bring your bikes to Mull for some serious traffic-free miles and a wilderness experience not found anywhere else in Britain. There's an excellent cycle ride to the island's main (and only) town at Tobermory. It's a 40-mile round trip, but taken over the whole day, and in decent weather, it isn't nearly as arduous as it is scenic. Tobermory is known for being the inspiration and setting for the kids' TV show *Balamory*, but the island was famous before that for its wildlife, and especially its population of sea eagles; they can usually be seen around Loch Frisa, where there are organised eagle-spotting trips, but also at several other coastal areas on the island.

For hikers, Mull's biggest attraction is Ben More, the only island Munro (a mountain with a peak over 3,000ft) outside of Skye. Much more accessible is Dun da Ghaoithe, Mull's second-highest peak, which rears up behind the site – a good half-day's walk, but one that offers life-affirming views and the chance to spot red deer and eagles. Back by the Sound your tent awaits, with a cosy congratulatory sundowner – to be enjoyed with *that* view.

COOL FACTOR Spectacular location, comfortable camping, easy access from the ferry.

WHO'S IN Tents, campervans, caravans, big groups, young groups, dogs – yes.

ON SITE 90 pitches, 30 with hook-up, some right by the sea, others with enchanting views to Ben Nevis. 16 Shielings and 2 cottages. Campfires allowed in a designated communal area. Excellent toilet and shower facilities with washbasins and disabled access. Swing, sandpit and games for children. Launderette. Astroturf tent pitches handy in poor weather, special tent pegs available if needed. Bike hire available.

OFF SITE You can walk along the beach to Duart Castle, (01680 812309; duartcastle.com), where the home baking in the tea room is legendary. Further afield, the island capital of Tobermory is a picturesque treat and is home to the Tobermory Distillery (01688 302647; tobermorydistillery. com). Or get the ferry to Oban for a mosey around the town. Many wildlife tour operators will collect from the site, including their neighbour Pete Hall of Mull Wildlife Tours (07780 601177; mullwildlifetours.co.uk).

FOOD & DRINK The Craignure Inn (01680 812305; craignure-inn.co.uk) does a decent pint, and this cosy pub also has a restaurant offering wild Mull venison, smoked trout from Tobermory, Mull Cheddar and Mull Brie. Across the bay, the Isle of Mull Hotel (01680 812544) has a fine swimming pool and spa. Tobermory offers a wide choice of eating options including the excellent Café Fish (01688 301253), where the freshest of fish is perfectly prepared.

GETTING THERE From the ferry, turn left on the A849 to Iona. After 400m, turn left opposite the church and past the old pier to reception – 800m in all.

PUBLIC TRANSPORT From Glasgow, rail or bus at noon, ferry at 4pm from Oban, arrive Mull 4.46pm; back at 10.55am ferry, arrive Glasgow by 4pm. Check times!

OPEN Camping March–November. Shielings April–October.

THE DAMAGE Tent and 2 people £17 (£3 discount if no car); extra adults £5.50, children £3, dogs £1.50; hook-ups £4.50; Shielings from £37/£231 per night/week for 2 adults; ensuite Shielings from £52/£312 per night/week.

sunart camping

Sunart Camping, Granite Square, Archaracle, Strontian, Argyll PH36 4HZ 01967 402080 www.sunartcamping.co.uk

To call Sunart Camping 'somewhat far-flung' is like saying the Sahara gets a tad toasty in the summer. Situated on the Ardnamurchan Peninsula on the Scottish Highlands' western extremities, Sunart Camping is one of the UK's most stunningly isolated camping spots. This small family-run, family-friendly site lies at the back of the sleepy lochside village of Strontian. Helmed by sprightly owners Tim and Lynn Coldwell, this unspoiled spot is the ideal base for exploring the islands of Oronsay and Càrna, the isles of Mull and Skye and the mighty Glen Tarbert.

Comprising a handful of grass pitches and hardstandings, Sunart is equally equipped for the canvas and caravan contingents. The cosy communal bothy is a nice touch, with comfy sofas and a wood-burning stove to see out the Highland elements (not to mention the midges – an inevitability in this part of the world). For those wanting the security of walls and doors, the brand new cedar camping cabins should do the trick.

These cosy little abodes come fully insulated with underfloor heating, plus double and bunk beds. The bigger six-person cabin also features an en suite bathroom (with flush loo and hot shower) and a small kitchenette.

The area is abuzz with wildlife you're unlikely to see in most other parts of the UK. The eponymous Loch Sunart is the shining centrepiece for all manner of amazing creatures, including Scotland's 'Big Five'; the otter, harbour seal, red squirrel, red deer and golden eagle. It's a short stroll into Strontian village, where there's a well-stocked shop and post office, and two fine restaurants at either end of the village (the loch-caught seafood in both is fantastic). Sunart's location right on the loch makes the site a great base for anglers and water sports enthusiasts. There's a free jetty on the shore and fishing tackle can be hired from the site, as can bikes for mountain biking in the forest.

COOL FACTOR Wonderful isolation, great wildlife and fabulous seafood!

WHO'S IN Tents, campervans, caravans, motorhomes, groups, dogs – yes. Glampers in the camping cabins.

ON SITE 15 pitches (6 with electric hook-up) and 12 serviced hardstandings. 3 heated cedar camping cabins (sleeping 4–6). Communal bothy with wood-burning stove. Facilities block has showers, hairdryers, laundry, microwave, fridge-freezer. Outside picnic areas, BBQs and pizza oven. Bike and fishing tackle hire available. Free Wi-Fi. Campfires are permitted off the ground and firepits are available to hire (logs for sale).

OFF SITE Strontian has a surprisingly lively social calendar for its size. Be sure to check out what's on at The Sunart Centre (01397 709228; sunartcentre.org). The views from Ardnamurchan Point are breathtaking: don't forget to visit the famous lighthouse (01972 510210; ardnamurchanlighthouse. com) – the most westerly part of the British Isles – and keep your eyes peeled for whales, dolphins and the occasional basking shark.

FOOD & DRINK The Ariundle Centre (01967 402279; ariundlecentre.co.uk) has a fully licensed tea room-cum-restaurant serving cooked breakfasts and evening meals. The Kilcamb Lodge (01967 402257; kilcamblodge.co.uk) in Strontian boasts a luxurious fine-dining restaurant and the less formal Driftwood Brasserie. Both enjoy stunning views over Loch Sunart. On the east side of the village, the Strontian Hotel (01967 402029; thestrontianhotel.co.uk) offers a similar set-up in its Dungallons Restaurant and Bothy Bar. The fresh, locally caught seafood in both places is exquisite.

GETTING THERE From the A82 take the short ferry journey over the Corran Narrows and, on leaving the ferry, bear left on to the A861 to Strontian. Turn right at the village green immediately after the police station. Follow the road round and take the first right at the crossroads. The entrance to the campsite is in front of you as the road bears right.

OPEN All year except February.

THE DAMAGE 1 person tent £6; 2–4 person tent £8; large tent £11; + £3 per person. Caravan/campervan £10 + £3 per person. Hook-up £3. Children up to the age of 15 free.

resipole farm

Resipole Farm, Loch Sunart, Acharacle, Argyll PH36 4HX 01967 431235 www.resipole.co.uk

Where can you go camping if you fancy spending half your time ruining your body in the name of physical exertion and the other half trying to improve your mind? Is there a campsite whose philosophy embraces both fast and slow lanes? A campsite where you can do extreme exercise one day, then an art course the next? It surely can't exist, can it? But it does, here at Resipole Farm, out on the western edge of the Highlands next to the shining shores of Loch Sunart.

Knowing that Resipole is a place frequented by outdoorsy, active types, we sent members of the *Cool Camping* (muddy) biking team to inspect the site, hoping to get their single-track minds improved in the process, as nothing is said to be utterly impossible.

What they found was an unmistakable 'activity aura' enveloping the whole site, with canoes and sailing boats being hauled to and from the loch, mountain bikers returning from a long day in the saddle in wonderfully filthy states, as well as plenty of folk who only want to get out there sometimes, but are happy to spend the rest of their holidays exertion-free.

Although this is a big campsite, which gets pretty busy in midsummer, the effect as a whole (thanks to big pitches and careful landscaping) is a pleasant environment that never feels too hectic or full. If it does get full they will always find room for those arriving on bike or on foot.

What really matters here, though, is not how big the pitches are, nor how superb the facilities, but what you can do to your body (and mind) in the world surrounding Resipole Farm. The boating potential has already been floated, but there is also a slipway for launching small powered craft into Loch Sunart, which is big enough for everyone to take advantage of.

For those whose concerns aren't as focused on all things outdoors, the campsite's cycle-friendly owners (bless 'em) run the Resipole Studios, which provide a hefty heap of culture to balance out all that adventure. Here campers can not only check out the various summer exhibitions and indulge their wallets on varying forms of art to stick on the walls back home, but they can even have a dabble at creating some artistic masterpieces of their own.

But enough of that art malarkey, and back to the important matter of biking, because this area is about as good as it gets for rampant cyclists, with the quiet lochside road giving access to rides as far as your legs will take you. Pedalling to the ruins of Castle Tioram makes a pleasant day out, Kentra Bay is amazing, and Ardnamurchan Point – there and back – is about 55 miles of pleasure and pain. With Ben Resipole peeping up out of the scenery just behind the site, it ain't half bad for walkers here either. Or landscape painters, for that matter.

COOL FACTOR Splendid location on the edge of Loch Sunart, in an unspoiled, largely undiscovered corner of Scotland.

WHO'S IN Tents, campervans, caravans, groups, families and active campers – yes.

ON SITE 60 hardstanding and grass pitches – all with superb views. Modern and comprehensive amenities, with showers, toilets, hot and cold washbasins, dish-washing, laundry and disabled facilities. Electric hook-ups are available and there's an onsite shop selling the essentials such as milk, bread, ice cream and chocolate.

OFF SITE There's enough to do on the water – canoeing, kayaking, sailing – and in the beautiful countryside around – biking, walking – to keep even the most active adventurer happy. Hire a boat with Ardnamurchan Charters (01972 500208; west-scotland-marine.com/BoatHire.html) and take to the majestic Loch Sunart and scan the waves for dolphins, whales and sea otters. The pictureque ruins of Castle Tioram and the sands of Kentra Bay make great targets for rides, as does the famous lighthouse at Ardnamurchan Point – Britain's most westerly point (see p.321). For the culture vultures among you, Resipole Studios (01967 431506; resipolestudios. co.uk) showcases some of the best contemporary Scottish art inspired by the stunning South Highlands.

FOOD & DRINK The Salen Hotel (01967 431661; salenhotel. co.uk) is just 2 miles away, and fortunately it's a pleasant place where decent food can be found. About 5 miles away, Ardshealach Lodge (01967 431399; ardshealach-lodge.co.uk) at Acharacle also has a good restaurant that offers 3-course evening meals from £20 per person.

GETTING THERE From the A82 Glasgow–Fort William road, travel 10 miles south of Fort William, cross Loch Linnhe by the Corran Ferry, then follow the A861 for about 20 miles to the site.

PUBLIC TRANSPORT Bus S48, run by Shiel Buses (01967 431272), travels between Fort William and Kilchoan and will stop at Resipole if required.

OPEN April–October.

THE DAMAGE Tent and 2 adults £20. Additional adults £4 each; children £3. Backpacker tent or cyclist and 1 person £8.

ardnamurchan

Ardnamurchan, Ormsaigbeg, Kilchoan, Acharacle, Argyll PH36 4LL 01972 510766 www.ardnamurchanstudycentre.co.uk

Ancient Celtic traditions say that over the western sea, beyond the edge of any map, lies the afterlife. Sitting at Ardnamurchan campsite it's certainly easy to believe, as you watch the sun torch the ocean between the scattered Hebrides, that you're as close as you can get to Heaven on Earth.

The site clings to the coast just a few miles from the tip of a rocky finger of land that's as far west as Britain goes. You approach it (slowly) via a ferry and a sinuous single-track road that hems in the crumpled and craggy landscape and makes getting here an escapade in itself. The site is situated to the west of the beautiful village of Kilchoan, on a small south-facing croft that has stunning views down the Sound of Mull to Morven and Mull. This far-flung location makes it the most westerly campsite on the British mainland.

Remarkably, it is the brainchild of one man, Trevor Potts, who has turned an old croft into this Elysian camping field. The site may seem rough-and-ready at first glance, a slice of wild hillside only just tamed, but as you settle in you'll appreciate just how much Trevor has done to make the site welcoming. Every pitch has been cut from the slope and levelled, and Trevor has recently vanquished a field of seven-foot-high bracken to open up a new camping area. Trevor also built the toilet block with recycled materials, and also built a replica of Shackleton's remarkable little boat next door. There is nothing fancy or arty about what Trevor has done here, but he did it all himself, and everything fits in neatly with the surroundings.

Pitches range from neat nooks with hook-ups near the washblock to wilder spots closer to the shore. If you camp right at the bottom of the slope you will be lulled to sleep by the wash of wave on rock. The foreshore is rough, rocky and just right for a scramble. You can catch creatures in the rockpools, throw stones at the waves or simply watch the ferries weaving their way along to nearby islands. The facilities are humble and homely, with surprisingly powerful showers. Flowers add a burst of colour to the whitewashed walls, and there can't be many washblocks that have their own whale skeleton.

So, what else does the Ardnamurchan Peninsula have to tempt campers? Well, some of the loveliest beaches on the planet can be found around the campsite's edges, as well as a remarkable remnant of a volcano nearby. Just a few miles away are the glorious sands of Sanna, lapped by turquoise waters. The drive there takes you through a jagged, almost extra-terrestrial landscape of steep cliffs and snaggle-toothed ridges. Further on around the coast, another age of history was brought back to life at Swordle Bay in 2011, when archaeologists unearthed a rare treasure – a Viking burial boat, virtually intact, although you can't see much more now than the mound of stones that marks the spot. You can, however, watch an occasional summer recreation of the boat's burial – an impressive sight. Back at camp, it's not hard to understand why people have been coming here for thousands of years.

COOL FACTOR The view; the wildlife that can be spotted (otters, pine martens, sea eagles asnd golden eagles); the beaches; the beautiful journey to get here.

WHO'S IN Tents, campervans, groups, dogs – yes. Large motorhomes, caravans – no.

ON SITE 20 pitches and 4 campervan hook-ups. Basic and quaintly ramshackle facilities, with toilets, showers, laundry and dish-washing facilities, 2 loos and 2 powerful showers. You can also hire 1 of 2 caravans and a bothy. Washing-up area with fridge. Internet access. No campfires.

OFF SITE You can join Trevor on one of his guided walks or attend one of his lectures on local geology and wildlife, stroll on the sandy beach at Sanna, and visit the lighthouse at Ardnamurchan Point (see p.321). Some of the loveliest beaches on the planet can be found around its edges, and a remarkable remnant of a (thankfully) extinct volcano. Abandon the car and take in the view with a walk around its impressive rim. Nearby Ben Hiant is a terrific wee mountain with superb views. You can also pop over to Tobermory on Mull by ferry from Kilchoan (0800 066 5000). It makes for a nice, genteel change from outdoor activities.

FOOD & DRINK There's a fine and fun coffee shop in an old stable at the Ardnamurchan Lighthouse. Bar meals and finer evening dining are on offer at the Kilchoan Hotel (01972 510200; kilchoanhotel.co.uk), 1½ miles away. Guests are encouraged to bring their own instruments along to create impromptu music in the public bar. There's also good food available at the Sonachan Hotel (01972510211; sonachan.com), on the way to Ardnamurchan Lighthouse.

GETTING THERE From the A82 take the ferry from Corran to Ardgour, the A861 for 25 miles to Salen, then take a left on to the B8007. On reaching Kilchoan, follow the lane along the coast and the site is almost at the end.

OPEN April–September.

THE DAMAGE £9 each person over 14 years, £4 for 14 years and under (under-5s free). Hook-up £4.

camusdarach

Camusdarach, Arisaig, Inverness-shire PH39 4NT 01687 450221 www.camusdarach.com

Camusdarach must surely be one of Britain's best all-round holiday destinations, but before getting into all the usual stuff, perhaps an explanation of the philosophy behind the running of the place may partially explain why a simple campsite can feel so thoroughly salubrious, and why everybody seems so relaxed and friendly while camping at Camusdarach.

Taking up the reins from previous owners, the Simpsons, new proprietors Jonny and Val Stuart-Orchard have continued the eco-conscious efforts of their predecessors. Everything is eco-driven and completely sustainable to retain the natural beauty of this extremely special place. Most of the day-to-day landscape management is done by a small flock of endangered Hebridean sheep, while the trendy and very plush toilet block (renewable softwood) releases effluents into gravel beds and wetlands planted with specific plants whose job it is to detoxify the environment they grow in. There has been no artificial landscaping of the two camping fields, because none is needed, and the whole philosophy of respecting nature and doing everything possible to fit in with the environment shines through in the everyday running of the site. It's informal and friendly, and campers are treated as intelligent individuals, all of which is partly responsible for that indefinable feeling of well-being. In turn, everybody respects their neighbours and the site.

However, no matter how well-run or eco-friendly a campsite may be, it is only really as good as the opportunities around it, and Camusdarach is engulfed by them. First and foremost is the seaside scenery the site nestles among, with miles of dunes giving way to blindingly white sandy beaches. You can walk for miles along the strands here, never really coming to terms with the fact that this really is north-western Scotland, not the Caribbean. The islands of Skye, Rum, Eigg, Canna and Muck punctuate the horizon across the azure waters, and you just can't help but feel good in this vision of paradise.

Many come here for a week and never move a motorised wheel for the whole duration, such is the basic appeal of the immediate surroundings. But another 'however' is due here, for the natural beauty of this area isn't restricted to the glorious seaside fringe. Visitors should turn their eyes inland to the lochs and hills for further inspiration, firstly towards Loch Morar, the deepest sheet of fresh water in Britain.

From this superb little campsite, set in seaside heaven, you can stumble out every day and gasp incredulously for weeks if the weather plays at all fair. And it often does here. There's nothing more to say and nothing more to write. You really have to come here to truly understand the feeling this place evokes.

COOL FACTOR Everything – the site, the location, the natural surroundings.

WHO'S IN Caravans, campervans, tents – yes.

ON SITE Grass and hardstanding pitches. Comfortable modern eco-block containing free showers, toilets, washbasins, disabled facilities, baby-changing, dish-washing and laundry. There is a small shop and takeaway, as well as a mobile shop that visits twice a week. Free Wi-Fi across the site.

OFF SITE Boat trips from Mallaig can be taken to the Isle of Skye on the ferry, or to Knoydart and Loch Nevis on the little boat (01687 462320) that carries supplies and mail to the outlying farms with no road access. Loch Morar offers kayaking and spectacular walks. Keep your eyes peeled for Morag, Nessie's lesser-known counterpart. The journey to Fort William from Mallaig by the '*Harry Potter*' train is a memorable one, giving an armchair view of big scenery en route. Next stop, Hogwarts!

FOOD & DRINK The onsite takeaway has everything from fresh croissants to bacon rolls, venison burgers and wood-fired pizzas. There is also an onsite shop stocking basic supplies and fabulous coffee. The Morar Hotel (01687 462346; morarhotel. co.uk), has a public bar equipped with a great selection of whiskies, and the Silver Sands restaurant with stunning views over the beaches of Morar.

GETTING THERE From the A830 Fort William–Mallaig road, take the B8008 through Arisaig and along the coast. The site is on the left about 4 miles north of Arisaig.

PUBLIC TRANSPORT Head to Fort William, where Shiel Buses (01967 431272) operate a service to Mallaig that stops at Arisaig's post office. It's a hefty walk from here, though, so it's best to book a taxi if you can. Just 5 miles from the campsite, the fishing port of Mallaig operates ferry services to Skye and the small isles. It's also just 3 miles from Arisaig, where boats can be taken daily to the Small Isles of Rhum, Eigg and Muck.

OPEN March–October.

THE DAMAGE £23 for a tent and occupants on a serviced pitch, including electric hook-up and grey water disposal. Booking is strongly advised, particularly during peak season.

loch ness shores

Loch Ness Shores, Monument Park, Lower Foyers, Inverness-shire IV2 6YH 01456 486333
www.campingandcaravanningclub.co.uk/lochnessshores

Dark, deep and narrow, Loch Ness stretches for over 23 miles between Fort Augustus and Inverness. Every inch of its crisp cold waters have been extensively explored in search of Nessie, the elusive Loch Ness monster, who continues to frustrate and beguile in equal measure. In all honesty 'Nessiemania' achieved overkill many moons ago, but Scotland's (if not the world's) most famous loch luckily has a natural beauty and an array of outdoor activities that keep campers coming back even if Nessie doesn't play ball.

Enjoying stunning views of the nearby forest and mountains is the appropriately named Loch Ness Shores. Located on the quieter south shore, near the village of Foyers, this 99-pitch, open-all-year campsite is run by the welcoming husband-and-wife team of Donald and Lyn, whose excellent local knowledge ensures campers make the most of their stay.

The site has impressive eco-credentials too. Innovative green techno logs are used to light and heat the onsite facilities, which include a decent amenity block (with underfloor heating) and home-from-home shower rooms.

The surrounding flora and fauna is one of Loch Ness Shore's major draws. With regular sightings of red squirrels, badgers, wild goats, otters, deer and over 40 species of wild birds, campers are advised to keep their binoculars at the ready. Wildlife hides are available and walks – ranging from a short leisurely stroll to Foyers Pier, to a wide range of forestry paths – offer fantastic rambling opportunities for all.

Open to both C&CC members and non-

members, Loch Ness Shores also offers the opportunity to 'glamp' in one of their five wooden wigwams, all boasting snug caravan-style beds. But whichever accommodation you opt for, you're sure to enjoy this beautiful, tranquil location in one of Britain's most scenic spots. So scenic, in fact, it's a wonder why Nessie hasn't dropped by for a cheeky weekend of camping. Ah well, Nessie's loss is most certainly your gain.

COOL FACTOR Dramatic scenery at an eco-friendly campsite that teems with wildlife.

WHO'S IN Tents, caravans, motorhomes, trailer tents, organisations, family groups, children, dogs – yes. Stag and hen parties – no.

ON SITE 99 pitches enjoying panoramic views across Loch Ness, 5 wooden wigwams, electrical hook-ups, farm shop, heated amenity block, parent-baby room, chemical disposal point, children's play area, drying room, Wi-Fi. One of only a few places around Loch Ness where you can launch your own boat. Hire electric bikes, canoes and boats with fishing permits if required.

OFF SITE Boots-n-Paddles (0845 612 5567; boots-n-paddles. co.uk) and Explore Highland (07808 071810; explorehighland. com) both offer various paddle-sport activities, including canoeing and river kayaking adventures. These are available for half or full day depending on your level of experience. Most activities are suitable for children between the ages of 10 and 18, when accompanied by an adult.

FOOD & DRINK The onsite shop sells fresh local produce, including BBQ food, coffee, cakes and meals prepared by a local butcher. The Waterfall Café (01456 486233; foyersstoresandwaterfallcafe.co.uk), a 20-minute walk away, is well stocked. The Craigdarroch Inn (01456 486400; thecraigdarrochinn.co.uk) has a cosy, traditional ambience, with wood panelling, high ceilings and open fires – and its bar and restaurant are an excellent source of good food and drink.

GETTING THERE From the A9, take the B862 to Dores, then turn right on the B852 to Foyers. From Fort William, leave the A82 at Fort Augustus, head right on the B862, and take a left on the B852 to Foyers Falls; follow the signs to Lower Foyers/ Loch Ness Shores.

PUBLIC TRANSPORT Train to Inverness, then a bus (every two hours on weekdays) to Lower Foyers at the site entrance.

OPEN All year.

THE DAMAGE From £5.35 per person to £24.05 for hardstandings with electric. Wigwams from £45 per night.

rothiemurchus

Rothiemurchus Camp and Caravan Park, Coylumbridge, Nr Aviemore, Inverness-shire PH22 1QH 01479 812800
www.campandcaravan.com

If you like trees – *seriously* like trees – then Rothiemurchus campsite is the type of spot you might go to and never want to come back. It's one of the best places in Scotland to enjoy swathes of indigenous Caledonian woodland, with a flurry of forests and wood-shrouded lochs, that has a real sense of being somewhere genuinely unspoiled and pristine.

The award-winning campsite is set within the boundaries of the Rothiemurchus Estate, which itself lies right on the edge of the remarkable Cairngorm Mountain massif, the vast mountain plateau that is the UK's largest national park. Babbling burns cut through the camp and make for a sublime experience; waking up on a bed of soft needles on a summer morning to the sound of rushing water and the smell of pine spiking the crisp air can't be overstated.

The Grant family has held the stewardship of the estate for over 400 years to the present day and its members have proved enlightened landowners, opening up the land for walkers, cyclists and tree lovers. Scotland's lingering feudal land ownership attracts its share of controversy, but Rothiemurchus is the type of inclusive estate that the Land Reform Act of 2003 was designed to encourage.

You can hire bikes from nearby and meander around the myriad paths, with an easy circular route taking in the twin lochs of Morlich and Loch an Eilein. The latter is one of the prettiest in the country, with a ruined castle sitting in the middle of the water and beaches fringing its edges. There are some more serious routes up past the outdoor activity centre at Glenmore which

stretch into the mountains on old drovers' trails, opening up remote lochs and isolated bothies. If that's all a bit too adventurous, just climb aboard the Cairngorm Mountain Railway, the funky funicular that eases up the mountainside revealing stupendous views with minimal effort. Be aware, though, that funicular users cannot walk on up to the summit.

Rothiemurchus is the sort of site that ticks so many different boxes. Forest camping at its finest, it works for those looking to get away from it all, those wanting to explore this enchanting place by bike or those who fancy a walk off into the challenging Cairngorm Mountains. And did we mention all the beautiful trees?

COOL FACTOR Trees, trees and more trees – and lots to do!

WHO'S IN Tents, tourers, motorhomes – yes. Dogs – no (except in tourers or motorhomes).

ON SITE 22 woodland and riverside pitches for tents plus 17 hardstandings for tourers and motorhomes in a separate area. There's a keycard-operated amenity block with hot showers, toilets, dish-washing area and laundry.

OFF SITE Archery, hiking, canoeing and more at the Rothiemurchus Centre (01479 812345; rothiemurchus.net), and Rothiemurchus Forest is yours to explore and enjoy. Glenmore Lodge (01479 861256; glenmorelodge.org.uk) is a serious outdoor activity centre with a particular emphasis on climbing and mountaineering, handy for the Cairngorms and some of Britain's finest ice climbing, as well as plenty of summer routes. Novices can either seek advice from the centre or enrol on one of its frequent courses. The Cairngorm Mountain Railway is a great way to enjoy the scenery with relatively little effort (01479 861261; cairngormmountain.org/funicularrailway).

FOOD & DRINK The Old Bridge Inn (01479 811137; oldbridgeinn.co.uk) is 2 miles away on the road to Aviemore – an atmospheric old inn with a fine log fire, specialising in local dishes such as peppered leg of venison, with plenty of whiskies and real ales on hand to wash it down. For a slice of cake and a nice cup of tea, The Druie Cafe Restaurant (01479 780200) in the heart of the forest takes some topping.

GETTING THERE Rothiemurchus campsite is just a couple of miles off the A9. Take the first turning for Aviemore and then follow the signs for Rothiemurchus. The site is visible after a couple of miles on the right-hand side.

PUBLIC TRANSPORT Regular bus services run from Aviemore to the Cairngorm Mountain Railway, passing the campsite on the way.

OPEN All year except November.

THE DAMAGE £9–£11 per adult per night and £2 for kids aged 5–16. Under-5s free.

glenmore

Glenmore, Aviemore, Inverness-shire PH22 1QU 01479 861271
www.campingintheforest.co.uk/glenmore

The extremities of the Scottish Highlands can mesmerise even the most experienced traveller. From the UK's deepest lake (Loch Ness), to its highest peak (Ben Nevis – 1,344 metres in case you're wondering), and all the way to the rugged and remote Shetland Islands, Scotland's unspoiled north challenges and inspires everyone who visits. Situated in the Highland's heart, Glenmore is a spectacular, wonderfully located campsite, with easy access to the sandy beaches of Loch Morlich, and one of the last original pinewood forests, the enchanting Caledonian. The landscape here is a little oasis of green and is one of the finest places in Britain for wildlife spotting, with deer, otters, golden eagles and even red squirrels regularly spotted by fellow campers. For such a large site (there are over 200 pitches), it never feels overcrowded; the majority of spaces are flat, secluded and come with fabulous forest views. While Glenmore may not be one of those sites that feature underfloor heating or fancy washing facilities, the toilets and showers are adequate for most needs and are clean and well maintained. Aviemore, a 15-minute drive away, is not only the gateway to the Cairngorms, but also the region's hub for transport, shopping and restaurants. Of course, the main attractions in this part of world are the broad mountain plateaus, serene lochs and deep valleys, but when bad weather puts the hills out of bounds, Aviemore quickly fills with hikers and cyclists (plus skiers and boarders in winter), recounting their latest adventure in the town's lively cafés and bars.

There cannot be many places to pitch that are more beautiful than Glemore. Many campers come here for a week and don't use a motorised wheel for their whole stay, such is the walking appeal of the nearby surroundings. Stumble out of your tent every morning and gasp in awe at the beauty that is the Scottish Highlands.

COOL FACTOR Authentic camping in the beautiful heart of the Scottish Highlands.

WHO'S IN Tents, caravans, motorhomes, trailer tents and dogs – yes.

ON SITE 206 spaces made up of standard and premium pitch types. Flushing toilets, showers, washbasins, parent and baby room, chemical disposal point, laundry, drinking-water taps, dish-washing facilities, payphone, battery charging and some disabled facilities.

OFF SITE Cairngorm Reindeer Centre (01479 861228; cairngormreindeer.co.uk) is a 10-minute walk from Glenmore, and visitors can feed and stroke the reindeer. Visit the Landmark Forest Adventure Park (0800 731 3446; landmarkpark.co.uk), which provides adventure for all ages. The Cairngorm Sled-dog Centre (07767 270526; sled-dogs.co.uk) is the only working sled-dog centre in the UK and one of only 5 in Europe. Take an exhilarating ride on a pooch-pulled buggy where you will enjoy the spectacular views of the mountains. Only 10 minutes from Glenmore, the Rothiemurchus Estate is also a top pick (see p.330 for all kinds of outdoor activities).

FOOD & DRINK The Happy Haggis (01540 662979; harkai.co.uk), established in 1974, is a family-run takeaway and restaurant in the heart of Aviemore serving good, honest food throughout the day. Mountain Café (01479 812473; mountaincafe-aviemore.co.uk) offers excellent views of the Cairngorm mountains and, coupled with excellent food created from local produce, is a great place to enjoy breakfast, lunch or some fresh, home-baked goods.

GETTING THERE From the A9 take the turn-off for Aviemore. At the first roundabout take the B9152 and follow signs for Glenmore Village/Cairngorm Mountain National for 7 miles – Glenmore is on the right.

PUBLIC TRANSPORT The overnight Caledonian Sleeper train between London and Scotland serves Aviemore train station (7 miles from Glenmore) from where you can get a bus to the campsite.

OPEN All year.

THE DAMAGE Prices per pitch per night including 2 adults start at £16.50.

lazy duck

Lazy Duck, Nethy Bridge, Inverness-shire PH25 3ED 01479 821092 www.lazyduck.co.uk

The Lazy Duck campsite is well named. Its resident Aylesbury Ducks are so relaxed that the site owners David and Valery once had to bring in nanny ducks as the Aylesburys were too lazy to bother hatching their own eggs. The site seems to have an equally soporific effect on campers, and new arrivals soon slip into a similarly relaxed state, with doing very little becoming the main aim of most days.

To call the Lazy Duck a campsite is perhaps a little misleading. It's more a chilled forest clearing, blessed with a sauna, wood-fired hot tub and a bush shower, where swings and hammocks dangle from the tall trees and man and duck idle side by side. It just happens to have plenty of room for four very lucky tents and their (maximum of three) inhabitants. With typical unassuming attention to detail, David and Valery and their team ask you to move on every three days to another spot to save the grass. Welcome new comforts include the Campers' Shelter, where you can relax by a chimenea in the evening and meet your fellow lotus-eaters. Other welcome additions are the Woodman's Hut, a seriously romantic log cabin-style getaway for two, and The Duck's Nest – an enviable retreat (again for two) right on the waterside complete with the ducks.

The views are sublime, with the heather moorland and patches of Caledonian forest stretching out before you and the peaks of the Cairngorms to the rear. The sauna is not just an afterthought either, with a small chill-out area by the sauna room where you can light a candle,

burn a little essential oil and listen to any of the collection of ambient CDs. The larch-built, wood-fired hot tub accommodates up to six.

Once you've managed to rouse yourself from this wanton relaxation, then even setting out on a walk requires little effort, as the Speyside Way, one of Scotland's designated network of long-distance trails, passes nearby. The area is also very popular with mountain bikers, and you can cycle on the Speyside Way itself, around the Abernethy Forest or the Rothiemurchus Estate. The forest and estate are both highly regarded, with a variety of terrains, from smooth forest roads to tough muddy single tracks through the thick trees. In winter there are ski slopes nearby; the Deans advise 'hutters' (there's no camping from November to May) to bring their own toboggan if they fancy a spot of sledging. Back at the campsite, one of the simple pleasures is just watching the eponymous ducks amble through their day. They are joined in the ponds and Fhuarain Burn by other birdlife, including mandarin, widgeon, goldeneye and whistling ducks. Red squirrel, roe and red deer, and the odd capercaillie can be spotted within the surrounding forest.

If you want to shun the laid-back ways of the Aylesburys, you can also tackle the Spey in a canoe or kayak, or just sample some of its famous produce on a choice of distillery tours – this is serious whisky country. After a few drams, a swing in a hammock is the perfect recreation at a site where relaxation is practically mandatory. Just ask those ducks.

COOL FACTOR A perfect place to enjoy the pleasures of doing nothing much.

WHO'S IN Tents (maximum 3 people) – yes. Caravans, campervans, dogs, big groups – no.

ON SITE 4 pitches for lightweight/expedition tents up to maximum 3 person. Campfires enouraged (in chimeneas). Wet weather cooking facilities. Sauna and wood-fired hot tub. Hammocks and swings. Toilet, bush shower and washbasin by the camping area. Washing-up space and a robust 'bush shower'. Free-range eggs plus veggies and salad. A communal area with a chimenea.

OFF SITE Of many distillery tours our favourite is Aberlour (01340 881249; aberlour.com), which is open for visits every day between April and October (otherwise Monday–Friday). The site is within the Cairngorms National Park (cairngorms. co.uk), which has numerous outdoor activities plus the Cairngorm Mountain Railway (see p.331). Ornithologists will enjoy the nearby RSPB reserve at Loch Garten (01767 680551), with its resident ospreys. The resort town of Aviemore is close by and also has plenty of wet weather options, shops, cafés and a swimming pool.

FOOD & DRINK Lazy Duck is the kind of place crying out for you to cook your own food on the open fire. A fishmonger visits on Wednesdays, and nearby Nethy Bridge has a post office and store and a superb butcher. For off-site sustanance, try the Old Bridge Inn in Aviemore (01479 811137; oldbridgeinn.co.uk) or the Mount View Hotel (01479 821248; mountviewhotel.co.uk) in the centre of Nethy Bridge.

GETTING THERE From Aviemore follow the A95 towards Grantown-on-Spey. After 8 miles, turn left towards Nethy Bridge. Enter the town down Station Road and do a quick left on to the B970, turn right and you'll find the campsite signposted on the edge of the village off the Tomintoul Road.

PUBLIC TRANSPORT Stagecoach Highlands run services to Nethy Bridge from Aviemore and Grantown-on-Spey.

OPEN May–October.

THE DAMAGE £15 for tent sleeping 1 person; £20 for 2; £25 for 3.

ythan valley

Ythan Valley, Smithfield, Ythanbank, Nr Ellon, Aberdeenshire AB41 7TH 01358 761400

Is there any part of Britain that remains unknown and undiscovered? Anywhere still anxiously awaiting (or dreading) a visit from its first tourist? Alas, probably not. But there are still a precious few hidden corners and secluded valleys in Scotland, free from any accommodation for the curious traveller. Ythan Valley was one such place, until David, Libby and daughter Iona decided to open a campsite in their meadow.

Despite its rather Welsh-sounding name, Ythan Valley campsite really is Scottish and can be found tucked away in a northeastern corner of Aberdeenshire. This undisturbed part of Scotland can't compete with the Highlands for dramatic scenery, and thus there are fewer tourists. Those who do venture here tend to hug the coastal margins rather than stray inland, where, in places such as Ythan Valley, visitors are usually limited to day-trippers.

But things have started to change since these five pitches at Smithfield Croft appeared, along with four beds in the onsite lodge. The campsite is tucked behind the croft on the edge of the small hamlet of Ythanbank, and from here the lucky and exclusively small number of campers can wander as lonely as clouds in the empty surroundings.

Camping here is a comfortable experience indeed, and the welcome extraordinarily warm and friendly. You get the impression that the campsite staff (the family) are really, at heart, doing this for the fun of it, and to share their rural backwater with new folk. This warm-hearted ethos extends across the daisy meadow to the theatrical conversion of an old coal shed – now a cosy campers' Wash House.

But that isn't all they do to make you feel at home; Libby does B&B, but not in the traditional sense. Here it's 'bread and breakfast'. The early morning sustenance they rustle up is varied and delicious and can even be delivered to your tent if you wish: full Scottish or veggie breakfasts, bacon butties, eggs-however and the speciality of the house – toast (or, more accurately, Libby's freshly baked bread, toasted).

Campers can order a fresh loaf every day in a bewildering number of varieties, so be sure to ditch the diet before you come here. Also, all this talk of being in the back of beyond, while it feels true enough on the spot, may not be wholly accurate. For instance, if you have a weakness for stately homes, Haddo House and Fyvie Castle are an easy drive or cycle away. Both boast landscaped gardens and rambling country parks with woodland and lakeside walks; ideal for working off all that baked breakfast goodness. The nearest settlement, Ellon, is just four miles away and, if campers still feel the need for the big city, Aberdeen is only 20 miles away. Positively local in other words.

However, with the welcome, space, tranquillity and completely unspoiled nature of the countryside on hand at Ythan Valley, it's tempting to just stay put and maybe tuck into a little bit more of that bread.

COOL FACTOR The welcome, the home-baked bread, the herbal bush showers, the roaming ducks and the beautiful rambling surroundings.

WHO'S IN Tents – yes. Caravans, campervans, dogs, big groups, young groups – no.

ON SITE Pitch numbers are limited – call to check there is a pitch available for you. Good facilities in the new quirky wash house with toilets, shower and washing-up sink.

OFF SITE Haddo House (08444 932179; NT) has gardens, a country park, produce shop and tearoom; Fyvie Castle (08444 932182; NT) is a medieval castle with amazing Edwardian interiors. The local craft beer producing BrewDog Brewery (01358 724924; brewdog.com) has a particularly popular tap room and you can do tours of the brewery too. The Glen Garioch Distillery (01651 873450; Glen Garioch Distillery) also does tours Monday–Saturday. Dunnottar Castle (01569 762173; dunnottarcastle.co.uk) is one of the most impressive sights on the Scottish coast.

FOOD & DRINK The Tolbooth (01358 721308) in Ellon is a traditional pub with a big selection of malt whiskies and no food to distract you. The Redgarth (01651 872353; redgarth. com) at Oldmeldrum has been CAMRA's Regional Pub of the Year numerous times and serves good food.

GETTING THERE Follow the A90 north from Aberdeen for 15 miles, then turn left onto the B9005 through Ellon. Continue along the road (including a right turn) to Ythanbank, go straight on in to the village (ignoring where the main road turns left), then right into the first narrow lane signposted to Schivas, then immediateley right into Smithfield's long drive.

PUBLIC TRANSPORT There's a regular and frequent bus service from Aberdeen to Ellon, from where there's an infrequent bus service to Ythanbank. Check the bus times beforehand with Traveline.

OPEN Spring, Summer and Autumn. The Little Lodge is also open in winter (weather permitting).

THE DAMAGE Tent with 1 person £9 per night; additional adults £5; children under 12 years £3. The Little Lodge log cabin is usually let on a weekly basis but can be let for a few days if needed.

glenbrittle

Glenbrittle, Carbost, Isle of Skye IV47 8TA 01478 640404 www.dunvegancastle.com

Poor Glenbrittle, it must be like having Miss World for a sister. Skye's Black Cuillin mountains are so jaw-droppingly beautiful that people often forget to enjoy the delights of the lowly glen at their foot. A thread of a road twists along a valley where red deer slip silently through the forests, a tumbling river forms exquisite pools of water and where, after seven sinuous miles, you will find one of the finest campsites in the country.

Glenbrittle campsite seems to have come to some peace agreement with its savage and towering mountain neighbours, allowing it to flourish quietly by their rocky flanks. The site is large but at the same time intimate, with long grass cropped into neat little sections that hold a few tents each. This, with the undulating terrain, gives the land a secretive feel: you could put 50 tents up and swear the place was half empty.

All of this makes selecting a pitch deliciously difficult. The view of the Cuillins is a gem, but no sooner do you align your tent towards it than you realise there are other treasures around. You could camp beside the riotous flowers that line the tiny stream, or next to the sleepy stretch of farmland inland from the campsite. Or how about next to a view of the beach that curves as firm and smooth as the belly of a young salmon? Whichever spot you fall in love with, you'll soon discover that this family has more than one beauty queen…

Glenbrittle is not one of those sites with shiny toilet blocks and vast children's playgrounds. The facilities at Glenbrittle have been upgraded, and the number of pitches has risen by 20, but the rugged simplicity of the site still attracts those in need of some serious R&R. It is a little like a Links golf course, with smooth broad fairways in which to pitch your tent and knee-deep rough in which to lose stray tent pegs.

Glenbrittle attracts an eclectic clientele from all corners of the world. You may stumble upon Scottish hippies singing 'Ziggy Stardust' around a fire on the beach, a gaggle of Polish climbers returning to the site, jangling their crampons and carabiners, or a quiet Japanese couple with a state-of-the-art tent and a worrying collection of sashimi knifes. Just don't let them see the Pot Noodle you're cooking up for your own supper.

Glenbrittle is probably most popular with climbers, who use it as a base for tackling the Cuillins, the mountain range that dominates the Skye skyline. Like a jaw full of broken teeth, it looms over Glenbrittle, blotting out the early sun. Every morning, plucky climbers can be seen setting off at dawn; climbing here is a serious business and not for the fainthearted. But even if you are not part of the crampon and carabiner crew, there are plenty of low-level adventures to be had along the peninsula. Whether you find yourself hanging from the rocks or simply relaxing on the beach, Glenbrittle is the perfect tonic for anyone who wants peace, tranquillity and a mobile phone with no signal.

COOL FACTOR Great views of the Milky Way and a beautiful beach on the doorstep.

WHO'S IN Tents, caravans, campervans, dogs, backpackers, groups – yes.

ON SITE Approx. 200 camping pitches available. Hardstanding with electric hook-ups also available. There is a lengthy beach, which is sheltered enough to be safe even for toddlers to have a paddle. There are washing-up facilities inside the shower and toilet blocks, washing machines and tumble-dryers, and cold water standpipes dotted around. The shop is well stocked and you can order piping hot bread and croissants for breakfast. Fishing permits can be purchased, a small selection of tents are available for hire and fishing equipment is available for rental or purchase. Wi-Fi is also available.

OFF SITE Discover the joys of Skye by hiking the infamous ridge trails or enjoy the pleasant quietness of its remote beaches. This is a real paradise for outdoor lovers, where bikers, hikers and kite-fliers have space to roam. If you're on the souvenir hunt, pay a visit to Skyeskyns (01470 592237; skyeskyns.co.uk) to pick up a few of the island's famous handcrafted wares or, on less outdoor-friendly days, visit the Hebridean stronghold of Dunvegan Castle (01470 521206).

FOOD & DRINK The campsite has its own shop, which is fully stocked with everything you might need. There is a coffee machine too. If you really need a bit of civilisation, head to the Sligachan Hotel (01478 650202; sligachan.co.uk), where there's a swanky restaurant and a cheaper bar. The Old Inn (01478 640205; theoldinnskye.co.uk) at Carbost, 8 miles back up the single-track access road, has regular live music throughout the summer and a lively atmosphere.

GETTING THERE Take the A87 to Sligachan and then the A863, turning by the hotel towards Dunvegan. After 5 miles take the B8009 for Carbost and, just before entering the village, turn left on to Glenbrittle's single-track road.

PUBLIC TRANSPORT There is a regular bus service which stops 50m from the site.

OPEN April–September.

THE DAMAGE Adults £9 per night; child £6. Electric hook-up £7. Day fishing permits per person £18.

sands

Sands Caravan & Camping, Gairloch, Wester Ross IV21 2DL 01445 712152 www.sandscaravanandcamping.co.uk

The shop at Sands is possibly the most remarkably stocked campsite store in the country. So much so that, as you check in, you might think the owners James and Marie have gone a wee bit over the top. But then you pitch your tent, breathe in the sea air, look out through the dune grass at the islands and mountains and realise that venison steaks, champagne and inflatable canoes are *exactly* what you need right now.

That's the thing about Sands – it keeps surprising you. The winding road that leads north out of Gairloch seems to be heading nowhere, then a sliver of grassy land gradually unfolds into a wide and welcoming apron bordered by swooping dunes and an epic seascape. Driving in, your first impressions are of a large caravan site, but campers have their own area of rolling duneland with plenty of tent-sized pockets for you to hide away in. This starts just down a winding track from the shop, and it's worth continuing along to check out the whole site before choosing your spot. Pitches range from secluded hollows to breezy eyries, while the spots in the southern corner are ideally placed by the site's own slipway – perfect for launching kayaks and heading out on other watery adventures.

There are also 10 heated wigwams should you fancy taking it a little easier for a few nights. These abodes come with firepits (campfires are not allowed anywhere else) and sublime views of the sunset as standard.

Wherever you are, it won't be long before you're winding your way through the dunes and down on to the beach to paddle in the irresistibly turquoise water. And even if this is surprisingly cold, don't worry – the shop sells wetsuits, too.

The beach, of course, is the campsite's glory, and during the day its gently sloping sands call one and all for a happy shift of castle-building, swimming and general larking about. When your work is done, you can perch in the grass at the top of the dunes, taking pride in your achievements and watching the blazing sunset over the far tip of Skye. This is a dreamer's place, and as the sun finally slides into the western ocean, the island of Longa drops into shadow, becoming a humpbacked sea monster settling down to rest for the night. With a beach to dig up, dunes to jump down, rocks to graze knees on and woods to go heffalump-hunting in, it's ironic that the campsite also has an adventure playground – it's not like it needs one. However, it's a beauty, and is set right in the middle of the site. Arrive when the sun is shining and you might also wonder why there is a games room. Well, it has been known to rain in the northwest of Scotland, and you may find yourself very glad of the owners' foresight. There is also a large indoor cooking and washing-up area, complete with several benches, and James and Marie have built a small café on site serving breakfast, lunch and evening meals. They are also planning to lay out a few mountain-bike tracks on some adjacent land. Like there isn't enough to do here already...

COOL FACTOR A great family site with a beautiful beachside location and serene views of Skye and the Hebrides.

WHO'S IN Tents, campervans, caravans, dogs on leads – yes.

ON SITE Newly refurbished washblocks are huge, clean and have underfloor heating. There is a large indoor kitchen and dining space, a dish-washing area, electric hook-ups, a laundry, a games room, bike and canoe hire and a children's adventure playground. The shop is very well stocked and is licensed. No campfires (except for wigwam guests).

OFF SITE The beautiful path to Flowerdale Falls, which are located 1 mile south of Gairloch, offers an energetic family ramble. The Gairloch Heritage Museum (01445 712287; gairlochheritagemuseum.org) is a great local museum that will have you stepping back in time. If you are visiting in early July, get your tartan out and put your best ceilidh shoes on for the annual Gairloch Highland Gathering.

FOOD & DRINK The Mountain Coffee Company in Gairloch (01445 712316) has a terrific selection of outdoor and adventure books, and the cakes are pretty thrilling, too. The food at the Old Inn at Flowerdale (01445 712006) is worth seeking out, and it tastes particularly delicious if you sit outside and enjoy it under the trees by the river. Tootle around the loch to the Badachro Inn (01445 741255; badachroinn. com), which snuggles by the seashore in a sheltered bay. The Melvaig Inn (01445 771212; melvaig-inn.co.uk), 6 miles from the campsite at Melvaig, is a bar-restaurant with wonderful views out to Skye that serves sandwiches and ploughman's lunches, cream teas and cakes, and pies and locally-caught seafood in the evening.

GETTING THERE Take the A832 to Gairloch. From there follow the B8021 coastal road north towards Melvaig. The Sands is 4 miles along this road on the left.

PUBLIC TRANSPORT There is a daily bus from Inverness to Gairloch, 4 miles from the site, but from there you will need to walk or hitch a ride.

OPEN April–October.

THE DAMAGE Tent and car + 2 people £15.50–£17.50. Extra adults £6.50, kids (5–16) £2.50.

lickisto blackhouse

Lickisto Blackhouse, 1 Lickisto, Isle of Harris HS3 3EL 01859 530485 www.freewebs.com/vanvon

Ever been to a party where you meet someone and you keep thinking you ought to be talking to your old pals but you're having so much fun that you spend the whole night happily wittering to your new chum? Lickisto is the campsite equivalent of that magnetic personality.

On the eastern coast of Harris, perched snugly above a sea loch, this campsite is perfect for exploring the island, from the wilds of the east coast or the breathtaking beaches of the west, but many campers barely leave the site, so drawn are they to its rock-star charisma. Harvey and John, its owners, have transformed a rough and rocky croft into a relaxing retreat, where the love they have lavished on their labours can be clearly seen and felt. Harvey is a fancy cook and bakes fresh bread for the camping guests every day before going off to work at his hair salon in Tarbert while John does all the handywork. Since acquiring Lickisto Blackhouse a few years ago, they've been slowly converting the place into one of the finest little campsites in the country.

The camping pitches are personally cut by John, and are separated from each other by wild grasses and heather, giving everyone their own individual space; plus there are a couple of yurts for lazybones, pitched high up on the site to give splendid ocean views. Each comes with a wood-burning stove, running water, futons (with linen), gas stove, carpets and candles. Harvey even pops a home-made loaf in, so don't forget your butter and jam.

The site has its own restored blackhouse, where you can cook a meal, play Jenga, have a shower or simply slouch on a leather sofa and dream. Pluck a fishing rod from the wall and you can try catching your supper from the loch. And guests are also free to enjoy the fruits (and veg) of the polytunnel – the lemon basil will be perfect should you hook a fish. Down by the sea loch there's a small landing cove if you want to turn up by boat or fancy having a waterside campfire. Around the communal table you're as likely to be rubbing shoulders with cyclists, canoeists and walkers as with people who've come by car. Lickisto is proud to be low-impact and small-scale, with a roof thatched with local heather, and wooden bridges and walkways made from telegraph poles discarded at the roadside.

When you arrive, John or Harvey is usually on hand to give you a tour. It's a seductive introduction and, as you wind down little paths between stands of high rushes and turn unexpected corners to reveal perfect pitches hidden behind flowering bushes, you may be forgiven for thinking Harvey is actually a white rabbit in disguise, leading you into Wonderland. The resident wildfowl are only too happy to make your acquaintance, and the ducks, in particular, have an engaging habit of wandering up and eyeing you in a way that clearly says, 'Have you finished with that biscuit?'. Down by the water of an evening, there's a good chance you'll see a local otter making his daily commute down the loch with his supper in his mouth. Rush hour at Lickisto – not to be missed.

COOL FACTOR A stunning oasis in the lunar landscape of Isle of Harris.

WHO'S IN Tents, campervans, dogs – yes. Caravans, big groups – no.

ON SITE 15 pitches, 4 campervan spaces with hook-ups and 2 gorgeous yurts. 'Bathroom byres' with 3 loos, 3 showers and loads of character. Blackhouse where campers can cook, chat and chill. The site is better suited to small or medium-sized tents: large 'multipods' could find it difficult to pitch. Bring midge repellent. Campfires allowed on the foreshore.

OFF SITE There are several art galleries on the east coast of Harris. You'll see why when you drive along the road. Pick up some genuine Harris Tweed in the shop at Tarbert. Visit the eagle observatory on the road to Huisinish, and make the effort to visit the Standing Stones at Callanish – they are older than Stonehenge and have an impressive **visitor centre** (01851 621422; callanishvisitorcentre.co.uk).

FOOD & DRINK Soak up some inspiration (and stunning home-baking) at the nearby Skoon Art Café (01859 530268; skoon.com). The Temple Café in Northton (07876 340416) is also worth a stop if you're exploring the island, making delicious food in as tiny a kitchen as you'll ever see. Back in Tarbert there's a swanky bar at the Hotel Hebrides (01859 502364; hotel-hebrides.com).

GETTING THERE From Tarbert take the A859 south, heading for Leverburgh. After about 4½ miles turn left at the sign for Roghadal. Follow the single-track road for 2½ miles, cross the bridge and, as you climb the hill, just before the bus stop, turn left. There are small discreet camping signs to direct you.

PUBLIC TRANSPORT The W13 bus runs from Tarbert Pier to Leverburgh, stopping not far from the campsite.

OPEN March–October (but by arrangement you can stay any time of the year).

THE DAMAGE Camping £12 per person, kids half-price, 'small 'uns free'. Price includes use of Blackhouse, free showers and fresh bread every day. Yurts £70 per night (extra person £20, larger kids £10).

sango sands

Sango Sands, Durness, Sutherland IV27 4PP 01971 511726 www.sangosands.com

Sutherland is the least populated place in Britain; and while journeying north to reach the isolated community of Durness, the emptiness and desolation may prove slightly unnerving for city-slickers on a rare trip north. For this reason, when the wide-eyed traveller finally rides into the wee village of Durness (population 400) it can feel like somewhere much, much bigger.

Travelling through the beautiful, slightly brutal scenery of this top northwestern corner of Scotland is a sensational experience and, taken slowly (stopping off at the other *Cool Camping* sites along the west coast, perhaps), it's a journey that will surprise, delight and sometimes shock. Once any sober mind has made it past Ullapool, it will be hard-pressed to recall any other place in Britain that quite captures the same essence of wilderness.

This is the setting for Sango Sands. It wouldn't matter if this campsite doubled up as the local bus shelter, for it offers succour to the weary traveller when it seemed that the world had ended.

Sango Sands teeters on the northern edge of Britain in glorious fashion, a fitting end to the trek through all that emptiness – and with a view out to infinity. Its unique north-facing location at the very top of Scotland means that in summer you can watch the sun both rise and set over the ocean. That is if you aren't lying in your sleeping bag, exhausted from the outdoor adventuring that is compulsory in this wild and windswept corner of the land.

If you can drag your eyes away from the view of mountains on two-and-a-half sides and the endless ocean on the other three (really, this is not an optical illusion) then the campsite itself is fairly ordinary. But you can't and it isn't.

There are several fields to camp in and the most picturesque spots are by the steep slopes above the beaches. There are other thoughtfully prepared areas for tents, which give children ample room to kick a ball away from nearby cars. It was in one of these quieter spots that we were joined for breakfast by a playful stoat. There are caravans littering the site in places, but they are almost invisible because the scenery is that big. There are several toilet blocks, and they are fine, but again pale in comparison to the location, which boasts an embarrassment of sandy beaches, with not one but two spectacular strands easily reached on foot from the site. The land and sea might meet here, but it's clear that they don't really get on. The beach is scattered with black rocks carved from ancient cliffs by centuries of northern storms. The power of the waves makes it a favourite spot of surfers and you can hire boards nearby if you fancy joining in. Or if the waves aren't too strong it is possible to swim.

That's the thing about Durness: it may be remote but there's a lot to do. A few miles west is the aptly named Cape Wrath, which you can visit by catching a ferry and then a minibus – there's a lighthouse, the highest sea cliffs in Britain and a thrilling sense of freedom. Then you can return to your tent on its cliff-top eyrie and stay awake for that late, late sunset.

COOL FACTOR Amazing scenery and location, teetering on Britain's northernmost tip.

WHO'S IN Tents, campervans, caravans, groups, dogs – yes.

ON SITE 120+ pitches, 64 hook-ups. 3 washblocks, 1 solely dedicated to showers. Waste disposal, dish-washing and laundry facilities. Fantastically, everyone has the use of a kitchen with free gas. Campers need to book if a hook-up is required. No campfires. Note: although the campsite itself is dog-friendly, the Oasis pub on the campsite is not.

OFF SITE Balnakeil craft village (balnakeil.wordpress.com) is an old MOD station that now has lots of individual galleries, cafés and workshops. Durness Golf Club (01971 511364; durnessgolfclub.org) welcomes visitors and has a terrific last hole over the ocean. Smoo Cave is the largest sea cave in Britain and just a 15-minute walk away. There is a peaceful public garden dedicated to John Lennon in Durness village – he regularly holidayed here as a boy. The beach surrounding the site is great for surfing.

FOOD & DRINK The Oasis Bar and restaurant, managed by the campsite owners, offers great food and local music, plus it's right next to the site! For what is audaciously billed as 'the best hot chocolate in the world', head to Cocoa Mountain Balnakeil (01971 511233; cocoamountain.co.uk). This spectacularly-set café and chocolaterie specialises in the brown stuff, from artisan truffles to its famous 'Mountain Mocha'.

GETTING THERE This is the far northwestern edge of Scotland – every route here is beautiful, but the quickest is probably the A9 north beyond Inverness then the A836 and A838 to Durness.

PUBLIC TRANSPORT There's a regular but infrequent bus service to Durness from Inverness.

OPEN April–October. Camping available at other times but without facilities.

THE DAMAGE Flat rates for adults £7, + first child £5, second child £3, additional children free. Hook-ups £4.

wheems organic farm

Wheems Organic Farm, Eastside, South Ronaldsay, Orkney KW17 2TJ 01856 831556 www.wheemsorganic.co.uk

Not for nothing did the poet and novelist George Mackay Brown say that the Orkney imagination was haunted by time. There's something otherworldly about the Orkney Islands. There's been a human presence here for thousands of years; the living in places like Skara Brae and the dead in the Neolithic burial chamber of Maes Howe, whose entry shaft is perfectly aligned with the setting sun on the winter solstice.

The land's been smoothed over by the prevailing winds, and the resulting views are of rolling hills and water, among the 70 islands that make up the archipelago. The dun hills are the tweed colour of a geography teacher's jacket and the sky can do everything from broody to menthol clear.

Wheems is owned and run by Mike, a landscape architect, whose outlook on life, the universe and camping is to keep things small, share in the beauty of the place and pass on his philosophy of eco-living. For those seeking creature comforts, Mike has constructed two solid wooden bothies, which are insulated with sheeps' fleece and have double-glazed doors that open on to a small deck that overlooks the bay – perfect for those travelling light or needing more comfort. Barbecues and small campfires are permitted, depending on the wind direction and the possibility of spark damage to neighbouring tents – if unsure do check with the owners first. Dogs are welcome as long as they are kept on leads.

COOL FACTOR Philosophically spot-on organic eco-camping with a warm welcome.

WHO'S IN Tents, campervans, dogs (on leads), small caravans, big groups, young groups – yes. Large caravans – no.

ON SITE 20 pitches, some with hook-ups; wooden camping bothies and a yurt. BBQs and small campfires allowed. 2 showers and 3 toilets in a wooden building by the bothy. Campers' kitchen has 2 small electric cookers and kettle, tables, chairs and a lawn with a stone bench. They also have a washing machine, large fridge, freezer, plus books and games for the kids.

OFF SITE Wander around the labyrinth of streets in Kirkwall, just a 20-minute drive away, or head to the tiny chapel on Lamb Holm, built by Itaiian POWs during the Second World War. They also built the causeways that link South Ronaldsay with the 'mainland'. Like most things here, it's a simple and unassuming place, but beautifully done.

FOOD & DRINK Organic fruit, veg and eggs are on sale in the site shop. The Creel (01856 831311; thecreel.co.uk) in St Margaret's Hope is one of Scotland's best restaurants, serving set 3-course menus for £40. Stop off also at the Murray Arms (01856 831205; murrayarmshotel.com) for one of their delicious local beers.

GETTING THERE The easiest route is the passenger ferry from John o'Groats to Burwick or the car ferry from Gills Bay to St Margaret's Hope. Follow the road from the ferry up through the village to the top of the hill and the main road to Kirkwall. Turn right then left (at the soldier's statue). Follow this road to the crossroads (where there's a postbox), straight over and the farm is on the left.

OPEN April–October.

THE DAMAGE Tent pitches £7–£15 per night + £3 per person; campervans from £9; bothies £35 (includes bedding and linen). Cars £2, dogs free.

index

50 WALKS IN

Gloucestershire

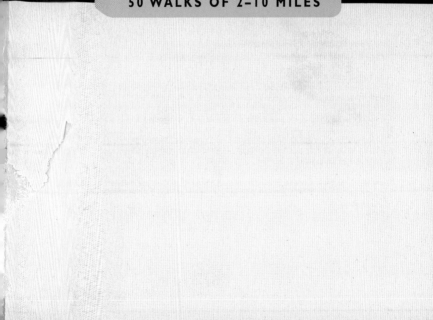

50 WALKS OF 2–10 MILES

First published 2002
Researched and written by Christopher Knowles
Field checked and updated 2008 by Nick Reynolds
Series Management: Bookwork Creative Associates
Series Editors: Sandy Draper and Marilynne Lanng
Series design concept: Elizabeth Baldin and Andrew Milne
Designer: Elizabeth Baldin
Picture Research: Vivien Little
Proofreaders: Pamela Stagg
Cartography provided by the Mapping Services Department of AA Publishing

Produced by AA Publishing
© Automobile Association Developments Limited 2009

Published by AA Publishing (a trading name of Automobile Association Developments Limited,
whose registered office is Fanum House, Basing View, Basingstoke, Hampshire RG21 4EA;
registered number 1878835)

A03627

ISBN: 978-0-7495-6052-2

A CIP catalogue record for this book is available from the British Library.

The contents of this book are believed correct at the time of printing. Nevertheless, the
publishers cannot be held responsible for any errors or omissions or for changes in the
details given in this book or for the consequences of any reliance on the information it
provides. This does not affect your statutory rights. We have tried to ensure accuracy in this
book, but things do change and we would be grateful if readers would advise us of any
inaccuracies they may encounter.

We have taken all reasonable steps to ensure that these walks are safe and achievable by
walkers with a realistic level of fitness. However, all outdoor activities involve a degree of risk
and the publishers accept no responsibility for any injuries caused to readers whilst following
these walks. For more advice on walking safely see page 144. The mileage range shown on the
front cover is for guidance only – some walks may be less than or exceed these distances.

Visit AA Publishing at www.aatravelshop.com

Colour reproduction by Keenes Group, Andover
Printed by Printer Trento Srl, Italy

Acknowledgements
The Automobile Association would like to thank the following photographers, companies and
picture libraries for their assistance in the preparation of this book.

Abbreviations for the picture credits are as follows: (AA) AA World Travel Library.

3 AA/D Hall; 9 AA/D Hall; 19 AA/K Doran; 21 AA/D Hall; 32/33 AA/D Hall; 47 AA/D Hall; 49
AA/S Day; 61 AA/H Palmer; 62 AA//R Rainford; 80/81 AA/D Hall; 101 AA/S Day; 102 AA/P
Baker; 128/129 AA/D Hall

Every effort has been made to trace the copyright holders, and we apologise in advance for
any accidental errors. We would be happy to apply the corrections in the following edition
of this publication.

Right: A footpath at Uley Bury (Walk 43)

50 WALKS IN

Gloucestershire

50 WALKS OF 2–10 MILES

Contents

Contents

Rating

Each walk is rated for its relative difficulty compared to the other walks in this book. Walks marked ✚✚✚ are likely to be shorter and easier with little total ascent. The hardest walks are marked ✚✚✚

Walking in Safety

For advice and safety tips see page 144.

Locator Map

Legend

→- - -	Walk Route	▨	Built-up Area
❶	Route Waypoint	▨	Woodland Area
– – –	Adjoining Path	🚹	Toilet
⛭	Viewpoint	🅿	Car Park
•	Place of Interest	🐟	Picnic Area
⌂	Steep Section	)(	Bridge

Introducing Gloucestershire

Gloucestershire has almost everything to make it a delightful county for discovering on foot. Within its boundaries are exceptionally varied landscapes. The Cotswolds, a region of gentle hills, valleys and gem-like villages, roll through the county. To their west is the Severn Plain, watered by Britain's longest river, and characterised by orchards and farms marked out by hedgerows that blaze with mayflower in the spring. Beyond the Severn are the Forest of Dean and the Wye Valley – this border country is a distinctive mix of Celtic and Anglo-Saxon traditions. All of these have been an inspiration to some of England's finest writers and composers. Together, they combine to create a notion of mellow rosiness that epitomises rural southern England.

Golden Villages

Gloucestershire doesn't have any real mountains: this is not a rugged county and will not suit the seekers of wilderness and rocky grandeur. The hills, though there are plenty of them, rise no higher than about 1,000ft (305m). What you do get from these hills, however, is a particular intimacy with the countryside. Climb out of Stanton, for example, and the views behind you, westward across the vale towards the Malverns and the Forest of Dean, are spectacular but never dizzy. Below you are fields of poppies and strings of golden villages, but you are never high enough to be isolated from their warmth.

What Gloucestershire lacks in rock it makes up for with an abundance of stone. Best known is the limestone of the Cotswolds, much of it a golden hue, which gives the villages of the region their widely admired charm. But there are also the standing stones of the Forest of Dean and the fossils in the Severn mud. Stone walls are everywhere on the hills and, even on the vale, stone has found its way into the fabric of some fine buildings, from churches to tithe barns.

Discover the Past

In Gloucestershire you are never far away from tangible remains of the past. There is something remarkable to see and touch from almost every era of British history, right up to our own time. Neolithic burial chambers are widespread, and so too are the remains of Roman villas, many of which retain the fine mosaic work produced by Cirencester workshops. There are several examples of Saxon building, including a chapel amazingly still intact, an array of medieval manor houses, and hundreds of villages visually unchanged for five centuries. In the Stroud valleys abandoned mills and canals are the mark left by the Industrial Revolution.

Gloucestershire has always been known for its abbeys, but most of them have disappeared or lie in ruins. However, few counties can equal the churches that remain.

These are many and diverse, from the 'wool' churches in Chipping Campden and Northleach, to the cathedral at Gloucester, the abbey church at Tewkesbury or remote St Mary's, standing alone near Dymock.

Castles and a Queen

If there is a shortage of anything in Gloucestershire, it is of castles. Well, you can't have it all; and yet even so, there are a couple of them. There is Sudeley Castle, where Catherine Parr is buried and, if you want the real medieval article, there is Berkeley, down on the vale.

Battles, with the exception of that at Tewkesbury, were usually fought elsewhere, leaving Gloucestershire to carry on being beautiful. I think that is what makes walking here a singular experience. Gloucestershire's natural advantages have been made use of, but never transformed into something ugly – on the contrary, people and nature have got together and created something that suits them both.

Using this book

Right: The landscape near Chedworth (Walk 25)

Empires and Poets at Adlestrop and Daylesford

*Embracing the legacies of Warren Hastings
and the poet Edward Thomas.*

DISTANCE *5 miles (8km)* **MINIMUM TIME** *2hrs 15min*

ASCENT/GRADIENT *230ft (70m)* ▲▲▲ **LEVEL OF DIFFICULTY** +++

PATHS *Track, field and road, 1 stile*

LANDSCAPE *Rolling fields, woodland and villages*

SUGGESTED MAP *OS Explorer OL45 The Cotswolds*

START / FINISH *Grid reference: SP 242272*

DOG FRIENDLINESS *Some livestock, but some open areas and quiet lanes*

PARKING *Car park (donations requested) outside village hall*

PUBLIC TOILETS *None en route*

Warren Hastings is a name that is simultaneously familiar and elusive; his role, however, in the making of the British Empire, was paramount. Born in the nearby village of Churchill, in 1732, he spent much of his childhood in Daylesford, where his grandfather was rector. When debt forced the sale of the manor, Hastings was sent to London for a career in commerce. He joined the East India Company, which was *de facto* ruler of India, and by 1773 he had attained the rank of Governor-General of Bengal, with the specific remit of cleaning up the corruption that was rife among the British and Indian ruling classes. His draconian methods were often resented but his determination and guile were effective. That India became the fulcrum of the British Empire was largely due to his work. Upon his return to England, he used his savings to repurchase Daylesford, where he died in 1818. The years before his death were bitter. A change in attitude to colonialist methods meant that Hastings was impeached for corruption. The seven-year trial bankrupted him and ruined his health, although he was eventually vindicated and made Privy Councillor to George III.

Spacious Parkland

Daylesford House was rebuilt by Warren Hastings to the design of the architect Samuel Cockerell, who had been a colleague at the East India Company. The building is in a classical style with Moorish features. The parkland around Daylesford House was laid out in 1787 by the landscape gardener Humphrey Repton in the spacious style of the day, made popular by Lancelot 'Capability' Brown. The village grew out of a need for cottages for estate workers. Similarly, Daylesford church was rebuilt by Hastings in 1816 as a place of worship for the estate workers. By 1860 the congregation had outgrown the church, so it was redesigned to accommodate it. Inside there are monuments to the Hastings family, while Warren Hastings' tomb lies outside the east window.

If Hastings represents the British Empire at its strongest then, in Adlestrop, you will find echoes of the changing world which signalled its decline. This characteristically rural small village, has come to be associated with one of the best-known poems in English, written by the war poet, Edward Thomas (1878–1917). Called simply *Adlestrop*, the poem captures a single moment as a train halts briefly at the village's station. Its haunting evocation of the drowsy silence of a hot summer day is all the more poignant when it is borne in mind that Thomas was killed by an exploding shell at Ronville near Arras in April 1917. Though trains still run on the line, the station was closed in 1964. You'll find the old station sign now decorates a bus shelter and the old station bench has the poem inscribed upon it.

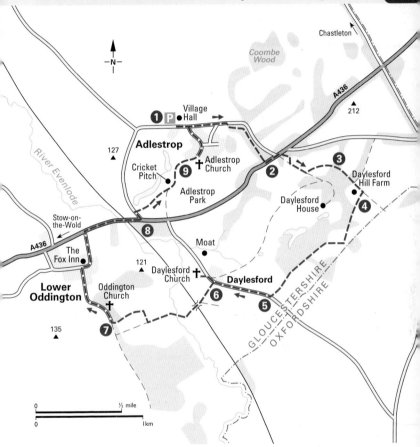

WALK 1 DIRECTIONS

❶ From the car park outside the village hall turn left along the road. Pass a road on the right, the bus shelter bearing the Adlestrop sign, and some houses. Some 200yds (183m) after another road, turn right over a stile. Follow a woodland path to the left and continue on this path until it meets a gate at a road.

❷ Cross the road with care and turn left along the verge. Before a road on the right and after West Lodge turn right through a wooden gate onto a path in the Daylesford Estate. The path curves left to a post and rail fence. Turn right alongside it as it curves to the drive. Turn left on to the drive, flanked by poplar trees, and after 100 paces turn left between post and rail fences.

3 Follow these to cross a bridge and follow a tree-lined avenue towards buildings. Traverse the farmyard and then turn right at Hill Farm Cottage, passing the estate office.

4 Walk along the drive between paddocks, soon following the estate wall. Pass the garden offices' gate and, as it goes sharp right, stay on the drive, reaching a road. Turn right at a gate.

5 Walk along the road, with the estate on your right, until you come to Daylesford estate village. Opposite the drive to Daylesford House is a shaded footpath leading to Daylesford church. After visiting the church, return to the road, turn right and retrace your steps and 95 paces beyond the phone box, turn right through a kissing gate.

6 Cross this field to a gate. Turn right on to a track and cross a

railway footbridge. Curve along the track through two field gates to cross an iron lattice-sided footbridge over the stream. Almost immediately turn right off the track, then left by the hedge to walk parallel to the track. At the end of the field turn left through a gate back onto the track, through a gate and then right, beyond the hedge. The path follows two sides of the field to a gate into a copse in the far corner.

7 At a track through the trees turn right and pass Oddington church. Continue, now on tarmac, to a junction in the village and turn right. Pass The Fox Inn and go to another junction. Turn right and walk on the pavement, where it ends, cross the road carefully to the pavement opposite.

8 Beyond the railway bridge, turn left along the Adlestrop road and turn immediately right through two kissing gates. Descend through Adlestrop Park to skirt to the right of the cricket pitch and head for a kissing gate to its right, in a tree gap.

9 Follow the track through a kissing gate and past Adlestrop church. At the next junction turn left through the village until you reach the bus stop. Turn left here to return to the car park at the start of the walk.

The Lost Villages of the Ditchfords

A walk among the ghosts of former medieval agricultural communities, abandoned since the 15th century.

DISTANCE 5 miles (8km)	**MINIMUM TIME** 1hr 45min

ASCENT/GRADIENT 130ft (40m) ▲▲▲ **LEVEL OF DIFFICULTY** ✦✦✦

PATHS Track and field, quiet lanes, ford or bridge, 2 stiles

LANDSCAPE Rolling fields, with good views at some points

SUGGESTED MAP OS Explorer OL45 The Cotswolds

START / FINISH Grid reference: SP 240362

DOG FRIENDLINESS Some livestock and some not very encouraging signs

PARKING Lay-bys on Todenham's main street, south of village hall

PUBLIC TOILETS None en route

There are cases of so-called 'lost villages' all over England and almost as many theories and explanations for their demise. The principal culprit is often said to be the Black Death, sweeping through the countryside in the 14th century and emptying villages of their inhabitants. However, this is by no means the only possibility and in the case of the Ditchfords there do appear to be other reasons for their disappearance. Ditchford is a name that was widespread in this area (perhaps because of their proximity to the Fosse Way – 'fosse' meaning ditch in Old English). Remnants of this, in the form of the names of houses and farms, are still evident on detailed maps, but of the three villages – Ditchford Frary, Lower Ditchford and Upper Ditchford – there is almost no trace.

Abandonment

A 15th-century witness, a priest from Warwickshire called John Rouse, wrote in 1491 that the Ditchfords had been abandoned during his lifetime. Changes in agricultural practices are thought to be the principal reason for this abandonment. As farming gradually became more efficient there was a disinclination to cultivate the stony soils of the more exposed and windswept upland areas.

At the same time, in the Cotswolds, the wool trade was rapidly supplanting arable farming, as the wolds were given over to sheep. Much of the land was owned by the great abbeys who, deriving a third of their income from wool, turned vast tracts of land over to summer pasture in the uplands and winter pastures on the more sheltered lower slopes. The result was that the villagers, mostly farm labourers who had for centuries depended on access to arable land for their livelihood, lost that access. They simply had to move elsewhere in search of work. Today there are no solid remains of any of the three villages. What you can see, however, is a series of regular rolls and shapes in the land that indicate settlement. Upper Ditchford, which stood on the slope near Neighbrook Farm, is the least obvious but you can see banked enclosures and terraces that probably supported buildings. The site is somewhat clearer in the case of Lower

THE DITCHFORDS

Ditchford, where there are terraces and the site of a manor house and moat. Ditchford Frary has left its name to a nearby farmhouse.

Surviving Village

Todenham survived the rigours of depopluation, and today is a quiet and unspoilt village situated on the edge of the Cotswolds. It's really a long, single road flanked by an assortment of houses and their leafy gardens. The manor house dates from the end of the Georgian period, while the church is worth a visit for its decorated and Perpendicular interior. Its features include a 13th-century font with the names of 18th-century churchwardens inscribed upon it.

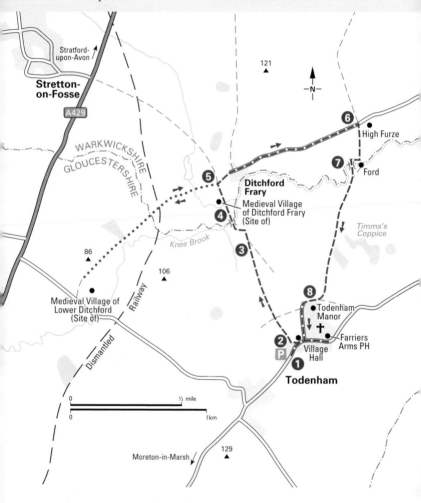

WALK 2 DIRECTIONS

❶ From a lay-by below Todenham village hall walk up towards the hall and turn left just before it. Continue along a gravelled drive between a house (The Retreat) and its garage and the go through solid timber gates.

❷ After 50 paces go right up the steps to a bank to a kissing gate.

THE DITCHFORDS

Pass into a field and head straight across. Go through another kissing gate on the far side, into a field of undulations indicating medieval ploughing. Continue on the same line to a stile – cross into the neighbouring field and, staying on its upper part, go straight ahead, in the direction of a large house.

❸ Cross another stile and join a farm track. Where the track goes into a field on the right bear left to pass to the right of a brick ruin, and cross a footbridge to a second footbridge with gates at each end.

❹ Cross this bridge and then go straight ahead, crossing a field (amid the earthworks of the site of Ditchford Frary) with a farmhouse ahead to the right. On the other side go through a field gate, cross another field and pass through a field gate to a farm track.

❺ If you wish to see the site of Lower Ditchford, turn left here onto the metalled track and keep going over the former railway line until you approach a road – the remains are to your left. Then return along the track. Otherwise turn right on the track and pass behind the farmhouse. The track becomes a metalled lane.

❻ After 0.5 mile (800m) just before High Furze farm turn right through a gate into a field. Follow its left margin until it dips down to a ford across Knee Brook. Turn right here and after 70 paces find a bridge on your left.

❼ Cross this ancient stone bridge and head uphill to the faint, grassy track that rises from the ford. By staying on this line, with the brook now to your right, you will come to a gate in the top corner. Go through on to a track that rises between tree lines and copses. After 0.5 mile (800m) you reach a junction opposite an entrance to Todenham Manor.

❽ Turn right here and follow this track as it curves left, around the manor between post and rail fences, and finally brings you back to the village with the village hall on your right. Turn left for the church and the Farriers Arms pub, or turn right to return to your car.

The Stone Secrets of the Windrush Valley

An insight into the character of Cotswold stone, which makes up the building blocks of the region's beauty.

DISTANCE 6 miles (9.7km)	**MINIMUM TIME** 2hrs 30min

ASCENT/GRADIENT 120ft (37m) ▲▲▲ **LEVEL OF DIFFICULTY** ✦✦✦

PATHS Fields, tracks and pavement, 14 stiles

LANDSCAPE Streams, fields, open country and villages

SUGGESTED MAP OS Explorer OL45 The Cotswolds

START / FINISH Grid reference: SP 192131

DOG FRIENDLINESS Some care required but can probably be off lead for long stretches without livestock

PARKING Windrush village

PUBLIC TOILETS None en route

Stone is everywhere in Gloucestershire – walk across any field and shards of oolitic limestone lie about the surface like bits of fossilised litter. This limestone, for long an obstacle to arable farming, is a perfect building material. In the past almost every village was served by its own quarry, a few of which are still worked today.

Golden Hue

Limestone is a sedimentary rock, made largely of material derived from living organisms that thrived in the sea that once covered this part of Britain. The rock is therefore easily extracted and easily worked; some of it will actually yield to a handsaw. Of course this is something of a generalisation as, even in a small area, the quality of limestone varies considerably in colour and in texture, suiting certain uses more than others. But it is for its golden hue, due to the presence of iron oxide, that it is most famous.

Slated

The composition of the stone dictates the use to which it will be put. Some limestone, with a high proportion of grit, is best suited to wall building or to hut building. Some outcrops are in very thin layers and are known as 'presents' because they provide almost ready-made material for roof-slates. When the stone needs a little help it is left out in the winter so that frost freezes the moisture trapped between layers, forcing them apart. The stone can then be shaped into slates. Because of their porous nature, they have to overlap and the roof is built at a steep pitch.

Construction Types

There are four basic types of traditional stone construction to be seen in the Cotswolds – dry-stone, mortared rubble, dressed stone and ashlar. The quality of Cotswold stone has long been recognised and the quarries here, to the west of Burford, provided building material for London's St Paul's Cathedral and several Oxford colleges.

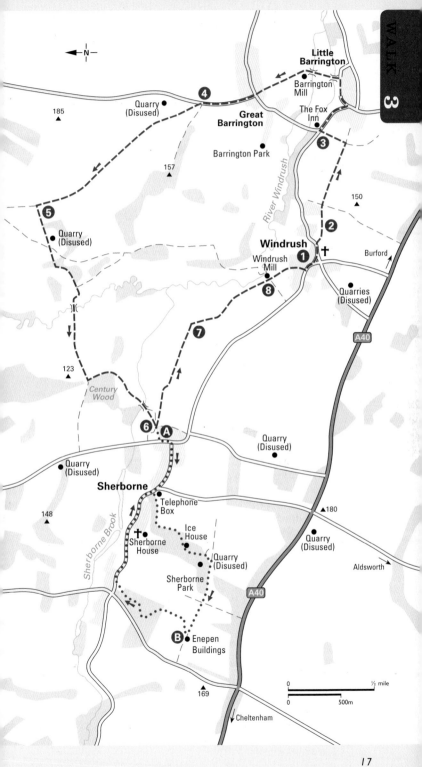

Little Barrington

Barrington Mill

Quarry (Disused)

185 ▲

④

Great Barrington

The Fox Inn

③

Barrington Park

River Windrush

157 ▲

150 ▲

⑤

②

Quarry (Disused)

Windrush

① ✝

Burford

Windrush Mill

⑧

Quarries (Disused)

⑦

A40

123 ▲

Century Wood

⑥ **Ⓐ**

Quarry (Disused)

Quarry (Disused)

Sherborne

Telephone Box

148 ▲

Ice House

Sherborne Brook

✝

Quarry (Disused)

▲180

Sherborne House

Quarry (Disused)

Sherborne Park

A40

Aldsworth

Ⓑ Enepen Buildings

169 ▲

0 ──── ½ mile

0 ──── 500m

↓ Cheltenham

WALK 3 DIRECTIONS

❶ Walk out of the village, keeping to the left of the church and, after about 100yds (91m), go right, opposite No 27, through a kissing gate into a field. Go across this field to the other side, keeping to the left.

❷ Go through the right-hand gate and continue across a series of stiles until you emerge in a large field at a wide grass strip (careful here, as it is used for 'galloping' horses) with the houses of Little Barrington opposite. Cross two thirds of the field, then turn left and head for the hedge at the bottom to the right of the cricket field.

❸ Go through a gap to the road. Ahead is The Fox Inn. Turn right, the pub car park on your left, enter Little Barrington and turn left along a 'No Through Road'. Pass Sundial Cottage on your left, the lane soon narrowing to a path. Where the path becomes a lane again, go left across a bridge, then another and pass to the right of Barrington Mill. Continue, eventually emerging in Great Barrington at a war memorial cross. Take the road in front of you, 'Little Rissington and Bourton-on-the-Water'.

❹ Where the stone park wall to Barrington Park on your left ends, go left on to a track and immediately right through a gate. Stay on this track for a little over 1 mile (1.6km) until, after climbing out of a dry valley, you come to a junction of tracks with large hedges before you.

❺ Turn sharp left and follow this track to the valley bottom and, where it turns hard left, go straight on and enter scrubby woodland. Cross the bridge over the River Windrush and follow a grassy track for two fields until, just before Century Wood, you turn left over a bridge with a stile at each end into a field. Follow the margin of the woods. Cross another bridge and a stile into a field and turn half right to the far corner. Through a gate, cross a footbridge and, after 50 paces, go through another gate and go half left to another stile.

❻ Take the track before you and then turn left over another stile. Cross this field parallel to the left-hand wall to go through a gate and walk along the right-hand margin of the next three fields.

❼ Continue to reach a stile at a corner. Go over into the next field and cross it on a right diagonal, walking in the general direction of a distant village. On the far side go through a gap into another field, with a stone wall on your right. Continue over a stone stile for several fields and pass by a stone barn to your right, at which point the River Windrush will appear to your left. Finally, pass a tin barn to your left-hand side, just as you arrive at a gate by a lane.

❽ Opposite, go up to a stile. Follow the perimeter of the next field as it goes right, ignoring a footpath into a field at the corner. Go beside a stone wall, over a stone stile on to a narrow track which leads into Windrush village.

Right: The Windrush River seen from The Fox Inn near Great Barrington

Sherborne
Sheep Village

Extend Walk 3 with a visit to a sheepish estate village.

See map and information panel for Walk 3

DISTANCE *3.25 miles (5.3km)* **MINIMUM TIME** *1hr 15min*

ASCENT/GRADIENT *210ft (65m)* ▲▲▲ **LEVEL OF DIFFICULTY** ✦✦✦

WALK 4 DIRECTIONS
(Walk 3 option)

The estate village of Sherborne originally belonged to Winchcombe Abbey. Huge flocks of sheep were gathered here for shearing, with much of the wool exported to Flanders and Italy. After the Dissolution of the Monasteries the estate was purchased by the Dutton family, who built themselves a fine house with the help of the eminent local quarryman, Valentine Strong. In the 19th century the house was rebuilt using estate stone but eventually it became a boarding school and has now been divided into luxury flats. The estate belongs to the National Trust. The village has some very pretty cottages, one of which, in the eastern part, has somehow acquired a Norman arch. From the road near the church there are sweeping rustic views across Sherborne Brook and its water-meadows, where once the medieval flocks of sheep would have grazed.

From Point **Ⓐ** turn right over a stile, following a path between cottages to a road. Turn left then right, into Sherborne. Enter the Sherborne Estate through a doorway beside the telephone box and follow the main path. Sherborne House will appear to the right. The path bears sharp left; after 150yds (137m) turn right. After a further 120yds (110m) turn left on to another gently ascending path. Stay left of a tree surrounded by a metal seat on a mound and enter a path on the far side to head for a gate. Go through the smaller of two gates, pass the old ice house and find a waymarker to a gate.

Follow the main path through the trees. At a gate, go through onto a farm track and turn right. Follow this for 0.5 mile (800m) to a gate at a farmyard, Point **Ⓑ**. Here you must turn back on yourself. Do this by turning right twice, through gates and gateways, to take a path initially with a fence (and dog waste bin) on your right.

This path soon bears left, descending, to enter conifer woodland beside a tree sculpture. Follow this wide path down until you come to a fork. Stay left and keep to the path as it skirts the woods, bearing right to flatten out at the bottom. Stay on it all the way to a doorway in a wall. Emerge at a road and turn right. Follow the pavement through the village for over 0.75 mile (1.2km), to turn left then right to return to Point **Ⓐ**.

Right: Poppies growing near Sherborne

Lechlade and the Thames

You are never far from the river on this route, centred on a once bustling crossroads in a quiet corner bordering Wiltshire and Oxfordshire.

WALK 5

DISTANCE 5.75 miles (9.2km)	**MINIMUM TIME** 2hrs 30min
ASCENT/GRADIENT Negligible ▲▲▲	**LEVEL OF DIFFICULTY** ✚✚✚

PATHS Fields, tracks and road, 8 stiles

LANDSCAPE Water-meadows, river and village

SUGGESTED MAP OS Explorer 170 Abingdon

START/FINISH Grid reference: SU 214995

DOG FRIENDLINESS On lead at locks; much birdlife beside rivers

PARKING Memorial Hall and sports complex off A361 north

PUBLIC TOILETS On Burford Street in Lechlade

WALK 5 DIRECTIONS

From the car park go south to the Market Square then walk west along the High Street and then left along Thames Street. Look around and you will see the high, slender spire of the majestic parish church, a constant presence throughout this walk even as the route strays into Wiltshire and Oxfordshire. The spire was perfectly described by the 16th-century writer John Leland as a 'pratie pyramis of stone'.

Ha'penny Bridge is a 1792 toll bridge – the toll house still stands. Cross the bridge and, at the end, drop down some steps on the

right to the riverbank. Walk ahead, with the river to your right, for just over 0.5 mile (800m) until, immediately after a bridge across the Thames, you see an old roundhouse among the trees on the far bank. Here the River Coln joins the Thames, alongside the now silted-up Thames and Severn Canal.

Lechlade was the upper limit for navigation on the Thames. In 1789, when the Thames and Severn Canal was completed, it became possible to move cargoes from ship to barge for the 29-mile (46.5km) journey across Gloucestershire.

Continue along the riverbank, cross a footbridge over a stream, and head across the field to find a kissing gate to the left of Inglesham House. The walk continues by turning left along the lane but, if you want to visit Inglesham church, turn right. This charming medieval building, much admired by William Morris, contains an exceptionally beautiful 13th-century *Madonna and Child*.

WHERE TO EAT AND DRINK

Lechlade has several venerable pubs to tempt the walker. Try the New Inn on the Market Place or the Red Lion on the High Street. These are both traditional coaching inns serving bar food and real ale. By the Thames is The Trout Inn which traces its origins to the 13th century.

LECHLADE

WALK

5

WHAT TO LOOK OUT FOR

At Buscot Lock, look for some plaques that compare the January 2003 flood level with those of 1947 and 1894. In Lechlade spend some time wandering the streets that run off from the market square. You will see some handsome buildings dating from the 17th to the 19th centuries.

At the end of the lane turn right, along the main road (using the verge). After 200yds (183m) turn left towards Buscot. In 0.75 mile (1.2km) turn left along the drive of Buscot Wick Farm. Just before the farmyard and cottages turn right along a drive and then go across some grass to a gate. Turn left around a house and within 100yds (91m) join a gravel track, towards a new milking shed. Look half right for near and distant black gates. Use these and a large oak to guide you across extensive pasture. At a tiny copse, skirt right for 50yds (46m), then two more stiles will see you to the road. Go through a gate on the other side, cross the field to a stile and turn left into the churchyard.

Buscot church contains a striking east window by the pre-Raphaelite artist Edward Burne-Jones, a pulpit partly made from a Flemish triptych and some delightful paintings. Leave by the lychgate and follow the riverbank to emerge at Buscot Weir. Here follow the concrete track if you want to visit the estate village of Buscot, which now belongs to the National Trust; there is a small shop and a pub on its short main street. Otherwise turn left then right to pass Lock Cottage and make your way across a succession of locks and bridges at Buscot Lock to a stile. Do not cross this but turn left to follow the Thames Path. Follow the river's meanderings until it brings you to a wooden bridge just beyond a 3-way post. Cross this and turn right to continue along the riverbank, noting the River Leach across to your right, which joins the River Thames just before St John's Bridge.

With both the River Coln and the River Leach flowing into the River Thames hereabouts, it is no surprise that there are a number of bridges. (Lechlade is in fact the only Gloucestershire town on the Thames.) Beneath the bridges, crowds of river pleasure craft have replaced the trading vessels of the past while, above, the bridges continue their function, bearing modern-day road traffic.

Walk beneath St John's Bridge, which dates from the 14th century and which takes its name from a former nearby priory. Pass St John's Lock, noting the statue of Father Thames that was built for the Great Exhibition of 1851 and which was moved here from its original site at Thames Head. Then enter the wide meadow ahead through a gate: the spire of Lechlade's parish church towers out of the flat landscape. The church was the inspiration for Percy Shelley's *Summer Evening Meditation*. Continue to the Ha'penny Bridge and Lechlade.

WHILE YOU'RE THERE

Just over 2 miles (3.2km) to the east of Lechlade is Kelmscot. The poet and craftsman, William Morris, the leading light of the Arts and Crafts Movement, lived in the Elizabethan manor house here from 1871 until his death in 1896. Morris is buried in the churchyard, and there is a charming carving of him on the village's Memorial Cottages.

Side by Side with the Eastleaches

Two churches, just a stone's throw apart across a narrow stream.

DISTANCE 4 miles (6.4km)	**MINIMUM TIME** 2hrs
ASCENT/GRADIENT 100ft (30m) ▲▲▲	**LEVEL OF DIFFICULTY** +++

PATHS Tracks and lanes, valley paths and woodland, 6 stiles

LANDSCAPE Villages, open wold, narrow valley and streams

SUGGESTED MAP OS Explorer OL45 The Cotswolds

START / FINISH Grid reference: SP 200052

DOG FRIENDLINESS Sheep country – dogs under control at all times

PARKING Village of Eastleach Turville

PUBLIC TOILETS None en route

These two Cotswold villages, sitting cheek by jowl in a secluded valley, carry an air of quiet perfection. And yet Eastleach Turville and Eastleach Martin are quite distinctive, and each has a parish church (though one is now redundant). St Andrews in Eastleach Turville faces St Michael and St Martin's across the narrow River Leach. Their origins lie in the development of the parish system from the earliest days of the Anglo-Saxon Church.

The Anglo-Saxon Kingdoms

The English parish has its origins in the shifting rivalries of Saxon England; for the one thing that united the various Saxon kingdoms was the Church. The first 'parishes' were really the Anglo-Saxon kingdoms. Christianity, the new power in the land, not only saved souls but also secured alliances. The Pope's aim was to invest more bishops to act as pastors and proselytisers, but at the same time their appointments were useful politically, helping to smooth the way as larger kingdoms absorbed their smaller neighbours. The number of appointments would also depend on local factors. Wessex, for example, was divided into shires and so a bishop was appointed for each one. Later the Normans appointed Archdeacons, whose job was to ensure that church buildings were maintained for worship. Over the centuries the assorted conventions and appointments that had accumulated through usage coalesced into a hierarchical English Church. For a long time, however, control was not tight. Missionaries, for example, would occasionally land from Ireland and found their own churches, quite independently of local potentates. Rulers and local landholders were certainly influential in the development of the parish system, but many parishes also derived from the gradual disintegration of the local 'minster', a central church on consecrated ground which controlled a group of client chapels. As population and congregations grew, the chapels themselves became new parish churches, with rights equal to those of the minster. This included the right to bury the dead in their own graveyard and administration of births and marriages.

THE EASTLEACHES

Tithe Payments

With the passage of time and the establishment of a single English kingdom, the idea of a parish had diminished geographically to something akin to its modern size. By the 10th century the parish had become the accepted framework for the enforcement of the payment of tithes, the medieval equivalent of an income tax. By the 12th century much of the modern diocesan map of England was established. So in the Eastleaches, all these developments come together and you find two parish churches virtually side by side. With politics, power and bureaucracy all playing a part, it's likely that the pastoral needs of the community were quite a long way down the list of factors which led to their creation.

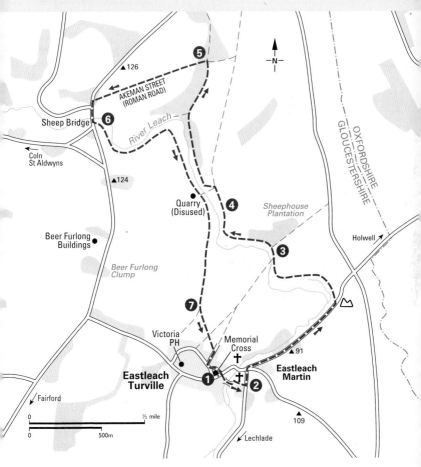

WALK 6 DIRECTIONS

❶ From the memorial cross in Eastleach Turville walk along the road with the river on your right. After a few paces locate a path on your right to cross the clapper bridge and follow the path into the churchyard of Eastleach Martin. Pass to the right of the church and emerge at a road.

❷ Turn left and then turn right at a junction, finally taking the lower road in the direction of Holwell. Walk on for perhaps

THE EASTLEACHES

600yds (549m) to where the road begins to rise steeply. Turn left here, pass through a gate into a field, and follow an obvious grassy track at the base of a slope for 0.5 mile (800m).

❸ This will bring you to a gate at the corner of Sheephouse Plantation. Go through the gate and follow the woods to your right. Continue to a gate at a field – do not go through this but continue forward with the field to your right. Soon you will reach a small area of scrubby trees, turn right here over a stile into a field and turn left.

WHAT TO LOOK OUT FOR

The little clapper bridge linking the two parishes is known locally as Keble's Bridge, after a family who were eminent in the area. John Keble, for whom Keble College in Oxford is named, was nominal curate for the two parishes in the 19th century. In the middle part of the walk the straight track to a road is part of Akeman Street, the Roman road that linked Cirencester with St Albans.

❹ Continue, passing through gates, until you come to a gated bridge on your left. Do not cross this but continue forward towards a gate at the edge of woodland. Go through and follow a woodland path until you emerge at a clearing. Walk to the other side to re-enter woodland and continue to a track.

WHERE TO EAT AND DRINK

Eastleach Turville has a lovely little pub, the Victoria, in the western part of the village. Nearby Southrop, to the south, also has The Swan, a creeper-clad old pub with real fires in winter and a wide choice of food. In Coln St Alwyns, to the west, you'll find The New Inn, everybody's idea of a classic Cotswold pub and serving excellent food.

❺ Turn left here and follow the track out of the woods and across fields until you come to a road. Turn left here, cross Sheep Bridge and, just before a turning to the right, go left into a field.

❻ Bear right along the valley bottom, then left and right again. This will bring you to a gate. Go through it, on to a track, and soon pass the gated bridge again. Follow the wall on your right as it curves up to a gate and then stay on the same line through gates until you reach a gate into the last field bordering Eastleach Turville.

❼ Turn half left across this field, heading for a gate just to the right of a prominent horse chestnut tree. Join the lane here, and keep left at the fork to return to your car at the start.

WHILE YOU'RE THERE

There are two places near by worth visiting while you are in the area. To the south is Lechlade, Gloucestershire's only settlement on the River Thames. There is a handsome market square, an idyllic riverside and several fascinating old streets to wander through. To the west is Fairford, a handsome village noted for its fine church containing one of the only sets of medieval stained glass in the country.

The Nabob of Sezincote and Bourton-on-the-Hill

Discovering the influences of India through the Cotswold home of Sir Charles Cockerell.

DISTANCE *3 miles (4.8km)*   MINIMUM TIME *1hr 30min*

ASCENT/GRADIENT *85ft (25m)* ▲▲▲   LEVEL OF DIFFICULTY ✦✦✦

PATHS *Tracks, fields and lanes, 7 stiles*

LANDSCAPE *Hedges, field and spinney on lower part of escarpment*

SUGGESTED MAP *OS Explorer OL45 The Cotswolds*

START / FINISH *Grid reference: SP 175324*

DOG FRIENDLINESS *Under close control – likely to be a lot of livestock*

PARKING *Street below Bourton-on-the-Hill church, parallel with main road*

PUBLIC TOILETS *None en route*

For anyone with a fixed idea of the English country house, Sezincote will come as a surprise. It is, as the poet John Betjeman said, 'a good joke, but a good house, too'. Built on the plan of a typical large country house of the era, in every other respect it is thoroughly unconventional. A large copper onion dome crowns the house, while at each corner of the roof are finials in the form of miniature minarets. The walls are of Cotswold stone, but the Regency windows and decoration, owe a lot to Eastern influence.

Hindu Architecture

Sezincote is a reflection of the fashions of the early 19th century. Just as engravings brought back from Athens had been the inspiration for 18th-century Classicism, so the colourful aqua-tints brought to England from India by returning artists, such as William and Thomas Daniell, were a profound influence on architects and designers. Sezincote was one of the first results of this fashion. Sir Charles Cockerell was a 'nabob', the Hindi-derived word for a European who had made their wealth in the East. On his retirement from the East India Company he had the house built by his brother, Samuel Pepys Cockerell, an architect. The eminent landscape gardener Humphry Repton helped Cockerell to choose the most picturesque elements of Hindu architecture from the Daniells' drawings.

Pavilion Inspiration

Some modern materials, like cast iron, were thought to complement the intricacies of traditional Mogul design. The garden buildings took on elements from Hindu temples, with a lotus-shaped temple pool, Hindu columns supporting a bridge and the widespread presence of snakes, sacred bulls and lotus buds. The Prince of Wales was an early visitor. The experience obviously made some impression as the intensely Mogul-influenced Brighton Pavilion arose not long after. Betjeman was a regular guest at Sezincote during his undergraduate days. 'Stately and strange it stood, the nabob's house, Indian without and coolest Greek within, looking from Gloucestershire to Oxfordshire.'

SEZINCOTE

Measuring Up in Bourton-on-the-Hill

This walks begins and ends in Bourton-on-the-Hill, a pretty village that would be exceptional were it not for traffic streaming through it on the A44. Nevertheless, there is quite a lot to see here. The church owes its impressive features to the fact that the village was formerly owned by Westminster Abbey, whose income was handsomely supplemented by sales of wool from their vast flocks on the surrounding hills. There is a fine 15th-century clerestory, lighting an interior notable for its substantial nave columns and a rare bell-metal Winchester Bushel and Peck (8 gallons/ 35.2 litres and 2 gallons/8.8 litres respectively). These particular standard English measures date from 1816, but their origins go back to the 10th century when King Edgar (reigned AD 959–975) decreed that standard weights be kept at Winchester and London. They were used to settle disputes, especially when they involved tithes. Winchester measures finally became redundant in 1824 when the Imperial system was introduced, though many Winchester equivalents remain in the United States. Further down the village, the 18th-century Bourton House has a 16th-century barn in its grounds.

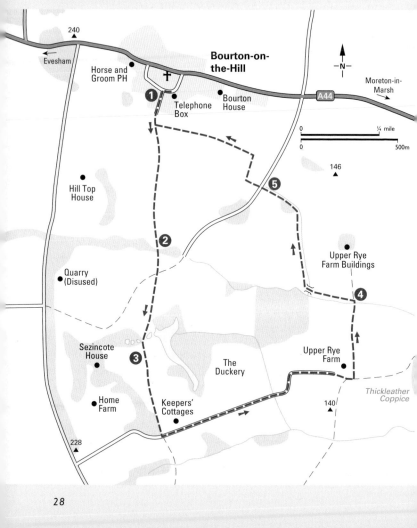

WALK 7 DIRECTIONS

❶ Walk up the road from the telephone box with the church to your right. Turn left down a signposted track between walls. Go through a gate into a field and then continue forward to pass through two more field gates.

WHILE YOU'RE THERE

Both Sezincote and Bourton House are open to the public but have a limited season, so check their opening hours in advance. Batsford Arboretum and Falconry is only a mile (1.6km) away, just off the road to Moreton-in-Marsh.

❷ Continue to a stile, followed by two kissing gates amid a tree belt. This is the Sezincote Estate – go straight ahead, following markers and crossing a drive. Dip down, keeping to the right of woodland, to two field gates among trees, with ponds on either side. Go ahead into a field, from where Sezincote House is visible to the right.

❸ Walk into the next field via a gate and go right to the end, aiming for the top, right-hand corner. Pass through a kissing gate

WHAT TO LOOK OUT FOR

As you start the walk look for a 'hole in the wall' just after the first gate. It consists of a tap located behind wooden doors just above ground, with the words 'Deo Gratias AD 1919', inscribed in the wall above. I presume this is in gratitude for the end of World War One. After Sezincote, as you walk down the road towards the farm, look for the buildings of the Fire Service Technical College, the main training centre for firefighters in the country.

WHERE TO EAT AND DRINK

The Horse and Groom is a handsome old pub at the top of the village. Recently refurbished, it serves good lunches. In Moreton-in-Marsh seek out the Marsh Goose, a restaurant specialising in good quality local produce.

to a narrow road and turn left. Walk down this road, passing the keepers' cottages to your left, and through a series of three gates. The road will bottom out, curve left then right and bring you to Upper Rye Farm. Pass well to the right of the farmhouse, go through a gate and, immediately before a barn, turn left along a track and a road.

❹ After a second cattle grid, go left over a stile. Follow the left edge of the field to a footbridge between step-through stiles. Go over it and turn right. Now follow the right-hand margin of the field to a stile in the far corner. Cross this to follow a path through woodland until you come to step-through stiles on each side of a footbridge and a field and continue on the same line to another stile.

❺ Cross a track to another stile into Sezincote's Millennium Oak Plantation and walk on. After a few paces, with Bourton-on-the-Hill plainly visible before you, turn right and follow the path to the next corner. Turn left and pass through three gates. After the third one, walk on for 60 paces and turn right through a gate to return to the start.

Regenerating Bourton-on-the-Water

*A walk on the wilder side of Bourton-on-the-Water
to see its natural regeneration.*

WALK

8

DISTANCE 4.75 miles (7.7km)   **MINIMUM TIME** 2hrs

ASCENT/GRADIENT 230ft (70m) ▲▲▲   **LEVEL OF DIFFICULTY** ✦✦✦

PATHS Track and field, can be muddy and wet in places, 18 stiles

LANDSCAPE Sweeping valley views, lakes, streams, hills and village

SUGGESTED MAP OS Explorer OL45 The Cotswolds

START / FINISH Grid reference: SP 169208

DOG FRIENDLINESS Some stiles may be awkward for dogs;
occasional livestock

PARKING Pay-and-display car park on Station Road

PUBLIC TOILETS At car park

Despite Bourton-on-the-Water's popularity the throng is easily left behind by walking briefly eastwards to a chain of redundant gravel pits. In the 1970s these were landscaped and filled with water and fish. As is the way of these things, for some time the resulting lakes looked every inch the artificial creations they were, but now they have bedded into their surroundings and seem to be an integral part of the landscape.

Migrating Birds

The fish and water have acted as magnets for a range of wetland birds, whose populations rise and fall with the seasons. During the spring and summer you should look out for the little grebe and the splendidly adorned great crested grebe, as well as the more familiar moorhens and coots, and mallard and tufted ducks. Wagtails will strut about the water's edge, swans and geese prowl across the water and kingfishers, if you are lucky, streak from bush to reed. Come the autumn, the number of birds will have increased significantly. Above all there will be vast numbers of ducks – pintail, shoveler, widgeon and pochard among them – as well as occasional visitors like cormorants. Either around the lakes or by the rivers you may also spy dippers and, in the hedgerows, members of the finch family.

Immigrant Birds

Should you get drawn into the village – as you surely will – keep listening for birdsong and you will hear some improbable 'visitors'. Bourton-on-the-Water has a large bird sanctuary which houses, among many other birds, one of the largest collections of penguins in the world. The reason for the presence of so many penguins in the Cotswolds is that the sanctuary's founder was also the owner of two small islands in the Falklands.

Long History

Penguins aside, Bourton-on-the-Water has a long history. The edge of the village is bounded by the Roman Fosse Way and many of its buildings are a pleasing mix of medieval, Georgian and Victorian. Although the village can become very crowded during the summer months, with the river banks at its centre like green beaches, strewn with people picnicking and paddling, it can still be charming. Arrive early enough in the morning, or hang around in the evening until the daytrippers have gone and you will find the series of bridges spanning the Windrush (one from 1756) and the narrow streets beyond them highly picturesque. They retain the warm honeyed light that attracts people to the Cotswolds. You'll see far fewer visitors in little Clapton-on-the-Hill, which overlooks Bourton. Make the brief detour just before Point ❺ to see its handsome green and tiny church.

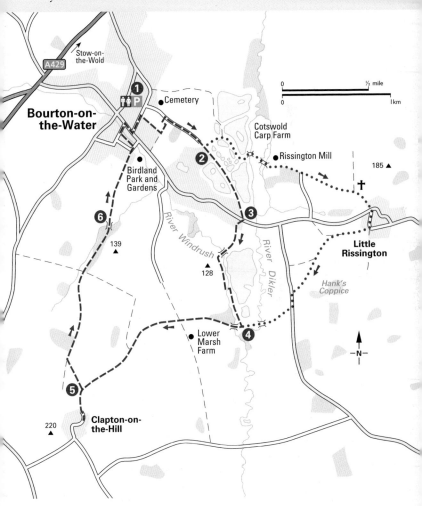

WALK 8 DIRECTIONS

❶ Opposite the entrance to the main pay-and-display car park in Bourton-on-the-Water locate a public footpath and continue to a junction opposite the village cemetery. Bear right to follow a lane all the way to its end. There are two gates in front of you.

2 Take the gate on the right-hand side, to join a grassy track. Follow the track between lakes to where it curves right. Leave the track to take a bridge and gate into a field. Go across the field, curving right to a kissing gate at a road.

3 Cross the road, turn right and immediately left on to a track. After 100yds (91m) go left through a kissing gate into a field and turn right. Use another kissing gate to return to the track, with a lake to your left. Just before a gate turn right over a bridge and left through a kissing gate on to a path alongside the River Windrush. Continue until the path comes to a kissing gate at a field. Turn left, go through another kissing gate and go left over a bridge before turning right. Soon walk beside a second lake.

4 Where this second, smaller lake ends (Point **B** on Walk 9) bear right to a stile, followed by a bridge and a stile at a field. Keep to the right side of fields until you come to a track. At a house go straight ahead, leaving the track, to a stile. In the next field, after 25yds (23m), turn left over a stile and then sharp right. Continue to a stile and then go half left across a field. Continue on the same line across the next field to a stile. Cross this and follow the right

margin of a field, to climb slowly to a junction of tracks. Turn left to visit the village of Clapton-on-the-Hill, or turn right to continue.

5 Follow a track to a field. Go forward then half right to pass right of woodland. Continue to a stile, followed by two stiles together at a field. Go half left across several fields and stiles. Keeping a stream to your left, walk for 0.25 mile (400m) through a deciduous plantation.

6 Cross the bridge and then go half right across a field to a bridge. Continue to more stiles and then walk along a grassy track between conifers towards houses. Follow a path to a road in Bourton. Walk ahead to the river and turn left, then right to return to the start.

Bourton, Clapton and Little Rissington

Extend Walk 8 with a diversion to Little Rissington.

See map and information panel for Walk 8

DISTANCE 6.25 miles (10km)	MINIMUM TIME 2hrs 45min
ASCENT/GRADIENT 344ft (105m) ▲▲▲	LEVEL OF DIFFICULTY ✦✦✦

WALK 9 DIRECTIONS
(Walk 8 option)

This walk takes you around further lakes, past a pretty mill and then up to Little Rissington, with its church that formerly served the nearby airfield – the original home to the Red Arrows display team.

At Point **Ⓐ** on Walk 8 bear left and, where the path forks, go right through a gate. After a few paces turn right along a narrow path, with a lake to your left. The path curves around the lake, coming to an end at a gate. Go through into a field and cross to a gate and stile. Cross the following meadow, bearing slightly to the right until you come to the banks of a stream.

Turn right, with the stream to your left, until you come to a stile and bridge on your left. Cross this and then another immediately after. With the wall of Rissington Mill close to your left, continue to a bridge and gate over a cut channel. Cross this field to a gate and drive.

Turn right, along it. Where the drive curves right, cross a stile on your left into a field. Go half right to a hedge, locate a bridge stile and cross into a field. Head up the field to the top corner and a stile. Then walk straight across the next field to a point just left of the church.

Turn right into the churchyard, walk around the church and leave on the other side to follow a path to a road at the edge of Little Rissington. Cross the road (moving left to do so safely) and follow the lane opposite through the village. Where the lane goes sharp left, continue along a track and, after 20yds (18m), turn right down a track at the edge of a field.

After 250yds (229m) go through a kissing gate, then after wooden rail fencing bear half left to a green gate. Go through and continue down to a stile. Cross this, turn sharp left to another stile and, in the next field, go half right. Follow this same line down a succession of fields to arrive eventually at a lane.

Turn left for 150yds (137m) and then turn right along a path. This will take you over stiles and then a bridge before arriving at the head of a lake. Cross to the other side, Point **Ⓑ**.

Fairford and the River Coln

Take this easy route from one of Gloucestershire's medieval wool towns to return by the river's edge.

DISTANCE 3.75 miles (6km)   MINIMUM TIME 1hr 30min

ASCENT/GRADIENT 15ft (5m) ▲▲▲   LEVEL OF DIFFICULTY ✦✦✦

PATHS Fields, tracks, riverside, can be muddy after rain, 6 stiles

LANDSCAPE Water-meadows, river and village

SUGGESTED MAP OS Explorer OL45 The Cotswolds or Explorer 169 Cirencester & Swindon

START / FINISH Grid reference: SP 152011

DOG FRIENDLINESS Good but lots of swans and ducks along riverside

PARKING On High Street near church or on Mill Lane

PUBLIC TOILETS Near parking

WALK 10 DIRECTIONS

This walk takes you out of town to the old gravel pits and back along the river. From The Bull Hotel walk up the High Street, with the church to your left (have a look at it at the end of the walk), and turn left into Mill Lane.

As the street name suggests, Fairford, like so many other small towns in the Cotswolds, owes its original importance to the medieval wool trade, and to one family in particular, the Tames. They were wool merchants and it was their money that embellished

St Mary's Church, one of the great Cotswold wool churches. The 16th-century writer and antiquary, John Leland, wrote, 'John Tame began the fair new chirche of Fairforde, and Edmund Tame finished it'. John Tame bought the manor and in fact rebuilt the church on the foundations of its predecessor, which had been built in Early English style.

Follow Mill Lane to the old mill and bridge. Then you come to a little garden flanked on two sides by an ancient shelter consisting of a stone slate roof supported by withered wooden pillars. About 150yds (137m) beyond this turn left over a stile into a meadow. Go straight across to the other side, pass through a gate and nip over a stile to a road.

Cross the road and enter Waterloo Lane, staying on this as it becomes a footpath. Where the football pitches come to an end, bear left along a footpath behind some houses. Stay on the path and

WHAT TO LOOK OUT FOR

As you pass the mill at the start of the walk look to the right and you will see what is left of the estate of Park House, which was demolished in 1955. The most obvious reminder is the elegant bridge beyond the mill pool. Keble House, on London Road, was the birthplace of poet and theologian, John Keble.

then continue along the side of a meadow. Cross a gravel driveway twice and soon reach a junction.

Turn left to enter a farmyard and then turn right, aiming for a point to the right of another cottage. Pass the cottage and cross a stile into a field. Bear left to be to the right of the river, to meet a stile at the edge of woodland. Cross onto a wide grassy track and continue close to the woodland, the river easing away to your left. Where the woods come to an end, bear half left to pass beneath the electricity cables and find a stile and bridge in the far corner, among bushes and trees.

Cross these, enter woodland and follow the footpath to a bridge across the river. On the other side, enter an area of lakes – former gravel pits. Walk anti-clockwise around the first lake and on the other side, 150yds (137m) after passing two protruding hedges, look for a path on the right between trees. Where this comes to an end turn left along a track. Keep going until you come to a bridge on your right. Cross this and then join the bank of the river.

While Fairford lies on the banks of the River Coln, where it meanders peacefully across a flat landscape of meadows and woodland, the town has an association with noise. Concorde was tested at the nearby airbase and, over the last few decades, it has served as a base for various military campaigns around the world. Every year there is a huge air tattoo here. Follow the river bank all the way to a bridge over the river. Turn right here.

St Mary's Church in Fairford was built in late Perpendicular style. It is a striking building but its most famous feature is the

WALK 10

WHILE YOU'RE THERE

It's difficult to avoid the presence of the military, particularly NATO's air forces, in the Cotswolds. So why not make the most of it and take in the RAF Benevolent Fund's annual international air tattoo, usually in July, at RAF Fairford.

near-complete set of medieval stained windows, perhaps unique in the country. They were made in the late 15th century (a few years before John Tame's death in 1500), probably by the Flemish craftsman, Barnard Flower, with the help of artisans. Flower was also employed by Henry VIII to work at Westminster Abbey and at King's College in Cambridge.

Follow the path you are on and it will lead you back into Fairford, to visit the church prior to returning to your car. The idea of the windows in St Mary's is to explain the Christian faith as if the onlooker were turning the pages of a picture book. They are arranged symmetrically. On one wall are windows depicting 12 prophets, opposite which are depicted the 12 apostles. The journey around the church, bathed in the magical light thrown down by the windows, is a memorable one. There are other things to admire here: John Tame's tomb, the amusing misericord seats in the chancel and the gravestone of Tiddles the cat in the churchyard.

WHERE TO EAT AND DRINK

There is a choice of several pubs and cafés in Fairford. The Bull Hotel, on the High Street near the church, is a nice old pub and convenient for this walk.

Blockley, Batsford and the Arboretum

*The exotic legacy of a 19th-century diplomat
adorns this part of the Cotswold escarpment.*

WALK 11

DISTANCE *5 miles (8km)* MINIMUM TIME *2hrs*

ASCENT/GRADIENT *410ft (125m)* ▲▲▲ LEVEL OF DIFFICULTY ✦✦✦

PATHS *Lanes, tracks and fields, 7 stiles*

LANDSCAPE *Woodland, hills with good views and villages*

SUGGESTED MAP *OS Explorer OL45 The Cotswolds*

START / FINISH *Grid reference: SP 165348*

DOG FRIENDLINESS *Some good lengthy stretches without livestock*

PARKING *In village street to west of church, north of post office*

PUBLIC TOILETS *On edge of churchyard, just off main street in Blockley*

England seems to be a country of trees. Walking through Gloucestershire you are surrounded by many native species but, when you visit Batsford Arboretum, you will encounter 50 acres (20.3ha) of woodland containing over 1,000 species of trees and shrubs from all over the world, particularly from China, Japan and North America. Public access to the arboretum is only possible via the A44 between Moreton-in-Marsh and Bourton-on-the-Hill, not from Batsford village itself.

The Japanese Connection

The arboretum was originally a garden created in the 1880s by the traveller and diplomat, Bertie Mitford, 1st Lord Redesdale and grandfather to the renowned Mitford sisters. Posted as an attaché to the British Embassy in Tokyo, he became deeply influenced by the Far East. Throughout the park there are bronze statues, brought from Japan by Bertie Mitford, and a wide range of bamboos. After the 1st Lord Dulverton purchased Batsford in 1920, his son transformed the garden into the arboretum we see today, with its 90 species of magnolia, maples, cherry trees and conifers. Batsford village is comparatively recent, having grown up at the gates of Batsford Park, a neo-Tudor house built between 1888 and 1892 by Ernest George. He built it for Lord Redesdale to replace an earlier, Georgian house. (It is not open to the public but is clearly visible from the arboretum.) Batsford church was constructed a little before the house, in 1862, in a neo-Norman style. It has several monuments to the Mitford family and a fine work by the sculptor Joseph Nollekens from 1808.

Silky Blockley

This walk starts in the unspoilt village of Blockley. It was originally owned by the bishops of Worcester but it didn't really begin to prosper until the 19th century. At one time no fewer than six silk mills, with over 500 employees, were driven by Blockley's fast-flowing stream. Their silks went mostly to Coventry for the production of ribbon. Blockley's history is both enlightened and superstitious. It was one of the first villages in the world to have electric light: in the 1880s Dovedale House was illuminated through Lord Edward Spencer-Churchill's use of water to run a dynamo. In the early part of that same century the millenarian prophetess, Joanna Southcott, lived in the village until her death in 1814. The tower of Blockley's substantial church predates the silk boom by only 100 years or so, but inside the church are several imposing monuments to the owners of the local mansion, Northwick Park. At least two of these are by the eminent 18th-century sculptor, John Michael Rysbrack (1694–1770).

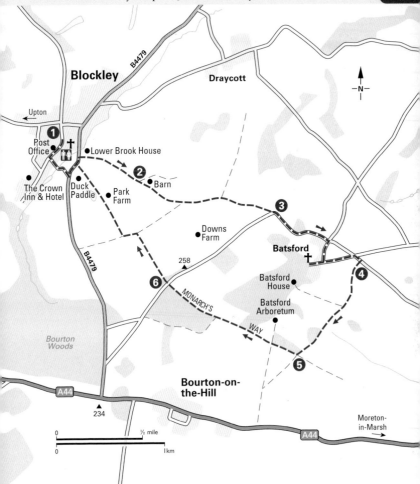

WALK 11 DIRECTIONS

❶ Leave the churchyard by the tower and walk through the village, turning left at School Lane. Follow this down across a stream and up to the main road. Turn left and, just before Lower Brook House, turn right on to

a lane walking up for 0.25 mile (400m) until the lane bears left.

❷ Continue ahead to pass to the right-hand side of a barn. In the next field follow its right-hand boundary to another gate. Pass through this to stay on the left side of the next field. Pass into yet

39

WALK 11

another field and then after 0.3 miles (480m) go half right to a gate leading out to a road.

❸ Go straight on and follow the road down to a crossroads. Turn right to pass through Batsford to a junction from where you can visit the church on the right. After visiting the church retrace your steps (there is no public access to the Arboretum from the village) to the junction and walk down the lime avenue then, at the next junction, turn right.

❹ After 100 paces turn right on to a footpath and follow this through a succession of fields, negotiating stiles and gates where they arise. Batsford House will be visible above you to the right.

❺ Finally, go through a gate into a ribbed field and turn right to a gate and kissing gate just left of a gate lodge at a drive. Cross this (the entrance to Batsford Arboretum), pass through a gate and follow the path up the field to a stile. Cross and continue to a track. Follow this up where it bears left. Turn right onto a path and almost immediately left at a wall, to continue the ascent with the park wall on your right. Keep going until you reach a stile to a road.

❻ Cross the road on to a track, then go through a gate and pass through two fields until you come to a path among trees. Turn left, go through another gate, and, after 140 paces, turn right over a stile into a field with Blockley below you. Continue down to a stile at the bottom. Cross into the next field and pass beneath Park Farm on your right. Go to the right of a pond to descend to a gate and stile, then follow a lane along the Duck Paddle, until you come to a road. Turn right and return to your starting point in the village.

Gardens around Mickleton

*A walk past Kiftsgate Court and Hidcote Manor Garden,
two early 20th-century creations of international repute.*

DISTANCE *5 miles (8km)*   MINIMUM TIME *2hrs 30min*

ASCENT/GRADIENT *625ft (190m)* ▲▲▲   LEVEL OF DIFFICULTY ✦✦✦

PATHS *Fields, firm tracks, some possibly muddy woodland, 5 stiles*

LANDSCAPE *Woodland, open hills and villages*

SUGGESTED MAP *OS Explorer 205 Stratford-upon-Avon & Evesham*

START / FINISH *Grid reference: SP 162434*

DOG FRIENDLINESS *On lead in livestock fields, good open stretches elsewhere*

PARKING *Free car park at church*

PUBLIC TOILETS *None en route*

This walk takes you within striking distance of two of the finest planned gardens in the country. The first, Kiftsgate Court, is the lesser known of the two but nonetheless demands a visit. The house itself is primarily Victorian, while the garden was created immediately after World War One by Heather Muir, who was a close friend of Major Johnston, the creator of the nearby Hidcote Manor Garden. Kiftsgate's gardens are designed around a steep hillside overlooking Mickleton and the Vale of Evesham, with terraces, paths, flowerbeds and shrubs. The layout is in the form of rooms and the emphasis is more on the plants themselves, rather than on the overall design. The steeper part of the garden is almost a cliff. It's clad in pine trees and boasts wonderful views across the vale below.

Major Johnson's Rooms

The second horticultural treat is Hidcote Manor Garden, part of the little hamlet of Hidcote Bartrim. This garden is the fruit of more than 40 years of work by Major Lawrence Johnson, an East Coast American who purchased the 17th-century manor house in 1907 and gave it to the National Trust in 1948. Many people consider it to be one of the greatest of English gardens, and certainly it is one of the most influential. Hidcote grew from almost nothing – when Major Johnson first arrived there was a just a cedar tree and a handful of beeches on 11 acres (4.5ha) of open wold. To some extent it reconciles the formal and informal schools of garden design. Hidcote is not one garden but several. Like Kiftsgate it is laid out in a series of 'outdoor rooms', with walls of stone and of hornbeam, yew and box hedge. These rooms are themed, having names such as the White Garden and the Fuchsia Garden. There is also a wild garden growing around a stream, as well as lawns and carefully placed garden ornaments that help to create a bridge between the order within and the disorder without.

Have a Butchers

This walk begins in Mickleton, at the foot of the Cotswold escarpment, below these two fine gardens. Clearly a Cotswold village, notwithstanding its mixture of stone, thatch and timber, the parish church at the village edge, lurks behind a striking house in the so-called Cotswold Queen Anne style. It has a 14th-century tower and a monument to the 18th-century quarry owner from Chipping Campden, Thomas Woodward. Near the hotel in the village centre is a Victorian memorial fountain designed by William Burges, the architect behind Cardiff Castle. There is also a fine butcher's shop here, a sight to behold, especially in autumn, when it's festooned with locally shot pheasant. This was also the birthplace of Endymion Porter, a patron of the Cotswold Olimpick Games on Dover's Hill (see Walk 13).

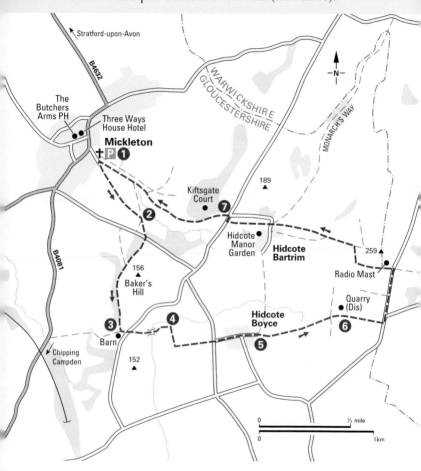

WALK 12 DIRECTIONS

❶ With your back to the church, turn right up a bank to reach a kissing gate to the left of Field House. Continue across a field on a right diagonal to a kissing gate at a thicket. Follow a path through trees and go through another kissing gate to emerge into a field

and follow its left margin to reach a kissing gate at the end.

❷ In the next field go half right to a gate in the corner. Cross a road and go up some steps to a stile or a gate. Turn right to walk around the edge of the field as it bears left. After 250yds (229m), take a path among trees, a steep

WHILE YOU'RE THERE

It would be a shame to miss the two fine gardens. Kiftsgate Court is open May to July, Saturday to Wednesday 2–6, and April, and August to September on Sunday, Monday and Wednesday 2–6. Home-made teas are available but dogs are not welcome. Up the road, Hidcote Manor Garden is owned by the National Trust and is open daily, 10.30–6.30. It is closed Thursday and Friday, March to November, except June and July, when it's closed Friday only. There is a good restaurant and plant sales centre.

bank eventually appearing down to the right. The path brings you to a field and then a Dutch barn.

❸ At the barn turn left briefly onto a track. Just about opposite the barn, keep left of a hedge, following the edge of a field to the bottom corner. Go through a gap to a bridge, with a stile on each side, cross a stream and turn left.

WHAT TO LOOK OUT FOR

In Hidcote Boyce some of the houses, though built of stone broadly in the Cotswold style, are unusually tall. The style is almost unique to the village.

❹ Follow the margin of the field as it goes right and then right again. Continue until you come to a field gate on the left. Go through this and walk until you reach another field gate at a road. Walk ahead through Hidcote Boyce. Where the road goes right, stay ahead to pass through a farmyard.

❺ Beyond a kissing gate take a rising track for just over 0.25 mile (400m). Where this track appears to fork, stay to the left to enter a field via a field gate. Bear left and then right around a hedge and head for a field gate. In an area of grassy mounds stay to the left of a barn and head for a gate visible in the top left corner.

❻ Follow the next field edge to a road. Turn sharp left to follow the

lesser road. Immediately before a radio transmission mast turn left on to a track and follow this all the way down to pass through Hidcote Manor Garden's car park entrance. Go straight on for 30 paces to turn left through a gate and then immediately right to walk a path parallel to the road with Hidcote's trees on your left. Through a beech copse enter a field through a kissing gate and cross it to a gate on the far side.

❼ At the road turn right and then, before Kiftsgate Court, turn left through a gate and descend through a field. Pass through some trees and follow the left-hand side of the next field until you come to a gate on the left. Go through this and cross to another gate ignoring a footbridge to your left. Follow the edge of the next field to a gate. Go through this and head towards Mickleton church and a path between walled graveyards to return to the start via a gate.

WHERE TO EAT AND DRINK

In Mickleton The Butchers Arms serves good pub food, and the Three Ways House Hotel is recommended for its puddings in particular. It's the home of the famous 'Pudding Club', where you can taste the finest in traditional English desserts. There is also a restaurant at Hidcote Manor Garden and a tea room at Kiftsgate Court.

Olimpick Playground Near Chipping Campden

Walk out from the Cotswolds' most beautiful wool town to Dover's Hill, the spectacular site of centuries-old Whitsuntide festivities.

DISTANCE *5 miles (8km))* **MINIMUM TIME** *2hrs*
ASCENT/GRADIENT *280ft (85m)* ▲▲▲ **LEVEL OF DIFFICULTY** +++
PATHS *Fields, roads and tracks, 8 stiles*
LANDSCAPE *Open hillside, woodland and village*
SUGGESTED MAP *OS Explorer OL45 The Cotswolds*
START / FINISH *Grid reference: SP 151391*
DOG FRIENDLINESS *Suitable in parts (particularly Dover's Hill) but livestock in some fields*
PARKING *Chipping Campden High Street or main square*
PUBLIC TOILETS *A short way down Sheep Street*

The Cotswold Olimpicks bear only a passing resemblance to their more famous international counterpart. What they lack in grandeur and razzmatazz, however, they make up for in picturesqueness and local passion. Far from being one of the multi-million dollar shrines to technology which seem so vital to the modern Olympics, the stadium is a natural amphitheatre – the summit of Dover's Hill, on the edge of the Cotswold escarpment. The hill, with spectacular views westwards over the Vale of Evesham, is an English version of the site of the Greek original.

Royal Assent

Dover's Hill is named after the founder of the Cotswold Olimpicks, Robert Dover. Established with the permission of James I, they were dubbed 'royal' games, and indeed have taken place during the reign of 14 monarchs. Dover was born in Norfolk in 1582. He was educated at Cambridge and then was called to the bar. His profession brought him to the Cotswolds but he had memories of the plays and spectacles that he had seen in the capital.

The Main Event

It is accepted that the first games took place in 1612, but they may well have begun at an earlier date. It is also possible that Dover was simply reviving an existing ancient festivity. Initially, at least, the main events were horse racing and hare-coursing. Other competitions in these early games were for running, jumping, throwing, wrestling and staff fighting. The area was festooned with yellow flags and ribbons and there were dancing events as well as pavilions for chess and other cerebral contests.

Annual Event

The Olimpicks soon became an indispensable part of the local Whitsuntide festivities, with mention of them even being made in Shakespeare's work.

CHIPPING CAMPDEN

Robert Dover managed the games for 30 years and he died in 1652. The games continued in a variety of forms throughout the following centuries, surviving several attempts to suppress them when they became more rowdy and seemed to present a threat to public order and safety. They finally became an established annual event once again in 1966.

Nowadays, the games are a more like a cross between pantomime and carnival, but they have retained their atmosphere of local showmanship. At the end of the events the spectators file down the road into Chipping Campden, where the festivities continue with dancing and music.

The Wool Town

It's worth lingering in Chipping Campden, possibly the most beautiful of all the Cotswold towns. A stroll along its curving High Street of stone houses is a must. The church, too, is particularly fine and it's also worthwhile searching out the Ernest Wilson Memorial Garden, on the High Street.

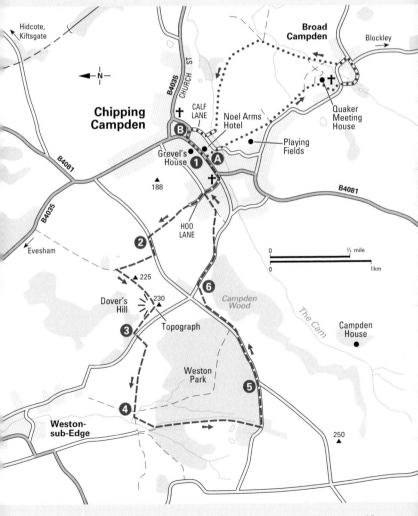

WALK 13 DIRECTIONS

① Turn left from the Noel Arms, continue to the Catholic church, and turn right into West End Terrace. Where this bears right, go straight ahead on Hoo Lane. Follow this up to a right turn, with farm buildings on your left. Continue uphill to a path and keep going to a road.

② Turn left for around 100 paces and then right to cross to a path. Follow this between hedges to a kissing gate. Through this turn left on to Dover's Hill, with extensive views before you, and walk along the escarpment edge, which drops away to your right. Pass a trig point and then a topograph. Now go right, down the slope, to a second kissing gate on the left.

WHILE YOU'RE THERE

Broadway Tower, with its associations with William Morris, stands about 4 miles (6.4km) to the south west of Chipping Campden. A Gothic folly, built in Portland stone in 1799, there is an interesting small museum inside and fine views across the vale.

③ Cross the road to a stile into a field. Cross this to a stile, then to a kissing gate by a horse shelter, then head to a gate in the bottom right-hand corner. Head straight down the next field. At a double stile go into another field and, keeping to the left of a fence, continue to another stile. Head down the next field, cross a track and then find adjacent stiles in the bottom left corner.

④ Cross the first one and walk along the bottom of a field. Keep the stream and fence to your right and look for a double stile

and footbridge in the far corner. Go over, crossing the stream, and then turn left, following a rising woodland path alongside the stream. Enter a field through a gate and continue ahead to meet a track. Stay on this track, passing through gateposts and over a stile, until you come to a country lane and turn left.

WHERE TO EAT AND DRINK

Chipping Campden has plenty of pubs, tea rooms and restaurants. Badgers Hall, on the High Street, does an exceptionally fine tea, while the Eight Bells, on Church Street, is a very relaxing pub.

⑤ After 400yds (366m) reach a busier road and turn left for a further 450yds (411m). Shortly before the road curves left, drop to the right on to a field path parallel with the road. About 200yds (183m) before the next corner go half right down the field to a road.

⑥ Turn right, down the road. Shortly after a cottage on the right, go left into a field. Turn right over a stile and go half left to the corner. Pass through a kissing gate, cross a road among houses and continue into Birdcage Walk, then turn right to return to the centre of Chipping Campden.

WHAT TO LOOK OUT FOR

On reaching Dover's Hill, the route almost doubles back on itself in order to observe legal rights of way. Spend a little time poring over the topograph – on a clear day there is much to identify. In Campden, look out for the 14th-century Grevel's House, opposite Church Lane. William Grevel is thought to have been the inspiration for the merchant in *The Canterbury Tales*.

Right: Looking across farmland to Chipping Campden

The Broad Way

Extend Walk 13 with a short diversion to nearby Broad Campden.

See map and information panel for Walk 13

WALK 14

DISTANCE *3 miles (4.8km)*   **MINIMUM TIME** *1 hr 15 min*

ASCENT/GRADIENT *180ft (55m)* ▲▲▲   **LEVEL OF DIFFICULTY** +++

WALK 14 DIRECTIONS
(Walk 13 option)

Chipping Campden's near neighbour, Broad Campden, does not have a spectacular high street, nor even much of a church. It does have some exceptionally pretty houses (several of which, unusually for the Cotswolds, are thatched), an attractive pub and a 17th-century Quaker Meeting House, all in a snug, overlooked fold of the Cotswold countryside.

From the High Street, walk through the arch next to the Noel Arms Hotel (Point **Ⓐ**) and continue ahead to join a path. Pass playing fields to reach a junction with a road. Go left here, into a field, then immediately right, to follow the field edge parallel with the road. After 500yds (457m) fork right to a gate. Enter a drive, walk past a house and then leave the drive to walk ahead to a gate. Pass through into an alley and follow it to pass the Quaker Meeting House.

Emerge at the green with the church to your left. At a junction continue ahead to walk for over 400yds (366m) through the village. The road bears left and straightens. After the turning for Blockley, go left down a road marked 'Unsuitable for Motors'. After 70yds (64m) turn right

along the drive of 'Hollybush'. Pass through a gate to follow the left edge of an orchard. At its lowest point note the metal kissing gate then go about 100yds (91m) further, to a stile and plank bridge. Cross these and turn right. Cross a tributary at the end of the field and, in the next field, go straight across, bearing right to a gap. Go up the next field to a metal kissing gate and pass into a field. Turn half left to pass to the right of a house.

Go through two metal kissing gates, then a third. Bear right, down to another stile in the bottom corner. In the next field go quarter left, with Chipping Campden church away to the right, to approach a stream near a stone arch. Do not cross the stream but, 100yds (91m) after the arch, turn right through a gate and follow the path as it turns left to a drive. Turn right and follow the drive to Calf Lane. Turn right and, at the top, turn left into Church Street (Point **Ⓑ**) to return to a junction with the main street (or right to visit the magnificent church). Turn left to return to the start of the walk.

Right: Flowers surrounding a pretty cottage in Broad Campden

WALK 15

Roman Ways at Condicote

Following the course of Ryknild Street across the high wolds.

DISTANCE 9 miles (14.5km)	**MINIMUM TIME** 3hrs 30min

ASCENT/GRADIENT 263ft (80m) ▲▲▲ **LEVEL OF DIFFICULTY** ✚✚✚

PATHS Track, field, estate road and country lanes, 5 stiles

LANDSCAPE Long views across high wolds, estate land, villages

SUGGESTED MAP OS Explorer OL45 The Cotswolds

START/FINISH Grid reference: SP 151282

DOG FRIENDLINESS Nice long stretches of track; some livestock in parts

PARKING Condicote village

PUBLIC TOILETS None en route

WALK 15 DIRECTIONS

During the first portion of this walk, you will be following the unmistakable line of a Roman road, Ryknild Street, which extended from the Fosse Way near Bourton-on-the-Water in a north-westerly direction, crossed Watling Street near Lichfield and turned north-east to terminate at Templeborough, near Rotherham. The stretch you will be walking along may not have changed much in 2,000 years, even if the ordered landscape that rolls away on either side would not, perhaps, be immediately recognisable to travellers of the era.

It is well known that the Romans built remarkably straight roads throughout Britannia, with a total length of about 10,000 miles (16,000km), most of which was built during the first 100 years of occupation – a mile (1.6km) of road every four days. Later roads were not as well built as the earlier ones – road building has always been an expensive business and the Romans sometimes found

it expedient not to insist on straight lines. Nonetheless, the overall level of skill involved was extraordinarily high.

Roman roads differed from their predecessors in the quality of the road building and the comprehensiveness of the road network. The basic aim was to link sites with water supplies, which were located a day's march apart (10–15 miles/16–24km). Alignments were laid out from hilltop to hilltop and then with intermediate points between. Some zig-zagging was permitted but only for good reasons – hill cuttings, for example, were rarely used, perhaps only as early military roads. Marshes were

---

WHERE TO EAT AND DRINK

The only place on the route is the Lords of the Manor Hotel in Upper Slaughter. This is a luxurious hotel with an excellent restaurant but at £49 for a 3-course meal (2008 prices) you may prefer to head into Stow-on-the-Wold.

not considered an obstacle and roads were built across them by the copious use of brushwood. Fording was preferred to bridges, presumably for reasons of cost and longevity.

WHILE YOU'RE THERE

South-east of Condicote is Donnington and, not far from it, the Donnington Brewery. This small, independent concern is not open to the public but, located alongside a small lake it must be one of the most picturesque breweries in the country. You can taste their excellent brews at the Fox in nearby Broadwell.

WHAT TO LOOK OUT FOR

Half-way through the walk you will pass through the domain of Eyford Park. You may be able to catch glimpses of this elegant house, built in 1910 in Queen Anne style by Sir Guy Dawber on the site of an earlier mansion.

The procedure for the construction of the road itself might consist initially of woodland clearance to the tune of a 90ft (27.4m) line, marked by ploughed outer ditches, followed by two more drainage ditches about 30ft (9m) apart that provided the outer limits of the road itself. Material from around about would be dug up and used to build up the roadway. On top of this would go local stone, followed by rubble, or gravel, which would then be cambered. Most of Ryknild Street may seem like a very straight farm track but its solid foundations are 2,000 years old.

From Condicote village green, take the road south out of the village, near the stone cross. Follow it to a junction and go straight ahead onto a track, the remains of Ryknild Street. As you might expect, the route is clear – follow this track for just under 2 miles (3.2km) to the B4068, passing a trig pillar early on and crossing roads with care where they arise. The section after the B4068 is a surfaced road which will bring you to a T-junction. Cross to a gate and then a field to a stile. In the next field, curve right to a stile at the edge of woodland. Cross an estate road to follow a woodland path to a gate at the edge of a field. Curve left to follow a fence down the field to a gate in the corner. Turn right along the road. After 100yds (91m) go left over a stile and turn immediately right.

Go through a succession of fields, finally dipping down to a gate and a bridge over a stream. Follow a path up to Upper Slaughter and turn left. At the village triangle turn right and head towards the river. After the last cottage on the left, turn left, with the river to the right, to follow a path past a house and then among trees. Follow this into grassland and up to gates beside Cress Cottage. Walk in woodland for 700yds (640m), initially descending, to the B4068. Turn left and walk along the road for about 350yds (320m), using the verge where possible. Just before cottages turn right onto a metalled drive rising up through trees. This will take you past Eyford Park. Stay on this in its various forms as track and drive for 1.5 miles (2.4km) to a road. At the road, turn right for 0.75 mile (1.2km) to a junction where a letter box is built into an attractive barn. Turn left. Follow this to another road. Cross over and continue until you come to the road on your left leading back into Condicote.

Musing on the Past at Northleach

A modest Cotswold market town is home to a pair of diverse museums.

DISTANCE 4 miles (6.4km)   **MINIMUM TIME** 1hr 45min
ASCENT/GRADIENT 165ft (50m) ▲▲▲   **LEVEL OF DIFFICULTY** ✦✦✦
PATHS Fields, tracks and pavement, muddy after rain, 3 stiles
LANDSCAPE Valley track, wolds and villages
SUGGESTED MAP OS Explorer OL45 The Cotswolds
START / FINISH Grid reference: SP 113145
DOG FRIENDLINESS Some clear stretches without livestock, few stiles
PARKING Northleach market place
PUBLIC TOILETS In market place

For a small market town to have one museum is unusual – to have two, as Northleach does, is remarkable. One, the Cotswold Countryside Collection, is closely associated with its surroundings; the other, Keith Harding's World of Mechanical Music, is one of those eccentricities that has, by happenstance, ended up here in Northleach.

Mechanical Music Museum

The World of Mechanical Music is in the High Street at Oak House, a former wool house, pub and school. There are daily demonstrations of all manner of mechanical musical instruments, as well as musical boxes, clocks and automata. Some of the instruments, early examples of 'canned' music, date back more than 200 years. The presentation is simultaneously erudite and light-hearted. (You may also listen to early, live recordings of concerts given by some of the great composers including Gershwin and Grieg.) This is something more than a museum – both serious historical research and highly accomplished repairs are carried out here.

House of Correction

To the west of the town centre, at a corner of a Fosse Way crossroads, lies the Cotswold Countryside Collection. It is housed in an 18th-century prison, or 'house of correction', built by a prison reformer and wealthy philanthropist, Sir Onesiphorous Paul. He was a descendant of a family of successful clothiers from Woodchester, near Stroud, who were also responsible for the construction of, what is now, the Prince of Wales's house at Highgrove. Paul's intentions were surely good, but conditions in the prison were still harsh and the treadmill was still considered effective as the unrelenting instrument of slow punishment. As well as a restored 18th-century cell block, you'll find the museum houses an interesting collection of agricultural implements and machinery, and displays plenty of fascinating photographs showing what rural life in the Cotswolds was once like. It is also the offices of the Chilterns Conservation Board.

NORTHLEACH

Then and Now

Northleach itself, like Cirencester and Chipping Campden, was one of the key medieval wool trading centres of the Cotswolds. Though once on a crossroads of the A40 and the Fosse Way, neither now passes through the town, the completion of the A40 bypass in the mid-1980s leaving the town centre a quiet and very attractive place to visit.

The main street is lined with houses, some half-timbered, dating from the 16th to 19th centuries. Many of these retain their ancient 'burgage' rear plots that would have served as market gardens. Above the market square is a tiny maze of narrow lanes, overlooked by the Church of St Peter and St Paul, the town's impressive 15th-century Perpendicular 'wool church'.

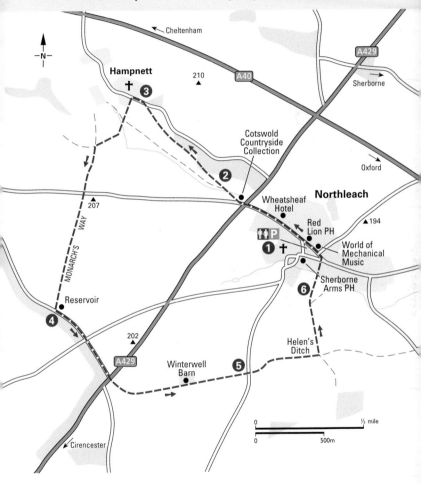

WALK 16 DIRECTIONS

1 From Northleach market place, with the church behind you, turn left and walk along the main street to the traffic lights at the A429. Cross with care, keep left of the Cotswold Countryside Collection and, immediately after passing the museum, turn right through a gate into a field. Go half right to cross a stream by a field corner and into the next field.

WALK 16

2 Aiming for a church tower go half right up the field to a gate. Pass through this into the next field and, keeping fairly close to the field's right-hand margin, head for a kissing gate on the far side. Pass into the next field and follow a path across it in the general direction of Hampnett church. This will bring you to a kissing gate at a road.

3 Turn left and almost immediately come to a concrete track on your left. To visit the church walk ahead and then return to this track. Otherwise, turn left down the track and follow it as it descends to pass farm buildings. Where the track begins to bear right, turn left to climb a track towards a gate. Go through it and continue to follow the track, eventually striking a road. Cross this to walk along another track all the way to another road by a reservoir.

4 At this road turn left and walk until you reach the A429. Cross with great care to a gate and then walk along a grassy track until you come to a farmyard. Walk through the yard and out the other side along a track to another road.

5 Cross to a track and follow this for 500yds (457m). Turn left through a gap in a hedge to enter a field and follow the left margin with a stone wall to your left. Northleach will soon come into view. Where the field comes to an end, go through a kissing gate and descend alongside a fence to a kissing gate beside a playground.

6 Go through and skirt tennis courts to cross a stream. Walk the length of an alley and, at the top, turn left to return to the starting point.

Guiting Power to the People

A gentle ramble in quintessential Gloucestershire, from a typical village with an atypical place-name and atypical ownership.

DISTANCE 6 miles (9.7km)   MINIMUM TIME 2hrs

ASCENT/GRADIENT 295ft (90m) ▲▲▲   LEVEL OF DIFFICULTY ✦✦✦

PATHS Fields, tracks and country lanes, 7 stiles

LANDSCAPE Woodland, hills and village

SUGGESTED MAP OS Explorer OL45 The Cotswolds

START / FINISH Grid reference: SP 094246

DOG FRIENDLINESS Fairly clear of livestock but many horses on roads

PARKING Car park outside village hall (small fee)

PUBLIC TOILETS None en route

It is remarkable how much detailed history is available about English villages, even ones, like Guiting Power, that are distinguished only by their comeliness. Looking from the village green, surrounded by stone cottages, with its church and secluded manor house, it is easy to imagine that very little has changed here in 1,000 years.

What's in a Name?

The eccentric name comes from the Saxon word 'gyte-ing', or torrent, and indeed the name was given not only to Guiting Power but also to neighbouring Temple Guiting, which in the 12th century was owned by the Knights Templars. Guiting Power though, was named after the pre-eminent local family of the 13th century, the Le Poers.

Over the years the village was variously known as Gything, Getinge, Gettinges Poer, Guyting Poher, Nether Guiting and Lower Guiting. Its current name and spelling date only from 1937. In 1086, the Domesday Book noted that there were 'four villagers, three Frenchmen, two riding men, and a priest with two small-holders'. Just under 100 years later the first recorded English fulling mill was in operation at the nearby hamlet of Barton to the north-east. In 1330 permission was given for a weekly market to be held at Guiting Power, which may explain the current arrangement of the houses about the green. Guiting had its share of the prosperity derived from the 15th-century wool trade, as the addition of the little tower to the church testifies.

Slow to Catch Up

And yet, in other ways, history was slow to catch up with small villages like Guiting. Its farmland, for example, was enclosed only in 1798, allowing small landowners such as a tailor called John Williams, who owned 12 acres (4.86ha) in the form of medieval strips scattered throughout the parish, to finally consolidate their possessions. Local rights of way were enshrined in law at this time. By the end of the 19th century the rural depression had reduced the population to 431, and it continued to decline throughout the

GUITING POWER

20th century. Nonetheless, it is recorded that apart from public houses (there were at least four), there were two grocers, two bakers, two tailors, two carpenters, two policemen and a blacksmith.

Local Village for Local People

There are still two pubs in Guiting Power but everything else, apart from the post office and a single grocery store, has disappeared. The village is unusual in that it hasn't succumbed to the inflationary effects of second homeowners from the cities pushing local housing beyond the reach of existing locals. Much of this is down to the far-sightedness of Moya Davidson, a resident in the 1930s, who purchased cottages to be rented out locally. Today these are managed by the Guiting Manor Amenity Trust. It has meant that younger people are able to stay in the village to live and work and there still a few families here who can trace their roots back in Guiting Power for several generations.

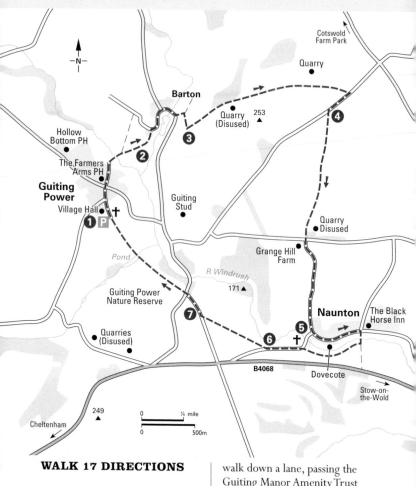

WALK 17 DIRECTIONS

❶ From the village hall car park walk down the road to the village green. Cross the road to walk down a lane, passing the Guiting Manor Amenity Trust Estate Office on the right. At the bottom go through a kissing gate into a field and turn right on to a path alongside a stream. Through a gate and over a footbridge, the path climbs towards a kissing gate. Don't cross the one in front of you but clamber over the one to your right into a field.

WHERE TO EAT AND DRINK

Guiting Power's two pubs are The Farmers Arms, just off the village green, and the Hollow Bottom on the Winchcombe side of the village. Naunton has the very pleasant Black Horse Inn.

② Turn left and walk straight across this field to another stile. Cross this and two more to pass a farmhouse in Barton village. Follow the lane down to a larger road and turn right. Cross a bridge and turn left up a track and, after 100yds (91m), turn right up another track.

③ After 140 paces bear left and walk along this track for about a mile (1.6km), until you reach another road passing a working quarry. Turn right, walk along here for about 250yds (229m) and turn left onto a stony track.

WHILE YOU'RE THERE

Located between Guiting Power and Stow-on-the-Wold is the Cotswold Farm Park, a sort of zoo specialising in rare breeds of British farm livestock. Animals include the Cotswold 'lion'. This breed of sheep was the foundation of the medieval wool trade and has fortunately been saved from extinction.

④ Follow this to a road, passing a quarry as you go. Cross the road and enter a lane descending past Grange Hill Farm. This quiet lane will bring you all the way into the village of Naunton.

⑤ At the junction turn left and walk along the village street for 500yds (455m) to The Black Horse Inn. Just before it turn right into Close Hill, a narrow lane. Over a bridge turn right to cross a stone slab stile to walk alongside the stream, the young River Windrush. Go over another stile and through two gates. The path becomes a village lane emerging near Naunton church. Turning left, follow the lane up out of the village.

⑥ After 0.25 mile (400m), through a kissing gate, turn right into a field. Turn left, walk to a stile and go into the next field. Cross this field, enter the next one and follow the path to the right of a wood to a gate at the road.

⑦ Turn right along the road and continue to a junction at the bottom. Cross the road to enter a field via a gate and walk straight across, aiming to the left of Guiting Power church. At the end go through a kissing gate and down some steps to pass to the right of a pond. Through a kissing gate walk across the next field and then through a kissing gate to walk to the left of the church via two further kissing gates and return to the start.

WHAT TO LOOK OUT FOR

The Norman doorway in Guiting church is an exceptionally rich golden hue. In Naunton, if you stroll back from The Black Horse Inn towards the church on the opposite side of the river, you will be rewarded with a view of a large but charming 17th-century dovecote which is occasionally open to the public. Many villages had dovecotes for eggs and winter meat.

The Woven Charm
of Bibury

*The outer charm of a weavers' village conceals
miserable workings conditions.*

> **DISTANCE** 6.25 miles (10.1km) **MINIMUM TIME** 2hrs 30min
>
> **ASCENT/GRADIENT** 165ft (50m) ▲▲▲ **LEVEL OF DIFFICULTY** +++
>
> **PATHS** Fields, tracks and lane, some muddy, one brief but steep descent, 5 stiles
>
> **LANDSCAPE** Exposed wolds, valley, villages and streams
>
> **SUGGESTED MAP** OS Explorer OL45 The Cotswolds
>
> **START / FINISH** Grid reference: SP 113068
>
> **DOG FRIENDLINESS** On lead throughout – a lot of sheep and horses
>
> **PARKING** Bibury village
>
> **PUBLIC TOILETS** Opposite river on main street, close to Arlington Row

Arlington Row is the picturesque terrace of cottages that led William Morris to refer to Bibury as the most beautiful village in England. It was originally built, it is thought, in the late 14th century, to house sheep belonging to Osney Abbey in Oxford. The wool was washed in the river and then hung out to dry on Rack Isle, the marshy area in front of the cottages. Following the Dissolution of the Monasteries the land was sold off and the sheep houses converted to weavers' cottages. Before mechanisation transformed the wool weaving industry, most weaving took place in the houses of the poor. Firstly, women and children spun the wool either at home or at the workhouse. Then it was transferred to the houses of the weavers, who worked on handlooms at home at piece rates.

A typical weaver's cottage might have had four rooms, with a kitchen and workshop downstairs and a bedroom and storeroom upstairs. There were very few items of furniture in the living rooms, while the workroom would have contained little more than a broadloom and the appropriate tools. The woven cloth was then returned to the clothier's mill for fulling and cutting. Work on cloth was often a condition of tenure imposed by landlords. The merchant landlord fixed a piecework rate and, provided that the work was satisfactory, the cottage could stay in the weaver's family from generation to generation. Weaving went on this way for some 200 years, until the introduction of steam power in the 18th century, after which it tended to take place in the Stroud Valley mills. Despite their unfavourable conditions, the cottage weavers resisted the change but to no avail.

Strictly speaking, much of what is considered picturesque in Bibury is in the neighbouring village of Arlington, but they are now indistinguishable. Apart from Arlington Row, there is plenty to enjoy in the village, especially the church, which has Saxon origins and is set in pretty gardens. Across the bridge is the old mill, open to the public. Nearby Ablington has an enchanting group of cottages, threaded by the River Coln. *A Cotswold Village* (1898), which describes local life in the late 19th century, was written by J Arthur Gibbs who lived at Ablington Manor. You pass the walls of the manor on the walk. In the village, are a couple of 18th-century barns.

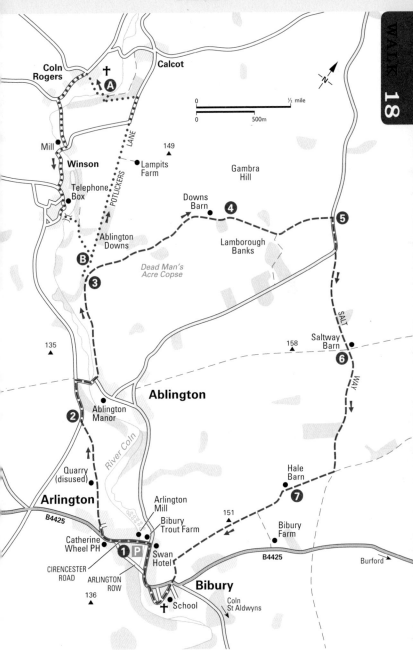

WALK 18 DIRECTIONS

1 From the parking area opposite Arlington Mill, walk along the Cirencester road, away from Bibury. Less than 100yds (91m) after the Catherine Wheel pub turn right along a lane and then keep left at a fork. Pass some cottages and go through gates and stiles into a field. Walk on the same line across stiles and fields until you pass to the right of a house to a road.

2 Turn right and walk down to a junction. Turn right into Ablington and cross the River Colne bridge. After a few paces, turn left along a track with houses on your right and a stream to your left. Continue to a gate and then follow the track, arriving at another gate after 0.5 mile (800m).

WHAT TO LOOK OUT FOR

Ablington Manor is to your right (behind high stone walls) as you cross the bridge in the village. Look out, too, not just for the 18th-century barns, but also for Ablington House, guarded by a pair of lions that once stood at the Houses of Parliament.

3 Go into a field and turn sharp right along the valley bottom. Follow a twisting route along the bottom of the valley. When you reach the next gate continue into a field, still following the contours of the valley. The route will eventually take you through a gate, just before Downs Barn and another gate immediately after.

4 Keep to the track as it bears right and gently ascends a long slope, with woodland to your left. When the track goes sharp right, with a gate before you, turn left through a gate on to a track. Follow it all the way to a road.

5 Turn right. After 300yds (273m), where the road goes right, continue straight on, to enter a track (the Salt

WHERE TO EAT AND DRINK

The Catherine Wheel is a pleasant pub on the Cirencester road in Arlington. The Swan Hotel has a good restaurant and also serves teas. Snacks are available at Bibury Trout Farm and at Arlington Mill.

Way). Continue along this via a gate for over 0.5 mile (800m), until you reach the remains of Saltway Barn.

6 Do not walk ahead but, immediately after the buildings, turn left into a field and then right along its right-hand margin. Walk on for just under 0.75 mile (1.2km), passing hedge and a plantation and, where the track breaks to the right, turn right through a gate in a stone field wall into a field; keep the wall on your right.

7 Walk on to pass to the left of the extended Hale Barn and its recent major earthworks. Enter a track, with the large buildings of Bibury Farm away to your left, and keep on the same line through gates where they arise. Eventually you will descend to a drive, leading you down to Bibury. Cross the road. Turn right, but in 30yds (27m) go half left, beside a telephone box, with a tiny green on your left. Near the church and school follow the curve round. Walk along the pavement into the village, passing Arlington Row on your left.

Right: Arlington Row, Bibury

On to Coln Rogers

Extend Walk 18 to a pretty part of the broad Coln Valley and two tranquil villages.

See map and information panel for Walk 18

DISTANCE *2.5 miles (4km)* **MINIMUM TIME** *1hr*

ASCENT/GRADIENT *213ft (65m)* ▲▲▲ **LEVEL OF DIFFICULTY** ✚✚✚

WALK 19 DIRECTIONS
(Walk 18 option)

From Point ❸ on Walk 18, instead of turning right along the valley, continue up the left side of the field (doing your best to avoid the enormous puddle that is usually there) and ascend to a gate. Go into the next field and keep to its right margin, coming to a gate at the far side. Go through into Potlickers Lane and walk along here, passing Lampits Farm on your right, all the way to a lane. Turn right along this lane (but do not follow the track on your right) in the direction of Calcot.

After 220yds (201m) turn left on to a track, with woodland tumbling away to your right. Ignore a path on your right that will appear soon after you start along here but, after 250yds (229m), turn right down a narrow path that steeples down the bank through the trees, bearing a little to the right.

At the bottom, Point ❹, you will emerge at a path beside the river, with a gate on your left. Turn left, through the gate. Follow the path along the river bank, with a large house to your left, to cross the river. Follow the drive to a lane. The interesting church on the right along here is of Saxon origin. About 100yds (91m) further on

reach a junction with a road. Turn left, following the lane through the village of Coln Rogers.

After 350yds (320m) bear left over a bridge and keep going along the road. Later, beside an old mill, this road goes sharp right, then left. Continue along the road to reach a junction in Winson.

Unusually for a village in the Cotswolds, Winson has several thatched cottages. Turn left and keep left at the village green. The large house overlooking the green was designed by Sir Robert Smirke, the architect responsible for the British Museum.

Go left, and stay left, until you reach a telephone box. Go beyond this but, well within 100yds (91m), turn left, through a gate and walk down a grassy paddock to another gate. Pass through to cross a bridge and follow a path through a plantation. At its boundary, Point ❸, turn right with the path and keep going to a gate. In the next field go half left, ascending, to the far corner. Go through a gate and enter the field back at Point ❸. Turn left along the valley floor to continue on Walk 18.

A Haul Around Hazleton and Salperton Park

An airy rural walk from a quiet village that owes its existence to medieval trading routes.

DISTANCE 4.5 miles (7.2km)   MINIMUM TIME 2hrs 15min

ASCENT/GRADIENT 360ft (110m) ▲▲▲   LEVEL OF DIFFICULTY ✛✛✛

PATHS Fields (muddy after ploughing), tracks and lanes, no stiles

LANDSCAPE Open wold, small valley, broad views and villages

SUGGESTED MAP OS Explorer OL45 The Cotswolds

START/FINISH Grid reference: SP 080179

DOG FRIENDLINESS Off leads over long, empty stretches of land

PARKING Hazleton village

PUBLIC TOILETS None en route

WALK 20 DIRECTIONS

The walk begins in the southern part of Hazleton, near the barn conversions at Priors Range, formerly Priory Farm (the part you will reach first if coming from the A40). Hazleton has a strictly rural feel to it. The village is situated on the route of the ancient Salt Way, which linked the salt workings in Droitwich (between Worcester and Birmingham) with the most convenient, navigable point of the Thames at Lechlade (see Walk 5), from where the salt could be transported to London.

Find a signpost to St Andrew's Church and take the lane, down then up, which passes to the left of the church. It has a Norman doorway and a 13th-century font. Much of the region known as the Cotswolds is associated with a stereotypical picture of England: villages made up of impossibly pretty cottages with roses around the door, sleepy pubs and lazy cricket matches. The picture is not entirely fanciful, but it tends to belie the fact that the area is also characterised by gently undulating hills, or 'wolds', here a Saxon word for open downland.

Leave the village and church behind by continuing on this lane, to reach a junction. Cross this to join an obvious farm track opposite. Remain on the track to pass to the left of a newer farmhouse, crossing a drive and then finding yourself in fields with woodland to your right. Keep going in the same direction. You will cross several fields and eventually follow the path through woodland that will bring you to a gate carved with 'Salperton'. Go through, along a broad, walled track to a lane.

WHILE YOU'RE THERE

Close to the nearby village of Notgrove, about 1.5 miles (2.4km) to the north west, is Notgrove Long Barrow. Much of it has been removed over the centuries, but nonetheless there is enough left to gain an impression of what it once was like.

The walk continues along the lane to the right, but to visit Salperton's church, turn left, over a cattle grid, then take the gated driveway to the right. The church stands right beside Salperton Park. This is a 17th-century manor house with 19th-century additions. Walk through the churchyard with several 17th-century table tombs. Once inside the church, its most noticeable aspect (to the right as you enter) is the wall painting featuring a dancing skeleton wielding a scythe. There are also monuments to the Browne family – presumably, former owners of Salperton. This little village, whose name derives from its proximity to the Salt Way, also lies on the wool-trading trail linking Chipping Campden, to the north, with the southern Cotswolds.

The main route turns eastwards along the lane for 0.75 mile (1.2km). Then, where the hedge on your right comes to an end, about 200yds (183m) before a barn, turn right into a field and walk straight across it to a gap. Go through this and strike half left to another gap leading into the neighbouring field. The fields here are exceptionally stony, even by Cotswold standards. It's easy to understand why medieval farmers favoured rearing sheep to the cultivation of crops.

Maintain the same line by going half right, aiming for a gap in the wall about half-way down this large field. Go through and continue in the same direction across another field to meet a wall. Turn left to walk along the side of the field, with the wall on your right-hand side. At the bottom turn right on to a track and walk to the right of Downs Barn. Continue to a gate and down a track close to a fence on your right for 275yds (251m). Then, when the field opens up to the right, carry on down to meet a fence, which you keep on your right as it goes a little left to a gate.

It is easy now to see the nature of wold country: small, sleek hills that five centuries ago would have been grazed by thousands of sheep producing the wool that was the most highly prized in Europe.

Go through into the field and follow its right margin, with a stream running beside you, for about 0.25 mile (400m) to a junction of paths and tracks. Pass through a gate and turn right through another, onto a bridleway. Stay on this, eventually passing through the farmyard of Lower Barn to join the lane – this will take you back into Hazleton.

Larks Above Down Ampney

*A route based on the birthplace of one of
Britain's best-known composers.*

DISTANCE *10 miles (16.1km)*   MINIMUM TIME *4hrs*

ASCENT/GRADIENT *100ft (30m)* ▲▲▲   LEVEL OF DIFFICULTY +++

PATHS *Fields, lanes, tracks, 9 stiles*

LANDSCAPE *Generally level fields and villages in all directions*

SUGGESTED MAP *OS Explorer 169 Cirencester & Swindon*

START / FINISH *Grid reference: SU 099965*

DOG FRIENDLINESS *On lead near livestock but plenty of stretches without*

PARKING *Down Ampney village*

PUBLIC TOILETS *None en route*

Ralph Vaughan Williams is considered by many to be England's greatest composer. He was born in 1872 in Down Ampney, where his father was vicar, spending the first three years of his life in the Old Vicarage. He studied music in London at the Royal College of Music with Parry, Stanford and Wood, who were the leading British musicians of the day. Then he studied in Berlin with Bruch and later in Paris with Ravel. This experience gave him the confidence to tackle large-scale works, many of which were based on English folk songs, which he had begun to collect in 1903. But Vaughan Williams was also interested in early English liturgical music, the result of which was his *Fantasia on a Theme by Thomas Tallis* (1910) for strings, which combines the English lyrical, pastoral tradition with the stricter demands of early formal composition.

Famous Works

Vaughan Williams went on to compose several symphonies, as well as a ballet based on the ideas of William Blake, and an opera based on *The Pilgrim's Progress* by John Bunyan. There were several sacred works, too, including a Mass and the Revelation oratorio. He also composed the score for the film *Scott of the Antarctic* (1948). One of his best-known hymn tunes is *Down Ampney* (1906), named in tribute to his birthplace. For many of us, however, Vaughan Williams is associated with two pieces in particular. The first is his version of *Greensleeves* (1928), the song said to have been originally composed by Henry VIII; and the second is *The Lark Ascending* (1914), the soaring work for violin and orchestra.

There are four Ampneys altogether. Down Ampney church is the finest and definitely worth a visit. It's crowned by a 14th-century spire and contains several interesting effigies. Adjacent to the church is Down Ampney House, a 15th-century manor house that was later redesigned by Sir John Soane. The prettiest of the villages is Ampney Crucis, which takes its name from the 14th-century cross in the churchyard. The head of the cross was only rediscovered in 1854, having been secreted in the church, probably to protect it from puritan zealots in the 16th or 17th century.

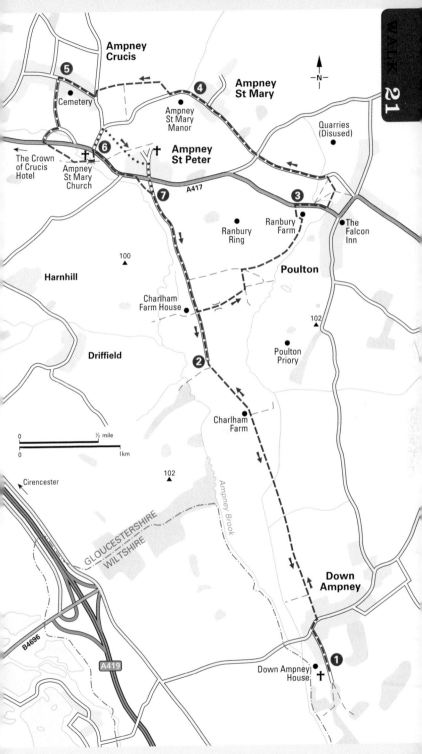

THE AMPNEYS

Ampney St Mary, the second Ampney you come to, is interesting because its original site was abandoned, leaving the little church you see today. Your route visits the fourth Ampney, Ampney St Peter, before returning to Down Ampney.

WALK 21 DIRECTIONS

❶ From the church walk to the centre of the village. At the main road turn right and after 130yds (119m) turn left along a lane. Continue through a gate on to a public bridleway and continue along the edge of three fields and across the fourth.

❷ Join a grassy track to Charlham Farm House. Turn right into a field and on the far side cross a bridge into another field. Cross to a gap and turn left onto a track. At a corner turn right to join a bridleway. Pass through a housing development to a road.

> **WHERE TO EAT AND DRINK**
>
> There are two pubs near the route, The Crown of Crucis Hotel in Ampney Crucis, and The Falcon Inn, just off the route when you get to Poulton. Continue along the road at Point ❸ and turn right.

❸ Turn right. After 320yds (293m) turn sharp left along a grassy path, then in 30yds (27m) turn right by a Thames Water facility. Enter a field and walk diagonally across it to a stone stile. Turn left along a lane to a junction. Follow the lane opposite through Ampney St Mary.

❹ Go through the village and after the entrance to Ampney St Mary Manor on your left, turn right over a stile into a field. Cross this half left to a gate and then walk down the left side of the field to a stile. Cross and walk diagonally across the field (due west). On the far side keep right of a wall and arrive at a gate at a road. Turn left and first right, into Ampney Crucis.

❺ After a cemetery on the left, turn left down a lane. At the bottom turn right to a main road. Cross to a stile. Enter a field and go quarter left under power lines to the river. Find a path leading to a bridge and the churchyard of Ampney St Mary. Leave this on the far side and meet the road.

❻ There are two possibilities here. The shortest is to turn right, pass a lane, then take a bridleway on the right. Go half left to a lane and turn right. The other route is longer but avoids traffic. Follow a lane opposite to a junction on your right. Turn right over a stile into a field. Go quarter left to a gate and then immediately right through a gate into a paddock. Cross to another gate and a stile. Go half left to a stile and then, after 30 paces, turn right through a gate. Cross a stile to the left and then go half right to a gate. Walk along the margin of a garden and after a gate turn left to emerge over a stile in Ampney St Peter. Turn half left to visit the church. Afterwards, turn right to cross the road and enter a lane.

❼ Stay on this lane as it becomes a track, from where you retrace your steps to Down Ampney and your car.

Around Cutsdean and Ford

The origins of the Cotswolds, once the focus of England's most valued export.

DISTANCE 6 miles (9.7km)	**MINIMUM TIME** 2hrs 30min
ASCENT/GRADIENT 265ft (80m) ▲▲▲	**LEVEL OF DIFFICULTY** ✦✦✦
PATHS Tracks, fields and lane, 5 stiles	
LANDSCAPE Open wold, farmland, village	
SUGGESTED MAP OS Explorer OL45 The Cotswolds	
START / FINISH Grid reference: SP 088302	
DOG FRIENDLINESS Best on lead – plenty of livestock, including horses	
PARKING Cutsdean village street	
PUBLIC TOILETS None en route	

Cutsdean can claim to be the centre of the Cotswolds, according to one theory about the origin of the name 'cotswold'. Today it is nothing more than a small, pretty village on the high, voluptuous wolds above the beginnings of the River Windrush. However, it may once have been the seat of an Anglo-Saxon chief by the name of 'Cod'. His domain would have been his 'dene' and the hilly region in which his domain lay, his 'wolds'. This is plausible, even if there is no verifiable record of a King Cod. Another explanation concerns the sheep that still graze many hillsides in the Cotswolds, a 'cot' referring to a sheep fold and 'wolds' being the hills that support them. (In Old English a 'cot' is a small dwelling or cottage.)

Lamb's Wool to Lion's Wool

Whatever the truth of the matter, the sheep remain, even if the species that in the Middle Ages produced the finest wool in Europe dwindled to the point of extinction. The ancestors of the 'Cotswold Lion' probably arrived with the Romans, who valued the sheeps' milk and their long, dense wool. The nature of the Cotswolds was perfect for these sheep: the limestone soil produces a calcium-rich diet, good for strong bone growth; and the open, wind-blasted wolds suited this heavy-fleeced breed, able to graze all year long on herbs and grasses. The hills teemed with Cotswold sheep; at one point the Cotswold wool trade accounted for half of England's income.

Distinctive Forelock

It is believed that the medieval Cotswold sheep differed a little from its modern counterpart. Its coat was undoubtedly long and lustrous, but it may have been slightly shorter than that of its descendants. It was the distinctive forelock and the whiteness of its fleece that inspired the nickname, Cotswold Lion, characteristics that persist in the modern sheep.

Under Threat

Why, then, did the fortunes of this miraculous animal plummet? To some extent this is a misconception, since serious decline occurred only with the

CUTSDEAN

move to arable farming in the Cotswolds in the mid-20th century. Demand for the wool was strong in the 18th and 19th centuries and the Cotswold was also prized for its meat and its cross-breeding potential. However, the market for long-stapled wool began to decline in favour of finer wool, and crop growing became more attractive to local farmers. Incredibly, by the 1960s, there remained only some 200 animals. Suddenly, it was clear that a living piece of English history was on the verge of extinction. The Cotswold Breed Society was reconvened and steps were taken to ensure the sheep's survival. Farmers have since rediscovered the animal's many qualities, and it is no longer quite such a rare sight on the wolds.

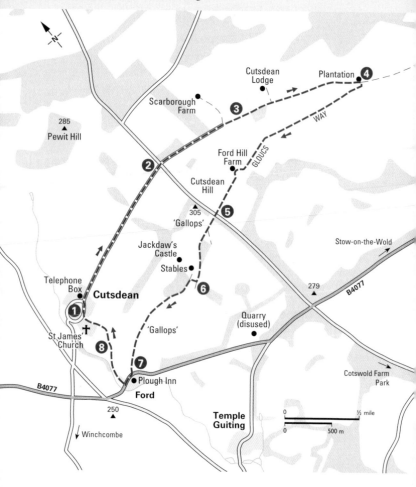

WALK 22 DIRECTIONS

❶ With the Church of St James to your right-hand side and, after a few paces, a telephone box away in a lane to your left, walk out of the village of Cutsdean past Stoneley. Continue uphill on this

straight country road for just over a mile (1.6km), until you come to a T-junction with another road.

❷ Cross this to enter another lane past a 'No Through Road' sign, at the margin of woodland. Beyond a second wood, where the track veers left towards a house, go straight on along a stony track.

❸ Eventually you come to a gate. Through this continue along the track, initially a wood to your right, to another gate, ignoring a footpath to the left at the brow of the hill. Through the gate the path has a stone wall on the left for a field and a half, the path then goes quarter right over the brow of a slope to head for a plantation.

❹ Emerging beyond the plantation turn immediately right at a track junction and right again, the plantation now on your right. Follow this track for 1.5 miles (2.4km), passing through Ford Hill Farm, all the way to a road.

❺ Across the road go through a gate, signed 'Jackdaw's Castle' and follow a tarmac lane which runs to the left of a 'gallops' used for training racehorses. Keep straight on where the track veers left into a neighbouring field.

❻ Soon after passing the stables of Jackdaw's Castle across to your

right, you need to turn sharp right at a footpath sign across the gallops area (watch out for horses) to join a tarmac track, where you turn left. The track descends gently for just under a mile (1.6km), the gallops and greensward to your left. Keep descending until you are near the bottom, at the beginning of a village. This is Ford: if you walk into the village you will see the welcoming Plough Inn directly in front of you.

❼ Otherwise turn right and, at a bend, turn right again to cross a car parking area to a stile. Over this walk along a grassy path, a post and rail fence to your right, a stream in a steep valley to your left, soon passing through a gate. The path leaves the fence and then descends through the copse to a stile.

❽ Cross the stile into a field and then go half right across it. Go down a bank, across a rivulet (possibly dried up in summertime) and up the bank on the other side to a stile. Cross into a field and turn left along the side of the field towards Cutsdean. Pass to the right of the church, which sits back across a wall to your left. At the edge of the village come to a stile: cross this to join a track. After 25 paces emerge on to the main street through the village and your starting point.

Stanton and Stanway from Snowshill

Discovering three of Gloucestershire's finest villages, which were saved from decline and decay.

DISTANCE 7 miles (11.3km)	**MINIMUM TIME** 2hrs 45min
ASCENT/GRADIENT 625ft (190m) ▲▲▲	**LEVEL OF DIFFICULTY** ✦✦✦
PATHS Tracks, estate grassland and pavement, 3 stiles	
LANDSCAPE High grassland, open wold, wide-ranging views and villages	
SUGGESTED MAP OS Explorer OL45 The Cotswolds	
START / FINISH Grid reference: SP 096341	
DOG FRIENDLINESS On lead – livestock on most parts of walk	
PARKING Snowshill village (free car park to north of the village)	
PUBLIC TOILETS None en route	

Villages in the Cotswolds are excellent examples of English vernacular architecture, but they have not always been prosperous. Many, like Stanton and Snowshill, were owned by great abbeys, but they passed to private landlords after the Dissolution of the Monasteries. Subsistence farmers were edged out by short leases and enclosure of fields. Villagers who had farmed their own strips of land became labourers. The number of small farmers decreased dramatically and, with the onset of the Industrial Revolution, so too did the demand for labour. Cheaper food flooded in from overseas and catastrophic harvests compounded the problem.

To the Cities

People left the countryside in droves to work in the industrial towns and cities. Cotswold villages, once at the core of the most important woollen industry in medieval Europe, gradually became impoverished backwaters. But the villages themselves resisted decay. Enlightened landlords, who cherished their innate beauty, turned them into restoration projects.

Enlightened Landlords

The three villages encountered on this walk are living reminders of this process. Snowshill, together with Stanton, was once owned by Winchcombe Abbey. In 1539 it became the property of Henry VIII's sixth wife, Catherine Parr and remained in her family until 1919. Then the estate was bought by Charles Wade. He restored the house and devoted his time to amassing an extraordinary collection of art and artefacts. Next on this walk comes Stanway, a small hamlet on a large estate owned by Lord Neidpath. The most striking feature here is the magnificent gatehouse to the Jacobean Stanway House, a gem of Cotswold architecture built around 1630.

Restored Houses

The village of Stanton comes last on this walk. It was rescued from decay in 1906 by the architect Sir Philip Stott. He bought and restored Stanton Court and many of the village's 16th-century houses.

SNOWSHILL

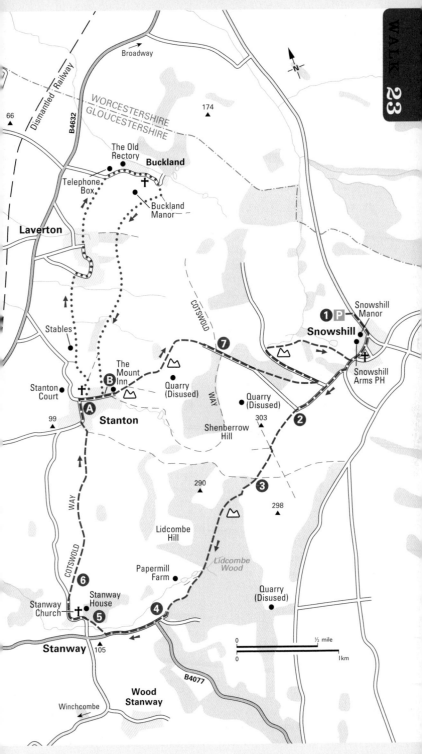

WALK 23 DIRECTIONS

1 From the car park walk into Snowshill village, descending to the right at a Y-junction past Snowshill Manor and the church on your left. After a 0.25-mile (400m) climb turn right down a lane signed 'Sheepscombe House'. After 0.25 mile (400m) at a right-hand bend on the crest of the hill turn left to a gate and enter a field.

2 Go half right to a gate. In the next field go half right to the far corner and left along a track. Take the second footpath on the right through a gate into a field and walk half left to another gate. Cross straight ahead through the field to another gate onto a track.

3 Walk down a stony track with a wood on your right. After 275yds (251m) turn right onto a track, veering right just before a stone barn. The track descends steeply through Lidcombe Wood. After 0.5 mile (800m), a farm comes into view to the right, after which the track bears left uphill. Continue along the track, which becomes a footpath, to a road.

4 Walk along the pavement and, after 500yds (457m), turn right through a gate into a small orchard. Walk half left across this, bearing slightly right, to arrive at a kissing gate. Go through this and walk with a high wall to your right, to reach a road.

5 Turn right and pass the entrance to Stanway House and church. Follow the road, shortly after another entrance turn right through a gate opposite a thatched cricket pavilion. Go half left to a stile and in the next large field go half right.

6 Now walk all the way into Stanton, following the regular waymarkers of the Cotswold Way. After 1 mile (1.6km) you will arrive at a gate at the edge of Stanton. Turn left along a lane to a junction. Turn right here and walk through the village, turning right at the war memorial. Where the road goes left, walk straight on, passing the stone cross and then another footpath. Climb up to pass Mount Inn. Beyond it walk up a steep, shaded path to a gate. Then walk straight up the hill on a stony track, climbing all the way to the top to meet a lane, passing through two gates.

7 Ignore the 'Cotswold Way' sign and walk down the lane for 250yds (229m) then turn left through a kissing gate into trees. Follow the path, going left at a fork. At the bottom cross a stile, continue to go through a kissing gate in the far corner by the road. Turn left and walk for 600yds (549m). Before a cottage turn right through a gate into a field. Descend to the far side and turn right through a gate. Walk on to a stile on your right, cross and turn left. Follow the margin of this grassy area to a track, then a gate and take the path to Snowshill.

Laverton and Buckland

Embrace two more gorgeous villages by extending Walk 23.

See map and information panel for Walk 23

DISTANCE 9.5 miles (15.3km)	MINIMUM TIME 3hrs 45min
ASCENT/GRADIENT 675ft (205m) ▲▲▲	LEVEL OF DIFFICULTY +++

WALK 24 DIRECTIONS
(Walk 23 option)

From Stanton stone cross war memorial, Point **A**, head for the churchyard, passing to the right of the church. In the corner turn right along an alley. At the end turn left and follow a path to a gate. Cross a plank bridge to a field and go left, to reach a stile in a gap. Now continue through gates and over stiles across several fields, many of which have been fenced to make paddocks, passing a substantial block of stables and an exercise yard. Maintain this line towards Laverton, a large hamlet liberally stocked with Cotswold stone architecture. Aim to the left of a house and turn right at the road. Follow the road through Laverton as it goes left, left and right. At a junction beside a tree within a circular seat, cross to enter a firm bridleway. Follow this to the main street of Buckland. Turn right and walk through the village. Shortly after a

telephone box and a footpath sign you will see, on your left, The Old Rectory – dating from the 15th century, it is the oldest medieval parsonage in Gloucestershire still in use. It has some fine stained glass and a timbered great hall. The 18th-century founder of Methodism, John Wesley, often used it as a base. Soon, to your right, is the church.

At the top, where the road curves left, go straight on to a kissing gate. Go through to a field and turn right. Pass handsome Buckland Manor (now a hotel) on the right. The neighbouring church contains medieval glass restored by William Morris, and a painted panel originally in Hailes Abbey. Go through another two kissing gates, then through a bridle gate and continue straight on. Pass through some trees to a gate. Stay on this same line, passing through a series of gates and stiles and crossing two brooks. You'll come to a large field on the flank of the hill. Follow markers here and, after 0.25 mile (400m), cross a stile beside a gate. Continue and pass a dense plantation to your right. At a stile beyond it, take the upper, contouring path (not one descending, half right). This leads you to a driveway which, in turn, takes you into Stanton, at another telephone box in the village centre, Point **B**.

Around Chedworth Villa

Finding out how wealthy Romanised Britons lived in the Cotswolds.

DISTANCE *4.5 miles (7.2km)*   MINIMUM TIME *2hrs*

ASCENT/GRADIENT *310ft (95m)* ▲▲▲   LEVEL OF DIFFICULTY +++

PATHS *Tracks, lanes, fields and woodland, 8 stiles*

LANDSCAPE *Meadows, streams, woods and shallow valleys*

SUGGESTED MAP *OS Explorer OL45 The Cotswolds*

START/FINISH *Grid reference: SP 052121*

DOG FRIENDLINESS *Quite good – plenty of quiet lanes and tracks*

PARKING *Car park in front of Chedworth church (restricted to congregation during services)*

PUBLIC TOILETS *None en route*

WALK 25 DIRECTIONS

From Chedworth church go through a gate to the right of the Seven Tuns pub. Beyond the stables behind the pub, enter a field and head for a stile in the far corner. Just a dozen paces further, another stile takes you left, through trees and over the dismantled railway.

The subject of this walk, the Chedworth Roman Villa, sits in a secluded, wooded stretch of the Coln valley, protected from the elements and with a good supply of water – the spring later

WHILE YOU'RE THERE

In the vicinity of Chedworth, you will probably notice signs for the 'Denfurlong Trail'. This self-guided walk makes use of a taped commentary that takes you around a dairy farm and describes the work involved. Daily milking takes place in the late afternoon. There are two possible trails to follow, the longer one requiring about two hours.

fed a temple to a water goddess. Despite our usual perception of a historically densely wooded Britain, the villa would have stood in open countryside.

Down the other side of the railway bear left, to bring you to a stile on your right. Go over into a field and walk down this to cross another stile. Take a stone slab across a stream then bear left up to a lane. Cross the lane and then, keeping left of the cottages, go up to a gate. Go on up the field to another gate and walk along a path ahead, passing through two more gates to arrive at a lane.

Turn right here and walk along the lane for 0.5 mile (800m), passing barns on the left. When you reach a point where there are footpaths to the left and right, turn left into a field and walk dead ahead, passing just left of a pair of trees and down beyond, to the edge of woodland.

Follow a track through the woods for 550yds (503m). Then,

CHEDWORTH

at a wooden footpath sign, go diagonally left up to a track and turn right. After 40yds (36m) turn left on a path that will soon bring you down to a road. Turn left here and, at a sharp corner, with Yanworth Mill to your right, walk straight on to enter a track. Follow this until it comes to an end at a road. Turn left and walk on to arrive at the Roman villa.

Although it was eventually the home of a well-to-do family, to begin with the villa functioned primarily as a farmhouse. The surrounding land was used for cultivating crops and raising animals. The resulting produce was distributed along the nearby Fosse Way. It was 200 years later that Chedworth was turned into the villa of a rich family. Steam baths were added and the common rooms were enlarged. The beautiful mosaic floors were laid down in the last part of the 4th century AD. It is believed that the occupants of the villa, in either of its incarnations, were almost certainly not from Rome – it is

more likely that they were native people who had thrown in their lot with the new rulers.

The Romans invaded Britain in AD 43 and appeared to have brought the area that is now Gloucestershire under their thrall within four years. The area west of the Fosse Way remained under military alert for another decade, but by AD 60 the Romans were established as rulers. The process of colonisation was a long one, but by the early part of the 2nd century AD the Romans and their subjects, known as the 'Romano-British', felt sufficiently at ease to begin the construction of small, timber-framed villas in the valleys of the Cotswold escarpment. Later villas were built of stone, but the features that have survived best in the centuries since are the magnificent mosaics that were made by craftsmen from Cirencester. Mosaics were still being constructed as late as AD 395. The Roman villa at Chedworth dates from about AD 120. It is open from March until mid-November, closed on Mondays (except bank holidays).

Carry on past the villa and enter woodland. Pass beneath an old railway bridge and within 150yds (137m) reach a crossroads of tracks. Turn left here and follow the main track until it takes you out of the woods, bringing you to a stile at the edge of a field. Go to the top of this field and take the gate directly in front of you. Soon take a stile ahead (not to the left) to reach wooden steps that descend quite steeply through trees to a stile at the edge of a field. Now walk ahead across this field until, just before a cottage on the right, you turn right to a stile beside it. Cross this and follow the lane back to the start.

Around the Lakes of the Cotswold Water Park

Through an evolving landscape in the southern Cotswolds

DISTANCE 5 miles (8km)   **MINIMUM TIME** 2hrs 30min

ASCENT/GRADIENT Negligible ▲▲▲   **LEVEL OF DIFFICULTY** ✦✦✦

PATHS Track, tow path and lanes

LANDSCAPE Dead flat – lakes, light woodland, canal and village

SUGGESTED MAP OS Explorer 169 Cirencester & Swindon

START / FINISH Grid reference: SU 048974

DOG FRIENDLINESS Good but be aware of a lot of waterfowl around lakes

PARKING Silver Street, South Cerney

PUBLIC TOILETS None en route

By their very nature, ancient landscapes and historic architecture evolve very slowly, changing little from one century to another. Can they resist the demands of a brasher era? In the Cotswolds the answer to this question is essentially 'yes'. Here building restrictions are strict – even, sometimes, draconian. The result, however, is a significant area of largely unspoilt English countryside; sometimes, thoughtful development has even enhanced an otherwise lacklustre skyline. The Cotswold Water Park, located in and around old gravel pits, is an example of this.

Recreational Gravel

Gravel has been worked in the upper Thames Valley, where the water table is close to the surface, since the 1920s. The removal of gravel leads to the creation of lakes and in the areas around South Cerney and between Fairford and Lechlade there are now some 4,000 acres (1,620ha) of water, in 133 lakes. They provide an important wetland habitat for a variety of wildlife. Most of these lakes have been turned over to recreational use of one sort or another, being a perfect place for game and coarse fishing, board sailing, walking, boating of various kinds, riding and sundry other leisure activities. Interestingly, this has been what is now called a private/ public enterprise. The landscaping has not just been a case of letting nature take over where the gravel excavators left off. The crane-grabs that were used for excavation in the 1960s, for example, left the gravel pits with vertical sides and therefore with deep water right up to the shoreline. As it happens, some forms of aquatic life flourish under these conditions, but in other lakes the shoreline has been graded to create a gentler slope, to harmonise better with the flat landscape in this part of the Cotswolds and to suit the needs of swimmers and children. In the same way, trees have been planted and hills have been constructed to offer shelter and visual relief. Old brick railway bridges have been preserved. Finally, a style of waterside architecture has been developed to attract people to live here. The landscape continues to evolve, just as the surrounding countryside has done for centuries.

South Cerney and Cerney Wick

The walk begins in South Cerney, by the River Churn, only 4 miles (6.4km) from the source of the Thames. Look inside the Norman church for the carving on the 12th-century rood. Later the walk takes you through Cerney Wick, a small village on the other side of the gravel workings. The highlight here is an 18th-century roundhouse, used once by canal workers.

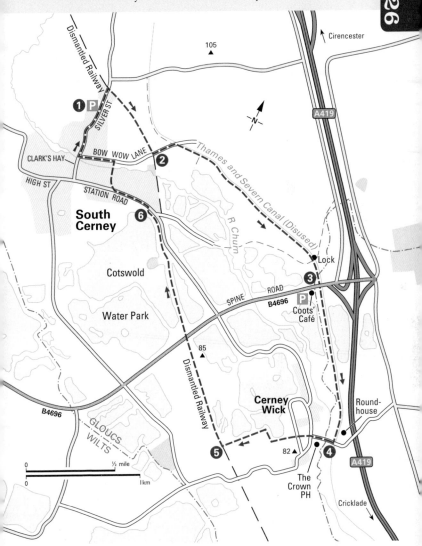

WALK 26 DIRECTIONS

❶ From Silver Street walk north out of the village. Just before the turning to Driffield and Cricklade, turn right onto National Cycle Route 45. Stay on this obvious path for 800yds (732m), to reach a brick bridge across the path. Turn right here up a flight of steps to reach a narrow road.

❷ Turn left and walk along here for 200yds (183m) until you come

WALK 26

to footpaths to the right and left. Turn right along a farm track, following a signpost for Cerney Wick. Almost immediately the shallow, overgrown remains of the Thames and Severn Canal appear to your left. When the track veers right into a farm, walk ahead over a stile to follow a path beneath the trees – the old canal tow path. Keep ahead through kissing gates as you pass the partly restored Wildmoorway Lower Lock, just before the Spine Road Bridge.

❸ Continue under the bridge and past Coots' Café until the path forks at an information panel. Here you have two choices: either continue on the tow path or take the path that skirts the lakes. If you take the lakeside path, you will eventually be able to rejoin the tow path by going left at a bridge after 600yds (549m). Continue until, after just under 0.5 mile (800m), you pass an old canal roundhouse across the canal to the left and, soon after, reach a lane at Cerney Wick.

❹ Turn right here and walk to the junction at the end of the road, beside The Crown pub. Cross to a stile and enter a field. Walk straight ahead and come to another stile. Cross this aiming to the left of a cottage. Cross the lane, go through a kissing gate and enter a field. Walk ahead and

follow the path as it guides you through a kissing gate and across a stile onto the grass by a lake. Walk around the lake, going right and then left. In the corner in front of you, cross into a field, then walk ahead towards trees and cross a stile to a track.

❺ Turn right, rejoining the old railway line and follow it all the way to the Spine Road. Cross with care, and continue along National Cycle Route 45. Stay on this all the way to another road and follow a path that runs to its left.

❻ Where the path ends at the beginning of South Cerney, continue along Station Road for 400yds (440m). A few paces past The Lennards on your right, turn right up the signposted footpath that takes you across a bridge and brings you to a lane called Bow Wow. Turn left here between streams and return to Silver Street and the start of the route.

WHAT TO LOOK OUT FOR

Disused transport systems feature greatly in this walk. For much of it you will be beside or close to the old Thames and Severn Canal (see Walk 33), or following the route of the old Andoversford railway line. The line linked Cheltenham and Swindon between 1891 and 1961. The roundhouse seen on the far side of the old canal as you approach Cerney Wick was used by lock-keepers and maintenance engineers. This design was a distinctive feature of the Thames and Severn Canal. Even the windows were rounded to afford the occupants maximum visibility of their stretch of canal. The downstairs would have been used as a stable, the middle storey as a living area and the upstairs held sleeping accommodation. The flat roof was also put to use collecting rainwater for the house's water supply.

Thomas Cromwell and Hailes Abbey

How an important abbey was destroyed by a King's Commissioner.

DISTANCE 5 miles (8km) **MINIMUM TIME** 2hrs

ASCENT/GRADIENT 605ft (185m) ▲▲▲ **LEVEL OF DIFFICULTY** ✦✦✦

PATHS Fields, tracks, farmyard and lanes, 4 stiles

LANDSCAPE Wide views, rolling wolds and villages

SUGGESTED MAP OS Explorer OL45 The Cotswolds

START / FINISH Grid reference: SP 051302

DOG FRIENDLINESS Mostly on lead – a lot of livestock in fields

PARKING Beside Hailes church

PUBLIC TOILETS None en route

In the decade from 1536 to 1547 just about every English religious institution that was not a parish church was either closed or destroyed – this was the Dissolution of the Monaasteries, Henry VIII's draconian policy to force the old Church to give up its wealth. The smaller monasteries went first, then the larger ones and finally the colleges and chantries. All their lands and tithes became Crown property. Much of them were sold off to laypeople, usually local landowners. The Church as a parish institution was considerably strengthened as a result of the Dissolution, but at the expense of the wider religious life. The suppression of the chantries and guilds, for example, meant many people were deprived of a local place of worship.

Hailes Abbey

Hailes Abbey was one of the most powerful Cistercian monasteries in the country, owning 13,000 acres (5,265ha) and 8,000 sheep. It was a particular target for reformers. In 1270 Edmund, Earl of Cornwall, the son of its founder, had given the monastery a phial supposed to contain the blood of Christ. Thomas Cromwell was the King's Commissioner responsible for seeing to the closure of the monasteries. He is reputed to have surveyed the destruction of the monastery from a vantage point near Beckbury Camp. There is still a fine view of the abbey from here, as you should find as you pass Point **5** on this walk. According to Hugh Latimer of Worcester, who had been working with him, Cromwell also spent an afternoon in 1539 examining the so-called 'blood'. Cromwell concluded that it was nothing more than an 'unctuous gum and compound of many things'. Once the valuables had been removed, local people took what was left.

The monastery lands were disposed of in a typical manner. First they were confiscated by the Crown and then sold to a speculator who sold the land on in lots. In about 1600 the site of the abbey was bought by Sir John Tracy, the builder of Stanway House. The monks were dispersed: a few managed to secure positions as part of the parish clergy, while others took up posts with the cathedrals at Bristol and Gloucester. Others returned to the laity.

HAILES ABBEY

Charming Remains

Hailes church is all that remains of the village of Hailes. It predates the abbey and survived the Dissolution, perhaps because it had been a parish church and was not directly linked to the neighbouring monastery. It is a church of real charm, sadly ignored by the many visitors to the monastery's ruins. Although very small, it has several special features, including a panelled chancel – floored with tiles from the monastery – and a nave with 14th-century wall paintings. Didbrook church also survived the upheavals. Built in Perpendicular style, it was rebuilt in 1475 by the Abbot of Hailes, following damage caused by Lancastrian soldiers after the Battle of Tewkesbury.

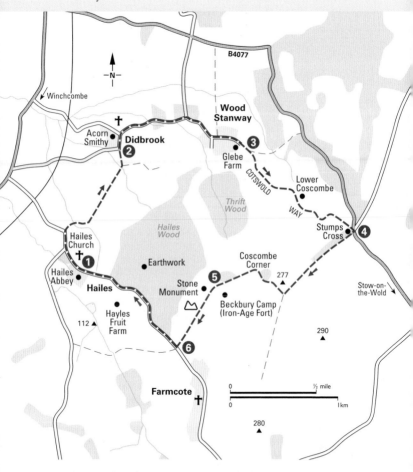

WALK 27 DIRECTIONS

❶ From Hailes church turn right and follow the lane to a T-junction. Turn right here and after 200yds (183m) turn right again onto a footpath through a gate. Walk aross an area of concrete, go over a stile next to a gate and follow a track as it goes right and left, turning at an old oak tree, eventually becoming a grassy path beside a field. Go over a stile, followed by a stile and footbridge. After about 75yds (69m) turn left, through a gate, and cross a field

HAILES ABBEY

WALK 27

WHAT TO LOOK OUT FOR

As you walk through the village of Didbrook, see if the blacksmith at the Acorn Smithy is open. In Wood Stanway, the wall of one of the first houses you pass to your left is covered in vines, producing a very healthy-looking crop of red grapes in the autumn, even though the English climate tends to favour white grapes.

WHERE TO EAT AND DRINK

Just near the end of the route is Hayles Fruit Farm. You can pick your own fruit, buy a variety of produce from the shop or you can have a light meal in the tea room. Winchcombe is the nearest town, offering many possibilities.

alongside the right-hand hedge to reach a gate at a road.

❷ Turn right and follow the road as it meanders through the pretty village of Didbrook then a stretch of countryside. At a junction turn right for Wood Stanway. Walk through this village, bearing left at a cherry tree on a grass island, into the yard of Glebe Farm.

❸ Ignore a bridleway sign and gate on the left and at a gate go onto a track on the left of a field and walk ahead, looking for a gate on the left. You are now on the Cotswold Way, well marked by arrows with a white dot or acorn. Cross into a field and go half right, keeping to the left of some electricity poles, to a gate in a hedge. Bear half left across the next field, heading towards farm buildings. Through a gate turn sharp right, up the slope (guide posts), to a gate on your right. Through this turn immediately left up the field to a guide post. Go through a gate. Follow the footpath as it winds its way gently up the slope. At the top walk along the crest, with a dry-stone wall to your right, to a reach gate at a road.

❹ Turn right and right again through a gate to a track. Follow this for 0.5 mile (800m), passing through a gate, until at the top (just before some trees), you turn right to follow another track for

50yds (46m). Turn left through a gate into a field and turn sharp right to follow the perimeter of the field as it goes left and passes through a gate beside the ramparts of an Iron Age fort, Beckbury Camp. Continue ahead to pass through another gate which leads to a stone monument with a niche. According to local lore, it was from here that Thomas Cromwell watched the destruction of Hailes Abbey in 1539.

WHILE YOU'RE THERE

Visit Hailes Abbey. You can rent a recorded commentary that explains the layout of the ruins. Farmcote church is another gem, little more than a chapel but ancient and uplifting. It's hard to find but worth the effort. Overlooking Hailes, it's located high up in a silent, tranquil corner of the wolds.

❺ Turn right to follow a steep path down through the trees. At the bottom go straight across down the field to a gate. Pass through, continue down to another gate and, in the field beyond, head down to a stile beside a signpost.

❻ Over this turn right down a lane, all the way to a road. To the left is Hayles Fruit Farm with its café. Continue ahead along the road to return to Hailes Abbey and the start point by the church.

Winchcombe and Sudeley Castle

A rewarding walk above a thriving Cotswold market town and the burial place of Henry's sixth queen – Catherine Parr.

DISTANCE	4 miles (6.4km) **MINIMUM TIME** 2hrs
ASCENT/GRADIENT	490ft (150m) ▲▲▲ **LEVEL OF DIFFICULTY** ✦✦✦
PATHS	Fields and lanes, 13 stiles
LANDSCAPE	Woodland, hills and town
SUGGESTED MAP	OS Explorer OL45 The Cotswolds
START / FINISH	Grid reference: SP 024282
DOG FRIENDLINESS	On lead (or close control) throughout – much livestock
PARKING	Free on Abbey Terrace; also car park on Back Lane
PUBLIC TOILETS	On corner of Vineyard Street

At the end of a long drive just outside Winchcombe is a largely 16th-century mansion called Sudeley Castle. The first castle was built here in 1140 and fragments dating from its earlier, more martial days are still much in evidence. Originally little more than a fortified manor house, by the mid-15th century it had acquired a keep and courtyards. It became a royal castle after the Wars of the Roses before being given to Thomas Seymour. Seymour lived at Sudeley with his wife, Catherine Parr – he was her fourth husband. Seymour was executed for treason. Queen Mary gave the property to Sir John Brydges, the first Lord Chandos. Sudeley Castle was a Royalist stronghold during the Civil War but was disarmed by the Parliamentarians. It was left to decay until its purchase in 1863.

Married at Nine Years Old

Catherine Parr, sixth wife of Henry VIII and the only one to outlive him, is buried in Sudeley's chapel. She was born in 1512 and educated in Henry's court. She was first married at nine, but widowed six years later. Back at court, she was at the centre of a group of educated women, using her influence with the King to protect her second husband, Lord Latimer, from the machinations of courtly politics. When Latimer died in 1543, Catherine was one of the wealthiest and best-connected women in England, and an obvious choice of wife for Henry. She looked after him and his affairs during the years until his death in 1547. Then she quickly married Seymour and moved to Sudeley where she died in childbirth in 1548.

Winchcombe

Winchcombe has a considerable history. In Anglo-Saxon times it was a seat of the Mercian kings and the capital of Winchcombshire. It became a significant place of pilgrimage due to the presence of an abbey established in 798 and dedicated to St Kenelm, son of its founder, King Kenulf. The abbey was razed in the Dissolution of the Monasteries, but the town's parish church survived. Of particular interest are the amusing gargoyles that decorate its exterior. They are said to be modelled on real local people.

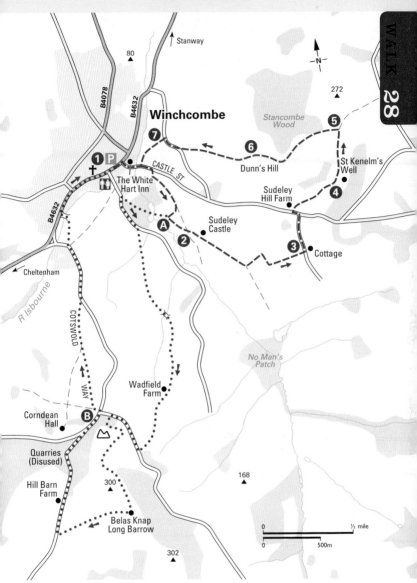

WALK 28 DIRECTIONS

❶ From the parking area on Abbey Terrace in Winchcombe, walk towards the town centre past a Lloyds TSB bank and turn right, down Castle Street. Where it levels out, cross a river bridge and after a few paces bear right to leave the road near the Sudeley Castle Country Cottages and

ascend to a kissing gate. Follow the path through the middle of a long field to a kissing gate. At a drive, with the castle visitor centre ahead, turn right for 50 paces, then left through a gate.

❷ Walk between fences, a play fort on the right, to a kissing gate. Follow the left fence past Sudeley Castle, then across its parkland

87

WHAT TO LOOK OUT FOR

In the church at Winchcombe, note the embroidery behind a screen, said to be the work of Catherine of Aragon, a wife of Henry VIII. Behind Sudeley Hill Farm, look out for St Kenelm's Well, largely rebuilt in the 19th century, a holy well connected with the martyred prince, patron saint of the vanished Winchcombe Abbey.

(guide posts). Over a stile in the far corner turn left and after 25 paces climb another stile and walk alongside the left-hand field boundary, then right at the corner alongside a fence. At the willows go left over stile and walk uphill beside hedging towards a cottage.

3 Through a gate turn left onto a lane and follow this to a junction, turning left. After about 50 paces and just before Sudeley Hill Farm turn right and over a stile. Head half left uphill and over another stile. Over this cross the middle of the field, then bear to the left of a cottage to a stile.

4 Over this you see St Kenelm's Well, a 17th- to 19th-century

WHILE YOU'RE THERE

There is enough to detain you for a day in Winchcombe itself. Not only can you visit Sudeley Castle (See Background to the Walk) which has gardens, a plant centre and exhibitions, but you will also find the fascinating Winchcombe Museum in the Victorian Town Hall building in the town centre. The Police Collection includes uniforms and equipment from a variety of police forces around the world, while the Folk Collection concentrates on the history of Winchcombe and its people.

building in a fenced enclosure. Pass to the left of this along a track. Cross a stream and go through a gate (or over the stile) and climb half right towards a gate at the right end of woodland.

5 At a woodland fence corner turn left, short of the gate, and go left alongside the fence, over two stiles alongside a small fenced field. Beyond this the path drops, fairly close to the woods on your right, and curves left to a gate. Through this continue alongside the wood, then a line of trees, to a gate and stile in the far corner.

WHERE TO EAT AND DRINK

Winchcombe has a large number of possibilities, ranging from pubs to tea rooms and restaurants. It also has a bakery (and a supermarket). If you visit Sudeley Castle, there's a good café.

6 Descend half right towards Winchcombe, heading to the furthest corner. Over a stile descend, a fence on your right. At the fence corner continue half right across the field. Through the hedge into the next field continue half left towards a gate. Over the nearby stile cross the field corner to another stile and a footbridge. Half left in the next field head for the gap to the right of a cottage. Through the gate turn right on to a lane, passing a heavily buttressed kitchen garden wall on your left.

7 After about 100yds (91m) turn left through a kissing gate and head across the field towards Winchcombe church tower. Then veer left before the river valley bottom to a kissing gate by a stone cottage. Follow this path to Castle Street and turn right over the river bridge and back into the town centre.

On to Belas Knap

An additional loop to Walk 28, visiting a well-preserved neolithic barrow.

See map and information panel for Walk 28

> **DISTANCE** *4.5 miles (7.2km)*   **MINIMUM TIME** *2hrs 30min*
> **ASCENT/GRADIENT** *574ft (175m)* ▲▲▲   **LEVEL OF DIFFICULTY** +++

WALK 29 DIRECTIONS
(Walk 28 option)

The Cotswolds are riddled with settlement remains from all eras, including early tombs. Of these, the huge green mound of Belas Knap, which means 'beacon hill', is the most evocative. It stands in a field overlooking Winchcombe.

From Point **Ⓐ** follow Sudeley Castle's drive all the way to a lodge and a road. Turn left. After 300yds (274m) go through a kissing gate on the right. Go half left to a stile and footbridge and cross two further fields on the same line. In the far corner of the third field cross a third footbridge to a field and follow its right-hand margin to a stile on the right. Go over, turn half left, steadily uphill, to the corner. Follow an enclosed path, pass Wadfield Farm and walk on a track to a road. Turn right. After 500yds (457m) turn left on to a steep path among trees. At a field turn left and follow its margin to the corner then right, to the top. Go through a gate and turn left. Eventually go through another gate to arrive at Belas Knap Long Barrow.

This barrow, or communal grave, dating to approximately 2500 BC, has a 'false' portal (apparently to warn off intruders) of breathtakingly exact dry-stone work. The real entrances to the burial chambers are at the sides. The tomb is constructed of slabs of limestone, covered in turf. Just who precisely was entombed here is unknown but it is surmised that ancestor worship was widely practised and that the mound was opened many times over the centuries to admit further generations of worthy souls. No doubt the whole community worked at its construction over many months and maintained it devotedly. It is possible that the barrow became the centrepiece of the settlement. In all, 38 skeletons have been found inside the tomb.

Leave the barrow on the opposite side and walk ahead until you come to a track. Turn right and descend for about 0.5 mile (800m) to a road at a sharp corner, Point **Ⓑ**. Go left over a stile into a field and descend half right to a kissing gate in fencing at the bottom. Turn right along a tarmac drive. When you come to a road turn left and, after 400yds (366m), go right through the left-hand kissing gate. Cross the field diagonally, then veer left to a kissing gate and footbridge. Beyond, go up a path to the road. Turn right and make your way back to Abbey Terrace.

Brockhampton, Whittington and Sevenhampton

What happened when the Black Death came to Gloucestershire.

DISTANCE 7.75miles (12.5km)   **MINIMUM TIME** 3hrs 30min

ASCENT/GRADIENT 280ft (85m) ▲▲▲   **LEVEL OF DIFFICULTY** ✦✦✦

PATHS Fields and tracks, 11 stiles

LANDSCAPE Woodland, wolds, villages and distant views

SUGGESTED MAP OS Explorer OL45 The Cotswolds

START/FINISH Grid reference: SP 010236

DOG FRIENDLINESS On lead only occasionally, in fields with livestock

PARKING Parking area at end of lane beyond Whitehall Farm, 2 miles (3.2km) north-west of Brockhampton

PUBLIC TOILETS None en route

WALK 30 DIRECTIONS

From the parking area walk along the lane towards Brockhampton for 1.25 miles (2km), to a road junction. After just 20yds (18m), turn right onto a footpath beside a field. Cross several fields as the path descends through undergrowth. Cross a field at the bottom to another stile and enter a large field.

Go forward, taking a rising, curving path, beside a plantation, leading to a fence on the left. Follow this and, at the point

WHILE YOU'RE THERE

Drive along the small lanes through the pretty countryside to the north and visit Winchcombe where you can visit Sudeley Castle or Belas Knap (see Walk 28/29). Alternatively visit the beautiful town of Cheltenham with its wide streets and acres of Georgian and Regency architecture.

WHERE TO EAT AND DRINK

In Brockhampton, the Craven Arms, passed near the walk's end, serves a good restaurant-style lunch. The pub stands next to all that remains of Brockhampton's old village brewery.

where telegraph poles on the right converge with the path, reach a stile on the left. Go over this onto a broad track. Follow it until you emerge in a large field. Cross this, curving slightly left to descend ever more steeply to a gate. Go through, follow the track to the bottom and bear right to a road.

Turn left and, at a junction opposite the Old School House, turn right towards Whittington Court for 200yds (183m), to a gate on the left. The house is mainly Tudor but there has been a manor house on this site since well before the Normans – a moated version is mentioned in the Domesday Book. Earlier stonework is still visible at the base of the walls. The Church of St Bartholomew stands adjacent to the house. If it is open it is worth visiting. You'll see the handsome brasses of Richard Coton – who built the present house – and his wife Margaret, as well as three Cotswold-stone effigies. It is said that the oak panelling in the chancel was made from the old pews of Sevenhampton church.

Take the middle path aiming just left of tall and broken trees, continuing on the same line over some grassy bumps to a stile on the far side.

The grassy bumps are all that remain of Old Whittington. Although the 14th-century Black Death devastated more towns than rural areas, a good quarter of Gloucestershire's population died. Many villages were abandoned and then resettled near by – Whittington is a good example.

Now follow the left margin of a succession of fields more or less on the same line. The path then crosses a field's middle line to a stile. It then descends into a thicket beside a lake. Keep right of this, then follow a clear path left of Syreford Mill to a track. Turn left and continue until you come to a lane. Cross the road to a track. Follow this as it passes houses and curves right into woodland. Walk through the woods to emerge at the edge of a field. Go ahead for 440yds (402m), across fields and through

a succession of gates, until, at a gated junction, you meet a good track descending from the right. Go through, turn left and follow this track down to a road. Turn left. Just before the ford at the River Coln turn right on to a grassy path. Follow this to a stile and a bridge. The path then climbs up a bank to a stile. Cross a field to a road and then enter Sevenhampton churchyard.

Sevenhampton was originally called Sennington and was located on the opposite hill until the plague's onslaught. Although small, the parish church's flying buttresses and impressive vaulting aspire to something greater. Sevenhampton Manor was built in 1550 and partially demolished in the 1950s.

Walk to the right of the church and then turn right into a newer burial area. Turn left to pass through two kissing gates into another field. Continue down beside a wall and enter the next field. Now go half right across the field to a kissing gate and follow a grassy path up into Brockhampton. Pass the former brewery, with its brick chimney, and then the Craven Arms pub, to a junction. Turn right, then left at the telephone box, signposted 'Rhodes Memorial Hall'. Where the road turns right, go straight ahead. Walk 0.75 mile (1.2km), crossing five fields by gates and stiles to a road. Turn left, then, just beyond Charlton Pool, turn left again. Stay on this until, 200yds (183m) before woodland, a wide track goes left. Soon enter conifers to rise steadily. A gate leads into open country for a further 0.5 mile (800m). Now walk in deciduous woodland for 400yds (366m) then fork left to the start.

A Ghostly Trail Around Prestbury

A gentle ramble around this unassuming old village which claims to be one of Britain's most haunted.

DISTANCE *3 miles (4.8km)*   **MINIMUM TIME** *1hr 30min*

ASCENT/GRADIENT *100ft (30m)* ▲▲▲   **LEVEL OF DIFFICULTY** ✚✚✚

PATHS *Fields (could be muddy in places) and pavement, 8 stiles*

LANDSCAPE *Woodland, hills and villages*

SUGGESTED MAP *OS Explorer 179 Gloucester, Cheltenham & Stroud*

START / FINISH *Grid reference: SO 972239*

DOG FRIENDLINESS *Lead necessary as some fields stocked with farm animals; some stiles have dog slots*

PARKING *Free car park near war memorial*

PUBLIC TOILETS *None en route*

The village of Prestbury, on the north-east fringe of Cheltenham, is reputedly the second most haunted village in England, with The Burgage its oldest and most haunted street. The largest building along it is Prestbury House, now a hotel. During the Civil War it was occupied by Parliamentary troops. Expecting Royalists camped on Cleeve Hill to send a messenger to Gloucester, they laid a trap. A rope was stretched across The Burgage. When the Cavalier rode through the village, he snagged on the rope and was catapulted from his mount. No doubt relieved of his despatches and interrogated, the unfortunate rider was then executed. A skeleton discovered near by in the 19th century is thought to be his. It is said that the sound of hooves can often be heard here, as well as a horse's snorting and stamping.

Exercise and Exorcism

More paranormal activity has been experienced in the hotel grounds, where they meet Mill Street. Here there have been sightings of rowdy parties of people in Regency dress. On this site, it turns out, there was once a fashionable meeting place, called the Grotto. It was where the local gentry would take their ease. By the time of its closure, in 1859, it had become known as a place of ill-repute.

Spectral abbots are regularly seen in Prestbury. The Black Abbot used to walk the aisle of St Mary's Church but, since his exorcism, he prefers the churchyard – a vicar came across him here, seated on a tombstone. The abbot has also been spotted in the early morning near the Plough Inn on Mill Street. In fact, there have been sightings of the Black Abbot almost everywhere in the village. Perhaps this may be explained by the fact that the Bishops of Hereford owned a palace here from the 12th century, while the Prior of Llanthony lived in the priory close to the church. There are several other haunted places you will come across in the village. At Sundial Cottage, in The Burgage, a lovelorn girl plays the spinet; the Three Queens house in Deep Street had to be exorcised; there are three stone cottages next to Three Queens, the middle one of which is haunted by soldiers from the Civil War, and the third of which is haunted by the Black Abbot. And another abbot (or perhaps the same one) with 'an unpleasant leer', is said to haunt Morningside House, next to the car park.

There is more to the village than ghosts, however. The manor of Prestbury, belonging to the Bishop of Hereford, was established by 899. Remains of the moated hall can still be found on Spring Lane, close to Cheltenham racecourse. The village is closely associated with the jockey Fred Archer, as a plaque on the King's Arms testifies, while the cricketer Charlie Parker, who played for England, was also born here.

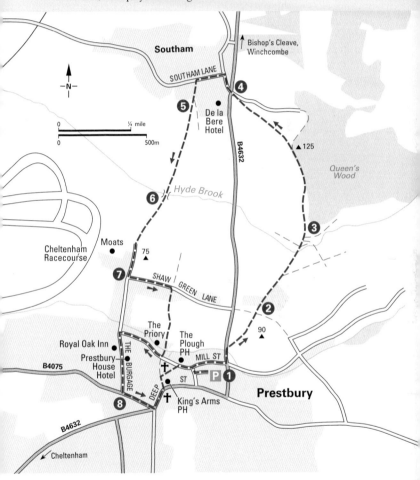

WALK 31 DIRECTIONS

❶ Leave the car park, turn right into The Bank and right again into Mill Street. At the main road turn left. After 100yds (91m) cross the road to a stile. Go into a field and go diagonally left to another stile.

❷ Cross this and follow the track that is ahead of you and slightly to your left. Where it goes right, cross a stile in front of you. Cross a field heading slightly to the right, to another stile. Go over this into a field and head for Queen's Wood in front of you.

3 Stay to the left of the woods. Eventually cross a track via two stiles and enter another field. Where the woods sweep uphill, keep straight on to drop through a field with old oak trees to a stile in the corner by the main road.

4 Ahead of you are the medieval buildings of the Hotel De La Bere. Cross the road and turn right. Follow the pavement as it bears left into Southam Lane. After 200yds (183m) turn left along a track to a gate. Go through this and a kissing gate to a field.

WHERE TO EAT AND DRINK

There are several pubs to choose from. The King's Arms welcomes children, The Royal Oak Inn also serves lunches and The Plough, on Mill Street, is a very fine old pub with a flagstone floor and a gorgeous garden. Prestbury House Hotel offers an excellent light lunch or dinner in a more formal setting.

5 Head across, bearing slightly right towards an oak tree, with the De La Bere on your left. Follow an obvious path across a series of paddocks and fields via stiles and gates, the path bypassing many of the kissing gates. Finally, at a kissing gate amid bushes in a corner, cross on to a track and follow this as it leads, via a low stile, to a footbridge and gate.

6 Cross and continue straight ahead into a field with a hedge on your right. Go over the brow of the slope through a kissing gate and down to a gate in the hedge to your right. Go through a kissing gate at the corner of the field to a track and follow this to a road.

7 Turn left along Shaw Green Lane. After about 400yds (366m)

WHILE YOU'RE THERE

Cheltenham, of which Prestbury is really a suburb, is a very handsome town and definitely worth a visit. It has fine Regency and Georgian architecture, as well as two excellent small museums, one in the birthplace of composer Gustav Holst (1874–1934), the other with features devoted to the arctic explorer Edward Wilson, and to the Arts and Crafts Movement.

turn right along a footpath passing between houses just past No 34. Eventually this will bring you out on to Mill Street, opposite the church. Turn right, to walk past the Priory and the brick wall that marks the site of the haunted Grotto, until you come to The Burgage. Turn left here, passing The Royal Oak Inn, Prestbury House Hotel and Sundial Cottage.

8 At the junction with Tatchley Lane turn left and then left again at mini-roundabouts into Deep Street, passing the Three Queens and the trio of stone cottages. Just before The King's Arms turn left on a footpath leading to the church. Turn right just before the church and pass through the churchyard to return to Mill Street, opposite The Plough. Turn right and then right again and return to the car park at the start.

WHAT TO LOOK OUT FOR

Don't forget that you are very close to one of Europe's greatest racecourses. As you walk across the fields towards Queen's Wood, you will have some wonderful views across the racecourse to Cheltenham. The Hotel De La Bere is a striking Elizabethan mansion that was once the home of Lord Ellenborough, a former Governor-General of India.

The Medieval Looters of Brimpsfield

A walk through a vanished castle and secluded valleys, taking in charming Syde and tiny Caudle Green.

DISTANCE 4 miles (6.4km)	**MINIMUM TIME** 2hrs
ASCENT/GRADIENT 180ft (55m) ▲▲▲	**LEVEL OF DIFFICULTY** +++

PATHS Fields, tracks and pavement, 18 stiles

LANDSCAPE Woodland, steep, narrow valleys and villages

SUGGESTED MAP OS Explorer 179 Gloucester, Cheltenham & Stroud

START / FINISH Grid reference: SO 938127

DOG FRIENDLINESS Some good, long stretches free of livestock

PARKING Brimpsfield Village Hall car park (in north-west of village)

PUBLIC TOILETS None en route

There is something poignant about a vanished castle. The manor of Brimpsfield was given by William the Conqueror to the Giffard family. In early Norman French a 'gifard' was a person with fat cheeks and a double chin. The Giffards built two castles, the first of wood on another site, and its successor of stone, near Brimpsfield church. In 1322 John Giffard fell foul of King Edward II, following a rebellion that was quelled at the Battle of Boroughbridge in Yorkshire – Giffard was hanged at Gloucester.

Plundering Populace

Consequently the family castle was 'slighted', that is to say, put beyond military use. In such circumstances local people were never slow to remove what was left for their own, non-military use. Now almost nothing remains of the castle apart from the empty meadow just before the church and some earthworks to its right. Some of the castle masonry found its way into the fabric of the church. On the stone shed to the left of the church there are details that appear to be medieval and which perhaps originally decorated the castle. The other possibility is that they formed part of a 12th-century priory, long since disappeared, that belonged to the abbey of Fontenay in Burgundy. Brimpsfield church, rather lonely without its castle, distinguishes itself on two counts. Several medieval tombstones, thought to commemorate members of the Giffard family, have been brought inside for their protection.

Mysterious Masonry

The other, highly unusual feature, is the huge base of the tower, which separates the nave from the chancel. It is not clear how this came about, but it is surmised that the east wall would originally have contained an arch over which a bell turret was built in the 13th century, requiring the addition of more masonry. When the turret was replaced by a 15th-century tower still more masonry was needed to keep it upright.

Syde overlooks the Frome Valley and perched on the valley slope, the early Norman church has a saddleback tower and a rustic, 15th-century

BRIMPSFIELD

roof. It's worth peering inside to search out the 15th-century octagonal font and the small round window featuring St James, dating from the same period. The box pews are from the 17th century. Don't miss the tithe barn just to the south of the church. Caudle Green is a typical example of a hamlet that has grown up around a single farm and expanded only very slightly over the centuries. It is dominated by an elegant 18th-century farmhouse overlooking the village green.

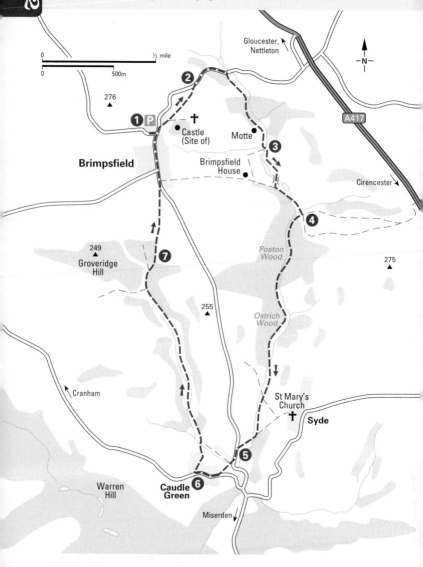

WALK 32 DIRECTIONS

1 From the Brimpsfield Village Hall car park head back into the village. By the bus stop, cross to a

gate, signed 'To Church'. Before you reach the church bear left to a stile. In the next field go half right to a corner and then go over a stile on to a road.

❷ Turn right and follow the road down to just before a cottage near the bottom. Turn right on to a drive. After 35 paces drop down to the left on to a parallel path which will bring you back on to the drive. Next, just before a cottage, turn left and go down into woodland to follow a path (the stream on your left). Follow this for 550yds (503m), ignoring a bridge on your left, to cross two stiles and emerge on to a track.

WHILE YOU'RE THERE

In nearby Miserden the Elizabethan mansion, Misarden Park, is set in pretty gardens; they are open on certain days throughout the summer months. Sir Edward Lutyens designed the war memorial here. Further west is Whiteway, where a group of libertarians from Essex established a proto-anarchist community, based on the ideas of Leo Tolstoy, in 1898.

❸ Turn left and follow the track as it rises to the right. After 100yds (91m), where the track bears left, go forward over a stile into a field with Brimpsfield House to your right. Go half right to another stile, pass a gate on your right and cross another stile at the next corner amid scrub. Follow the path to cross a bridge and bear left up to a track. Follow this for 250yds (229m), until you come to a crossways, just past two pollarded willows.

❹ Turn right through a gate to follow a footpath along the bottom of a wooded valley. After 0.75 mile (1.2km) the track will become grassy. Where houses appear above you to the left, you can go left up the slope to visit the church at Syde. Otherwise remain on the valley floor and continue until you come to a gate. Go

WHERE TO EAT AND DRINK

There is nowhere on the route where refreshment is available, unless you divert to the Golden Hart at Nettleton Bottom. Otherwise you can seek out the Carpenter's Arms in Miserden to the south, or the Black Horse in Cranham to the west.

through it, then over a stile to pass to the left of a cottage. Follow a drive up to a road.

❺ Turn left and follow the road until it turns sharp left. At this point turn right over a stile into a field and walk up a steep bank and over a stone stile to arrive on a road in Caudle Green.

❻ Turn right. At the green, just before a large Georgian house ahead of you, and follow a winding path in woodland down to the valley bottom. Over a stile, turn left, go through a bridle gate, and follow the path along the valley bottom on the same line for 0.75 mile (1.2km) until you come to a stile at a field.

❼ Walk along the edge of a wood, then up the valley to a stile. Over this continue alongside a hedge until you come to a stile at a road. Turn left to re-enter Brimpsfield village, continuing past a telephone box, go left at the war memorial and back to the Village Hall.

WHAT TO LOOK OUT FOR

The little stream encountered at points during the walk is the infant River Frome, which, in its later, stronger stages to the south, runs through the Stroud Valley. As you ascend the valley into Syde look out for the old sheep dip just below the village.

Sapperton and the Thames & Severn Canal

Sapperton, both the focus of a major engineering project and a cradle for cultural change.

DISTANCE 6 miles (9.7km)	**MINIMUM TIME** 3hrs
ASCENT/GRADIENT 345ft (105m) ▲▲▲	**LEVEL OF DIFFICULTY** ✦✦✦

PATHS Woodland paths and tracks, fields, lanes and canalside paths, 18 stiles
LANDSCAPE Secluded valleys and villages
SUGGESTED MAP OS Explorer 168 Stroud, Tetbury & Malmesbury
START / FINISH Grid reference: SO 948033
DOG FRIENDLINESS Good – very few livestock
PARKING In Sapperton village near church
PUBLIC TOILETS None en route

Sapperton was at the centre of two conflicting tendencies during the late 18th and early 20th centuries – the Industrial Revolution and the Romantic Revival. In the first case, it was canal technology that came to Sapperton. Canal construction was widespread throughout England from the mid-18th century onwards. Investors poured their money into 18th-century joint stock companies, regardless of their profitability. Confidence was high and investors expected to reap the rewards of commercial success based on the need to ship goods swiftly across the country.

Tunnel Vision

One key project was thought to be the canal that would link the River Severn and the River Thames. The main obstacle was the need for a tunnel through the Cotswolds, the cost of which could be unpredictable. But these were heady days and investors' money was forthcoming to press ahead with the scheme in 1783. During the tunnel's construction, the diarist and traveller John Byng visited the workings. With obvious distaste he wrote, 'I was enveloped in thick smoke arising from the gunpowder of the miners, at whom, after passing by many labourers who work by small candles, I did at last arrive; they come from the Derbyshire and Cornish mines, are in eternal danger and frequently perish by falls of earth.'

Legwork

The Thames and Severn Canal opened in 1789. The Sapperton Tunnel, at 3,400yds (3,109m) long, is still one of the longest transport tunnels in the country. Barges were propelled through the tunnel by means of 'leggers', who 'walked' against the tunnel walls. Yet the canal was not a success. The cost of maintaining the tunnel led to the closure of the canal in 1911.

The Arts and Crafts Movement

It isn't just the great canal tunnel that is of interest in Sapperton. Some of the cottages here were built by disciples of William Morris (1834–96). He was the doyen of the Arts and Crafts Movement in design. It aspired to reintroduce to English life a simple yet decorative functionality, in part as a reaction to the growing mass-production methods engendered by the Industrial Revolution. Furniture makers and architects like Ernest Gimson (from Leicestershire), Sidney and Ernest Barnsley (from Birmingham), and Norman Jewson, all worked in Daneway, at Daneway House. Gimson and the Barnsley brothers are buried at Sapperton church.

You'll find the finest example of the Arts and Crafts vernacular-style architecture in Sapperton is Upper Dorval House. The entrance to the western end of the Sapperton Tunnel is in the hamlet of Daneway, a short walk along the path from the Daneway Inn.

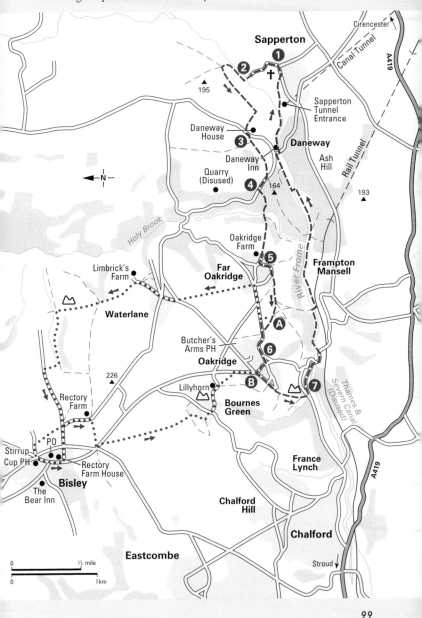

WALK 33 DIRECTIONS

1 With the church to your left, walk along a 'No Through Road'. This descends rapidly and, by the entrance to a house at the bottom, turn left on to a footpath. This turns right and into woodland.

2 Cross a stream and continue left uphill into woodland. Take the main path and, where it forks, go left uphill. Climb to a junction of tracks. Turn left at the guide post and stay on the track mainly in woodland for 0.5 mile (800m) to a gate at a lane.

3 Turn left and then immediately right over a stile (opposite Daneway House). Cross another stile and walk along a wide grassy area, with a fence to the right, to a kissing gate at a lane. Turn right for 250yds (229m) then turn left over a stile.

4 Walk down a drive. Just before the house go left through a hedge and turn immediately right, following a path to a gate. Cross this, then a stile and bridge, a field, and a stile into woodland. Follow a path to a stile at a field and cross half right, heading for farm buildings. Pass through a gate and go left of Oakridge Farm to a stile on to a lane.

5 Turn left and pass a junction, signed 'Trillis'. At a sharp right corner go ahead into a field. Walk to a stile at the far end. Cross the next field and find a stile in the top right corner. Go straight ahead to follow the left margin of the next field to a stile at a road. Turn left along the road to descend through Oakridge.

6 At bottom of the hill, the road bears left, then take the right fork uphill. At a crossroads turn right towards Bisley, climbing steeply to another crossroads (Point **B**). Turn left. At the village green go to its end and bear right to a stile. Enter a field, keep close to a hedgerow on the left-hand side and cross three further stiles. Bear right across a field to a stile into woodland. Soon, over another stile, descend steeply and turn left onto a footpath, which you follow to a junction. Turn left, descending to reach a road.

7 Turn left then, at a junction, turn right to cross a bridge. Bear left and after 50 paces turn left again over a footbridge with a stile at each end, then right on to a footpath, the canal tow path. Follow the canal for 600yds (549m) with one kissing gate. Go right across the canal bridge and turn left back on to the canal tow path for 1.5 miles (2.4km), passing through three kissing gates and over a modern footbridge, to reach a road by the Daneway Inn. Turn right over a bridge and then left to continue by the canal. Cross over one stile to the Sapperton Tunnel. Walk above the tunnel's portico to a field. Over a stile bear half right up to a kissing gate. Go left on to a path and walk up to a lane which leads back into Sapperton. Turn left and then right at the churchyard to return to the start.

Right: The restored entrance to the Thames and Severn Canal

Queen Elizabeth I and the Bisley Boy

Extend Walk 33 for a much longer walk, to visit Bisley, one of the Cotswolds loveliest villages.

See map and information panel for Walk 33

DISTANCE 11 miles (17.7km) **MINIMUM TIME** 5hrs

ASCENT/GRADIENT 740ft (225m) ▲▲▲ **LEVEL OF DIFFICULTY** +++

WALK 34 DIRECTIONS
(Walk 33 option)

From Point **Ⓐ** go half right to a stile. Turn left along a track to a road and turn right. After 0.25 mile (400m), at a crossroads at Far Oakridge, turn left on to a track. At a junction follow 'Bisley 1.5' down for 100yds (91m). Take the left-hand 'no through road'. Pass to the left of Limbrick's Farm. At a spinney fork left for 50yds (46m) to a gate.

Go up a big field to a stile at some woodland. Follow a steep path down to a stile. Descend a field, turning left before the bottom. Walk through fields, and beside small ponds, eventually turning right at a waymarker, up to a road. Turn left for 750yds (686m).

Your 'Bisley loop' begins at this junction. Go half right along a track. Cross the field ahead to turn left along a walled path to metal railings at a road. Cross carefully, watching for traffic, and descend some steps into the middle of Bisley village.

In Bisley, legend says, the real Queen Elizabeth I is buried. Apparently, during a visit as a young girl, she fell ill and died. A local boy who closely resembled her took her place and went on to become queen…

Turn left and within about 250yds (229m), at Rectory Farm House, turn left, uphill, to a junction. Enter the road opposite and follow it as it goes sharp right. After 400yds (366m), opposite Rectory Farm, turn right through a gate and cross fields to a road, ignoring the road junction. Cross to a stile and then a paddock to another stile. Go half right across two fields and then keep this line to a gap. Go through, and find a waymarked corner gap. Go half left, bisecting the field. At the next stile, with farm buildings ahead, go half left towards woodland. Go down a path to a small field. Go half right to cross a track and a stile. Cross to a path beside houses and descend into Bournes Green.

When you strike tarmac turn briefly right to a junction, then turn left. At the next junction descend a grassy bank to follow a road down and up further, to a corner, opposite Lillyhorn. Take the stile and path up through trees to another stile. Cross one more field and the next stile gives onto a road. Here turn right and within 300yds (274m) rejoin Walk 33 at a diagonal crossroads, Point **Ⓑ**. (Turn right towards Point **❼**.)

Turbulent Tewkesbury

*Tracing the military movements that culminated
in the Battle of Tewkesbury.*

DISTANCE *4 miles (6.4km)*   **MINIMUM TIME** *1hr 45min*

ASCENT/GRADIENT *35ft (10m)* ▲▲▲   **LEVEL OF DIFFICULTY** ✚✚✚

PATHS *Fields, pavement and lanes, 3 stiles*

LANDSCAPE *River, distant hills and town*

SUGGESTED MAP *OS Explorer 190 Malvern Hills & Bredon Hill*

START/FINISH *Grid reference: SO 891325*

DOG FRIENDLINESS *Traffic on main roads so on lead – otherwise quite good*

PARKING *Several car parks, most convenient on Gander Lane*

PUBLIC TOILETS *Gander Lane car park or on main road
near Tewkesbury Abbey*

WALK 35 DIRECTIONS

The walk begins at Gander
Lane, north east of Tewkesbury
Abbey. This spectacular Norman
construction dominates the town,
which is situated at the confluence
of the Rivers Severn and Avon. It
was partly this geography which
made Tewkesbury the site of one
of the most important battles in
English history.

Walk away from the town centre.
Cross the River Swilgate and
continue to a pair of iron gates.
Stay on the tarmac path as it
traverses the area known as the
Vineyards, where the monks of

WHAT TO LOOK OUT FOR

As you walk around the town,
look out for the narrow alleys
– with their entertaining names
– that lead off Tewkesbury's main
streets. They owe their existence
to the tendency for the Severn
to flood, forcing the population
to make the best use of
available space.

the abbey once cultivated grapes
but now home to several sports
clubs. Notice a commemorative
plinth on your right and keep to
the left of the cemetery. It was
along here that a Lancastrian army,
consisting of over 6,000 men,
stood on 4th May 1471, facing
towards the south.

The conflict between the Houses
of York and Lancaster had already
lasted for 20 years. The Yorkist
Edward IV was in exile and the
Lancastrian Henry VI had been
restored to the throne through
the machinations of the Earl of
Warwick. In April 1471 Edward
returned to England, defeated
Warwick and imprisoned Henry.
Margaret of Anjou, Henry's
consort, headed for Wales to
drum up further support, but
at Tewkesbury, a crossing point
of the Severn, her army was
intercepted by Edward.

Skirt the cemetery and you will
soon arrive at a road. Cross the
road and turn right towards a
house, taking the path that runs

along its left flank. This will bring you on to Gloucester Road, at a point where a wing of the Yorkist army stood. Turn left along the pavement. Go 100yds (91m) beyond a bus stop then turn left along a path, towards houses. At the end turn right to follow another path, turning left at a corner. This brings you to a gate on your right into Margaret's Camp. The field, named after Margaret of Anjou, is believed to be where the Lancastrian army bivouacked before the battle.

Cross the field to a gate on the far side, emerging onto a road beside houses. Turn right along a cycle path, return to Gloucester Road and turn right again, passing Gupshill Manor across the road. Now a restaurant, Gupshill Manor is where Queen Margaret is said to have stayed the night before the battle. After 700yds (640m), at the second bus stop, cross to the stile beside it and enter a field. Walk to the other side. Ignore the 'Battle Trail' sign to your right and go 50yds (46m) to cross a stile leading over a small brook. This is thought to be the point where King Edward stood. Continue ahead between a fenced-off barn conversion and a house, Crosslands, to reach a lane. In the field before you stood the wing of the Yorkist army led by Edward's brother, the Duke of Gloucester, later Richard III.

Turn right and continue to a junction, close to where the first clash of the battle occurred. Margaret's army suffered a bloody defeat at the hands of Edward and the Yorkist cause remained safe until the Battle of Bosworth in 1485. Turn right and after about 50yds (46m) turn left through a kissing gate into Bloody Meadow, where the remnants of the Lancastrian right wing were slain. Pass through trees to a stile and then on to a road. Turn right and pass a depot and meet Gloucester Road yet again. Opposite are the Vineyards, into which the Lancastrians fled, some taking refuge in the abbey. After two days they were given up and were executed in the abbey grounds.

Turn left and follow the pavement until you come to The Bell Hotel at the corner of Mill Street. Turn left here, down to the Abbey Mill. Now cross on to The Ham. Turn right to follow the bank of the Mill Avon. Just before a flour mill, turn right over a footbridge across the Mill Avon. Turn left and follow this as it curves right. Now Red Lane, this will bring you to the High Street with its famous timber-framed houses. Turn right here and walk the length of the street. Then go half right along Church Street, and left into Gander Lane.

WALK 36

Painswick's Traditions

From the Queen of the Cotswolds through the Washpool Valley.

DISTANCE 7.5 miles (12.1km)	**MINIMUM TIME** 3hrs 30min
ASCENT/GRADIENT 705ft (215m) ▲▲▲	**LEVEL OF DIFFICULTY** ✦✦✧

PATHS Fields, tracks, golf course and a green lane, 20 stiles

LANDSCAPE Hills, valleys, villages, isolated farmhouses, extensive views

SUGGESTED MAP OS Explorer 179 Gloucester, Cheltenham & Stroud

START / FINISH Grid reference: SO 865095

DOG FRIENDLINESS Off lead along lengthy stretches, many stiles

PARKING Car park (small fee) near library, just off main road, Painswick

PUBLIC TOILETS At car park

Local traditions continue to thrive in Painswick, the 'Queen of the Cotswolds'. These are centred around its well-known churchyard, where the Victorian poet Sydney Dobell is buried. The churchyard is famously filled, not only with the 'table' tombs of 18th-century clothiers, but also with 99 beautifully manicured yew trees, planted in 1792. The legend goes that only 99 will ever grow at any one time, as Old Nick will always kill off the hundredth. Should you be minded to do so, try to count them. You will almost certainly be thwarted, as many of them have grown together, creating arches and hedges.

This old tale has become confused with an ancient ceremony that still takes place here on the Sunday nearest to the Feast of the Nativity of St Mary, in mid-September. This is the 'clipping' ceremony, which has nothing to do with cutting bushes or flowers. It derives from the old Saxon word, 'clyping', which means 'embrace' and is used in conjunction with the church. Traditionally, the children of the village gather together on the Sunday afternoon and join hands to form a circle around the church or churchyard, and advance and retreat to and from the church, singing the *Clipping Hymn*. Perhaps this ceremony is the distant descendant of an a pagan ceremony involving a ritual dance around an altar bearing a sacrificed animal. The children wear flowers in their hair and are rewarded with a coin and a bun for their efforts. There was, and maybe still is, a special cake baked for the day, known as 'puppy dog pie', in which a small china dog was inserted. Was this a reminder of the ancient ritual sacrifice? There are yew trees in other gardens in the village, many older than those in the churchyard, and one of which is said to have been planted by Elizabeth I.

The other famous tradition that continues to be observed in the area takes place further along the escarpment, at Cooper's Hill. Here, on Spring Bank Holiday Monday, the cheese-rolling races take place. From a spot marked by a maypole, competitors hurtle down an absurdly steep slope in pursuit of wooden discs representing Gloucester cheeses. The winner, or survivor, is presented with a real cheese; but the injury rate is high and there has been a lot of controversy about whether the event should continue.

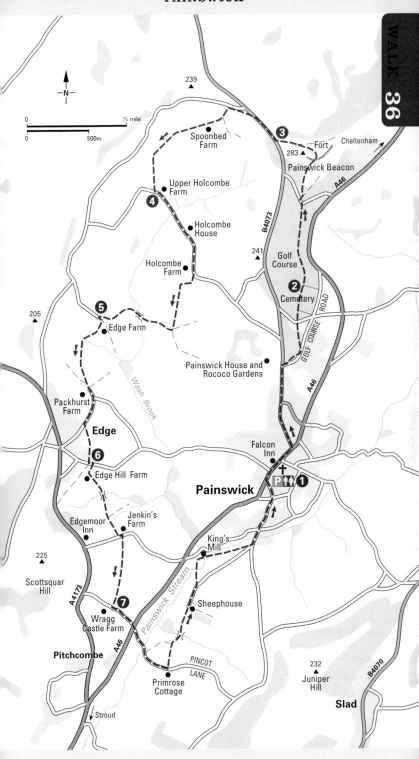

WALK 36 DIRECTIONS

❶ Turn right out of the car park and right along the main street. Turn left along Gloucester Street, join another road and continue uphill, then go right onto Golf Course Road. Bear left on to a track, joining the Cotswold Way, through the car park, turn left into a lane and then, after 50 paces go left into woodland and across a fairway (look out for golf balls).

❷ Keep to the left of a cemetery, then cross another fairway to a path. Continue to a road. After 50 paces turn right, leaving the track after 60 paces. Walk along the left edge of the golf course to the top, passing to the right of a trig point. Descend the other side and turn left down a path. At a track go left to a road, aiming for the gap in the trees visible from the trig point.

❸ Turn right and descend to a bus stop. Here cross to a path amid trees. Beyond a gate turn left down a track to Spoonbed Farm, and descend bearing right at a track junction. Pass the farm to a gate, then take a path to a field. In a second field keep left of an ash tree to reach a stile. Through a new copse and after another stile cross a field to the right of Upper Holcombe Farm to a stile.

❹ Turn left onto a lane for 0.5 mile (800m) to Holcombe Farm. Here continue straight on along a track, passing some gates at a bend on the left. Continue and at a stile go left into the next field. Cross a stile and bear right to another stile. Over this turn right into a green lane which leads to a footbridge with a stile at each end. Bear right alongside the stream and soon bear left uphill to a stile. Over this follow the left-hand field margin curving uphill to a stile.

❺ Turn left along a track towards Edge Farm and fork right at farm buildings to a gate. Over a stone stile cross two fields to a gate arriving at a road. Bear right at a Y-junction. Opposite a house turn left over a stile, bear half right to another stile and onto a path between a hedge and fence to enter Edge.

❻ Turn left, then sharp right at the post-box and go past the village hall. Before the farmhouse turn left over a stile, then another and descend along the field margin to a footbridge. Over this ascend a field to a stile in the opposite hedge, then head for a gate at a track, to the right of a farm. Go through this and through another gate opposite and then along field edge to a kissing gate on to a lane. Turn left and, after 30 paces, turn right via a gate on to a track. The track becomes a path to a stile. Cross fields on the same line, then over stile and quarter left to a field gate and then another, passing right by a house to a road.

❼ Turn left, descend to cross the A46 and walk along Pincot Lane. At Primrose Cottage turn left over a stile and then cross to another. Descend to cross a footbridge, climb and cross the field to a gate, left of Sheephouse. Walk along the drive and where it forks go left down to King's Mill. Bear right through a gate and over the weir, then a stile, and walk alongside the stream to arrive at a lane, via two more stiles. Turn left to return to Painswick.

Walking with Rosie in the Slad Valley

A stroll through the countryside around Slad,
backcloth to Laurie Lee's most popular novel.

> **DISTANCE** 3.75 miles (6km)   **MINIMUM TIME** 2hrs
> **ASCENT/GRADIENT** 425ft (130m) ▲▲▲   **LEVEL OF DIFFICULTY** ✦✦✦
> **PATHS** Tracks, fields and quiet lanes, 17 stiles
> **LANDSCAPE** Hills, valleys and woodland
> **SUGGESTED MAP** OS Explorer 179 Gloucester, Cheltenham & Stroud
> **START / FINISH** Grid reference: SO 878087
> **DOG FRIENDLINESS** Mostly off lead – livestock encountered occasionally
> **PARKING** Lay-by at Bull's Cross
> **PUBLIC TOILETS** None en route

The Slad Valley is one of the least spoiled parts of the Cotswolds, notwithstanding its invariable association with the area's most important literary figure, the poet Laurie Lee (1914–97). And yet he is not instantly remembered for his poetry but for *Cider With Rosie* (1959). This autobiographical account of a Cotswold childhood has, for thousands of students, been part of their English Literature syllabus.

A Childhood Gone Forever

For anyone coming to the area, *Cider With Rosie* is well worth reading, but it is especially pertinent here as it is largely set in Slad, where Lee was brought up and lived for much of his life. The book charts, in poetic language, the experiences of a child living in a world that is within living memory and yet has quite disappeared. Some of the episodes recounted in the book are said to have been products of Lee's imagination but, as he said himself, it was the 'feeling' of his childhood that he was endeavouring to capture.

A Spanish Odyssey

The story of his life is, anyway, an interesting one. He spent a considerable time in Spain and became involved in the Spanish Civil War and the struggle against Franco. Afterwards he established a reputation as a poet, mixing with the literati of the day. He was never very prolific – much of his energy appears to have been poured into love affairs. He did, however, write plays for radio and was involved in film-making during the Second World War. But it was with the publication of *Cider With Rosie* that he became a household name. Readers from all over the world identified with his magical evocation of rural English life and the book has not been out of print since. To some extent Lee became a prisoner of a *Cider With Rosie* industry. The picture of an avuncular figure living a bucolic idyll was not a strictly accurate one – much of his time was spent in London. He was susceptible to illness all his life. Nonetheless, in his later years he managed to complete his autobiographical trilogy. His second volume, *As I Walked Out One Midsummer Morning* (1969) describes his journey from Gloucestershire

SLAD VALLEY

to Spain as an itinerant fiddle player. The third, *A Moment of War* (1991), recounts his experiences there during the Civil War. Lee died in 1997 and is buried in Slad churchyard. Many of the places in and around the village mentioned in *Cider With Rosie* are readily identifiable today. Although it is no longer possible to frolic in the roads with impunity, the valley remains as beautiful as it ever was.

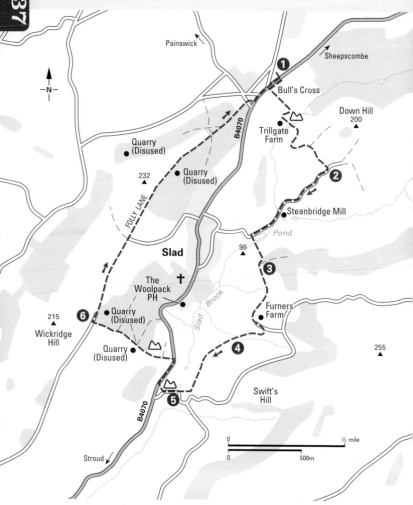

WALK 37 DIRECTIONS

❶ From Bull's Cross walk to the south end of the lay-by and turn left on to a tarmac-covered footpath, the Wysis Way. Follow it down and, immediately before Trillgate Farm turn left over a stile into a field. Go half right, down the field and up the other

side, to a gate and stile at the top. Turn left along a track. Where it joins another track stay right and continue to a lane.

❷ Turn right and walk to the bottom. Pass Steanbridge Mill and if you want to visit Slad, follow the lane into the village. To continue the walk turn left immediately after the large pond along a restricted byway and walk to a stile. Cross into a field, with a hedge on your right, and continue to a stile at the top.

❸ Cross and follow a path to another stile. Follow the left side of the next field and go over another stile, then continue along the path. Pass through a gate on to a track, stay to the right of Furners Farm and curve left. About 30yds (27m) after the curve turn right over a stile on to a wooded path and after 130yds (118m) go right again over a stile into a field. Walk ahead, with the farm above you and to the right. Cross another stile and then keep to the right of a small pond.

❹ At the top of the pond cross a stile into a field. Go half left across it to a gate and stile. In the next field head straight across its lower part. At a point where a telegraph pole stands close to a hedge, turn right over a stile on to a track. Turn left to meet a lane.

❺ Turn right and follow the lane to the valley bottom. Start to climb the other side and at a corner go over a stile on your right by The Vatch Cottage. Ascend steeply, skirting the garden, to another stile at the road. Turn right along the pavement. After 150yds (137m) bear left on to a public footpath and climb steeply. At a junction of footpaths bear left and continue to a field. Follow the margin of the field up to a stile, then follow the path as it weaves between a dry-stone wall and the edge of woodland.

❻ At the top go over a stile, turn right on to Folly Lane and continue to a junction. If you want to go into Slad, turn right, otherwise continue ahead on to a path that will soon take you through the Frith Wood Nature Reserve. Walk through the woods, finally emerging at your starting point at Bull's Cross.

Weaving Along the Stroud Valley

Discover the impact of the Industrial Revolution in the Cotswold valleys.

DISTANCE 6 miles (9.7km) **MINIMUM TIME** 3hrs

ASCENT/GRADIENT 495ft (150m) ▲▲▲ **LEVEL OF DIFFICULTY** ✚✚✚

PATHS *Fields, lanes, canal path and tracks, 3 stiles*

LANDSCAPE *Canal, road and railway, valley and steep slopes, villages*

SUGGESTED MAP *OS Explorer 168 Stroud, Tetbury & Malmesbury*

START / FINISH *Grid reference: SO 892025*

DOG FRIENDLINESS *Good, with few stiles and little livestock*

PARKING *Lay-by east of Chalford church*

PUBLIC TOILETS *None en route*

Wool has been associated with the Cotswolds for centuries. During the Middle Ages the fleece of the 'Cotswold Lion' breed was the most prized in all of Europe. Merchants from many countries despatched their agents to purchase it from the fairs and markets of the wold towns in the northern part of the region – most famously Northleach, Cirencester and Chipping Campden. Woven cloth eventually became a more important export and so the industry moved to the southern Cotswolds, whose valleys and faster-flowing streams, which were suited to powering woollen mills.

Mechanisation

The concentration of mills in the Stroud area was evident by the early 15th century. Indeed, its importance was such that when a 1557 Act of Parliament restricted cloth manufacture to towns, the villages of the Stroud area were exempted. By 1700 the lower Stroud Valley was producing about 4.59 million square metres of cloth every year. At this time the spinning and weaving was done in domestic dwellings or workhouses, the woven cloth then being returned to the mill for finishing. The Industrial Revolution was to bring rapid change. There was great opposition to the introduction of mechanical spinning and shearing machines. This was heightened in 1795 by the development of the improved broadloom with its flying shuttle. The expectation was that, as well as compelling weavers to work in the mills, it would bring mass unemployment. Progress marched on, however, and by the mid-19th century there were over 1,000 looms at work in the Stroud Valley. They came with their share of political unrest too, and in 1825 and 1828 strikes and riots broke out. The industry went into decline as steam replaced water power and it migrated northwards to the Pennines. By 1901 only 3,000 people were employed in the cloth industry, compared with 24,000 in the mid-17th century. Today, only one mill remains.

Graceful Elevations

This walk begins in Chalford, an attractive village built on the steep sides of the Stroud Valley. Its streets are lined with 18th- and 19th-century clothiers' terraces and weavers' cottages. On the canalside the shells of woollen mills are still plentiful.

The 18th-century church contains fine examples of craftsmanship from the Arts and Crafts period of the late 19th century. Nether Lypiatt Manor is a handsome manor house now owned by Prince and Princess Michael of Kent. Known locally as 'the haunted house', it was built in 1702 for Judge Charles Cox. Its classical features and estate railings, all unusual in the Cotswolds, inspired wealthy clothiers to spend their money on the addition of graceful elevations to their own houses.

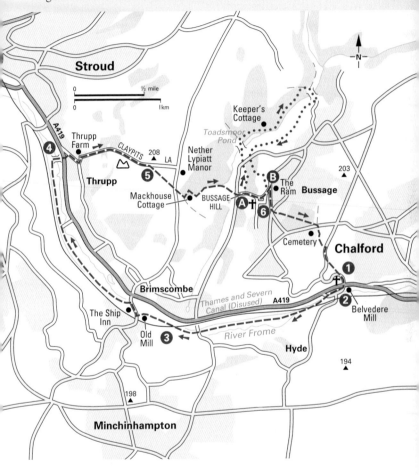

WALK 38 DIRECTIONS

❶ Walk towards Chalford church. Immediately before it, cross the road and locate a path going right, towards a canal roundhouse. Note the Belvedere Mill across to your left and follow the tow path beside the Thames and Severn Canal on your right.

❷ Cross a road and continue along the tow path as it descends steps. Now follow this path for about 2 miles (3.2km). It will soon disappear under the railway line via a gloomy culvert, so that the railway will now be on your right, beyond the old canal. Old mills and small factories line the route.

3 Shortly before arriving in Brimscombe the tow path passes beneath the railway. Soon after, it becomes a road leading into an industrial estate. At a road opposite a large, old mill, turn left, to come to a junction. Cross and turn right. Immediately after The Ship Inn turn left along a road among offices and workshops. Continue straight on along a path, with factory walls to your right. The canal reappears on your left. As you walk on into the country you will pass beneath three brick bridges and a metal footbridge.

4 At the next bridge, with a hamlet on your left, turn right to follow a path to the A419. Cross this and turn left. Beside the bus stop turn right up a short path to meet Thrupp Lane. Turn right, and at the top, turn left into Claypits Lane. Turn right just before Thrupp Farm and climb up steeply.

5 After a long climb, as the road levels out, you will see Nether Lypiatt Manor in front of you. Turn right, beside a tree, over a stile into a field. Go half left to the far corner. Cross a stone stile and follow a narrow path beside trees to a road. Descend a lane opposite. Where it appears to fork, follow the 'Mackhouse Cottage' sign, descending. Enter woodland, descending steadily,

and fork right near the bottom. Keep a pond on your left and cross a road to climb, steeply again, up Bussage Hill. After 100yds (91m) pass a lane on the left (Point **A** on Walk 39). At a pair of signs indicating speed de-restriction (!) fork left. Soon notice a woodland path on the left, Point **B**, but continue on the road to The Ram. Turn right.

6 Walk for nearly 0.25 mile (400m) to a telephone box then, at a bus shelter, turn left to follow a path among houses into woodland. Go ahead until you meet a road. Turn left and immediately right down a path beside a cemetery. Descend to another road. Turn right for 100yds (91m) – care needed on this short road stretch – then turn left down a steep lane among trees, leading back to Chalford. At the bottom turn left to the lay-by.

Spinning Off into the Toadsmoor Valley

Extend Walk 38 with a visit to this relatively inaccessible little valley.
See map and information panel for Walk 38

DISTANCE *8 miles (12.9km)* **MINIMUM TIME** *4hrs*

ASCENT/GRADIENT *565ft (175m)* ▲▲▲ **LEVEL OF DIFFICULTY** +++

WALK 39 DIRECTIONS (Walk 38 option)

The Cotswolds, for all their obvious charm, manage to conceal plenty of happy surprises. Many of these are only really accessible on foot – the Toadsmoor Valley is one.

From Point **Ⓐ** turn left along a track and follow it to a road. Cross this to a lane and follow this down, right, to a bridge and a ford.

This exquisite wooded valley runs between the Golden Valley at Brimscombe and a point just west of Bisley. In the past there were mills here, now long gone, although the weavers' cottages that preceded the mills remain. Cross and stay on the track as it bears right with Toadsmoor Pond on your right.

This pond spreads along the valley bottom at the foot of a steep slope covered in tall trees. In the autumn these are a breathtaking sight. The pond is a haven for wildlife, including the grey heron, the largest of European herons. Follow this track for just under 0.75 mile (1.2km), passing to the right of Keeper's Cottage. (On the lake side of the track, opposite Keeper's Cottage, is a formal landscaped garden, something of a surprise in the midst of nature's exuberance.) Walk on nearly 0.5 mile (800m), until the track rises to a country lane. Turn right to cross a bridge and then, opposite a house on the left, enter an initially tarmac track on the right. This will climb steadily and take you high above the valley.

The steep, winding lanes that characterise this part of the Cotswolds were just wide enough to accept pack animals laden with spun or woven wool. Go past another house, beyond which lies a good path through woodland. Follow it to a road on the left.

Cross the road (crossed earlier on Walk 39) to steps leading up to a stone stile. Cross to woodland and follow a rising path which eventually leads to a stile. Go over into a field and ascend with a hedge on your right, but, at the first hedge across the slope turn right and walk along the left side of a field to arrive at a stile at the edge of woodland. Cross over to a woodland path and follow it to a steep lane in Bussage. Here, Point **Ⓑ**, turn left, to rejoin Walk 38.

Around Tetbury Town and Country

This handsome Cotswold town has kept its appeal without allowing conservation to leach it of its character.

DISTANCE 3.5 miles (5.7km)   **MINIMUM TIME** 1hr 30min

ASCENT/GRADIENT 100ft (30m) ▲▲▲   **LEVEL OF DIFFICULTY** ✦✦✦

PATHS Fields, lanes and tracks, 8 stiles

LANDSCAPE Rolling hills, farmland and town

SUGGESTED MAP OS Explorer 168 Stroud, Tetbury & Malmesbury

START/FINISH Grid reference: ST 890931

DOG FRIENDLINESS On lead in town and in one section with animals

PARKING Several car parks in central area near church

PUBLIC TOILETS Old Brewery Lane or behind The Snooty Fox

WALK 40 DIRECTIONS

The centre of Tetbury is built around the Market Place, dominated by the pillared Market House. Built in 1655, it was later enlarged to accommodate the town's fire engine and lock-up.

The Police Bygones Museum, on Long Street in the former Police Station, contains a collection of relics of Cotswold law enforcement in the old cells.

From the centre of the town pass the Market Hall on your right and then The Snooty Fox. Walk down Chipping Street and then pass The Priory Nursing Home on your left. The road, now The Chipping, descends and passes the steep Chipping Steps on your right. 'Chipping' is an old English word for market. The area close to the steps, lined with weavers' cottages, was for centuries the site of 'Mop Fairs', where the unemployed could offer their services for domestic and farming posts. Over the wall on your right is the street called Gumstool Hill.

The hill is used for the annual woolsack races and at one time there was once a ducking-stool or gum-stool here, used for the punishment of 'scolds'.

Tetbury's most attractive aspect is its streets of stone houses of all styles and of all ages. In the main they are used today as they always have been – as residences and places of work. Tetbury's early prosperity was based on the wool trade, but in the 18th century industrial demand for fast-flowing water, which Tetbury was unable to provide, led to the town's decline. As with other towns and villages in the Cotswolds, this did have one happy consequence – Tetbury has not been blighted by inappropriate development. Unusually, however, its modern prosperity and vitality are not

WHILE YOU'RE THERE

Visit Westonbirt Arboretum, just over 3 miles (4.8km) to the south of Tetbury. It has one of the largest collections of trees and shrubs in the world.

dependent exclusively on tourism. On the contrary, tourism here is the gilt on the gingerbread, which makes it a pleasant place to visit.

At a road junction just before The Royal Oak fork right along a lane, signed 'Lark Hill'. Keeping to the left of a transformer station, follow this lane all the way to a gate into Preston Park. Go through and walk straight ahead. Go to the top of a knoll and then descend on the other side, keeping to the right of a fence to cross a stream by a stone bridge. Continue along the path to a gate. Go through, crossing the dismantled railway, and then half left up a bank to another gate. Go through and ahead to follow a path along a grassy area of shrubs. Follow this around to the right, then pass between Little Larkhill Cottage and Little Larkhill Farm, to join their shared track. Stay on this and follow it all the way to a lane, where you turn right.

Stay on this for 0.6 mile (1.1km) – look out for the ruin of a brick-built gun emplacement – and then, opposite a track on the left, turn right over a stile into a field. Walk along the field edge, skirting a pond, then carry on to find another stile, in the general direction of Tetbury church. The parish church is in complete contrast with almost every other church in the Cotswolds. It is a striking example of late 18th-century Georgian Gothic. Its spire is one of the highest in the country and its interior is delicate and simple.

Go over the stile and cross the field to a gate. In the next field head for some farm buildings but, just before them, turn right through a gate into a farmyard. Turn left to walk through the farmyard and continue on to a track. Just before the cottages complex of The Folly Farm, find a stone stile and a metal kissing gate, both under a tree on the right. Once through these take the fenced path to meet the main road beside the hospital.

Turn right along the pavement to a minor road on the left, just before a bridge. Follow this down until, after a stone bridge, you turn right up to a kissing gate. After just 10yds (9m) turn right, taking a path under trees then through a deciduous plantation to a stile. Cross this and continue on the same line to come to the A433. Turn sharp right beside this and follow a descending track – this was the original road into Tetbury. At its end you will emerge to the right of the arched road bridge. Turn left, through the far arch, and then bear right up a path. Turn right, towards the church, then left for the centre of Tetbury.

All Saxons and Severn at Deerhurst

An easy walk by the river to discover a rare, complete Saxon chapel on the banks of the Severn.

DISTANCE 3.25 miles (5.3km)	**MINIMUM TIME** 1hr 30min

ASCENT/GRADIENT 115ft (35m) ▲▲▲ **LEVEL OF DIFFICULTY** +++

PATHS Fields, pavement and riverbank, 12 stiles

LANDSCAPE Hills, villages and river

SUGGESTED MAP OS Explorer 179 Gloucester, Cheltenham & Stroud

START/FINISH Grid reference: SO 868298

DOG FRIENDLINESS Off lead except near occasional livestock

PARKING Car park (small fee) outside Odda's Chapel

PUBLIC TOILETS None en route

Deerhurst, a small, pretty village on the banks of Britain's longest river, the Severn, is endowed with a chapel and a church of particular, if not unique, significance. Both buildings hark back to that poignant period of English history immediately before the Norman Conquest. At the time of their arrival, in the 5th and 6th centuries AD, after the withdrawal of the Romans, the Saxons were a pagan people. But they were gradually converted through the influence of St Augustine and the preaching of the British or Celtic church. Deerhurst was in the Saxon kingdom of Hwicce, an area that was converted to Celtic Christianity by Welsh missionaries.

A Visit to Rome

In AD 800 Aethelric, ruler of Hwicce, was inspired by a visit to Rome – on his return he set aside a large acreage of land at Deerhurst for the construction of a monastery. The monastery became the most important in Hwicce and indeed one of its monks, Alphege, was to become Archbishop of Canterbury in the early 11th century. The monastery, however, was partially destroyed by the Danes in the 9th century. Although a small monastic community stayed on, it was finally levelled at the time of the Dissolution of the Monasteries. Nonetheless, the monastery church at Deerhurst, once as important as Gloucester and Tewkesbury, has survived as the finest Saxon church in England. It contains some 30 Anglo-Saxon doors and windows as well as a 9th-century font. The Deerhurst Angel, located outside on the east wall, dates from the 10th century.

Odda's Chapel

A short distance from the church is Odda's Chapel, one of only a handful of wholly Saxon buildings left in England. It takes its name from Earl Odda, a kinsman of Edward the Confessor. When his brother, Aelfric, died at Deerhurst in AD 1053, Odda had this chapel built, to be used as an oratory and to be served by the monastery monks. It owes its survival entirely to chance. The monastery, and the chapel, eventually became the property of Westminster Abbey. The chapel was later deconsecrated and subsumed into the adjoining abbot's house. After the monastery's dissolution in 1540 the abbot's house became a farmhouse and the existence of the disused chapel was quite forgotten. It was only in 1885, during restoration work on the house, that the chapel was rediscovered and its significance understood. The building you see today is one of great simplicity – a stone room with high walls and only two windows – but its antiquity, location, and its almost pristine state seem somehow awe-inspiring.

Near by, and also visited on this walk, is the scattered village of Apperley. Here you'll see some very fine, timbered houses, one of which is the post office. The Coalhouse Inn, on the river bank, was built in the 18th century to cater for the bargees who were transporting coal from the Forest of Dean up-river to Gloucester and Tewkesbury.

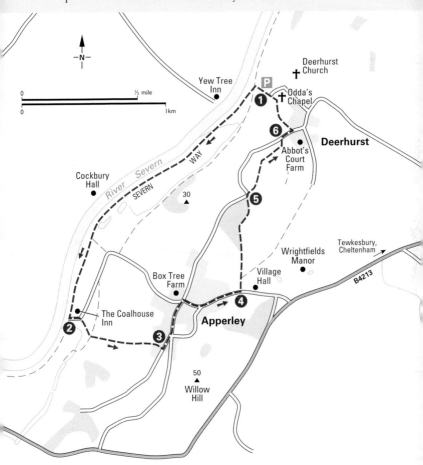

WALK 41 DIRECTIONS

❶ With Odda's Chapel behind you, turn left and then right through a gate to walk along a track as far as the river bank. Turn left to follow the Severn Way.

Continue through a number of gates and over stiles, following an obvious path (sometimes a little overgrown), with the river always close by on the right. Eventually you reach The Coalhouse Inn, set back a little to the left.

W A L K 41

❷ Turn left after the pub to follow a road. Once behind the pub turn right on a track for a few paces. When it veers left go straight ahead to a stile and cross into a field. Continue to another stile. In the following field go uphill to find another stile at the top, beside a gate. Go over and follow the right-hand margin of the field to another gate. Go through, and continue to the road in Apperley.

❸ Turn left to walk through the village. At a four-way signpost turn right, away from Box Tree Farm, heading along Sawpit Lane, towards Tewkesbury.

❹ Just before the village hall turn left and walk across the playing fields to a stile. Cross and stay on the same line to arrive at another stile. Now follow the right-hand margin of a field and, later, a plantation, as it eventually curves right and brings you to a stile at a lane.

❺ Go over to the lane and turn sharp right to a gate. Once in the field turn left to come swiftly to another stile. Cross this to enter another field and then walk down, crossing another stile to the right of a house. Go ahead then, after passing new barns on your right, find a stile and finger post in the hedge to your left. (Odda's Chapel is visible beyond.) Go over to a road and turn right.

WHILE YOU'RE THERE

At Twigworth, towards Cheltenham, you will find Nature in Art which is, uniquely, an art gallery and museum dedicated exclusively to nature-inspired art of all kinds. It has a cafè too. In nearby Tewkesbury (see Walk 35) you can visit Tewkesbury Abbey, which boasts the largest Norman tower in Europe.

❻ Continue to a flood gate. Turn left to walk atop further flood defences alongside a private garden. Cross a stile into a meadow and continue diagonally right, heading for a stile and gate beside Odda's Chapel and the timbered building next to it. This will bring you to a gate by your starting point.

WHAT TO LOOK OUT FOR

This part of the River Severn is much used by river craft of all sorts (although commercial traffic has completely disappeared). Look out for sailing craft from the sailing club on the far bank, rowing boats and, sometimes, beautifully painted longboats that have been rented by holiday-makers.

Severnside at Ashleworth and Hasfield

A fine walk along the banks of the River Severn, visiting a huge, and beautifully-preserved, tithe barn.

DISTANCE 7.25 miles (11.7km)   **MINIMUM TIME** 3hrs 15min

ASCENT/GRADIENT 65ft (20m) ▲▲▲   **LEVEL OF DIFFICULTY** ✦✦✦

PATHS Tracks, fields, lanes and riverbank, 20 stiles

LANDSCAPE Flat: river, meadows, woods, farms, villages and distant hills

SUGGESTED MAP OS Explorer 179 Gloucester, Cheltenham & Stroud

START/FINISH Grid reference: SO 818251

DOG FRIENDLINESS Not much livestock but many stiles

PARKING Grass verges in vicinity of tithe barn

PUBLIC TOILETS None en route

Medieval tithe barns, such as the impressive example at Ashleworth, still survive around the country in surprisingly large numbers. In many cases they are still in use, even if the original purpose for which they were built has long been an irrelevance. They date back to the period before the 16th century, when the great monasteries owned much of the land that was not held by the Crown. Around Ashleworth the land belonged to Bristol Abbey. The local people who worked the land were their tenants. There were different categories of tenant who, in return for working the land of their landlord, were allowed access to common land and also to work a certain amount of land for themselves.

Medieval Taxes

Whatever category they belonged to, they all shared one special obligation and that was the payment of tithes, or taxes, to the abbey. This was most often in the form of produce, stored in the tithe barn, which usually stood close to the church and the abbot's residence. If the abbot was not in permanent residence then he would make regular visits with his entourage to ensure that the tithes were paid correctly and on time. The presence of a huge tithe barn here, in what today is a comparatively remote village, has a geographical explanation. Ashleworth is situated at an easily fordable part of the river – an important consideration before the era of easy transportation. There had been a church at Ashleworth since before the compilation of the Domesday Book. A manor house certainly existed during the Norman period, and no doubt before. The barn, and Ashleworth Court next to it (which was used as an administrative centre), date from the late 15th century.

Kings and Queens

The limestone barn is 125ft (38m) long, consisting of ten bays – this is an enormous building by any standards. If you look up to the stone slate roof you can only marvel at the deceptively simple timber braces that support it. In this barn 'queen post trusses' are used, that is, a trellis of posts standing

ASHLEWORTH

vertically from the horizontal tie beams, as opposed to a 'king post truss', consisting of a single vertical post. The bays would have been used to store both tithes and also the normal produce of the farm. Had you wandered through the barn 500 years ago you would have seen different types of grain, honey, dairy produce and, of course, Cotswold wool, all of which would have been subsequently shipped downriver. Ashleworth Court, next door, is a fine example of a medieval stone building barely changed since the time of its construction. The black and white, timbered Manor House, built as the abbot's residence, stands a short distance along the road.

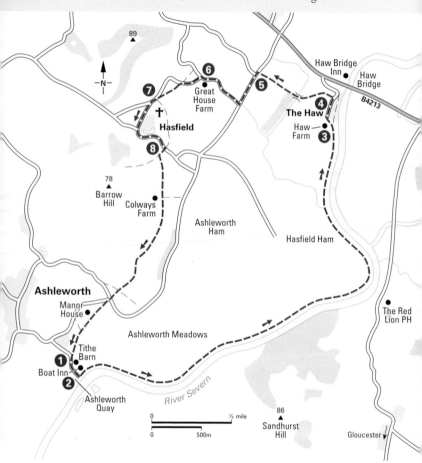

WALK 42 DIRECTIONS

❶ From the tithe barn walk along the road towards the River Severn, passing the Boat Inn on your left-hand side.

❷ At Ashleworth Quay turn left over a stile to walk along the river bank. Follow it for a little over

3 miles (4.8km). In general the path is obvious, but where it sometimes appears to pass through gates, you may find they are locked and that you should instead be using a stile closer to the river. Sandhurst Hill will come and go across the river, followed by The Red Lion pub (sadly also out of reach across the river).

3 Eventually you will pass Haw Farm. Immediately after it follow a track that leads left, away from the river, and then passes to the left of a number of houses and cottages. The track becomes a lane and the Haw Bridge will appear before you.

WHILE YOU'RE THERE
Visit Gloucester, a city whose beauty it is still possible to discern, notwithstanding years of unsympathetic development. Gloucester Cathedral is of enormous historical and architectural interest, while the old docks, though no longer commercially operational, have been rescued from oblivion – the former warehouses have been turned into museums and shops.

4 Just before the lane goes left turn left over a stile into a field. Walk straight on and then, as the field opens up at a corner, bear half left to arrive at a wooden stile in a wire fence. Go half right to a stile and green metal gate crossing a drainage channel. Continue straight on across two fields.

WHAT TO LOOK OUT FOR
The River Severn can flood quite badly and you will notice a number of damage limitation devices built in the vicinity of Ashleworth and elsewhere. In the past floods have reached as far as the church every two or three years. The worst flood, however, was in 1947. The level the water reached is recorded on the wall of the south aisle.

5 This will bring you to a lane where you turn left. Within 400yds (366m) turn right along another lane, until you reach Great House Farm.

6 Stay on the lane as it bears left. Then, after passing two houses, cross left into a field. Head downhill, half right, to a corner and rejoin the lane.

7 Turn left and continue into Hasfield, keeping left for Ashleworth. Turn left to visit the church and return to carry on through the village, still heading towards Ashleworth.

8 Before a row of cottages on the right, turn right at a footpath sign. Follow a good farm track, soon crossing a stile to walk parallel with it to Colways Farm. Beyond it, begin with a hedge to your left, later drifting right to cross two footbridges, then stiles over wire fences and beside a pylon. At a lane go over a stile just left of the road opposite. Head across to a gap. Now follow the path on the right side of fields all the way back to a point just before the tithe barn.

WHERE TO EAT AND DRINK
Early on the route, beside the river at Ashleworth Quay, is the Boat Inn, an exceptionally unpretentious and comfortable pub. There are also two pubs nearby: just off the route on the B4213 at Haw Bridge is (unsurprisingly) the Haw Bridge Inn, and in Ashleworth village is The Queen's Arms.

Uley and its Magnificent Fort on the Hill

The vast bulk of the ancient fort of Uley Bury forms the centrepiece for this walk along the Cotswold escarpment.

DISTANCE *3 miles (4.8km)*   MINIMUM TIME *1hr 30min*

ASCENT/GRADIENT *345ft (105m)* ▲▲▲   LEVEL OF DIFFICULTY ✦✦✦

PATHS *Tracks and fields*

LANDSCAPE *Valley, meadows, woodland and open hilltop, 2 stiles*

SUGGESTED MAP *OS Explorer 168 Stroud, Tetbury & Malmesbury*

START / FINISH *Grid reference: ST 789984*

DOG FRIENDLINESS *Suitable in parts but livestock on Uley Bury and in fields on extension to Owlpen*

PARKING *Main street of Uley*

PUBLIC TOILETS *None en route*

Uley is a pretty village, strung along a wide street at the foot of a high, steep hill. It is distinctive for several reasons. It has its own brewery, which produces some fine beers including Uley Bitter and Uley Old Spot. In the past the village specialised in the production of 'Uley Blue' cloth, which was used in military uniforms. And then there is Uley Bury, dating back to the Iron Age and one of the finest hill-forts in the Cotswolds.

Peaceful Settlements

There are many hundreds of Iron Age forts throughout England and Wales. They are concentrated in Cornwall, South West Wales and the Welsh Marches, with secondary concentrations throughout the Cotswolds, North Wales and Wessex. Although the term 'hill-fort' is generally used in connection with these settlements, the term can be misleading. There are many that were built on level ground and there are many that were not used purely for military purposes – often they were simply settlements located on easily-defended sites. Broadly speaking, there are five types, classified according to the nature of the site on which they were built, rather than, say, the date of their construction. Contour forts were built more or less along the perimeter edge of a hilltop; promontory forts were built on a spur, surrounded by natural defences on two or more sides; valley and plateau forts (two types) depended heavily on artificial defences and were located, as their names suggest, in valleys or on flat land respectively; and multiple-enclosure forts were usually built in a poor strategic position on the slope of a hill and were perhaps used as stockades.

Natural Defences

Uley Bury, covering about 38 acres (15.4ha), is classified as an inland promontory fort and was built in the 6th century BC. It falls away on three sides, the fourth side, which faces away from the escarpment, is protected by specially constructed ramparts which would have been surmounted by a wooden palisade. The natural defences – that is, the Cotswold escarpment, facing west – were also strengthened by the construction of a wide and deep ditch, as well as two additional ramparts, an inner one and an outer one, between which the footpath largely threads its course. The three main entrances were at the northern, eastern and southern corners. These, vulnerable parts of the fort, would have been fortified with log barriers.

Although some tribespeople would have lived permanently in huts within the fort, most would have lived outside, either on other parts of the hill or in the valleys below. In an emergency, therefore, there was space for those who lived outside the fort to take shelter within. Eventually the fort was taken over by the Dobunni tribe – Celtic interlopers from mainland Europe who arrived about 100 BC – and appears to have been occupied by them throughout the Roman era.

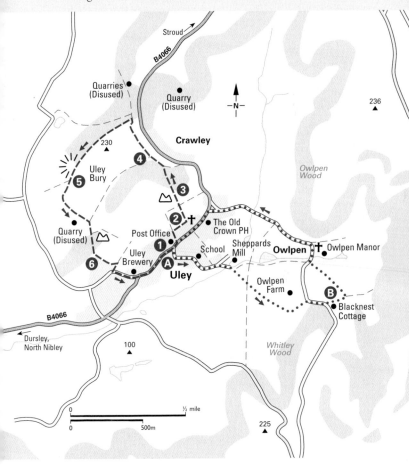

WALK 43 DIRECTIONS

1 From the main street locate the Uley Stores (on your left as you walk up the street). Walk along the narrow lane (to the right, as you look at the stores).

Pass between houses as the lane dwindles to a track. Immediately before a stile turn right along a public footpath heading towards Uley church.

ULEY

❷ When the churchyard can be seen on the right, turn left up a narrow path beside a cottage. This rises fairly sharply and brings you to a kissing gate. Pass through into a meadow. Climb steeply up the grassland towards woodland.

❸ At the treeline veer left of the woods. In a corner on the far left go through a gate and follow a winding woodland path uphill. When you come to a fence stay on the path as it bears left. Go

WHAT TO LOOK OUT FOR

There are magnificent views westward from the summit of Uley Bury. You should easily be able to see the esturary of the River Severn, as well as the Tyndale Monument. Look out too for the brewery in Uley and the statue of a pig outside it. This is a Gloucester Old Spot, a breed of pig peculiar to the county, now making something of a comeback.

through a gate to emerge from the woods. Stay on the path as it rises across grassland.

❹ Follow the perimeter of the ancient Uley Bury in an anti-clockwise direction, with steep drops to your right. When you meet a junction of paths go left along the edge of the hill, with views to the west. After about 600yds (549m), at a curve, you will see a stile that invites you to descend.

❺ Ignore this stile; instead continue ahead. At the next corner go over a stile and continue to skirt the bury. When you have gone a further 250yds (228m), to the bury's south-eastern point, bear right on a bridleway that descends between hillocks. Continue, dropping quite steeply through bushes to a gate (not the gate and stile visible 50yds/46m to your right). Descend to a stile.

❻ Walk along the tarmac path, all the way to a cottage and then a kissing gate. Go through this and pass beside the cottage to arrive at a lane. Turn left here and follow the lane, soon passing the Uley Brewery, to reach the main road. Turn left, passing South Street (Point ❹ on Walk 44), to return to the start.

WHILE YOU'RE THERE

Two sites are worth a closer look while you're in the area. Near by is the little village of North Nibley, over which towers the 111ft (34m) Tyndale Monument. Built in 1866 this is a tribute to William Tyndale (c1494–1536). He was born at Dursley near Gloucester, and was the first to translate the New Testament of the Bible from Latin into English. It is possible to climb to near the top of the tower for magnificent views. Just to the north of Uley Bury, and still on the escarpment, is Uley Long Barrow, better known as Hetty Pegler's Tump. This is a neolithic chambered tomb some 180ft (55m) in length. A narrow stone doorway leads into a passage, off which four semicircular chambers would have contained cremated remains.

Over the Fields to Owlpen Manor

Extend Walk 43 to the other side of this idyllic valley to see a picturesque manor house.

See map and information panel for Walk 43

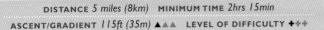

> **DISTANCE** 5 miles (8km) **MINIMUM TIME** 2hrs 15min
> **ASCENT/GRADIENT** 115ft (35m) ▲▲▲ **LEVEL OF DIFFICULTY** ✦✦✦

WALK 44 DIRECTIONS
(Walk 43 option)

From Point **Ⓐ** turn right to walk along South Street. Follow the road as it goes left and passes the school. Keep going until it forks, at which point go right, heading for Sheppards Mill. Keep to the right of the mill (now converted to a private dwelling) and come to a stile. Head for the seen gate, with a fence to your left. Beyond this, proceed uphill, edging slightly left to a stile. Cross a third field. Climb over a stile and turn left, to pass the cluster of buildings of and around Owlpen Farm. You may see some llamas here.

Cross the stile and turn right, uphill for 150yds (137m). Just before Blacknest Cottage, turn left through a gate into a field. Go straight down, looking for a gate ahead of you at a protuberant corner of a fence, Point **Ⓑ**. Pass through into the next field and then go half left, aiming for a point to the left of Owlpen church below you, just to the left of Owlpen Manor. Keep going to the far side of the field, from where you will have a fine view of the manor house.

This is an impossibly idyllic scene. To your left, the broad valley

sweeps grandly southwards, its sides covered densely in trees, with the village of Uley asleep at the feet of the fortified hill. Before you is a picturesque, 15th-century manor house (with additions from later centuries), bedded into a green hollow. In fact, the foundations of the house are far earlier, dating back to 1080. The house was restored in the 1920s by Norman Jewson, an influential member of the Arts and Crafts Movement in Sapperton and Daneway (see Walk 33). The house's charming name is actually a corruption of 'de Olepennes', the family that owned the manor until 1490. The Victorian church has a colourful interior, and a number of brasses commemorating members of the Daunt family, who succeeded the de Olepennes as lords of the manor, remaining until 1805.

Locate a stile in the very bottom corner, concealed by a young plantation, and drop down to a lane. Turn right, pass the entrance to the church (which can be visited by following signs), and follow the lane all the way back to Uley. At the main street turn left to return to Point **Ⓐ**.

Overleaf: Looking south-west at Uley Bury

Little Sodbury's Fort and Horton Court

Encountering the ancient and the medieval along a new way.

DISTANCE *3.75 miles (6km)*   **MINIMUM TIME** *1hr 45min*

ASCENT/GRADIENT *245ft (75m)* ▲▲▲   **LEVEL OF DIFFICULTY** ✚✚✚

PATHS *Tracks, fields, woodland and lanes, 7 stiles*

LANDSCAPE *Meadows and open hilltop*

SUGGESTED MAP *OS Explorer 167 Thornbury, Dursley & Yate*

START/FINISH *Grid reference: ST 759844*

DOG FRIENDLINESS *Livestock in initial fields, thereafter reasonably good*

PARKING *Considerate parking in Horton village*

PUBLIC TOILETS *None en route*

WALK 45 DIRECTIONS

Walk up the hill out of Horton. About 50yds (46m) before a road junction turn right on to a track towards Little Sodbury. After 20yds (18m) go left through a fence to a path. Continue to a stile, to follow the Cotswold Way, between horse paddocks.

Around 55 years elapsed between the birth of the notion of a continuous route through the Cotswolds and the 'official' opening of The Cotswold Way in 2007. Its status as a 'National Trail' is shown by the distinctive

WHILE YOU'RE THERE

In this southern part of Gloucestershire you are not far from the city of Bath, one of the most beautiful cities in Europe and now a UNESCO World Heritage Site. Above all it is a city of elegant Georgian architecture, but there are many other attractions including the Roman Baths and new spa baths, the abbey and many museums and galleries.

acorn waymarker. (You may, in places, see the older white dot.) Many improvements, such as the installation of metal kissing gates and the building of sturdy wooden footbridges, have been made.

Cross the field in front of you and come to a stile on the far side. Descend a steep bank then reascend, passing a small reservoir. Go ahead across pasture for 0.25 mile (400m), easing right towards a hedge, and find a stile in the corner just before a cottage. Cross onto a path and turn left to follow a path to a lane in Little Sodbury. Turn right and, at the next junction, left. Pass Little Sodbury church on your left and continue along this lane for 550yds (503m). At a junction, fork left along what is really the drive to Little Sodbury Manor. After a few paces turn right onto a path, then, at a triangle of young conifers, bear left as the path rises up the slope and brings you to the fortified-looking walls of a farmhouse. To visit Little Sodbury hill-fort, turn right and then left through a kissing gate. The fort is

HORTON

considered to be one of the finest
in the Cotswolds, (see Background
to Walk 43).

Turn left and, at the end of the
wall, turn right through a gate.
Turn left across gravel and then
cross a paddock to a gate. Go
through to a field and cross half
right to a ladder stile. Go over
to a lane and cross to enter New
Tyning Lane in front of you.
Follow this for 700yds (640m),
until you come to a junction. Turn
right along Hall Lane. Follow the
road for 80yds (73m) then, at a
corner, leave the road to enter
a lane. Pass the fort at Horton
Camp then some houses. About
300yds (274m) beyond Top Farm,
at a left bend with a passing place,
turn left before gates, on a path,
marked by a low wooden post,
through woodland. Follow this to
the bottom, to a stile at a field.
Cross to another stile at a lane and
turn right. Walk down the lane, as
far as the (unnamed) entrance to
Horton Court.

Founded in 1140, Horton Court
is one of the oldest inhabited
buildings in the Cotswolds, and
probably the oldest rectory in
England. The original limestone
house was little more than a single
great hall, which still survives,
although the house was greatly
embellished and extended under
the ownership of William Knight

in the 16th century. He was both
Bishop of Bath and Wells and
Chamberlain to King Henry VIII.

Horton Court is just one of
several historically important
sites and landmarks encountered
on the Cotswold Way. In total
the Way runs for just under 100
miles (161km), keeping close
to the Cotswold escarpment,
between Chipping Campden in
the north and Bath in the south.
A route along the Cotswold edge
was first mooted in the early
1950s but only in 1968, when
Gloucestershire County Council
carried out a recreational survey,
was the idea resurrected. In
1970 it was decided to create the
Cotswold Way, based on existing
roads and public rights of way.
Amendments were made over the
following years, with enthusiastic
voluntary help from the Cotswold
Warden Service. In 1983 the first
official application for national
status was made. It took another
15 years before the go-ahead was
finally given, and, along with it,
entitlement to grant aid for its
creation and maintenance.

Immediately, at this sharp right
corner, turn hard left to a
bridleway. Cross a field, then pass
through a hedge to reach a gate.
Continue to another gate and
then follow a hedge to a kissing
gate. Veer left to the corner of a
protruding hedge and then onto a
kissing gate near some houses. Go
through this and follow the path
back into Horton.

Seeking the Severn Bore at Arlingham

A long but fairly level walk along the river where Britain's regular tidal wave rushes in.

DISTANCE 7.5 miles (12.1km)	**MINIMUM TIME** 3hrs 30min
ASCENT/GRADIENT 85ft (25m) ▲▲▲	**LEVEL OF DIFFICULTY** ✦✦✧

PATHS Tracks, fields and lanes, 8 stiles

LANDSCAPE River, meadows and distant hills

SUGGESTED MAP OS Explorer OL14 Wye Valley & Forest of Dean

START/FINISH Grid reference: ST 708109

DOG FRIENDLINESS Good, despite stiles, some long, empty stretches; lead on Severn bank

PARKING Arlingham village

PUBLIC TOILETS None en route

The River Severn is at its most impressive around Arlingham – in its lower reaches before opening up to the Bristol Channel. Here Gloucestershire juts out into the river to form a large promontory, forcing the river into a huge sweeping loop, widening to well over half a mile (800m) at certain points. To the west it is overlooked by the Forest of Dean ridge, to the east by the Cotswold escarpment.

Bore Formula

Shallow and placid though it might appear here, the River Severn has a capricious nature. The area has been devastated by floods in the past, most notably in the 16th century. The Severn Bore, for which the river is justly famous, is a tidal wave that is formed a little way downstream, where the river narrows at Sharpness. The fundamental cause behind the bore is the combination of a large volume of tidal water, funnelled into a quickly narrowing channel, hastening on to rock rising from the riverbed. A wave is created, which is then free to roll on to the Severn's middle reaches. Flooding, however, is rarely a problem here now, as the flood control measures you see as you walk have succeeded in containing the river. It does, though, continue to create havoc every winter further upstream. Significant sea tides at the river's wide mouth make the Severn Bore such a spectacle. In fortnightly cycles over the course of each month the tides reach their highest and lowest points. Near the Severn Bridge the second highest rise and fall of tide in the world has been recorded (the first is in Canada, on the Petitcodiac River). Once a month, for a few days, the spring tides occur, reaching a height of 31 feet (9.4m) at Sharpness. Whenever the tides reach 26ft (8m) or more, a bore will be unleashed.

Exciting Boring

Because of its tendency to extremes, the Severn can be a dangerous place. The shallow and placid-seeming stream, that may invite you to paddle on a summer's day, can be transformed almost instantaneously into a swirling current capable of knocking you off your feet and carrying you away. Nonetheless, there are those who love to ride the bore. Surfers and canoeists ride it for the thrill but the waves will sometimes reach almost 10ft (3m) and travel at 12mph (19kph), finally losing its impetus near Gloucester. Annual tables are produced that predict the best days for seeing the bore but, in truth, much depends on luck.

WALK 46 DIRECTIONS

❶ From the centre of the village, with The Red Lion Inn at your back, walk along a 'No Through Road'. Pass the church and continue along the road. It becomes a track which brings you to a kissing gate. Go to the top of the bank.

2 With the River Severn on your right, turn left through a kissing gate. Continue along this route, passing through kissing gates where they arise, until you see Hock Cliff in front of you. Pass into the field that begins to slope up towards the cliff.

3 Turn sharp left to walk down the bank and along the left side of a field. Cross a bridge into the next field. When the field edge swings right go ahead and left to a footpath sign beyond a farm track. Follow this path running between hedges.

4 Cross a road and enter the 'No Through Road' in front of you. Follow it towards some houses. Just before a gateway turn left through two kissing gates into a field. Follow its right-hand side to a stile and then continue on the same line. Just beyond two big houses on your right and about 100yds (91m) before some

farm buildings, turn right over a stile into a field. Crossing this diagonally brings you to a kissing gate and a lane.

5 Turn left and follow the lane through Overton for just over 0.5 mile (800m). Where the road goes sharply right beside a long house, turn left to rejoin the Severn Way. The path will lead away from the river briefly, among trees, to emerge at a stile beside a meadow. Continue walking ahead, maintaining your direction, passing through gates, always with the River Severn on your right and again ignoring any paths leading inland.

6 The footpath will soon take the form of a raised bank, or dyke. It reaches its northernmost point then swings to the south, just after passing a farm – the town of Newnham should now be clearly visible on the opposite bank. Continue to a pub, The Old Passage Inn, on your left.

7 Beyond the inn take the long, straight lane on your left, which leads across the flood plain, all the way back to Arlingham.

The Wartime Poets of Dymock

A quiet backwater on the border with Herefordshire was once home to some of the finest poets of the early 20th century.

DISTANCE *9.25 miles (14.9km)*   MINIMUM TIME *4hrs 15min*

ASCENT/GRADIENT *100ft (30m)* ▲▲▲   LEVEL OF DIFFICULTY +++

PATHS *Fields and lanes, 27 stiles*

LANDSCAPE *Woodland, hills, villages, rural farmland and streams*

SUGGESTED MAP *OS Explorer OL14 Wye Valley & Forest of Dean and Explorers 189 Hereford & Ross-on-Wye and 190 Malvern Hills & Bredon Hill*

START/FINISH *Grid reference: SO 673292 (on OL14)*

DOG FRIENDLINESS *Stiles and some livestock but plenty of off-lead potential*

PARKING *Northern end of Kempley Green, beside telephone box and bus shelter*

PUBLIC TOILETS *None en route*

Dymock lies in a frequently overlooked, remote corner of Gloucestershire, on the border with Herefordshire. In the years leading up to the First World War this pretty, unspoilt area became the home and inspiration to a group now known as the Dymock Poets. Some went on to lasting fame, others have been all but forgotten. The first to settle in Dymock, in 1911, was Lascelles Abercrombie. He was followed by Wilfrid Gibson and then by the American poet Robert Frost. Edward Thomas rented a cottage here in 1914 and all played host to John Drinkwater, Rupert Brooke and Eleanor Farjeon. Were it not for the Great War, they may well have continued living and working here, united as they were by a love for the English countryside and a respect for each other's abilities. As it was, their friendship was the catalyst to a considerable body of work, much of which can claim to have been inspired by experiences and friendships gained at Dymock.

Forgotten Talent

Abercrombie lived at a cottage called Gallows, at Ryton, to the east of Dymock. Forgotten though he is, at the beginning of the 20th century he was hailed by the *Times Literary Supplement* as a great talent. It was his move to Dymock that was emulated by Gibson, who settled at the Old Nail Shop in Greenway Cross. Gibson, too, is now unknown, but at the time he was the best-read poet in the country. His move to Dymock led to frequent visits by Brooke and Drinkwater. The four of them contributed to a quarterly called *New Numbers*, published from Ryton in 1914 and which contained some of Brook's poems. Robert Frost, who became involved through a review of his poetry by Abercrombie, rented a cottage called Little Iddens while Edward Thomas (who immortalised the Cotswold village of Adlestrop in his most famous poem, see Walk 1) lived in a cottage near by, called Old Fields. It was Frost who persuaded Thomas to concentrate on his poetry rather than his prose.

Dymock and the Man of Ross

Dymock, which has a number of attractive timber houses, was also the

DYMOCK

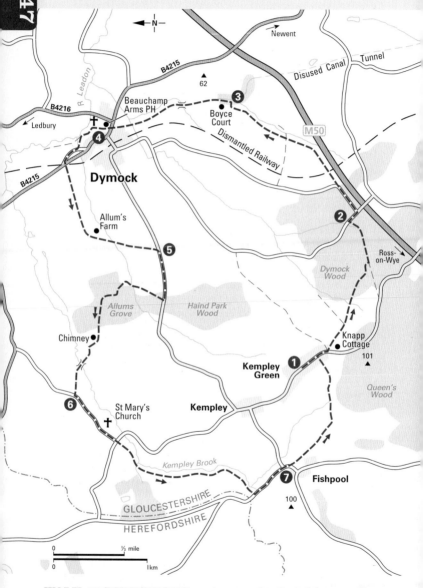

birthplace of John Kyrle, the so-called 'Man of Ross'. A local justice and benefactor to the town of Ross-on-Wye in neighbouring Herefordshire in the late 17th and early 18th century, he acquired his moniker though his countless good deeds. These included securing a spire and bell for the parish church. Kyrle was actually the Earl of Ross by birth, but his good work earned him respect as a common 'man of Ross'.

WALK 47 DIRECTIONS

❶ Walk through Kempley Green and turn left just before Knapp Cottage. Take the right-hand of two paths. Cross stiles, pass a barn and then enter an orchard. Enter Dymock Wood to follow a path and Daffodil Way signs for over 0.5 mile (800m) to a road.

② Turn right and then left before a motorway bridge. Where this road bears left, proceed through a gate into fields and follow the route down to a stream. Turn left before it. Cross a track and stiles, pass through a gate and walk straight along a track for 600yds (549m) towards Boyce Court.

③ Just before it veer right, then go ahead beside a derelict canal, through woodland to a lane. Turn right over a bridge and immediately left onto a path beside the stream. Continue, staying first right and then left of the stream, all the way to Dymock.

④ Go into the churchyard and out the other side, through a gate into a field. Turn half left and take the second bridge on the right. Then bear half left to a stile. Turn right along a disused road and cross the B4215. Follow a track, leaving it to keep to the right of Allum's Farm. Pass a barn and go half left across the field to a gate. Enter an orchard, turn right and follow its left margin and then that of a field, to a road.

⑤ Turn right. After 600yds (549m) turn right into a field alongside woodland. After 120yds (110m) go half right over a mound to soon enter the woods. Turn right and follow the boundary to a stile. Turn left, shortly re-entering woodland. Follow a path, to a stile. Cross a field, keeping to the left of a chimney, and then right into a field. Look for a stile on

WALK 47

your left, cross into the adjacent field and then turn right to find a bridge across the stream. Go half left across fields to a road.

⑥ Turn left past St Mary's Church. At the next T-junction go into the field ahead. Proceed into the next field and continue for over 0.75 mile (1.2km) with the stream on your left across several fields to a lane. Turn left to a junction at Fishpool.

⑦ Turn right, after 50yds (46m) turn left over a stile. Curve right and then pass a series of stiles to aim to the right of a cottage. Follow the path through poultry enclosures and then bear left over stiles so that a house is on your right. Go right into a field. Turn left and follow the same line, ascending gently, to Kempley Green. Turn left, back to the start.

WHAT TO LOOK OUT FOR

The isolated St Mary's Church, which was once the parish church of Kempley, contains some fine 14th-century mural fragments depicting a wheel of life and St Michael weighing souls. The chancel contains the most complete set of Romanesque wall paintings in England. Completed between 1132 and 1140, they had been painted over and were not rediscovered until 1872.

Along Offa's Dyke

Exploring the Saxon King's earthwork
along the Celtic border.

DISTANCE 4.5 miles (7.2km)	**MINIMUM TIME** 2hrs 15min
ASCENT/GRADIENT 740ft (225m) ▲▲▲	**LEVEL OF DIFFICULTY** +++

PATHS Tracks, fields, lanes, stony paths and river bank,

LANDSCAPE River, meadows, woodland, farmland and village

SUGGESTED MAP OS Explorere OL14 Wye Valley & Forest of Dean

START/FINISH Grid reference: ST 540011

DOG FRIENDLINESS Off lead for long stretches, but occasional livestock

PARKING Lay-by near telephone box in Brockweir or The Old Station, Tintern, on other side of river (fee)

PUBLIC TOILETS None en route (except at The Old Station)

Offa's Dyke is a massive earthwork constructed by King Offa, the ruler of the Saxon kingdom of Mercia, in the 8th century AD. The dyke represented the western frontier of his kingdom and ran for about 170 miles (274km) from Chepstow in the south (near the confluence of the Wye and the Severn) to Prestatyn in the north. Its basic construction consisted of a bank of earth, 20ft (6.1m) high and 8ft (2.4m) wide, with a ditch at the foot of its western flank. Even today the frontier between Wales and England runs largely along the course of the dyke. (On this stretch the River Wye forms the present-day boundary between Gloucestershire and Monmouthshire.) The construction of the dyke was felt to be necessary because, after the Romans decamped and the Angles and Saxons invaded, Britain was divided into a number of warring kingdoms. Among these Mercia finally became pre-eminent in England, but the Celtic Britons clung tenaciously to their western mountains. Under Offa, Mercia absorbed other kingdoms and its king became *de facto* ruler of the English in England.

Definitive Boundary

It is not thought that the dyke was conceived as a fortification – it was more a means of definitively marking the boundary between Mercia and its neighbouring kingdoms. Nor was it the first of its kind. Other Saxon rulers had defined their kingdoms in a similar fashion, but none had done so on the scale undertaken by Offa. It is an impressive achievement for its time. The Offa's Dyke Path, opened in 1971, is more or less the same length as the dyke itself but only rarely do the two coincide precisely.

Brockweir was once the most important port of the River Wye. Together with the River Severn, the River Wye was the main trade route serving the Forest of Dean. Timber, iron and coal from the Forest were brought to Brockweir, loaded at the wharf and shipped downstream to Chepstow. A horse-drawn tram that brought the goods from the mines also served the port. Brockweir was also a centre of shipbuilding. All of this came to an end with the arrival of the railway in the late 19th century.

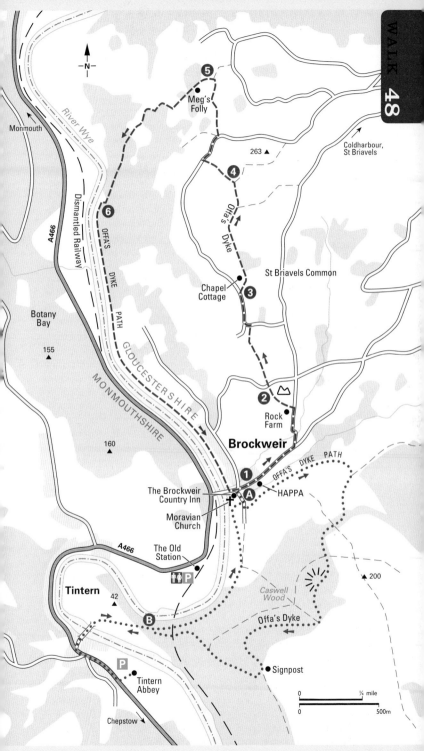

WALK 48

River Wye

Monmouth

A466

Dismantled Railway

OFFA'S DYKE PATH

MONMOUTHSHIRE

GLOUCESTERSHIRE

Botany
Bay

155 ▲

160 ▲

5 Meg's
Folly

263 ▲

Coldharbour,
St Briavels

4

Offa's Dyke

6

St Briavels Common

Chapel
Cottage

3

2

Rock
Farm

Brockweir

1

OFFA'S DYKE PATH

HAPPA

The Brockweir
Country Inn

A

Moravian
Church

The Old
Station

A466

Tintern

42 ▲

B

Caswell
Wood

▲ 200

Offa's Dyke

Signpost

P

Tintern Abbey

Chepstow

0   ¼ mile
0   500m

WALK 48 DIRECTIONS

WALK 48

❶ Walk uphill out of Brockweir until you reach a junction on your left, signposted 'Coldharbour'. Turn left along this narrow lane for about 200yds (183m). At a corner beside Rock Farm turn left on to a track, marked 'Offa's Dyke Path', which narrows and climbs to a lane.

❷ Cross this and continue your ascent until you reach another lane. Turn left here and follow the lane for 200yds (183m), to pass a cottage on the right, followed by some ruined stone buildings. Turn right along a lane.

❸ Keep to the right of Chapel Cottage onto a path, still ascending. When you reach a wider track, fork left. This dwindles to a path, continuing to climb, until it brings you to another track, beside a stone stile. Turn left again.

❹ After 50yds (46m), before a gate, fork right to a metal kissing gate into a field. Cross the field to a similar gate, to the left of a

house. In the next field stay to the left of a farm and come to a third kissing gate at a lane. Turn right to climb gently. It levels out and then, where it starts to climb again at a corner, turn left on to the right-hand path, heading towards Oak Cottage (hand-painted sign). Descend until you arrive at a lane before a house.

❺ Turn left here to follow a track that descends to a house called Meg's Folly. Continue down, to the right of the house, alongside its garden boundary, ignoring a signposted path after 25yds (23m). After a further 250yds (229m) this time fork right to take the signposted path, descending more steeply. In 80yds (73m), at a low wooden marker post, turn left. This waymarked path now zig-zags down, beside slabbed dry-stone walls. Keep an eye out for loose pebbles among the forest debris on the path. Eventually the path straightens and steepens. You will reach the edge of the woods and another metal kissing gate. Beyond it flows the River Wye, which is tidal here.

❻ Turn left through the metal kissing gate and follow the river back to Brockweir. As you approach the village keep close to the river to enter a path that will bring you on to a lane leading up to the road at Brockweir Bridge. Turn left to pass The Brockweir Country Inn, Point **Ⓐ**, and return to the start.

Tintern Abbey

Extend the walk up to Offa's Dyke and on to Tintern Abbey.
See map and information panel for Walk 48

DISTANCE *4.25 miles (6.8km)* **MINIMUM TIME** *2hrs 30min*
ASCENT/GRADIENT *740ft (225m)* ▲▲▲ **LEVEL OF DIFFICULTY** ✦✦✦

WALK 49 DIRECTIONS
(Walk 48 option)

On reaching the Brockweir Country Inn, Point **A**, from the river, turn right. After 50yds (46m) turn left with the buildings of the Horse and Pony Protection Association (HAPPA) to your left. Climb up this track, passing through gates where they arise. Enter a field with a large barn in it. Bear right, entering an enclosed path, running to the right of a field. Follow this to the stile beside a gate at the top. Turn right for perhaps 50yds (46m) to a low wooden post, taking the second worn path diagonally uphill. At the next post go briefly right, then scramble up the bank. Now on Offa's Dyke, turn right, following a clear path through woodland.

Pass any stiles that arise and cross any tracks. The path at one point will take you to the edge of the woods with a field to your left. About 600yds (549m) after that you come to another junction. In front of you, although the path continues to the Devil's Pulpit (a look-out point), you should turn right at the signpost to follow a stony track towards Tintern.

The ruined abbey, founded in 1131, and immortalised in the poem *Tintern Abbey* by William Wordsworth, belonged to the Cistercian order. What is left is the defiantly noble shell of the abbey church, built in English Gothic style between 1270 and 1325. The abbey was 'dissolved' in 1537.

The path is quite clear, bringing you to an obvious track. Turn right and, within 50yds (46m), turn half left onto a footpath descending through woodland. When this meets another footpath at a T-junction turn right, continuing to a track and a stone parapet, Point **B**. To visit Tintern Abbey, turn left here, following the track out of the woods to a bridge, crossing over the River Wye into Wales and turning left. Otherwise, turn right here, along the track in the direction of Brockweir.

When the woodland to your right ends continue for 150yds (137m). Seek a stile down to the riverside. Turn right to continue to a stile at the Moravian church at Brockweir. The Moravian Church, which has its origins in what is now a region of the Czech Republic, is a free church whose precepts influenced John Wesley, creator of the Methodist Church. Pass to the right of the church and then left back to Point **A**.

Staunton's Stones

*A walk among massive stones within the woods
of the Forest of Dean.*

DISTANCE 6.25 miles (10.1km)	MINIMUM TIME 3hrs
ASCENT/GRADIENT 655ft (200m) ▲▲▲	LEVEL OF DIFFICULTY ✦✦✦

PATHS *Forest tracks and paths, 2 stiles*

LANDSCAPE *Woodland, hills and village*

SUGGESTED MAP *OS Explorer OL14 Wye Valley & Forest of Dean*

START/FINISH *Grid reference: SO 541125*

DOG FRIENDLINESS *Very good*

PARKING *Parking apron on forestry road adjacent to main road (or on disused
road section 400yds/366m west)*

PUBLIC TOILETS *None en route*

WALK 50 DIRECTIONS

From the parking area head along a track into the woods. Where the track curves sharply left, turn right on to another track. Follow this for just under 0.75 mile (1.2km), until you see large boulders on your right. Turn right to follow a waymarked path up the slope passing first the Suck Stone and then, at the top, Near Hearkening Rock (not the smaller slab to the left).

These are just two of the many giant stones that you will pass on this walk. Composed of a quartz conglomerate – a mixture of

WHAT TO LOOK OUT FOR

In the village of Staunton look out for the curious round enclosure on your left as you pass through the village. This is the village pound where animals were kept before being sent to market, and where strays were secured for their owners to collect them on paying a fine.

quartz and Old Red Sandstone – they have mostly been formed by natural weathering over millions of years. The Suck Stone is thought to be one of the largest single boulders in the country with estimates of its weight varying from 4,000 to 14,000 tons. From Near Hearkening Rock, keen-eared listeners are supposed to be able to hear messages whispered from the Buck Stone (seen later on the walk).

Go up behind Near Hearkening Rock and, with your back to it, follow an initially gravelled path through the trees for 150yds (137m) to a forest track. Turn left and immediately right, onto a path. After 200yds (183m) you come to a T-junction. Turn left and go right at a fork to continue to a forest track in a further 50yds (46m). Cross this diagonally to walk with a high wire fence on your left. Creation of the Lady Park Wood National Nature Reserve – so designated to allow natural succession of its oak-lime woodland – is not the

FOREST OF DEAN

first incidence of 'conservation' in the Forest's history. Back in 1668 depletion of the trees prompted a Dean Forest Reforestation Act.

The Forest of Dean is all that remains of the woodland that sprouted at the end of the Ice Age. Clearance began in about 4000 BC, as farmers established settlements. By the Iron Age the Forest had become an important source of minerals. The Normans imposed controls on deforestation, but in the 17th century the Forest was opened to private individuals and soon there were only a few hundred oaks left. Charles II ordered 11,000 acres (4,500ha) of oak to be planted and the Court of Verderers was set up to manage them. There are now some 27,000 acres (10,900ha) of oak, chestnut and other native trees.

When the fence turns left veer right, following a path steeply to the valley bottom. Turn right, away from the sign 'River Wye and Biblins' (an adventure centre), for just under 1 mile (1.6km). At a crossroads turn right. After 100yds (91m), just before a telegraph pole, turn left onto a rising path, which you follow as it intersects other paths and arrives at a track at a bend. You will hear traffic to your right. Turn left and follow this for 550yds (503m). At another crossways of tracks turn right on to a grassy path for 120yds (110m). Turn right along a path and continue to the Long Stone beside the A4136. The Long Stone is artificial, probably created during the Bronze Age. Some 7ft (2.1m) high, it is thought to have been part of an ancient cemetery.

Turn right for a few paces and then cross the road to enter the woods on another path. Follow this to emerge at a junction of forest tracks. Turn left to follow the rising track. Where it begins a shallow curve to the left, fork right on to a newish track between conifers. Take this for 150yds (137m). Turn right and follow this broad path down to a farm track and onwards to Staunton. At a junction turn left, away from the main road and through the old village. Curve sharply right, up to the White Horse Inn. Turn left along the pavement and then left on a curving 'No Through Road'. At the stile and '15mph' sign ascend to follow a climbing path to the Buck Stone. This used to be celebrated as the 'rocking stone', poised on its 3ft (90cm) apex, but in 1885 some lads heaved it over.

Go through the gate only to visit the Buck Stone; otherwise keep the wall closely on your right. Emerge left of Buckstone Lodge after 150yds (137m). Go down to a track and turn right. At the entrance to the Buckstone Activity Centre turn right on a falling path. Where the path divides just before a telegraph pole go right. Take a path left alongside a fenced and felled plantation to return to the road. Cross and turn right to return to the start.

Walking in Safety

All these walks are suitable for any reasonably fit person, but less experienced walkers should try the easier walks first. Route finding is usually straightforward, but you will find that an Ordnance Survey map is a useful addition to the route maps and descriptions.

RISKS

Although each walk here has been researched with a view to minimising the risks to the walkers who follow its route, no walk in the countryside can be considered to be completely free from risk. Walking in the outdoors will always require a degree of common sense and judgement to ensure that it is as safe as possible.

- Be particularly careful on cliff paths and in upland terrain, where the consequences of a slip can be very serious.

- Remember to check tidal conditions before walking on the seashore.

- Some sections of route are by, or cross, busy roads. Take care and remember traffic is a danger even on minor country lanes.

- Be careful around farmyard machinery and livestock, especially if you have children with you.

- Be aware of the consequences of changes in the weather and check the forecast before you set out. Carry spare clothing and a torch if you are walking in the winter months. Remember the weather can change very quickly at any time of the year, and in moorland and heathland areas, mist and fog can make route finding much harder. Don't set out in these conditions unless you are confident of your navigation skills in poor visibility. In summer remember to take account of the heat and sun; wear a hat and carry spare water.

- On walks away from centres of population you should carry a whistle and survival bag. If you do have an accident requiring the emergency services, make a note of your position as accurately as possible and dial 999.

COUNTRYSIDE CODE

- Be safe, plan ahead and follow any signs.

- Leave gates and property as you find them.

- Protect plants and animals and take your litter home.

- Keep dogs under close control.

- Consider other people.

For more information visit www.countrysideaccess.gov.uk/things_to_know/countryside_code